THE BOOK OF ORDERS

OF

KNIGHTHOOD

AND

DECORATIONS OF HONOUR.

THE BOOK OF ORDERS

OF

KNIGHTHOOD

AND

DECORATIONS OF HONOUR

OF ALL NATIONS

COMPRISING AN HISTORICAL ACCOUNT OF EACH ORDER,
MILITARY, NAVAL, AND CIVIL, FROM THE EARLIEST TO THE PRESENT TIME,
WITH LISTS OF THE KNIGHTS AND COMPANIONS OF EACH BRITISH ORDER.

EMBELLISHED WITH

Fac-Simile Coloured Illustrations of the Insignia

OF THE VARIOUS ORDERS.

EDITED BY

SIR BERNARD BURKE

ULSTER KING OF ARMS.

The Naval & Military Press Ltd

Published by

The Naval & Military Press Ltd
Unit 5 Riverside, Brambleside
Bellbrook Industrial Estate
Uckfield, East Sussex
TN22 1QQ England

Tel: +44 (0)1825 749494

www.naval-military-press.com
www.nmarchive.com

In reprinting in facsimile from the original, any imperfections are inevitably reproduced and the quality may fall short of modern type and cartographic standards.

INTRODUCTION.

THE desire to possess honorary distinctions has shown itself in various shapes, from very remote times, and among nations strangely dissimilar; and to be able to wear them on the person as evidence of some particular qualification in the individual, or acknowledgment of important service rendered by him to his country, has been an object of human ambition, almost from time immemorial. The value of these incentives to exertion was found out by every government that could maintain pretensions to civilization, and as society assumed the more regular elements of organization, such personal distinctions multiplied in all the settled States of the Old and New World. Objects, trivial in their nature, when applied to this purpose, assumed a new and absorbing interest, and at opposite parts of the globe similar badges of superiority were equally prized and coveted. Such were the Button of the Mandarin, the Fleece of the Spanish Grandee, and the Garter of the English Knight. Other forms were pressed into the service, and chains, ribbons, medals and crosses formed part of their insignia. In the various Continental Courts, honorable decorations have become numerous, extending even to the artizan class of the community, among which skilful workmanship furnishes a claim to such distinction; others of a purely military character are distributed to private soldiers—while civilians may aspire to a recognition of intrepidity in the medal given " for saving from danger." Indeed, Merit in almost every form, is acknowledged and rewarded.

In our own country, orders are few, and are sparingly distributed, and medals only bestowed by the Sovereign for eminent military or naval service; this renders them more prized by their possessors, and more precious in general estimation. An addition has recently been made to the very limited list, in the shape of a decoration for rewarding particular acts of valour; this, however, like the others, belongs exclusively to the Military and Naval services. Civil Merit has been less considered—the Orders of the Bath and the Garter being out of the reach of a very large majority of talented civilians, falling occasionally only to some skilful diplomatist, or influential statesman. A few private Societies to some extent supply the omissions of the State—the Humane Society providing the 'Saving from Danger' medal, and more than one scientific and learned Association, in a like manner, recognising superior intelligence and skill. These are decorations, however, which not being recognized by the Sovereign, are of course not worn at Court.

Within the last few years, the number of such objects of ambition accessible to our countrymen, has been greatly increased from foreign sources, particularly from India, France,

Turkey and Sardinia, which Governments have bestowed them liberally, in acknowledgment of merit or daring in certain hazardous services. This has drawn greater attention to the Honorary Decorations and Orders of other countries. Hitherto, however, our knowledge of them has been extremely imperfect; no English publication existing which represented them to the eye, or included the entire series. The value of an authority on such a subject, in which the reader can ascertain who has been decorated, and what is the character of the decoration, must be obvious. To supply this desideratum, a full account has been compiled from the best authorities, of all the orders, with a description of every distinction now worn at home and abroad; and trustworthy lists have been appended, brought down to the latest announcements, of the English recipients of both. The Illustrations will speak for themselves. It is only necessary to add, that every possible care has been taken to render the volume worthy of general patronage.

THE BOOK OF ORDERS OF KNIGHTHOOD

AND

Decorations of Honour.

DUCHIES OF ANHALT-KOETHEN, ANHALT-DESSAU, AND ANHALT-BERNBURG.

THE ORDER OF ALBERT THE BEAR.

THE Order common to the three Anhalt Duchies, is 'Albert the Bear,' founded by Prince Sigismund I. about 1382, and renewed, on the 18th November, 1836, by the Dukes Henry, Leopold Frederick, and Alexander Charles, "in honour," as the patent says, "of their illustrious ancestors, and for the purpose of being presented as a token of honour and distinction to their meritorious subjects." The Order consists of three classes: Knights of the Grand Cross, Commanders, and (simple) Knights.

The decoration of the Grand Cross (Plate 2. Tab. I. No. 2) is worn across the right shoulder, towards the left side, by a green watered ribbon with two poppy-coloured stripes, and is accompanied by a star (No. 1). The Commanders wear it round the neck, suspended by a similar but narrower ribbon (No. 3), while the Knights suspend it at the button-hole, by a ribbon of a like character, not so broad.

In connection with the Order is a gold and silver Medal of Merit. The impression on it is the same as on the former, viz. : 'Albert der Bär, reg. 1123—1170,' (Albert the Bear, reigned from 1123 to 1170), on the obverse; and " Fürchte Gott und scheue Niemand' (Fear God and no one besides), on the reverse. (Plate 2. Tab. I. Nos. 4 and 5).

To the branch of Anhalt-Koethen specially, belong—

1. The Initial Decoration, founded by the late Duke Ferdinand. The initial was originally an 'F,' but, since the accession of Duke Henry in 1830, it has been changed into an 'H.' The decoration is set in brilliants, and is presented for long faithful service. It is worn round the neck, suspended by a ribbon of white and green colours; and has only one class.

2. Medal of Merit, Loyalty, and Attachment. (Pl. 3. Tab. II. Nos. 8 and 9.) It was founded in 1835 by Duke Henry, and is divided into two classes: Gold and Silver. It is worn suspended by a white watered ribbon with a green stripe near each edge.

3. The War Medal for the campaigns of 1813, 1814, and 1815 (No. 10). It was founded in 1819, by Duke Ferdinand Frederick, and distributed amongst the troops who were engaged in one or all of the battles of those campaigns. It is of iron, with the initial 'L' (that of 'Louis,' the then reigning Duke) on the obverse; and the legend, 'Den Vaterland's Vertheidigern 1813, 1814 und 1815' (To the defenders of the Fatherland, 1813, 1814, and 1815) on the reverse.

It is worn suspended by a white ribbon with four narrow green stripes (No. 7).

The Anhalt-Dessau branch possesses (besides the one common to all three) the 'Cross of Volunteers for the campaigns of 1813, 1814 and 1815.' (Tab. II. No. 10). It was bestowed in 1823 by Duke Leopold Frederick on all those who already in possession of a mark of military distinction in the shape of a ribbon, founded and presented by his predecessor, Leopold Frederic Francis, in 1816. On the reverse is the inscription, 'Anhalt's tapfern Kriegern, 1814—1815' (To Anhalt's brave warriors, 1814—1815).

The third branch of the ducal house of Anhalt-Bernburg has also founded a War Medal for the campaigns of 1814 and 1815. It is of iron, with the initials of the Duke Alexius Frederic Christian on the obverse, and the inscription, 'Den Vertheidigern des Vaterlandes, 1814—1815' (To the defenders of the Fatherland, 1814—1815) on the reverse. It is worn suspended by a green watered ribbon with two broad white stripes and edgings (No. 6).

Suspended by a similar ribbon, is also worn a Golden Medal of Civil Service, the obverse of which is the same as that of No. 6. The inscription on the reverse marks the cause of the distinction, which is: 'Für fünfzig-jährige Diensttreue' (For fifty years' loyal service).

To the above three classes of the Order 'Albert the Bear,' a fourth class was added, on the 24th February, 1850, at Dessau, the residence of the present oldest reigning Duke. It possesses a second class Commanders. All the four classes wear the insignia as given in Table I. Nos. 2 and 3, in addition to the old family escutcheon of the Behrings, viz.: on the obverse, a bear with a crown and collar placed upon a rising wall towards the left; in the middle scutcheon are seen the Anhalt Arms, while the reverse exhibits below the eye or catch, the Ascanian Arms. The only distinction of the three classes consists in their different sizes. The Knights of the Grand Cross wear it across the right shoulder suspended by a broad ribbon of the colours given in the Table, accompanied by a star (No. 1) fastened to the left side of the breast. The Commanders of the 1st Class wear it round the neck, accompanied by a star, in the form of a cross, the rays of which are connected with each other by golden wreaths of rue, while the middle is the same as that of the star of the Grand Cross. The (simple) Knights wear it at the button-hole.

The oldest member of the ducal family is Grand Master of the Order, but he consults the other Dukes on all important matters connected with the Order.

DECORATIONS OF HONOUR.

Anhalt's Decoration of Merit, for saving from danger, was founded in December, 1850. It consists of a silver medal, and contains, on the obverse, the bear, crown, and inscriptions of the former insignia, and on the reverse an oak wreath, with the legend: 'Für Rettung von Gefahr' (For saving from danger). It is worn at the button-hole, suspended by a green watered ribbon with two narrow red stripes.

On the 29th October, 1847, a new decoration was created at Anhalt-Koethen, for distinguished service by the Anhalt-Koethen Contingency to the German Bund. The death of the Duke, however, which occurred on the 23rd November, 1847, by which the male dynasty became extinct, retarded the publication of the patent until the 9th December, when Duke Leopold Frederick of Anhalt-Dessau ordered that the decoration should contain the initial of the deceased Duke, though he postponed the distribution until after a final convention, relating to the government, was concluded with Duke Alexander Charles of Anhalt Bernburg.

It is a military decoration bestowed for a certain number of years' service; those spent in campaigns count double, while those passed in prison go for nothing. To the third class belong sergeants and privates; the badge consists of a

ANHALT. *Table I.* PLATE 2.

Hurst and Blackett, London. 1858.

ANHALT. *Table* II.   PLATE 3.

black iron buckle mounted in silver: the middle contains the Arms of the ducal house, with the initial 'H' to the right, and the cypher 'IX' to the left (indicating nine years' service). That of the second class is a silver buckle with a black edge, and the cypher 'XV' (fifteen years' service) on it. That of the first class is a similar buckle, but of gold, mounted in silver, with the cypher 'XXI' (twenty-one years' service) on it.

The decoration for officers consists of an octagonal golden cross (worn with the same ribbon); the round middle scutcheon is white enamelled, and contains on the obverse the initial of the Duke, with the ducal crown above it, and on the reverse the cypher 'XXV' in gold (indicating twenty-five years' service, including the period of subordinate rank).

Also in Anhalt-Dessau was established, on the 1st of February, 1848, a similar decoration of honour: known as the Military Distinction for Anhalt-Dessau.

For sergeants and common soldiers, the badge is a silver buckle; the centre contains the ducal arms, with the initial of the Duke to the right, and the cypher 'XII' (for the second class), or 'XX' (for the first), to the left. It is worn on the left side of the breast, suspended by a green ribbon, the half-width of which protrudes on each side of the buckle. For officers and military surgeons, the decoration is a golden octagonal cross, white enamelled in the middle, bearing on the obverse the initial of the Duke, with the ducal crown above it, and on the reverse the cypher 'XXV,' both in golden letters; it is likewise worn by a green ribbon upon the left side of the breast.

When the decoration of the higher class is obtained, that of the inferior must be returned.

AUSTRIA.

THE ORDER OF THE GOLDEN FLEECE.

The 'Order of the Fleece' was founded by Philip le Bon (Duke of Burgundy and the Netherlands), on the 10th January, 1429, the day of his marriage with the Princess Isabelle of Portugal. The number of the members was originally fixed at thirty-one, including the sovereign, as the head and chief of the institution. They were to be: 'Gentilshommes de nom et d'armes sans reproche.' In 1516, Pope Leo X. consented to increase the number to fifty-two, including the head.

After the accession of Charles V., in 1556, the Austro-Spanish, or rather, the Spanish-Dutch line of the house of Austria, remained in possession of the Order. In 1700, the Emperor Charles VI. and King Philip of Spain both laid claim to it. The former, however, on leaving Spain—which he could not maintain by force of arms—took with him to Vienna the archives of the Order, the inauguration of which he solemnized there, in 1713, with vast splendour; but Philip V. of Spain declared himself Grand Master, and formally protested, at the Congress of Cambrai, (1721), against the pretensions of the German Emperor. The dispute, though subsequently settled by the intercession of France, England and Holland, was frequently renewed, until the Order was tacitly introduced into both countries, and it now passes by the respective names of the

AUSTRIA. Table I.   PLATE 4.

Hurst and Blackett, London. 1858

Spanish or Austrian 'Order of the Golden Fleece,' according to the country where it is issued.

The principal provisions of the statutes of the Order, now in force in Austria, are:

1. The uncontrolled power of the head to create any number of members, from the Catholic and ancient high nobility of the realm. (If a Protestant, the consent of the Pope must first be obtained).

2. The duty of the members to assist the head in war and other perilous situations.

3. The prohibition against members entering any foreign service without special permission.

4. By high treason or cowardice in war, the Order to be forfeited.

5. All disputes between members to be settled amicably by the Chapter.

The insignia of the Order consist of a Golden Fleece hanging on a golden blue-enamelled flint stone, emitting flames of fire, and borne, in its turn, by a ray of fire. On the enamelled obverse are inscribed the words (from Claudian) 'Pretium laborum non vile' (Not a bad reward for labour). (Plate 4. Tab. I. No. 1.)

The members were originally enjoined to wear the decoration constantly round the neck by a golden chain, the links of which were equally to consist of fire-stones and rays (Tab. I. No. 8). The chain having, however, been found too cumbersome for the wearer, Charles V. allowed the substitution of a red ribbon, by which the insignia may be worn either round the neck, or at the button-hole. At present, it is usually worn round the neck, except on solemn occasions, when the chain is worn over the collar round the neck.

The costume of the Knights on particular solemn occasions consists of a long robe of deep red velvet lined with white taffetas, over which is thrown a long mantle of purple velvet, lined with white satin, and richly trimmed with embroidery, containing fire-stones and steels, emitting flames and sparks. On the hem, which is equally of white satin, are repeatedly embroidered in gold, the words, 'Je l'ay empris' (I have accepted it—the Order). The original inscription was: 'Autre n'auray' (I will have no other—Order), which was, however, substituted by the former phrase, by Charles the Bold, son of the founder. The head is covered by a cap of purple velvet, equally set with gold embroidery, and behind which is attached a little hood. The shoes and stockings are red.

The annual festival of the Order is celebrated at Vienna on St. Andrew's Day (30th November), or on the following Sunday, when the Emperor and all the Knights, then present at Vienna, repair in procession and full costume to the Court Chapel to hear Divine Service, and thence return to the castle to dine at open table in the 'Knights' Saloon.'

The Chapter meets in the Court Chapel every year on the 6th January.

THE ORDER OF MARIA-THERESA.

This is a purely military Order, founded by the Empress Maria Theresa in 1757, in acknowledgment of the valour, wisdom, and loyalty displayed by her officers in the memorable contests of her reign. Her Royal Consort, the Emperor Francis I., took upon himself the office of first Grand Master; and that high dignity is fixed by the statutes (published 1758) to belong to the sovereigns of Austria for ever after.

The claims to the Order rest chiefly on personal military merit, irrespective of birth, duty, favour, family connection, or long service.

The number of members is unlimited; but it hardly amounts, at the present moment, to a hundred.

All superior officers (including ensigns and cornets), indiscriminately, and without regard to religion, rank, or other circumstances, are eligible for the Order.

Originally, there existed only two classes: Knights of the Grand Cross, and simple Knights; but the Emperor Joseph II. added (1765) a third class—that of Commanders.

The badge of the Order (Plate IV. Tab. I. Nos. 3 and 4) is an octagonal cross, enamelled white, and set in gold. The centre, also in gold, contains the Austrian Arms, surrounded by a white margin, in which is inscribed the word: 'Fortitudini' (For valour), in golden letters. The reverse shows, on white ground, the initials, in monogram, 'M. T. F.' (Maria Theresa [and] Francis), encompassed by a golden ring and laurel wreath. The ribbon has the colours of the Austrian Arms, and is divided into three stripes—the middle being white, and the two extremes poppy-colour.

The Knights of the Grand Cross wear the insignia on a broad ribbon of the same colour, across the right shoulder towards the left hip, while the left side of the breast is adorned with a star, the face of which represents the Order, embroidered in silver, resting on a laurel wreath (No. 2). This star was added by the Emperor Joseph II. in 1765.

The Commanders wear the decoration round the neck, on a somewhat smaller ribbon, and without the addition of the star; while the simple Knights suspend it from the button-hole by a ribbon about an inch and a half wide.

The Order is held in high estimation, on account of the rareness of its distribution. It is, according to the injunctions of the founder, reserved for extraordinary exploits of military success and skill.

THE APOSTOLIC ORDER OF SAINT STEPHEN.

St. Stephen, intended originally to be the National Order of Hungary, also owes its institution to the Empress Maria Theresa, and was designed as a reward for civil distinction and merit. It was founded on the 5th May, 1764, on the day when the presumptive heir to the throne, the Archduke Joseph (afterwards the Emperor Joseph II.), was crowned King of Rome. The name was given in honour of the founder of the Hungarian kingdom, St. Stephen. By the statutes, the Grand Mastership of the Order is vested in the Crown of Hungary, and the College is to consist of a hundred noble Knights distinguished by merit. They are divided into: Knights of the Grand Cross (to the number of twenty), Commanders (to the number of thirty), and Knights simple, (to the number of fifty).

The badge (Plate IV. Tab. I. Nos. 6 and 7) is an octagonal cross, green-enamelled, with a golden edge, and containing another cross in the red-enamelled centre. On the obverse of the middle scutcheon is seen the Apostolic silver cross within a golden crown placed on a green mountain, bearing on both sides the initials of the founder: 'M. T.' (Maria Theresa), with the legend: 'Publicum Meritorum Præmium' (Public reward of merit). The white-enamelled reverse of the scutcheon exhibits a cross of oak-leaf, with the legend: 'Sto. St. Ri. Ap.' (Sancto Stephano, Regi Apostolico). Above the cross is appended the Hungarian crown of gold. Green and red are the two national colours of Hungary, while the Apostolic cross indicates the renewed Apostolic title of the founder of the Order.

The Order is suspended by a red ribbon with green borders, and is worn by the Knights of the Grand Cross—if laymen—across the right shoulder, and, if ecclesiastics, round the neck.

The Grand Cross Knights wear in addition, on the left side of the breast, a cross embroidered with silver, in the centre of which is seen the obverse of the badge, surrounded by a wreath of oak-leaves (No. 5.)

The Commanders carry the decoration, suspended by a narrow ribbon, round the neck, without the star; while the Knights wear it, by a small and narrow ribbon, at the button-hole.

The Grand and Commander-crosses are to be presented only to persons of high and ancient nobility, or to high functionaries of the State; while that of the Knights may be conferred upon the inferior nobility.

The annual festival is celebrated on St. Stephen's Day (26th December), or on the following Sunday.

The Costume of all the Knights, at public processions, consists of a long mantle of green velvet, bordered with ermine, and lined with crimson taffetas. The under-garment and the cap are of crimson velvet; the latter is edged with ermine, and ornamented with heron-feathers, placed in a red and green enamelled sheath.

The under-garment of the Knights of the Grand Cross is richly covered with embroidered oak leaves, while that of the Commanders, and simple Knights, has an embroidered border, the only distinction being in the size of the border, which, in the last, is somewhat smaller. (Plate V. Tab. II. No. 14.)

The embroidery represents oak leaves closely joined to each other, being emblematic of honour for civil services.

The Knights of the Grand Cross wear, in addition, on the festivals, or on any other solemn occasion, a golden collar, the links consisting alternately of the initials of St. Stephen and the founder of the Order, with the Hungarian crown between them. In the centre is the Golden Eagle, the bearing of the house of Austria, with the inscription: 'Stringit Amore' (United by love).

Only the Grand Cross Knights and the presumptive heirs to the throne, or other members, by special permission of the Grand Master, are free to adorn the insignia with precious stones.

The most distinguished officers of the Order are, besides the Grand Master: 1st, the Prelate appointed by the Grand Master from the higher clergy, who performs Divine Service on their festival days; and 2nd, the Chancellor, who addresses the meeting when the Chapter is held, or when a new Knight is created, who reads the oath to be taken, sits at the side of the Grand Master on solemn occasions, reports the state of affairs, orders the issue of decrees, and is also the keeper of the Seal. The Chancellorship of the Order is always vested in the Court-Chancellor of Hungary.

Every Knight of the Grand Cross becomes, on his election, a Privy-Counsellor of the State; and every Commander a titular Privy-Counsellor. The simple Knights may, at their desire, be created Barons, and even Counts, according to circumstances.

In decrees, the Grand Master styles the Knights of the Grand Cross, 'Cousins.'

Every aspirant to the Grand Cross must prove his *Sieze Quartiers*, that is, his noble descent through, at least, four generations; but the Grand Master may make exceptions in favour of individuals of particular merit and distinction.

At the nomination of candidates, and after the latter have taken the oath of the Order (kneeling before a crucifix), the Grand Master addresses them in Latin, as follows:

"Quam juris jurandi religione prompti novistis observantiam
"et fidem, illam, ut strenuos ac honoratos decet Equites, omni
"loco ac tempore vos integram servaturos prorsus non ambi-
"gimus. Recepturi igitur de manu Nostrâ per Nos vobis

"designatum Ordinis Signum, eorum, quæ nunc religione "spopondistis inviolabilem memoriam conservate. Nos autem "gratiam et benevolentiam Nostram vobis confirmamus." (We doubt not, for a single moment, that you will steadfastly adhere, as becomes brave and honourable knights, to the vow of respect and loyalty made by your oath. In receiving, therefore, from our hands the insignia of the Order destined for you, keep the contents of your solemn oath inviolably in your memory, while, on our part, we assure you of our favour and benevolence).

The Grand Master has power to dispense with the oath in some particular cases.

The nomination of a new member usually takes place on St. Stephen's Day. At the moment of investiture, the Grand Master addresses the candidate in the following words: "Accipe Signum Ordinis Equitum S. Stephani, publicum singularium" (the last word is only used at the nomination of a Grand Cross Knight), "meritorum tuorum testimonium ac "præmium, illudque semper adpensum gerito, ut nempe quid "Deo, Nobis Domuique Nostræ, atque Ordinis hujus dignitati "debeas, honoris, quem a Nobis, accepisti, magnitudine moni- "tus, nunquam ignorare possis." (At the nomination of the other Knights—of Commanders and simple Knights—the form is: "Honoris, quod a Nobis hodie accepisti, insigni monitus," &c.) (Receive the insignia of the Order of St. Stephen as a public testimony of your [peculiar] merits, and wear them always about you, to remind you constantly of the distinguished honour bestowed upon you to-day by us, that you may never forget what you owe to God, to ourselves, to our house, and to the dignity of the Order).

The Diploma is given to the Knights of the Grand Cross in the form of a book, and to the other Knights in the form of a patent.

THE ORDER OF LEOPOLD.

As the Order of St. Stephen was exclusively destined for the nobility, the Emperor Francis I. founded, on the 7th January, 1808—the day after his marriage with his third wife, Louise of Modena—a new Order, named after the Emperor Leopold II., and extended it to all meritorious subjects, civil or military, without regard to rank or birth.

The first distribution of the Order took place on the 8th January, 1809.

The Austrian Emperors are the sole Grand Masters, and have full power to confer the Order upon any one they please.

The badge (Plate II. Nos. 10 and 11) is an octagonal red enamelled cross of gold, and white encasement. On the obverse of the round red centre are, in monogram, the initials 'F. I. A.' (Franciscus Imperator Austriæ), while in the white mounting are the words: 'Integritate et Merito' (For integrity and merit). The reverse is white, surrounded by a golden oak wreath, and containing the motto of the Emperor Leopold II.: 'Opes regum corda subditorum" (The riches of kings are the hearts of their subjects). Between each of the four arms of the cross are seen three oak leaves with two acorns, while the whole is surmounted by the imperial crown of Austria.

This Order is also divided into three classes. The Knights of the Grand Cross wear the decoration across the right shoulder, suspended by a red ribbon with white stripes at the borders, loosely hanging towards the left hip. Close to it, on the left side of the breast, is a silver octagonal star, the centre of which contains the obverse of the cross insignia. (Plate V.

AUSTRIA. *Table II.* PLATE 3.

Hurst and Blackett, London. 1858.

Tab. II., No. 9.) On festival days, the cross is worn upon the breast, suspended by a golden neck chain, the links of which consist alternately of the monogram initials ' F. L,' (Francis and Leopold) with the Austrian crown above them, and of wreaths of oak leaves.

The Commanders wear their cross round the neck, suspended by a smaller and rather narrower ribbon (about an inch wide), while the Knights (simple) wear the cross of a smaller size, at the button-hole of the left breast, by a narrow ribbon of about half an inch wide.

The uniform or costume with the exception of the mantle, is for all classes red and white, (the national colours of Austria). The coat with an upright collar, breeches, shoes, and cap, are all of red velvet. The coat is lined white, and edged with golden embroidery four inches deep, representing garlands of oak leaves. The shoes are adorned with bows of gold lace instead of buckles. The body is girded with a white silk sash richly trimmed with golden fringes hanging over the sword, which is adorned with gilt bronze, the hilt forming a cross. At one side of the pommel are the initials ' F. I. A.' and at the other, the foundation year of the Order. The scabbard is covered with red velvet. The cap is adorned with white feathers, and with a golden cord, which is twisted round it three times. The neck-collar, four inches wide, is of cambric linen, it falls down the neck, and is trimmed with gold lace. The gloves, of white leather, have large gauntlets adorned with golden fringes. The white velvet mantle—the symbol or knightly purity and virtue—distinguishes the various classes by its length and width, as also by the depth of its golden embroidery, and by the trimming of white silk plush in imitation of ermine.

The cross of the Officers is set in a large golden medal, encircled by the legend. It is worn round the neck suspended by the ribbon. The ceremonies of nomination are nearly the same as those of the 'Maria Theresa Order,' while the Oath is made in German, as follows:

"I, *N. N.*, swear to God, to observe, at all times, and on "all occasions, until the end of my life, inviolably and most "strictly, my duty of loyalty and veneration towards His "Majesty, the reigning Emperor, as Grand Master of the "Sublime Order of Leopold, as also towards his illustrious suc-"cessors, and the whole Arch-Ducal House of Austria, and to "contribute, to the best of my power, to all and everything "that may conduce to the safety, glory, and growth of the "Austrian Empire, as also to prevent, on the other hand, as "much as lies in my power, everything that might tend to "injure the power of the Order, and its legitimate representa-"tives. I finally swear, to act up strictly to the laws and "statutes of the Order, as well as to the commands of His "Majesty, as Grand Master of the Order, and to wear con-"stantly about me the insignia of the Order. So help me "God."

The Grand Master has the power to dispense with the oath in some individual cases. Candidates unacquainted with the German may take the Oath in Latin. In handing over the insignia to the candidate, the Grand Master says (in Latin or German):

"We are convinced that you will, as becomes a valiant and "upright knight, always keep faithfully the promises in your "oath. Receive, therefore, the badge of the Order of Leopold "as a reward of your merits, and which you are bound always "to wear about you, that the mark of honour bestowed upon "you may always be present to your mind, and remind you of "what you owe to God, ourselves, our House, and the dignity "of the Order."

Without special permission (which is, however, never refused) no foreign order can be worn at the side of that of Leopold. The festival is always held in the Court Chapel on the first Sunday after Twelfth-day.

The rights and privileges of the members are the same as those of the Order of St. Stephen. No one can be honoured with the latter without previously possessing the corresponding degree of the Order of Leopold, so that every class of the latter must precede that of St. Stephen.

THE ORDER OF ELIZABETH THERESA.

The Order of Elizabeth Theresa, the second Military Order of Austria, was founded, in 1750, by Elizabeth Christina, relict of the Emperor Charles VI. The number of the Knights was originally limited to twenty officers, from the rank of Colonel up to that of General, who had loyally served the House of Austria for a term of thirty years; but it was increased to twenty-one in 1771, by the daughter of the founder, the Empress Maria Theresa, at the time when the Order was renewed and underwent some modifications.

The Order consists of three classes, the first of which numbers six, the second eight, and the third seven Knights; it is endowed with a revenue of 16,000 fl. (£1,600), out of which the members receive pensions of 1000 (£100), 800 (£80), and 500 fl. (£50) respectively. When a vacancy occurs, by decease or otherwise, the War Department sends in a list of eligible candidates, having exclusive regard to merit, without distinction of birth, country, religion, or the possession of any other order, and from that list the Emperor makes his choice.

The badge (Plate 5, Tab. II. No. 15) is an octagonal star set in gold, the points of which are enamelled partly red and partly white; in the middle is an oval scutcheon with a golden edge, round which is inscribed: 'M. Theresa parentis gratiam perennem voluit' (*Maria Theresa wished to give perpetual duration to the gracious favour of her mother*), while the centre contains, beneath the Imperial crown, the initials in monogram, 'E. C. and M. T.' (*Elizabeth Christina and Maria Theresa*). All the Knights wear it, without further distinction, appended to an Imperial Crown at the button hole of the left side, suspended by a black silk ribbon.

Annually on the 19th November (the feast of St. Elizabeth) solemn high mass is held in the Church of the Augustine Friars, at Vienna, in the presence of all the Knights, Generals, Staff and Sub-Officers of the Vienna garrison. The Catholic Knights are bound to say three times every day, a *Pater Noster* and *Ave Maria* for the deceased founder, and the reigning sovereign; while the non-Catholic Knights pay annually three ducats by way of alms for the Invalid Institution at Vienna.

THE ORDER OF THE IRON CROWN.

On the 17th March, 1805, the States-Council of the Italian—previously Cis-Alpine—Republics, changed the form of government into a Monarchy, electing Napoleon as the first hereditary King of Italy. He was crowned as such at Milan, on the 20th May of the same year. The crown used, on that occasion, was that of the ancient Longobardian Kings, which had been preserved in the Treasury of the church at Monza, near Milan. It consists of a golden hoop about four fingers wide, finely chased, and adorned with precious stones in the form of an antique diadem, behind which is attached an iron ring of about one finger wide, which, according to tradition, had been forged from the nail of Christ's Cross, and from which the title is derived. Napoleon founded, in commemoration of his coronation, and at the same time as a reward for those who were to distinguish themselves in his new kingdom, on the 5th June, 1805, an Order, for the decoration of which he adopted the figure of the 'Iron Crown,' and called it 'Ordine della Corona di Ferro' (Order of the Iron Crown). The reigning Kings of Italy were—by the statutes—to be Grand Masters of the Order. The number of the Knights was originally limited to six hundred and twenty, divided into three classes: Dignitaries (twenty), Commanders (one hundred), and Knights (five hundred), all of whom were to be in the enjoyment of pensions. By an Imperial decree of the 19th December, 1807, the number was increased—owing to the increased extent of the kingdom—to thirty-five Dignitaries, one hundred and fifty Commanders, and eight hundred Knights, exclusive of foreigners and members of the Imperial family. Frenchmen, generally, were not to be considered as foreigners. The pension of the first class was fixed at 3000, of the second at 700, and of the third at 300 lire.

The badge was the Iron Crown, the middle of which contained the French Eagle with raised wings. Round the ring of the Crown was the legend: 'Dio me la diede, guai a chi la tocca' (God has given it to me, woe to him who dares to touch it!) while the front exhibited the effigy of Napoleon.

The decoration of the first class (Dignitaries) was of gold, worn by them across the right shoulder, suspended by a broad ribbon of orange colour and green borders, and accompanied by a star at the left side of the breast. The Commanders had it also of gold, while that of the Knights was only of silver; it was worn by the two latter at the button-hole of the left side, suspended by a small ribbon, and without the addition of the star. After the fall of Napoleon, the Order was forgotten, until 1815—16, when the Emperor Francis I., during his visits to his new Italian provinces, re-introduced it in a modified form;

its first distribution took place at Milan on the 12th February, 1816—the birth-day of the Emperor. The order then received the name: 'Austrian Order of the Iron Crown,' and by the statutes published on the same day, it was provided, that—

1. The function of Grand Master should be inseparably vested in the Imperial Crown of Austria, and the nomination of members solely dependent on the will of the Emperor.

2. No one should be allowed to claim or petition for the Order.

3. The Knights to be divided into three classes, without any further distinction beyond that of the number, which was limited for the first class to twenty, the second to thirty, and the third to fifty, exclusive of the princes of the Imperial House.

4. All individuals of merit and distinction to be eligible for the Order.

The decoration of the previous Order was abolished, and that of the new one (Plate 5. Tab. II. No. 13) now consists of a golden crown (of the same form as the Iron Crown), upon which is placed the Austrian eagle on both sides, bearing on the obverse a blue scutcheon upon the breast, with the letter F (Francis) in it, and on the reverse the year 1816 (the year of its foundation).

The Knights, of the first class, wear the decoration across the right shoulder suspended by a broad gold-yellow ribbon with dark blue borders, in addition to a star, embroidered in silver, on the left side of the breast, the centre of which contains the Iron Crown, and round the blue edge are inscribed the words: 'Avita et Aucta' (Ancient and extended). (Plate 5. Tab. II. No. 12).

On solemn occasions the decoration is worn by a gold chain round the neck, the links of which consist alternately of the letters in monogram 'F. P.,' the Iron Crown, and a wreath of oak leaves. (Plate 6. Tab. III. No. 16).

The second class suspend the order round the neck, and the third at the button-hole—each without the star.

The Knights are not allowed to adorn it with brilliants, without special permission of the Grand Master.

The tri-coloured costume, (yellow, blue, and white) consists of a yellow velvet under-garment reaching down to the knees, and laced by a silver cord from the right arm down to the hip, while the lower part is left open. The whole is lined with white taffetas, and edged with silver embroidery. Hose and stockings are of one piece, of white silk; the shoes are of white velvet, lined with yellow satin, while bows of blue satin with silver fringes are used instead of buckles. The cap is of blue velvet with white lining, to which is attached a collar of blue velvet, falling and extending over the shoulders, and a flap twisted round with silver cords. The costume finishes with a mantle of blue velvet, richly embroidered, and fastened by a clasp on the right shoulder, while the left part is adorned with a star. Above the mantle is a straight ruff of lace. The mantles differ in size. That of the first class has a long train; that of the second barely reaches to the ground, while that of the third only extends to the middle of the leg. The sword is straight, the handle forms a cross, and is adorned with silver mountings, while the scabbard is of blue velvet. It is suspended from a sash of similar velvet with silver embroidery, and rests in a sword pocket.

The ceremonies of the nomination are the same as with all other Austrian Orders.

The annual festival is held on the first Sunday after the 7th April—the day when the Lombardo-Venetian kingdom was established.

THE ORDER OF THE STAR CROSS.

The House of Austria has always boasted of being in possession of a small piece of the genuine Cross of Christ; and the Emperors Maximilian and Frederic III. used to wear that relic about their persons, enclosed in a cross of gold. After the death of the latter, Leopold I. his successor, presented it to the widowed Empress Eleonore, daughter of Duke Charles II. of Mantua, to comfort her in her widowhood; she kept it very carefully locked in a small box, adorned with crystal and enamel, and covered with silk. It happened that in the night of the 2nd February, 1668, a fire suddenly broke out in the Imperial Castle at Vienna, just below the apartments of the Empress Eleonore, and it soon reached the Imperial apartments, from which she escaped with considerable difficulty, before they were entirely consumed. On the following day search was made for the relic, and it was discovered amongst the ruins fortunately untouched by the conflagration, with the exception of the metal which was partly melted.

The Empress was so rejoiced at the incident, that she ordered a solemn procession on that occasion, and resolved to found a Female Order, not only—as the statutes say—to commemorate the miraculous event, but also to induce the members to devote themselves to the service and worship of the Holy Cross, and lead a virtuous and religious life in the exercise of religion and works of charity.

Pope Clement IX. confirmed the new Order and its rights in his Bull: 'Redemptoris et Domini nostri' (28th June, 1668), confiding to the Prince Bishop of Vienna, its spiritual management. The Emperor Leopold I. not only sanctioned its statutes, but took the Institution under his special protection;

AUSTRIA. *Table III.* PLATE 6.

Hurst and Blackett, London, 1858.

while the Empress Eleonore declared herself (18th September, 1668), its founder and chief patroness. The Order received the name of 'Community of noble ladies,' under the title of 'the Star Cross;' and the members were styled 'Crossbearers, or ladies of the Star Cross,' (after a constellation of that name at the South Pole).

This Order is only bestowed on Princesses, Countesses, and other high-born ladies.

The Empress, or a Princess of the Austrian House, is head patroness, who nominates the members, and selects two from amongst them for her assistants.

Their number is unlimited, and entirely dependent on the pleasure of the head patroness.

The festival of the Order is celebrated twice a year; on the day when the Cross was found (3rd May), and on Holy-rood-day (14th September). Mass for the departed souls of the patroness and members is usually held on the 6th February.

The decoration of this Order (Plate 6. Tab. III. No. 22) which, by the bye, has been altered four times since the reign of Empress Maria Theresa—has the form of an oval medal with a broad blue-enamelled edging; it encompasses the Austrian eagle with golden claws, upon which rests a green enamelled golden cross, mounted in brown wood. Upon it is, in black letters upon white ground, the motto of the Order: 'Salus et Gloria' (Hail and glory). It is worn on the left side of the breast, suspended by a bow of black silk ribbon. The festival days (3rd May and 14th September), are set apart for the nomination of candidates, when the insignia are placed upon the altar, ritually consecrated and presented by the patroness, who is seated, to the candidate ladies, who are in a kneeling position before her.

THE TEUTONIC ORDER.

In the earlier part of the 12th century, about the time when, in the East, the Knights of various countries began, after the model of the monks, to form themselves into different Orders, for the purpose of vanquishing the infidels, and protecting and supporting, with all the energy and enthusiasm inspired by vows of chastity, poverty and obedience, the numerous pilgrims on their way to the Holy Sepulchre; a pious German, whose name is now lost, built at Jerusalem a hospital for the pilgrims of his native country—the then existing Orders of the Templars and of St. John, having thought fit to devote their care exclusively to the comforts of the French and Italian pilgrims. This hospital soon counted for its patrons several wealthy merchants and Knights, and being consecrated by the Patriarch, a chapel was joined to it, devoted to the Blessed Virgin; it soon became an important asylum for German warriors, especially in 1189 at the siege of Acre, when the founder, assisted by contributions from German merchants at Lübeck and Hamburg, took care of the sick and wounded soldiers, who lay in tents before that place.

In 1191, Frederick of Suabia, on his arrival, after the death of Frederick of Barbarossa, with the rest of his army before Acre, deemed it advisable to secure to the institution a more solid basis. He gave it a constitution, and prescribed to the Knights and merchants assembled, regulations, the general outlines of which he formed after those of the Order of St. Augustine, while the rules and laws concerning the sick and poor he borrowed from the Knights of St. John, and those relative to war and peace from the Templars. He conceded to it all the rights and . privileges peculiar to these Corporations or Colleges, and gave it, under sanction of Pope Coelestin III. the name of: 'the Order of the German House of the Holy Virgin at Jerusalem,' choosing for the insignia, a black cross with white mountings, worn upon a white cloak.

By the provisions of the original statutes, only native Germans of blameless character and nobility were admissible. The members were, moreover, to be unmarried and to remain single the whole of their lives; they were also to give up to the Order all their private property, and to devote themselves exclusively to the service of God, the sick and the poor, and to the defence of the Holy Land. Their food was originally bread and water, and their couch only a sack of straw, all of which, together with their garment, were regularly distributed amongst them by the Grand Master.

After a long series of eventful vicissitudes, the Order attained its culminating point, and assumed at the same time quite a different character under the Grand Master Herman of Salza, who well knew how to turn to account the disputes between Pope Honorius III. and the Emperor Frederick II., as also the warlike events in the provinces which now form a part of Eastern Prussia.

The Duke Conrad of Masovia and Cujavia, having, in his religious zeal, attempted to force Christianity upon his pagan neighbours the Prussians, was met with such an obstinate resistance from them, that he was in his turn threatened with an invasion of his own dominions. In this dilemma he called to his assistance, in 1226, the Teutonic or German Knights, offering them in return for their service, the concession of important rights and privileges; while the Pope and the Emperor granted them the possession of all the lands they might conquer from the heathens during the war. Herman had just returned from his third Crusade to Palestine, and settled at Venice after the loss of Acre, the head-quarters of his Order. He so adroitly managed the opening crusade against the heathen Prussians, that thousands from all lands and countries rallied under his flag, by which the Order received an immense increase in members and property, from Germany, Italy, Sicily and Hungary. The war was successfully carried on under his General, Balk, who within a few years built the towns of Pulen, Thorn, Marienwerder, Elbing, and others. The Order soon possessed large districts of land on the Baltic Sea, governed by a Land Master, while the Grand Master fixed his residence at Marburg in Hessia.

During these complicated but fortunate events, the Order had assumed a new form and character. Instead of the original names of 'Brothers' and 'Hospitalers,' the Knights were now called Masters, and, indeed, acted as such in the strictest sense of the term. They became imperious, tyrannical, despotic, and led a voluptuous and luxurious life at the expense of their Prussian subjects, who figured as the most wretched, oppressed, and miserable creatures in Europe. Nowhere in Europe was bondage carried to such a cruel extent as under the rule of these German Knights, who were intoxicated by war, and plunged in sensual enjoyments. Hence the continued insurrections, devastations of towns and lands, complaints, treaties, and difficulties; hence the despised decrees of the Pope and the Emperor, the incessant disputes with the clergy and bishops of rank, and the subversion of the rules, statutes and laws of the original Constitution, which form the greatest portion of the history of the Order, and which finally resulted in prostration and an exhaustion of its strength and power, especially after the terrible battle near Tannenberg against the Poles and Lithuanians, (15th July, 1410), in which the Grand Master, Ulrich of Jungingen, and thirty thousand of his followers, lost their lives.

In 1440, the towns of Dantzig, Elbing, Thorn, and the nobility of several adjoining provinces concluded a formal treaty amongst themselves against these ruthless masters, while in 1454 the whole of Western Prussia, headed by King Casimir IV., rose against them, and after a war of twelve years, which cost above three hundred thousand human lives, the Order was obliged to sign a treaty which left it in possession of only half of Prussia, and placed it under the supreme authority of Poland. But having repeatedly violated this treaty, the Order was virtually abolished by the peace of Cracow (1525), the whole of its landed property having been granted as a fief of Poland to the then Grand Master, Albert, Margrave of Brandenburg.

Thenceforth its chief resided at Mergentheim in Franconia, under the title of Administrator in Prussia, Grand Master of the Teutonic Order in Germany and Italy, and Spiritual Prince of the Empire and member of the Franconian district, while his possessions consisted of Mergentheim, with fifteen thousand German square miles, and thirty-two thousand inhabitants, partly Catholics and partly Protestants. By the peace of Lüneville, (9th February, 1801), the Order lost the bailiwicks, Coblentz, Altenbriesen, and Bourgogne, and though it received in return the abbeys and cloisters of Austrian Voralberg, and the diocese of Augsburg and Constance, the peace of Presburg (1805) invested the Emperor of Austria with all the rights, dignity, and revenues appertaining to its Grand Master.

In 1809, Napoleon entirely abolished the Order in the Rhenish provinces, and the different European princes appropriated to themselves the possessions belonging to their respective territories, a spoliation to which Austria was compelled to consent in the ensuing treaty of peace. At the Congress of Vienna, the Chapter House at Francfort-on-the-Maine, together with the domains, revenues, and privileges attached to it, were returned to the Order then existing in Austria and Prussian Silesia.

It having thus come under the protection of Austria, the statutes were modified in accordance with its new relations, and by an Imperial decree of the 28th June, 1840, it is provided, that—

1. The German Order is to exist in Austria as an independant spiritual and knightly Order, but shall be considered and treated at the same time as a direct fief of the Austrian Crown.

2. The Emperors of Austria are always to be considered as its patrons and protectors.

3. The rights and duties relating to the administration of its possessions, are to be the same as those of any private property in Austria according to the laws of the land.

4. The Order and its relations are not to be subject to the inspection of the civil authorities, except in special cases where his Imperial Majesty should think proper to require from it an account of its financial position and internal regulations.

5. The property of the Order, whether moveable or not, is not to be mortgaged or disposed of, without the special consent of the sovereign.

6. As regards taxes and other state, and provincial, burdens, its possessions are to be considered as secular property in every respect.

7. Its head is to bear the title of 'Grand Master of the Teutonic Order.'

8. At every accession of a new Emperor, or appointment of new Grand Masters, the latter are bound to petition for, and receive solemnly a renewal of the fief. They are considered and treated as Spiritual Vassal Princes of Austria, and enjoy the rank and rights of the most ancient Order of the realm

above all the Secular and Spiritual Princes whose dignity dates subsequent to the foundation of the Teutonic Order.

9. Though by their vows, monks, the Knights may remain in the enjoyment and free disposal of their private property, except in gifts amounting to more than 300 ducats, when the consent of the head must first be obtained.

10. No member is to be security or guardian for other persons, without special dispensation from the head.

11. Wills and legacies by the members must bear the sanction of the head, without which they are void.

12. If the head or a member should die intestate, his personal property falls to the Order, without its being obliged to pay his debts.

13. Only in matters strictly belonging to the Order, the members are to be under the jurisdiction of its legitimate authorities, while in every other respect they stand under the civil authorities of their local districts or provinces.

The insignia (Plate 6. Tab. III. No. 20) are worn round the neck, or (No. 19) as a cross, with silver embroidery, upon the breast. On solemn occasions, the Knights wear a white mantle decorated with a similar, or even larger cross.

THE ORDER OF MALTA (ST. JOHN).

This famous Institution, the predecessor of the Teutonic Order, occupies in history a far more important page. Its origin falls in the time when Jerusalem was still in the hands of the Mahometans, A.D. 1048. A number of merchants from Amalfi, by consent and gift of the Khalifs, founded, not far from the Holy Tomb, a Benedictine cloister, consecrated to the Holy Virgin, with a chapel in honour of St. John the Baptist, and a hospital for the reception of pilgrims, which they confided to the management of the monks. In 1099 Godfrey of Bouillon having conquered Jerusalem, gave to the hospital a constitution, endowed it with considerable lands and capital, and released the monks from the duties of its management, which now devolved upon several of the Knights of his army, who soon formed themselves into a spiritual order, that was confirmed, in 1113, by Pope Paschal II.

The members, who made the vows of obedience, chastity and poverty, divided themselves into three classes.

1. Knights, warring against the infidels, and protecting the pilgrims.

2. Priests, managing the spiritual affairs of the Order.

3. Brother servants entrusted with the care and nursing of the sick in times of peace, who served as inferior warriors in times of war. Subsequently, a fourth class was created for subordinate menial duties and labours—that of Donatists.

The original costume of the Order was a black coat, a cloak with a pointed hood, adorned on the left side towards the heart with a small white cross, (that of the Donatists with only half a cross), as also with a golden cross in the middle of the breast. In war, the Knights wore splendid armour, and a red over-garment adorned with a silver cross.

The Knights of St. John, in conjunction with the Templars and other Knights, (with whom they lived, however, in continual conflicts) succeeded for a long time in keeping in their hands the tottering throne of Jerusalem, for which cause they fought with such admirable zeal, that many places in the Holy Land have now become monuments of their valour—more especially Jerusalem (1152), Ascalon (1153), Balbais (1118), Hittin (1187), &c.; nor did they retire—as the other Knights and secular Princes did—from the campaign even after Soliman had, in 1187, conquered Jerusalem. They greatly harassed the Turks, first from Margat, then from Acca (Ptolemais), in which last place

AUSTRIA. Table IV. PLATE 7.

Hurst and Blackett, London. 1858.

they maintained themselves for nearly a whole century. After the loss, however, of Ptolemais, the last refuge of the Christians in the Holy Land, Villiers, the Grand Master, saved himself with the remnant of the Knights in the island of Cyprus, where king Lusignan consigned to them the half demolished town of Limisso.

There they built a fleet, and soon became one of the first maritime powers in the Mediterranean. In 1308, their power was increased by its union with the Order of St. Samson of Jerusalem. The Grand Master, Villaret, now resolved to remove his residence to Rhodes, which the Saracens had taken from the Greek Emperor Andronicus. The Pope approved of the plan, promised support, and vested in him the right of appointing the future Archbishop of Rhodes. The knights succeeded in conquering (15th August, 1309) the island, whence they called themselves the 'Knights of Rhodes.' The Council of Vienna conceded to them (1311) the greatest part of the possessions of the dissolved Order of the Templars, at which period their power may be said to have reached its zenith.

In a glorious battle (1321) Gerard du Pius, the Vicar General of the Order, destroyed the great Moslem fleet, and in conjunction with the Venetians and the King of Cyprus, the Knights conquered (1341) Smyrna; which Timur, however, wrested from them after an obstinate resistance. The same Vicar General freed the King of Armenia from the Turks (1347), destroyed the fleet of the Egyptian pirates in the harbour of Alexandria, and conquered that town (1365). He likewise destroyed, near the island Longo, the fleet of Sultan Al Nager al Daher (1440), and repulsed successfully four years afterwards a second attack of the Sultan upon Rhodes. Even Muhamed II. when he besieged (1480) Rhodes with one hundred thousand men, and one hundred and sixty ships, was compelled to raise the siege, after having suffered heavy losses; and when after his death, the fraternal disputes about the crown and empire compelled the younger Prince Zizim (1482) to take refuge at Rhodes, placing himself under the protection of the Grand Master, the latter demanded and received 35,000 ducats from the victorious Bajazeth for the annual support of his younger brother, besides 10,000 ducats as indemnity for the expenses of the last war.

In 1485, the Order received a further accession of wealth and power, by the Pope's grant of the possessions of the abrogated Order of the "Sacred Tomb" and "St. Lazarus." In 1501, the Grand Master d'Aubusson was appointed Generalissimo of the troops of the combined Princes against the Mahometan pirates; and a few years afterwards, the Grand Master, Emmerick of Amboise, fought and won the great naval battle against the Egyptians, near the Port Lajazzo in Caramania.

Internal dissensions, however, added to the arbitrary dispositions of the Popes, greatly tended to weaken the power of the Order in latter times. Soliman II. attacked Rhodes in 1522, with a fleet of four hundred sails, and an army of one hundred and forty thousand men. That place was defended only by six hundred Knights, and four thousand five hundred soldiers of the Order. The Sultan would probably have raised the siege of a place which was so obstinately defended by the brave Knights, who repeatedly inflicted heavy losses upon his troops, had it not been betrayed by the Chancellor of the Order, Andreas of Amaral, who, out of revenge for not having been elected Grand Master, pointed out to the enemy a weak point in the fortifications, by which the Turks entered, as the head of the traitor was falling by the hand of the executioner. The brave Knights, even at that critical moment, obtained terms of capitulation and free retreat. They left their residence, now a complete ruin, which they had gloriously maintained for nearly two hundred and twenty years, in fifty vessels which brought them, and four thousand inhabitants of the place to Candia. Thence they repaired to Venice, Rome, Viterbo, Nizza, Villafranca, and Syracuse; until 1530, when the Emperor Charles V, enfeoffed them with the island of Malta, together with Tripolis, and the islands of Gozzo and Comino, under the condition that they should wage an incessant war against the pirates and infidels.

In this their new residence, they served for a long time for Europe, as a strong bulwark against the Turks; they were courted by the monarchs of Protestant Europe, despite the slur cast upon their religious principles, ever since the introduction of the Reformation in England, Germany, and the Northern States of Europe, and notwithstanding the loss of Tripolis (1552) which was wrested from them by Dragut, the Saracen General. During the whole of the 17th century, it was, indeed, by their assistance alone that the European powers, each and all, were enabled to make head against the powerful Turks, and finally succeeded in expelling them from Candia, Prevesa, St. Maura, Koron, Navarin, Modon, and Chio.

Nor are there wanting brilliant pages in their history as late even as the middle of the eighteenth century, though the Order had then greatly suffered by the moral degeneration of its members. The events, however, of 1761, by which Malta and the Order were only saved from total destruction by the intercession of France, sufficiently testified to the utter decline and fall of that gigantic institution, while the Turks, themselves, thenceforth began to look at the Knights of Malta no longer as dangerous enemies, but as mere troublesome, factious, and quarrelsome neighbours, whom they were obliged to spare and leave unmolested, simply because they were protected by the great powers of Europe.

The French Revolution deprived the Order of all their privileges and possessions in France, (19th September, 1792) while in 1798, Malta fell into the hands of Napoleon by the cowardly capitulation of Baron Hompesch, their Grand Master. Though the Emperor Paul of Russia declared himself in the same year Grand Master, and though Malta was conquered by England in 1801, it was never returned to the Order, which was deprived, at the same time, of its possessions in Germany, by the Princes of the Rhenish Confederation.

Having thus lost all political importance, the Order was no longer headed by a Grand Master, but by a deputy Grand Master, who resided from 1805 to 1814 at Catanea and afterwards at Ferrara. In more recent times, some of its possessions in Lombardy, Parma, Modena, Lucca and Naples, were restored. The Order still exists in those states, as also in Bohemia, Russia, and Spain, though under a modified constitution, and in separate bodies. Since 1831, the Deputy Grand Master has resided at Rome.

The members are divided into professed Knights, *i. e.* Knights who have really sworn to the constitution and made the vows prescribed by the statutes, and honorary Knights who are merely allowed to wear the dress and insignia without strictly belonging to the Order. The favour is granted to Catholic noblemen of honourable reputation, and of noble descent by both parents. The first class only exists in countries where the Order is still in possession of some landed property.

The costume of the Knights of the first class, consists of a frock-coat of scarlet cloth, with white lining, facings, collar, hat and plume. That of the second class is a similar coat, but with black velvet lining, facings and collar, and a black hat and plume. Both classes have white hat flaps, epaulettes with thick golden tassels, buttons, spurs, and hat string equally of gold, pantaloons of white casimir with golden trimmings.

The decoration (Plate 7. Tab. IV. Nos. 23 and 24) is a white octagonal cross suspended by a black ribbon; but the embellishments attached to it, are different in the different countries where the Order exists under royal authority. (*See* Spain and Prussia).

MEDALS AND DECORATIONS OF HONOUR.

1. *The Civil Cross of Honour.*—This, of all the decorations of honour in Austria, deserves peculiar notice. It was founded by the Emperor Francis I. in 1814, and distributed personally by him on the 26th May, 1815. It occupies the first rank in public estimation next to the Orders of Theresa and St. Stephen, and forms a sort of transition from Orders to decorations of inferior degree. It was conferred as a civil honour for zeal and merit displayed during the critical years of 1814 and 1815.

A committee of several Ministers of State, under the Presidency of the Minister of Justice, Count Wallis, had been formed to judge of, and enquire into the merits of the candidates.

Only two hundred out of four thousand competent candidates were honoured with the Cross. The strict and rigid enquiry into the merits of the candidates has caused this distinction to be highly prized by the public.

Upon the obverse of the Cross (Plate 7. Tab. IV. Nos. 25 and 29) are the words: 'Libertate Europæ asserta 1813—14' (Europe's liberty maintained), and upon the reverse: 'Grati Principes et Patria, Franciscus Imp. Aug.' (the Prince and country are grateful). It was presented in gold and silver, and is worn at the button-hole, suspended by a black ribbon with dark yellow borders.

2. *The Military Medal of Honour*, also called *Medal of Valour or Merit.*—It was founded by the Emperor Joseph II. as a reward for sub-officers and privates, and is divided into gold and silver medals, according to the respective degree of merit and distinction.

To the first is attached an increased pay of fifty per cent; the medals may be worn even after the owners have quitted the military service, in which case the possessors of the golden one enjoys the additional amount of half-pay connected with it.

On the obverse (Tab. IV. No. 28) is seen the effigy of the Emperor with his name, and on the reverse (No. 27) the inscription: 'Der Tapferkeit' (To valour), surrounded by a laurel wreath. It is worn suspended by a ribbon of red and white stripes. At the death of the owner it passes to his heirs, who have the option of exchanging it for money, in which case the War Treasury pays for the golden medal 35 fl. 28 kr. (about £3 10s.); or for the silver, 1 fl. 26 kr. (3s).

3. *Cross of Honour for Military Chaplains*, was founded by the Emperor Francis I. on the 26th November, 1801, for spiritual duties performed on the field of battle under perilous circumstances. It is worn suspended by a striped ribbon of red and white, has the form of a square cross, and is edged with trefoil leaves. Upon the round scutcheon are the words: 'Piis Meritis' (For pious services). (Tab. IV. No. 21).

4. *The Civil Medal of Honour* is of gold and of three different sizes, and is conferred on individuals of both sexes. The largest exhibits, upon the obverse, the effigy of the founder, the Emperor Francis I., with the inscription: 'Franciscus Austriæ Imperator,' while the reverse represents a temple, with the inscription: 'Austria ad imperii dignitatem evecta' (Austria raised to Imperial dignity).

The two smaller medals show on the face the effigy of the Emperor, with the inscription: 'Franciscus Aust. Imp. Hun. Boh. Gal. Lod. Rex. A. A.' (Tab. IV. No. 31), the reverse, the Scales of Justice, Sceptre, and Mercury's staff, and above them a crown with the inscription: 'Justitia Regnorum Fundamentum' (Justice is the foundation of empires). These medals are worn on the left side of the breast, suspended by a red ribbon. Of particular distinction is the great medal suspended by a golden chain.

5. *The Cross of the Bohemian Nobility.*—It was conferred, 1814, by Francis I. on those of the Bohemian nobility, who had formed, during the war of that year, a volunteer body guard, which accompanied the person of the Emperor throughout the whole campaign. It is bestowed on no one else. It is red enamelled, bears in the centre the white Bohemian lion, with the inscription: 'Nobilibus Bohemis bello gallico fidis corporis custodibus Franciscus Augustus, MDCCCXIV.' It is worn on the left side of the breast, suspended by a ribbon of three equal stripes, red in the middle and white at the two extremes.

6. *The Military Decoration of* 1814 (Tab. IV. No. 30), is a cross of the same shape as the Civil Cross of Honour, but rests, in distinction, on a laurel wreath; is cast from the French guns captured in the war, and is worn at the button hole suspended by a dark yellow ribbon with black borders. It belongs indiscriminately to all uniforms of the military who served during the campaigns of 1813 and 1814, and may be worn by them even after their retiring from service. The owners are also allowed to have their names engraved on the edge of the Cross. There were originally only one hundred thousand of them manufactured, viz. four thousand large, six thousand middling, and nine

hundred thousand small ones. The number has since, no doubt, considerably increased.

7. *The Distinction and Badge of Confidence.*—To mark the merit of soldiers from the degree of sergeant downwards, as also to promote re-engagements in the army, distinction plates were introduced, worn on the left side of the breast. Native soldiers may receive them when still in service, or have re-enlisted after having completed the prescribed term of service. The forms are: (Plate 6. Tab. III. No. 18) for the first, and form No. 17, for the second re-engagement.

THE ORDER OF FRANCIS-JOSEPH.

This Order (Plate 8. Tab. V. Nos. 32 and 33) was founded by the present Emperor Francis Joseph I. as a public acknowledgment of distinguished merit, indiscriminately for all classes of society. The first statutes were published on the 2nd December, 1849; but were modified in the succeeding year on the 25th December, 1850. They provide: 1. The annual festival of the Order to be held on the anniversary of the accession to the throne of the present Emperor.

2. The Order to bear the name: The Order of Francis Joseph, with the motto 'Viribus unitis.'

3. The Order to be conferred on individuals of distinguished merit, without regard to birth, religion or rank.

4. The members to be nominated by the Emperor himself, their number being unlimited.

5. The dignity of Grand Master to be inseparably vested in the Austrian Crown.

6. The Order to consist of three degrees: Knights of the Grand Cross, Commanders, and Knights.

AUSTRIA. *Table V.* PLATE 8.

Hurst and Blackett, London. 1858.

7. The badge of the Order to be a gold enamelled Cross, externally octagonal and bent forward.

The Cross in itself is red, with a golden ring round it. The middle scutcheon is circular and white surrounded by a golden stripe, and contains on the obverse the two letters F. J. (Franciscus Josephus). Between the four arms of the cross is visible the two-headed crowned eagle in gold, partly enamelled black, holding in his two beaks a golden chain, in the lower links of which is the motto: 'Viribus unitis.' The reverse of the cross is the same as above described, with the only difference that (the year) 1849 is substituted for the letters F. J.

The Knights of the Grand Cross wear the badge by a deep red ribbon, four inches wide, across the right shoulder, and at the side of it, on the left breast, an octagonal silver star, the centre of which contains the decoration as described above in the obverse of the Cross.

The Commanders wear it round the neck, suspended by a similar red ribbon about two inches wide.

The simple Knights suspend it on the left side at the button hole, suspended by a similar ribbon about one and a half inches wide.

On ordinary occasions, the members may wear the Cross in a diminished form at the button hole, suspended by a small golden chain.

The form of the chain is described in "Bavaria," (Plate 16. Tab. VI. A. B. and C.) Fig. A. exhibits the large chain of the Grand Cross Knights; Fig. B. that of the Commanders; and Fig. D. the smallest one of the Knights. The centre scutcheons of the eagles in Fig. B., and the scutcheons with the golden crown in Fig. C. are white enamelled, while the letters *F. I.* in Fig. D. are red enamelled.

Members are not allowed, without special permission, to wear the Order adorned with precious stones, though they are at liberty to do so with their family crests.

The grant of the Order does not entitle the wearer to any degree of nobility, or any other hereditary distinction.

THE CIVIL CROSS OF MERIT

was founded on the 16th February, 1850, as a substitution for the previous 'Civil Medal of Honour.' The Cross consists of four classes. The first is of gold with a crown above it (Plate 8, Tab. V. No. 34); the second is likewise of gold but without crown; the third is of silver with a crown; and the fourth of silver without a crown.

The Cross is worn at the button hole, or in a knot, on the left breast, suspended by a deep red ribbon.

BADEN (GRAND-DUCHY).

The Family Order of Loyalty.—This Order, the highest in the Grand Duchy, was founded by Margrave Charles William of Baden, Durlach and Hochberg, on the 17th June, 1715—the day on which he laid the foundation stone of his castle at Karlsruhe, and which is still the annual meeting day of the Chapter. The Order was renewed on the 8th May, 1803, by the Elector, afterwards Grand Duke Charles Frederick, Margrave of Baden, on the occasion of the electoral dignity being transferred to the reigning house of Baden. It has since been divided into two classes: Knights of the Grand Cross and Commanders. But by the new statutes of the 17th June, 1840, only the first class was retained, numbering in it, no one but reigning Princes, Princes of blood, or such eminent men in the Grand Duchy who bear the title 'Excellency,' or are already in possession of the Order of the Zähring Lion, or have peculiarly distinguished themselves by extraordinary acts of loyalty or valour. The class of Commanders has ceased to exist ever since 1814.

The badge (Plate 9. Tab. I. Nos. 1 and 2) is an octagonal Cross with the ducal crown above it, enamelled red, and two C's in monogram connecting each of the four corners. The same initial is seen on the white centre, where it is represented leaning on green rocks, surrounded by the motto of the Order: 'Fidelitas' (Loyalty). On the reverse of the Cross are the arms of Baden. It is worn by a broad orange-coloured ribbon with silver borders, by the Knights of the Grand Cross across the right shoulder, and by the Commanders round the neck. On the left side of the breast is, in addition, attached a silver octogonal star, to which is appended the same Cross of the above description, except that the motto and the middle scutcheon are of orange colour.

THE CHARLES FREDERICK ORDER OF MILITARY MERIT.

As the name indicates, the Order was founded for reward of military merit, by the Grand Duke Charles Frederick, on the 4th April, 1807. It is designated as a reward—as the patent says—'for the exploits of officers who might have neglected them with impunity, or were performed by them with peculiar skill, wisdom, courage, and decision.' It consists of three classes: Knights of the Grand Cross (to which only Generals are admitted), Commanders, and Knights. The number of the members is unlimited. The Grand Duke is Grand Master of the Order, and has the right to confer it on whomsoever he pleases without consulting the Chapter. The latter meets every year on the 20th November, when the claims of the respective candidates are examined, and taken into consideration. The chairman, on that occasion, is generally the Grand Duke, or in his absence the senior Knight of the Grand Cross. The three oldest members of the three classes enjoy a pension of 400, 200, and 100 fl. (£40, 20, and 10) respectively.

The badge of the Order is the Cross (Plate 9. Tab. I. No. 4) suspended by a ribbon of three stripes, yellow in the middle and red at the extremes, and with white borders. Both the size of the Cross, and the width of the ribbon differ in each of the three classes. It is worn by the Knights of the Grand Cross

BADEN. Table I. PLATE 9.

Hurst and Blackett, London. 1858.

BADEN. Table II.   PLATE 10.

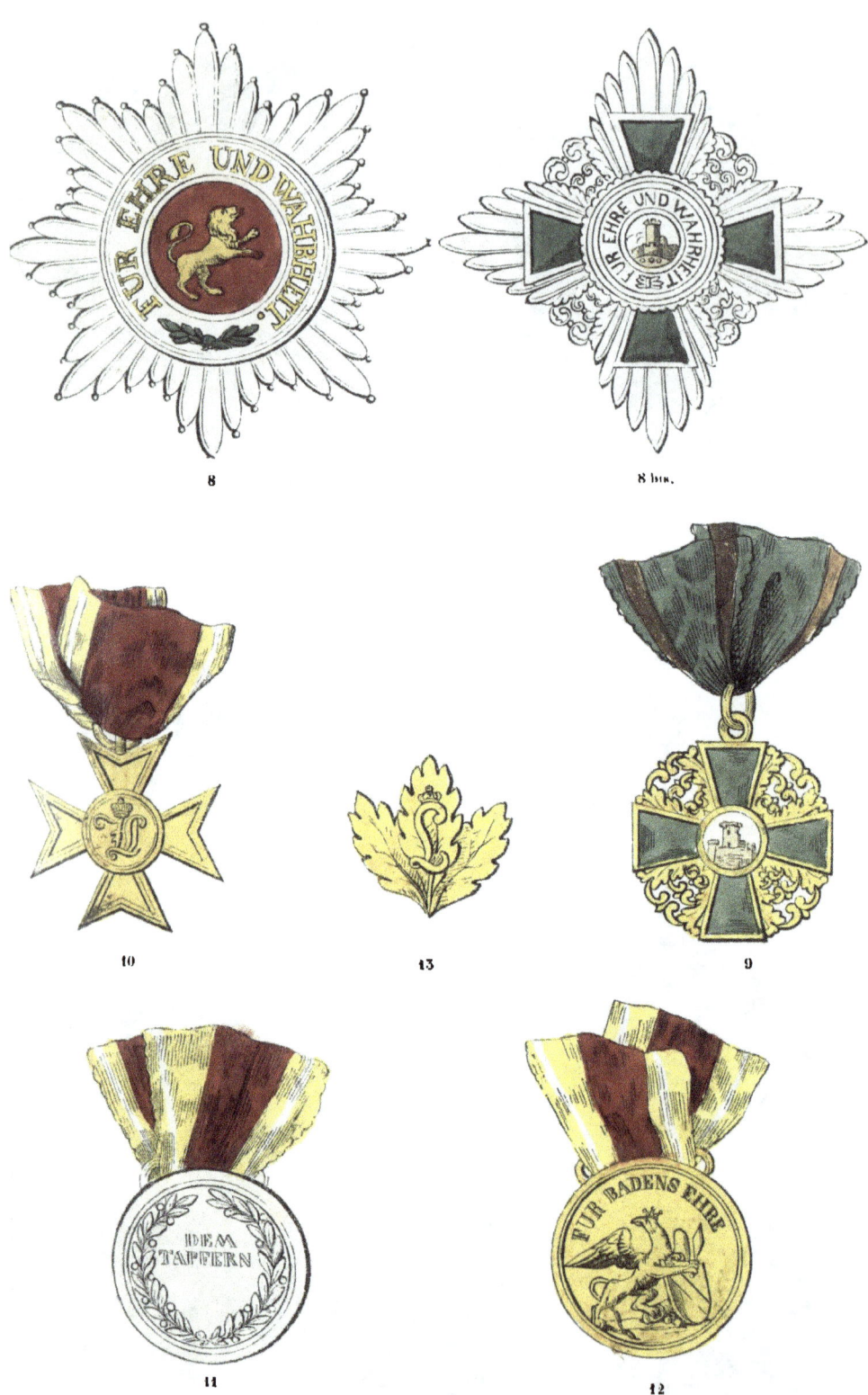

Hurst and Blackett, London. 1858.

across the left shoulder towards the right hip; by the Commanders round the neck, and by the Knights at the button hole of the left side. The Cross is accompanied by a silver star (Tab. I. No. 3) attached to the left side of the breast, and the centre of which resembles the reverse of the Cross; it is presented to the Knights of the Grand Cross at their nomination, while the Commanders only receive it when they occupy the rank of Generals, or are about to be promoted to that rank.

The Order was last conferred in 1820.

Equally with the above Order, was founded for sub-officers and privates, and under similar qualifications, the *Military Medal of Merit*, which is worn (Plate 10. Tab. II. Nos. 11 and 12) at the button hole of the left breast. It is presented either in gold or in silver. To the former is attached an increase of double pay, and to the latter of half pay.

ORDER OF THE LION OF ZAEHRINGEN.

The Grand Duke Charles founded this Order in 1812, on the anniversary christening or namesday of his consort, Stephanie of Beauharnais (niece of the Empress Josephine). He named the Order after the Ducal House of Zähringen, the ancestors of the reigning family of Baden. The badge is a golden Cross, the intervening spaces of which are joined with golden clasps, while the green enamel in the middle of the obverse represents the ruins of the original castle of Zähringen in a round field with a golden ring (Tab. II. No. 9). The reverse shows upon a similar field of red colour a lion rampant in gold.

The Grand Master is the Grand Duke; the Order has four classes: Knights of the Grand Cross, and Commanders of first and second classes, and Knights. The Princes of the House of Baden are born Knights of the Grand Cross. The number of the members is unlimited.

The Order is worn by the Knights of the Grand Cross across the right shoulder by a green ribbon with orange coloured borders, accompanied by an octagonal silver star; the round red scutcheon in the middle contains a golden lion in a fighting position, with the inscription: 'Für Ehre und Wahrheit' (For honour and truth) (Tab. II. No. 8). Knights who are already in possession of the Family Order of Loyalty, wear a Grand Cross round the neck.

The Knights of the first class wear, besides, a square silver star with the Cross of the Order upon it, and surrounded by a red ring, with the above inscription.

The simple Knights wear the decoration at the button-hole.

As a particular distinction, the decoration of the Commanders and Knights is often adorned with an oak leaf (Tab. II. No. 13). This is the case since 1826.

The first chapter was held three years after its foundation, in 1815, at the time of the Vienna Congress. The size of the Cross varies with the different classes.

DISTINCTION OF MERIT FOR OFFICERS, SUB-OFFICERS, AND PRIVATES.

This Order was founded on 18th February, 1831, by Grand Duke Leopold, as a public acknowledgment for long and loyal service in the army.

1. Officers who have served in the line twenty-five years (including the years of lower rank) receive the small golden Cross (Plate 10. Tab. II. No. 10).

2. Privates and sub-officers receive a buckle with a red ribbon, of yellow stripes, and white borders. It has three classes: for twelve, eighteen, and twenty-five years service; the respective buckles (Plate 9. Tab. I. Nos. 5, 6 and 7) are of iron (mounted in silver), silver or gilt.

The Cross is worn by the officers at the button-hole, suspended by the same ribbon as above; while the buckles of the other classes are worn on the left side of the breast.

Since the foundation of these latter badges of distinction, the 'Military Order and Medal of Charles Frederick' were discontinued to be conferred for service of twenty-five years, and the claim thereto is now confined to its original destination: viz. to 'valour in war.'

THE MEDAL OF CIVIL SERVICE

in gold (value 18, 12, and 6 ducats) shows on one side the effigy of the Grand Duke, the founder, and is worn at the button-hole, suspended by an orange coloured ribbon. It was founded in the reign of Grand Duke Charles Frederick, and is conferred on civil officers of inferior rank for long and loyal service, as well as on private individuals who have given assistance in accidents of fire and water, or distinguished themselves in the useful arts and industry.

DECORATION FOR FIELD SERVICE

was founded 27th January, 1839. It consists of a bronze medal, representing on the obverse, a vulture holding in his left claw the Baden crest, and in the right a sword, with the inscription 'Für Baden's Ehre' (For Baden's honour), while the reverse contains the words: 'Für treuen Dienst im Kriege' (For faithful service in war) surrounded by an oak wreath. It is worn upon the left breast by an orange coloured ribbon, with red and white borders. It is conferred on soldiers in the line, or in the landwehr, who have made at least one campaign.

BAVARIA.

THE KNIGHTLY ORDER OF ST. HUBERT.

Duke Reinhold IV. of Liege and Guelderland having died in 1423 without issue, his duchy, Gueldern, fell to Arnold of Egmont, while Adolph of Berg became possessor of the Duchy of Liege. But Arnold, believing that Adolph had taken the lion's share in the inheritance, attempted at first to right himself by force of arms. He consented, however, afterwards to a compromise, and a truce of ten years. But, when after the death of Adolph in 1437, his cousin, Gerhard V., Count of Ravensberg, inherited the Duchies of Liege and Berg, Arnold re-appeared with his old claims, and entered with an army into the territory of Liege. In confidence of his right, Gerhard gave him battle (3rd November, 1444) near Ravensberg in Westphalia, in which he was victorious, and completely routed his foe. In commemoration of that happy event, which took place on the feast of St. Hubert, (3rd November), Gerhard founded an Order which he placed under the patronage of that saint, and gave it originally the name of the Order of the Horn, the Knights being used to wear a golden chain composed of bugle-horns.

The Order flourished until 1609, when the male dynasty of the Liege house became extinct at the death of John William. Since then, the Order was forgotten for nearly a whole century owing to the pending disputes about the inheritance, as also to the intervening Thirty Years' War, and it was at last rescued from oblivion by the Elector of the Palatinate, John William of the House of Neuburg, on the 29th September, 1708. Having inherited a part of the territory to which the Order previously belonged, he declared himself Grand Master of the revived institution, gave it a constitution and new statutes; and bestowed upon the first twelve Knights of the Grand Cross, who were Colonels in the army, the possession of small tracts of land. The Order consisted under the Elector, as Grand Master, of twelve Counts or Barons, and an unlimited number of Princes and noblemen who did not belong to any other order. The nomination was vested in the Chapter, who voted by majority; the candidates elected were obliged to pay 100 ducats entrance fee for the poor. The Knights wore a large red ribbon, and upon the breast a silver Cross within a gold embroidered star with the inscription: 'In Fidelitate constans' (Constant in loyalty). The two successors of John William still further enlarged the statutes; but the last and still prevailing ordinances are those promulgated by Maximilian Joseph IV. (first King of Bavaria) on the 18th May, 1808.

He declared the Order the first in the kingdom, and brought it into connection with that of Civil Merit, by decreeing that candidates must be members of six years' standing of the latter. The Order counts now only twelve Knights from the ranks of Counts and Barons, exclusive of the Sovereign, and the members whom the latter may, in addition, choose to nominate from among the Princes, both native and foreign. The Chapter is annually held either on the 29th September, the day of the renewal of the Order by the Elector, John William, or on the 2nd February (the festival of the Virgin Purification). The entrance fees are now 200 ducats in gold (about £100) for Princes, and 100 ducats

BAVARIA. Table I.   PLATE II

Hurst and Blackett, London. 1858

(£50) in gold, besides 100 rixthalers (£20) for Counts and Barons.

The insignia of the Order consist: 1. Of a star (Plate 11. Tab. I. No. 1) worn by the Knights embroidered in silver upon the left breast. Upon that star is attached a cross embroidered with silver and interwoven and mounted in gold; it contains in the middle a round field of flame coloured, or poppy-red velvet, with the motto of the Order: 'In Treu vast' (Constant in loyalty) in golden Gothic letters.

2. Of a poppy-red ribbon, about three and a half inches wide, with narrow green borders, worn across the left shoulder towards the right hip, on which is suspended an octagonal large cross, white enamelled and blazing with gold, while between each of the arms of the cross are seen three golden points, and above the whole the royal crown. The central field represents, on the obverse, the history of the conversion of St. Hubert, with the above motto in a red ring. The reverse contains the Imperial ball, with the Cross in the shape of a globe, and with the inscription: 'In memoriam recuperatæ dignitatis avitæ, 1708' (In memory of the restoration of the original dignity, *i. e.* the Order). (Tab. I. Nos. 2 and 3). This great Cross, together with the large chain, as described in § 3, are, however, only worn on certain festivals, nor is it allowed to adorn the chain with precious stones. The daily decoration of the Knights (by fine of 20 thalers for each omission) is a small Cross, which may be adorned with a few precious stones in proportion to its size.

3. Of a golden chain of forty-two links, of which twenty-one represent, in oblong squares, the history of the conversion of St. Hubert; while the other twenty-one, which are alternately red and green, contain the Gothic initials in monogram, of the words: 'Treu vast.'

The costume, on festival days, is the Imperial mantle dress

i. e. a black collar, a sash of the same colour; narrow, short breeches with poppy-red garters and bows, and a short black mantle after the old Castilian fashion, plume and sword.

THE KNIGHTLY ORDER OF SAINT GEORGE.

The origin of the Order cannot be shown with historical accuracy. The statements of the Bavarian chroniclers, that the Order was brought over to Germany from the Holy Land, as early as the twelfth century by Welf I., Otto III. and IV. and Eckart II., are, at least, not sufficiently warranted by historical records. The same may be said of the alleged renewal of the Order by the Emperor Maximilian I., who is said to have founded an Order of St. George in 1494, previous to the campaign against the Turks. These questionable traditions are, however, closely connected with the strictly historical account of the second renewal, or rather first foundation of the Order by the Elector Charles Albert, afterwards the Emperor Charles VII., who received it as a pious legacy from his father, Max Emanuel. The latter had, during his campaigns against the Turks, solemnly resolved to renew it as a military badge of distinction; but this he was prevented by death from accomplishing. His intention was, however, carried out by his son, who founded on the 24th April, 1729, the knightly Order of St. George, imposing upon the members the duty of venerating that saint, and believing in the Immaculate Conception of the Virgin.

He gave statutes to the Institution, and richly endowed it with large priories, prebends, and afterwards with provostships; and Pope Benedict XIII. confirmed the Order, by a Bull, granting to it all the honours, privileges, and advantages which had been conceded by previous Popes to all the high Orders of Germany. After the extinction of the Louis line of Bavaria, the Elector Charles Theodore adopted it (1778) as a Palatinate-Bavarian institution, while his successor Maximilian Joseph sanctioned it as a royal Bavarian Order, only second in rank to that of St. Hubert. King Louis made some alterations in the constitution in 1827.

The King is the Grand Master while the Crown Prince is first Grand Prior, and the next Prince second Grand Prior. The Chapter comprises six Knights of the Grand Cross, twelve Commanders, and an unlimited number of Knights, some of whom are nominated by the Grand Master as Honorary Knights of the Grand Cross..

Since 1741, a spiritual class has been added, consisting of a Bishop, a Provost, four Deans, and a number of Chaplains, who enjoy the distinction of Papal House Prelates. This class has been instituted and confirmed by the Bulls of Popes Benedict XIV. (6th October, 1741), and Pius VI. (30th April, 1782). The candidates must prove their Catholic descent, and the Order consists of two languages: the German and a foreign; the latter, however, counts only about one third of the members. The possession of another Order excludes the reception of this, without the special permission of the Grand Master. In the oath, the candidates confess to believe 'in the Immaculate Conception of the Virgin without the original, or birth-sin.' The Order celebrates, therefore, besides its anniversary, the 24th April, the 8th December, as the festival of the Holy Conception of the Virgin. The costume on these occasions consists of a long robe of bright blue velvet, with a train and without sleeves, more or less embroidered with silver, lined with white satin or Gros-de-Naples, and with a velvet collar of the same colour. Upon this robe is the star of the Order embroidered on the left side (Plate 2. Tab. I. No. 5). Beneath is worn an undergarment opening by buttons to the half of the bosom. Short breeches of white satin, and similar rosettes, trimmed with silver fringes, white silk stockings, and white cordwain shoes, a high round hat of black felt with a silver sling of six, three or four cords, white leather gloves, a ruff of white lace buttoned in the front and hanging down upon the breast by the two ends, and finally a white satin sash round the body and fastened in a ring on the left side, with a short Knight's sword in a white belt, complete this elegant costume.

The badge (Plate 2, Tab. I. Nos. 6 and 7) is worn by a broad sky-blue ribbon with white and dark blue borders, by the Knights of the Grand Cross upon the breast, and by the Commanders and Knights round the neck. The size differs with the degree of rank. The decoration represents on the adverse (No. 7) the Immaculate Conception of the Virgin, and on the reverse St. George on horseback together with the dragon. In the four corners of the Cross, on the obverse, are seen the initials of the words: 'Virgini immaculatæ Bavaria immaculata' (Immaculate Bavaria to the immaculate Virgin); on the reverse is the motto of the Order: 'Justus ut Palma florebit' (The just will flourish like a palm tree). Upon the chain of which there are three links in Plate 2, Tab. II. No. 11 are distributed the words: 'In Fide, Justitia et Fortitudine' (In faith, justice and valour).

THE MILITARY ORDER OF MAXIMILIAN JOSEPH.

On the 8th June, 1797, the Elector Charles Theodor, founded a military decoration of honour, which King Maximilian Joseph transformed into a royal Order under the above title, on the 1st March, 1806, the day when the Bavarian Prince assumed the title of King. It is formed after, and to the same purpose as the Baden Order of Military Merit of Charles Frederick. That the Order is held in high estimation, is owing

BAVARIA. *Table II.* PLATE 12.

to the extra advantages and privileges attached to it. The six senior Knights of the Grand Cross, the eight senior Commanders, and the fifty senior Knights receive an annual pension of 1500, 500, and 300 fl. (£150, £50 and £30) respectively. Every Bavarian commoner becomes ennobled with his nomination, and if his father and grandfather were also members of the Order, the nobility becomes hereditary in the family. The funeral of a deceased member is attended with ceremonies prescribed for that of one rank above his own. To these personal privileges, King Louis added (27th February, 1835) the following benefits for the children of the members. An annuity of 300 fl. (£30) is granted every year to eight children of living or deceased members, namely: to males until their twenty-fifth year of age, and to females until they are married, or in some way provided for, otherwise the grant continues for life; and the same is the case also with males if incapable of gaining a livelihood from physical defects or infirmities.

The decoration is a gold white enamelled cross with golden rays in the corners, placed under a royal crown. The blue enamelled middle shows on the obverse the initials in gold of the royal founder, Maximilian Joseph, and on the reverse, equally in gold, the motto of the Order: 'Virtuti pro patriâ' (To valour for the fatherland). The Knights wear it (Tab. II. Nos. 9 and 10) upon the left side of the breast, suspended by a black ribbon with narrow white and blue borders. The Commanders wear it round the neck, while the Knights of the Grand Cross suspend it across the right shoulder, or round the neck, and have, in addition, attached upon the left breast an embroidered star (Tab. II. No. 8). The size of the decoration accords with the class occupied by the members.

CIVIL ORDER OF MERIT OF THE BAVARIAN CROWN.

This Order was also founded by King Maximilian Joseph on the 19th May, 1808, and is of the same character for civil servants as is the Military Order of Merit for the military. "It is meant," according to the statutes, "to confer an honourable distinction on the servants of the state, and on the citizens of all classes of society who should have distinguished themselves by prominent virtues and merits."

It consists of three classes: Grand Cross Knights, Commanders, and Knights. The three classes were originally to consist respectively of only twelve, twenty-four and one hundred members, but the number was subsequently (8th October, 1817) increased to twenty-four, forty, and one hundred and sixty, exclusive (in the first class) of those Knights on whom was at the same time conferred the Order of St. Hubert. This Order, like the Military one of Merit, entitles the candidate to personal or hereditary nobility. The three degrees are conferred by recommendation of the Council of the Order.

By the original law, the total funds of the Order were to be applied to the annual pensions of a certain number of members of all classes, but in 1824, the founder decreed that a part should be set aside for the support of twenty children of the members of the three classes, each to the annual sum of 250 fl. (£25). King Louis (1834) increased that sum to 300 fl. (£30), and the number of the recipients (1835) to thirty-eight.

The decoration consists of an octagonal white enamelled Cross, encompassed by an oak wreath under a royal crown. The middle of the obverse contains a golden crown upon white and blue rucs, with the legend in golden letters within a red ring : ' Virtus et Honos ' (Virtue and honour.) The reverse shows the effigy of the founder, with the inscription: ' Max. Jos. Rex Boyvariæ ' (Max Joseph, King of Bavaria.) This large Cross (Tab. II. Nos. 13 and 14) which differs in size with the various degrees, is worn suspended by a blue watered ribbon, with narrow white borders, by the Knights at the button hole, by the Commanders round the neck, and by the Knights of the Grand Cross across the left shoulder towards the right hip. The latter wear, in addition, upon the left breast an embroidered star (Tab. II. No. 12). No. 22 in Plate 13, Tab. III, represents three links of the middle part of the chain, the central link of which contains the initial of the founder. The oval intervals contain alternately the initials of the motto: ' Virtus et Honos.' Connected with the above Order is:

THE MEDAL OF CIVIL MERIT.

This medal, in gold, is bestowed on State-functionaries below the rank of Counsellor of Board or College. It gives no claim to nobility or support for children. To simple citizens it is presented in silver. Plate 15, Tab. V. No 32, contains the effigy of the founder with the inscription ' Max Jos. König von Baiern ' (Max Joseph, King of Bavaria). The reverse shows within a laurel wreath, the words : ' Dem Verdienste um Fürst und Vaterland ' (For merit of Prince and country). It is worn at the button hole of the left side, suspended by a silk ribbon one inch wide composed of two white and three bright-blue narrow stripes.

This medal supplies the place of several previous ones of a similar character, introduced by Charles Theodor (1794 and 1798), and by the Elector Max Joseph (1805) during the French war.

THE ROYAL LOUIS ORDER.

'Für ehrenvolle fünfzig Dienst-jahre' (For honourable service of fifty years), is the inscription upon the reverse of the Cross, impressed in golden letters upon white ground within a green enamelled laurel wreath—thus plainly indicating the object of the founder. It was created on the 25th August, 1827 (the date is given in the four corners of the reverse). The obverse bears the effigy and crown of the King in gold upon a white enamelled ground, while in the four corners of the Cross are the words: 'Ludwig König von Baiern' (Louis King of Bavaria) (Plate 14, Tab. IV. Nos. 27 and 28). The fifty years service required may have been spent partly or wholly in the service of the court, government, war department, or in the church of the country, or its incorporated provinces. For officers, the years of campaign count double, while those spent in inactive service count for nothing. The decoration is only conferred on individuals who bear the title of Counsellor. For those of lower rank, the badge consists of a gold medal (Plate 15, Tab. V. No. 30) with the same inscription as the Cross. Both are worn at the button-hole, suspended by a crimson ribbon with sky blue borders. The ribbon of the Cross is somewhat broader than that of the medal.

THE ST. MICHAEL ORDER OF MERIT.

This Order is one of those the objects and statutes of which have undergone manifold modifications in process of time. Its founder, Joseph Clemens, Elector of Cologne and Duke of Bavaria, introduced it on the 29th September, 1693, as a

BAVARIA. Table III. PLATE 15.

Hurst and Blackett, London. 1858.

Knightly Order exclusively for Catholics of noble descent, and imposed upon the members the duty of "defending religion and the honour of God." When Bavaria became a kingdom, and Maximilian Joseph I. began to introduce reforms in the several Orders of the state—as already seen in those of St. Hubert, St. George, and Max Joseph—he added, in the present Order, (11th September, 1808) the duty of "defending the fatherland." The statutes limited the number of the Knights of the Grand Cross to eighteen (who form the Chapter), of Officers to eight, and of Knights to thirty-six, all of whom must belong to the Catholic religion. The Grand Master was, however, free to nominate fourteen honorary members without regard to birth, rank, or religion. So it stood until the death of the Grand Master, Duke William of Bavaria in 1837. The new statutes date from the 16th February of that year, when the Order was erected into an Order of Merit, without distinction of birth, rank or religion, enlarging the claims thereto, to loyalty, patriotism, and distinction of useful works generally. Nobility is not *ipso facto* the result of the nomination. Since 1837, the number of the Grand Crosses for natives is fixed at twenty-four (exclusive of those conferred on the Knights of St. Hubert), of Commanders at forty, and of Knights at three hundred. The Order is now in so far connected with that of St. Michael, that the latter follows in rank the corresponding degree of the former.

The decorations (Plate 13, Tab. III. Nos. 16 and 17) are those of the Grand Crosses and Commanders, showing on the obverse in gold-relief St. Michael in warlike attire, surrounded by flashes of lightning. His shield bears the inscription ' Quis ut Deus ?' (Who is like God ?) The Cross of the (simple) Knights bears upon the face the initials of those three words. The four corners of the crosses of all classes are mounted in gold, containing in gold characters the initials: P. F. F. P. of the words 'Principi Fidelis Favere Patriæ' (True to the Prince and attached to the country). The Cross itself is azure blue, octagonal, and covered by a royal crown. The reverse (in all classes) contains in blue enamel the word 'Virtuti' (To virtue) upon a golden ground.

The Knights of the Grand Cross wear besides, upon the left breast, a golden cross upon a star of silver rays with the above motto 'Quis ut Deus?' (Plate 13, Tab. III. No. 15). Of the width of the ribbon by which the Order is suspended, two thirds are dark blue, and one third rose colour, in equal proportions for both ends. The Knights of the Grand Cross wear the Order across the right (since 1844 upon the left) shoulder, suspended by the above ribbon about three and a half inches wide; the Commanders wear it in smaller size round the neck by a somewhat narrower ribbon, while the Knights have it, in still smaller proportions, fastened to the coat.

Plate 14, Tab. IV. No. 29, represents the chain which the members formerly used to wear upon their costume on festival days, while the new statutes mention neither costume nor chain.

In 1846, the total number of the members was fixed at four hundred and sixteen, viz. thirty-six Grand Crosses, sixty Commanders, and three hundred and twenty Knights.

THE ORDER OF ST. ELIZABETH.

The first Consort of the Elector Charles Theodor of the Palatinate, Elizabeth Augusta, daughter of the Palatine Joseph Charles Emanuel of Schulzbach, founded this Order for ladies in honour of her sainted patroness and namesake, on the 18th October, 1766, as a purely charitable institution for the poor. It was confirmed on the 31st January, 1767, by Pope Clement XIII. and endowed with various indulgencies. The Catholic

BAVARIA. *Table IV.* PLATE 14.

Hurst and Blackett, London. 1858.

religion and the Seize Quartiers—the proof of noble descent running through sixteen generations of their own or their husband's ancestors—are indispensable conditions for candidates. The Grand Mistress is, however, empowered to nominate an unlimited number of ladies, from princely houses and her own court, as also six other married or widowed ladies of noble, though not ancient, descent. The nomination takes place either on Easter, or on St. Elizabeth's day (19th November). The entrance fee is four ducats. The badge (Tab. IV. Nos. 25 and 26) is a white enamelled Cross, representing on one side St. Elizabeth dispensing charity to the poor, and on the other the initial of the founder. It is worn on the left breast by a blue ribbon with red borders. No member can appear in public without it, except by fine of one ducat.

The King appoints the Grand Mistress; the present one is the Duchess of Leuchtenberg.

FEMALE ORDER AND INSTITUTION OF ST. ANN AT MUNICH.

The Order was founded by the relict of the Elector Maximilian III., Maria Anna Sophie, from her own private property, in 1784, for the benefit of the Bavarian nobility. The number of members was originally limited to ten single ladies, after the completion of their 15th year, who could prove their noble descent through sixteen generations. They were to live together in the establishment under the guidance of the Deanness, and perform, moreover, daily, at certain hours a choral service. Its existence under such regulations was but short, and in 1802, the Elector, afterwards King Max-Joseph IV., was induced to decree the discontinuance of convent life, especially as regarded the living under one roof. He left, however, to the inmates their allotted benefices or pensions, and even allowed them to make eligible marriages. The number of members who were endowed for life with pensions, he raised from ten to eighteen; ten of whom (all noble born) were to receive 1000 fl. (£100) each, two 500 fl. (£50) each, and six others (the daughters of commoners but civil officers of a certain rank) also 500 fl. (£50) each. The Lady Abbess of the establishment was to be, at least, a Princess of the reigning house. The costume worn, when at Court or before the Lady Abbess, remained unaltered; it consisted of a black garment, and of the insignia, the description of which will be given presently.

The financial position of the institution rendered, however, in 1825, a further reform indispensable. By a decree of the 10th February of that year, the benefices or pensions were reduced to 800 and 400 fl. respectively (to £80 and £40). By this and other means, the administration was enabled to increase the number of the members to twenty-five in the first, and forty-two in the second class, a third of whom were to be the daughters of military officers. The present Abbess is the Princess Adelgonde of Bavaria.

The costume of the Order is a black dress trimmed with lace, and a long black velvet mantle with a hood; the hood of the Abbess is trimmed with ermine. The badge (Plate 13, Tab. III. Nos. 18 and 19) is a gold Cross white enamelled, and enchased in blue, with rounded sides, and golden rings in the corners. It represents on the obverse the Virgin, and on the reverse the patron Saint of Bavaria, St. Benno, both in gold on white enamel. In the points of the obverse are distributed the words 'Sub tuam Præsidium' (Under thy protection), and of the reverse: 'Patronus Noster' (Our patron Saint).

FEMALE ORDER OF THE ST. ANN INSTITUTION AT WURZBURG.

By the will of the Countess Anne Maria of Dernbach, born Baroness Voit of Rieneck, in 1683, her estates were, in case her Consort should die without issue, to be applied to the foundation of an establishment for unmarried ladies of the Franconian nobility. It happened, that Count Dernbach died 1714, without direct heirs, and the Prince Bishop of Wurzburg, John Philip, therefore acted up to this disposition in the Countess's will. He founded the establishment, and fixed the number of the members at six, including the Abbess. They were bound to live under one roof, while the indispensable conditions of their admissibility were, the Catholic religion, descent of sixteen noble generations, *i. e.* eight on each of the parent's sides (the Franconian race in preference), and an age varying from twelve to sixteen years. Adoration of God, celebration of the memory of the founder, and education in all noble virtues and spiritual sciences, were the objects of the establishment. The Prince Bishop Frederick Charles confirmed these statutes 1793, while a considerable donation made in 1756 by Count Ostein, permitted an increase of the members to seven, including the Abbess.

When, at the beginning of the present century, the ancient relations of the German empire ceased to exist, and the principality of Wurzburg, like many other petty states, lost its independance, and became incorporated with Bavaria, the Elector Max-Joseph IV. abolished this institution, (4th April, 1803) but united it, after a few months, with the one at Munich, allowing from its revenues the pensions of twelve members, four at 800 fl. (£80), for native nobility, and eight at 400 fl. (£40), for state functionaries.

The peace of Pressburg (26th December, 1805), having restored the independance of Wurzburg by creating it a Grand-Duchy, its Sovereign, Prince Ferdinand Archduke of Austria, re-established the institution at Wurzburg by a convention with Bavaria (29th April, 1807), and gave it in 1811 new statutes. In 1814, though Wurzburg fell again to the share of Bavaria, the institution retained its independance, nor were its statutes materially altered, except that the number and title of the members were in so far modified, that instead of four members (as fixed in 1811), the number was now fixed at an uncertain number of honorary ladies, twelve noble ladies with pensions of 800 florins each, and twenty non-noble ladies with pensions of 400 florins each.

These pensions were granted until their marriage, and if married with royal consent, one year's pension was allowed by way of dower.

The badge (Tab. III. No. 20) is a gold Cross, white enamelled, and its broad sides rounded. The obverse represents in gold upon white enamelled ground St. Ann, and upon the points are distributed the words: 'In ihren edlen Töchtern' (In her noble daughters), while the reverse bears the crest of the founder. It is worn upon the black dress suspended by a red ribbon with silver borders.

THE ORDER OF THERESA.

"To grant to a certain number of unmarried noble ladies, a distinction of honour, as also a pension by which their income may be increased," so says the introductory part of the Patent. Theresa, late Queen of Bavaria, founded (12th December, 1827) the above Order, endowing it, from her own private property, with a revenue sufficient to allow an annual pension to twelve members, six of whom at 300 fl. (£30), and the other six at 100 fl. (£10). The reigning Queen (even as a widow) is always to be Grand Mistress of the Order, or by her choice, and by consent of the King, some Princess of the royal house. The pretension—as in the previous one—to the Order, is nobility of ancient Bavarian descent, and an age above ten years. The candidates must also show that their own private income does not exceed annually the sum of 300 fl. All Christian sects are admissible. The pension ceases with marriage; but if suitably married according to their rank, they are allowed to wear the insignia in future as 'honorary ladies,' though the pension is discontinued.

The badge (Plate 14, Tab. IV. No. 23, front; and No. 24, reverse) is a Cross, worn by a bow of a white-watered ribbon with two sky-blue stripes, fastened to the left breast, and on gala days when at Court, a similar broad ribbon is thrown across the right shoulder towards the left hip. The costume is a dress of bright blue silk.

MILITARY DISTINCTION AND DECORATIONS OF HONOUR.

The Military Medal of Honour, was founded by the Elector Max-Joseph IV. (22nd November, 1794) in gold and in silver, to reward sub-officers and soldiers for brave conduct in war. With the silver medal the pay is increased one half, and with the golden it is doubled. It does not, however, increase with promotion, while, on the contrary, it diminishes with pension, and ceases altogether with discharge.

The medal (Plate 15, Tab. V. No. 33, obverse; and No.

34, reverse) is worn on the left breast, suspended by a black ribbon with white and bright blue borders.

2. *Decoration of Honour and Distinction for Military Surgeons*—was founded by a military decree (8th November, 1812) by King Max-Joseph; it is in gold and silver, the former weighing ten ducats and measuring one five-eighths Bavarian inches in diameter.

It is worn on the left breast on the same ribbon as the previous, (Tab. V. No. 31), and represents on the obverse the effigy of the founder, with the inscription: 'Maximilianus Josephus Rex Bejoariæ' (Max-Joseph, King of Bavaria), and on the reverse: 'Ob Milites inter Prælia et Arte et Virtute servatos' (for saving soldiers in war by art as well as by courage). The Patent says: 'To claim this important reward, it is absolutely necessary that the candidate surgeons must have given their professional aid upon the field of battle or in the hospitals, without shrinking from the dangers around them, and have performed their duties with skill, presence of mind, and sympathy with the suffering wounded, &c., &c.' The gold medal is presented (by the King in person) to established surgeons of regiments; and the silver to surgeons of batallions and to mere practitioners. To the medal is attached a pension of 300, 200, 150, and 100 fl. (£30, £20, £15, and £10), the first two, to four owners of the golden medal, the third to eight, and the fourth to all the other possessors of the silver medal.

3. *The Military Cross for the Years* 1813 *and* 1814. (Plate 13, Tab. III. No. 21).—It is a Cross cast from the metal of guns, and founded on the 4th December, 1814, in commemoration of the War of Liberty of that period. It was distributed 27th May, 1817, not only amongst the troops who had actually made the campaigns of the two years; but also amongst those who had entered the service as late as the following year (1815). It is worn on the left breast, the Bavarian Field-Marshal, Prince

BAVARIA. Table V. PLATE 15.

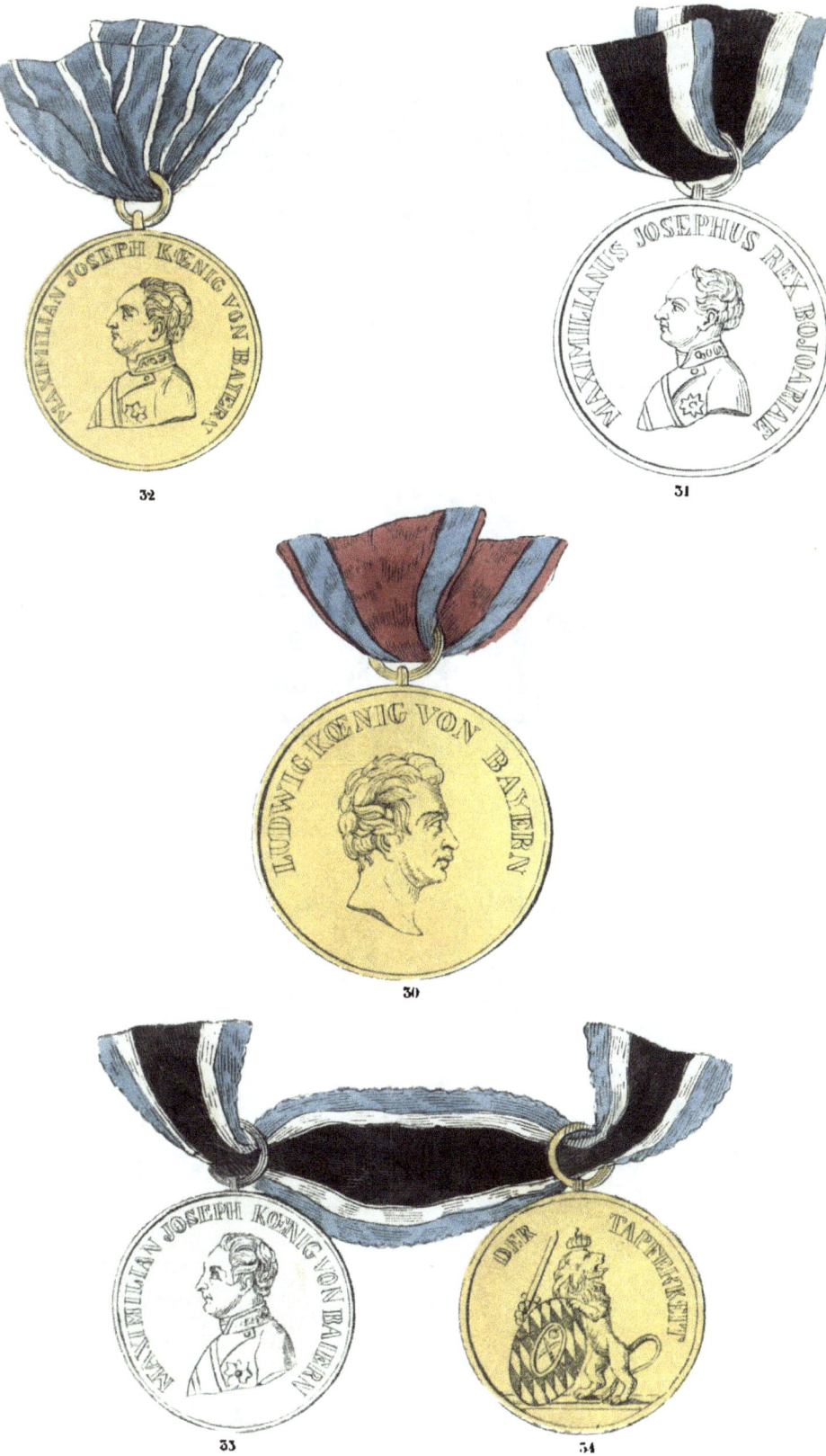

BAVARIA. Table VI. (AUSTRIA. Table VI.)　　　PLATE 16.

35

36　　37

AUSTRIA.

A.　　　　　　　　　　　　B.

C.

Hurst and Blackett, London. 1858.

Wrede, was, however, allowed to wear it round the neck. It is also suspended on the standards of the regiments who served at that period.

THE ORDER OF MAXIMILIAN FOR ART AND SCIENCE.

It was founded 28th November, 1853, by King Maximilian II. as a distinction for prominent talents in the Arts and Sciences, and more especially for German savans and artists. It is divided into two parts: the Arts and the Sciences. The decoration consists of a Gothic Cross, enamelled dark blue with white edges, and four rays in the corners, and surrounded by a wreath of laurel and oak leaves. The middle of the Cross forms a shield, the front of which exhibits the effigy of the founder, with the inscription, 'Maximilian II. König von Baiern,' while the reverse represents either an owl (as symbol of science) or—for the division of the Arts—Pegasus, with the inscription, 'Für Wissenschaft und Kunst' (For science and art). Within the points of the Cross are to be seen the words '28th November, 1853' (the foundation day). It is worn round the neck, suspended by a dark blue ribbon with white borders (Plate 16. Tab. VI. No. 35).

The King is Grand Master of the Order. The Chapter consists of seven or nine members, who annually meet in November to deliberate on the merits of the candidates. The number of members is limited to one hundred, with a due regard to the proportion of the two departments, the arts and sciences. The Order is not hereditary, and the insignia are returned, after the demise of a member, to the Minister of State of the Royal Household and Foreign Affairs.

BELGIUM.

THE ORDER OF LEOPOLD (CIVIL AND MILITARY).

This Order was founded on the 11th July, 1832, and has been divided, since 1838, into five classes—Knights of the Grand Cross, Grand Officers, Commanders, Officers and Knights. The nomination is made by the King, as Grand Master. Members of the two Chambers, who receive the Order from other motives than merely military distinction, are subject to a new election. Privates and sub-officers who are Knights of the Order, enjoy, until their promotion, an annual pension of 100 francs (£4). The motto of the country, 'L'union fait la force' (Union constitutes power) is also that of the Order.

The decoration, differing in size only, is the same for all degrees. For the four first classes, however, it is in gold, while for the fifth class it is in silver. The illustrations (Plate 17. Tab. I. Nos. 1 to 5), give the half of the official size of the insignia. The first class wear the star (No. 1) on the left breast, and the decoration (No. 3), suspended by a flame-coloured watered ribbon, thrown across the right shoulder towards the left hip. The second class wear the star (No. 2), upon the left breast. The third suspend the cross (No. 4), round the neck. The fourth suspend it at the button-hole by a bow or knot (No. 5), while the fifth class wear it also at the button-hole, but without a bow, and suspended by a much narrower ribbon.

BELGIUM. Table I.　　　　　　　　　　　　　　PLATE 17.

Hurst and Blackett, London. 1858.

Illustration 6, represents the reverse of the insignia. The gold chain worn on solemn occasions by the Knights of the Grand Cross (No. 3) consists alternately of the crown or lion, and the initials in monogram L. R. (Leopoldus Rex).

The insignia of the military members of the Order are distinguished by two crossed swords of gold (with the Knights only of silver), fixed, with the first class, in the centre of the star, adorned with the motto of the Order and the Belgian Lion, and with the three other classes below the crown above the star.

By decree 8th November, 1832, the administration of the Order is transferred to the Minister of Foreign Affairs.

THE IRON CROSS AND MEDAL.

The foundation of this Order had, in fact, preceded the former, which was conferred, in 1835, upon sixteen hundred and two Belgian citizens who had taken an active part in the Revolution, many of whom had previously received the iron medal (Plate 18. Tab. II. No. 9). The form and inscription of the Cross are represented Tab. II. No. 7 (front), and No. 8 (reverse). It is worn suspended by a red watered ribbon, with black and yellow borders. The above-mentioned medal shows upon the obverse the Belgian Lion with the inscription, 'Aux défenseurs de la patrie' (To the defenders of the fatherland), and upon the reverse, the year 1830 in the centre of the sun, which is encompassed by the arms of the nine Belgian provinces, and the inscription, 'Indépendance de la Belgique' (Independence of Belgium).

MEDAL FOR DEEDS OF SELF-DEVOTION OR SACRIFICE.

A private society in one of the provinces of the Netherlands, in 1825, first distributed medals for deeds of self-devotion. The

Belgian government introduced the same into Belgium after the revolution. The expenses are included in the annual budgets. The medal is distributed in gold, silver gilt, and silver. The intrinsic value is 100, 50 to 60, and 30 to 40 francs. It is worn at the button hole by a tri-coloured ribbon, black, red and yellow.

The front of the medal (Tab. II. Nos. 11 and 12) represents the effigy of the King, with the inscription, 'Leopold Premier, Roi des Belges.' The reverse shows in the middle a crown, beneath which is, each time when presented, engraved, the name, domicile, and the cause of the reward, of the recipient. The legend is 'Dévouement, Courage, Humanité—Récompense publique' (Self-devotion, courage, humanity—public reward).

By a decree of the 19th April, 1849, the following bye-laws were added:

1. The medal is in future to be adorned with a crown.
2. The distribution of the colours of the ribbon by which the medal is worn suspended at the button-hole is shown (Plate 19. Tab. III. Nos. 14, 15 and 16).

MEDAL FOR VACCINATION.

It originated in Holland in 1818, for the encouragement of vaccination. The value of the gold medal is 50 gulden (about 4 guineas), and is presented to medical practitioners who have gratuitously vaccinated more than one hundred children in the course of the year.

The same medal (Tab. II. No. 10) is now also introduced in Belgium.

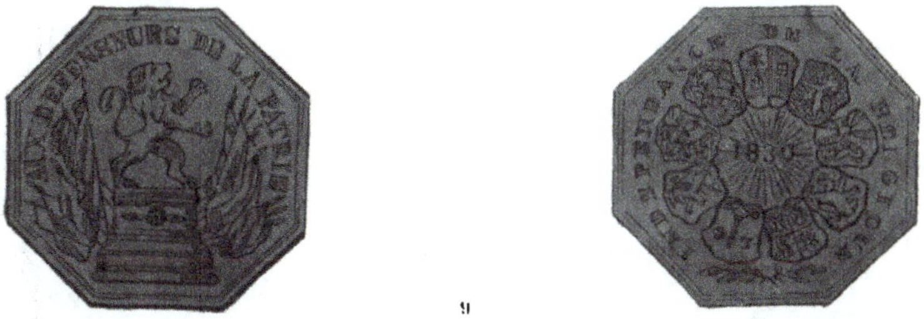

BELGIUM. *Table III.* PLATE 19.

14

15

15

16

Hurst and Blackett. London. 1858.

MEDAL FOR ARTIZANS, MECHANICS AND THE WORKING-CLASSES.

The following royal patent was issued on the 7th November, 1847:

1. A decoration with the symbols of commerce and industry, is to be issued under the name, " Reward for artizans, mechanics, and the working classes." The name of the recipient and the year when granted to be impressed on the reverse.

2. There are to be two classes, one for a gold, and the other for a silver medal.

3. It is to be worn on a small chain of the same metal on the left side of the breast (Plate 19. Tab. III. No. 13).

4. It is exclusively designed for mechanics who join skill to irreproachable conduct.

5. The jury appointed at the Industry Exhibition, is to report on their various merits.

6. The skill of the mechanic or artizan is to show itself in a work distinguished for fine form, wholly or mostly of his own production.

7. The first reward is the silver medal, while the gold is to be awarded to increased progress and skill, after the receipt of the former.

8. The number of the members is limited to one thousand; two hundred to the gold, and eight hundred to the silver medal.

In 1848, the reward was also extended to agricultural talent and improvement, on the occasion of the Agricultural Exhibition.

The number of the latter is fixed at five hundred for the gold, and twelve hundred for the silver medal.

BRAZIL.

THE ORDER OF PEDRO.

Don Pedro I. established this Order, named from himself, soon after he assumed the title of Emperor of Brazil. It is the highest in the empire, has only one class, and was only presented to reigning sovereigns.

Beneath an imperial gold crown is seen a radiating golden pentagonal star, upon which rests another pentagonal star, white enamelled with gold edges, and with gold little balls at each corner. The blue enamelled broad ring has two narrow gold edges, with the legend: 'Fundator del Imperio dal Brazil' (Founder of the Brazilian empire), while the white enamelled centre of the star shows a gold Phœnix bearing within its silver face the letters P. I. (Pedro I.), and in its claws an antique crown. This Order is worn by a broad green watered ribbon with white borders, across the right shoulder towards the left hip (Plate 20, Tab. I. No. 2).

A similar star, but without crown (Tab. I. No. 1), is besides worn on the left breast.

In October, 1842, this Order received its first statutes, and was, by them, divided into three classes, consisting of twelve Knights of the Grand Cross, fifty Commanders, and one hundred Knights. The Princes of the imperial family are, by birth, Knights of the Grand Cross.

BRAZIL. Table I. PLATE 20.

Hurst and Blackett, London. 1858.

THE ORDER OF THE CROSS OF THE SOUTH.

This Order, which is divided into four classes, Knights of the Grand Cross, Dignitaries, Officers, and Knights, was also founded by Don Pedro I. on the 1st December, 1822, instituting the reigning Emperor as Grand Master. The decoration (Tab. I. No. 4) is a pentagonal white enamelled Cross, resting upon a green laurel wreath with broad edges mounted in gold, and the ten points of which bear little gold balls. The gold scutcheon in the centre of the obverse, shows the effigy of the Emperor Don Pedro in relief, and is surrounded by a dark blue ring with gold edges, and the legend 'Petrus I. Braziliæ Imperator' (Pedro I. Emperor of Brazil). The four stars which form this curious constellation of the South Cross, are exhibited upon the sky blue centre of the reverse, which is also surrounded by a dark blue ring with gold edges, and the legend, 'Præmium bene Merentium' (Reward of the well deserving). This Cross is surmounted by a gold imperial crown, and is worn by a sky blue ribbon (more or less broad according to the degree of the wearer) by the Knights of the Grand Cross across the right shoulder, by the Dignitaries round the neck, and by the Officers and Knights upon the left breast.

A pentagonal radiating star of gold below an imperial golden crown, the middle face of which contains the same as the reverse of the Cross, distinguishes the owners of the three higher classes, and is worn by them upon the left breast (Tab. I. No. 3).

The particular characteristic of the Order is, that Princesses, Duchesses, and other high born ladies, are not excluded from it.

THE ORDER OF THE ROSE.

Was founded by Don Pedro on the 17th October, 1829, the day of his second marriage with the Princess Amalie Eugenie Napoleone of Leuchtenberg and Eichstadt, daughter of the celebrated Prince Eugene, Duc de Leuchtenberg. It was destined as a reward for both civil and military merit.

The Order, of which the Emperor is Grand Master, has eight real, and eight honorary Knights of the Grand Cross, sixteen Grand Dignitaries, thirty Dignitaries, and an unlimited number of Commanders, Officers and Knights. The heir presumptive to the throne, or Crown Prince, is at once Knight of the Grand Cross and Dignitary, while the other Princes of blood are only the former. Only those with the title Excellency, are admissible to the Grand Cross, while the Grand Dignitaries receive the title (Excellency) with their nomination. The Dignitaries are chosen from those who are already styled, Senhor, while with the nomination of Commander, the candidate receives the title (Senhor.) The Officers receive, with the Order, the rank of Colonel, and the Knights that of Captain.

The insignia (Tab. I. No. 6) consist of a white enamelled hexagonal star with gold edges, the six points of which bear small balls; the star is fastened by the upper point to a gold imperial crown, surrounded by a wreath of full blown roses. Upon the white ground of the front are seen the letters, P. A. (Pedro and Amalie), encompassed by a broad golden ring or circle, with the legend, 'Amore Fidelios' (Love and fidelity). The gold centre of the reverse shows the date of the foundation, while the blue ring round it has the words, 'Pedro e Amalia.'

The Order is worn by a rose coloured or pink ribbon, with

BRAZIL. *Table II.* PLATE 21.

7

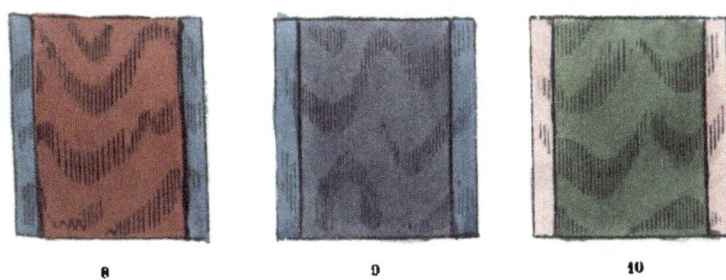

8 9 10

Hurst and Blackett, London. 1858.

white borders, the width of which varies with the various degrees of the wearers. The Knights of the Grand Cross wear it across the right shoulder, the Dignitaries round the neck, and the three other classes upon the left breast.

The five superior classes wear, besides, upon the left breast, a star (No. 5) exactly resembling the obverse of the Order, except that it is much larger, and is in addition surmounted by a gold crown, for the Knights of the Grand Cross and Dignitaries. The eight real Knights of the Grand Cross wear, besides, on solemn occasions, a gold chain of roses worked in enamel.

THE ORDERS OF ST. BENEDICT OF AVIZ AND ST. JACOB OF THE SWORD, AND THE ORDER OF CHRIST.

These three Orders had followed the royal family at their emigration from Lisbon to Rio Janeiro, and were retained by the colony, after John VI. was recalled to the capital of Portugal. They became national in Brazil by decree, 20th October, 1823, and by subsequent usages. The insignia were only in so far altered that the crown of Portugal was exchanged for that of the empire, and the borders of the ribbons of the Orders of Christ (Plate 21. Tab. II. No. 6), and St. Jacob (No. 7) were changed into blue, and those of St. Benedict (No. 8) into pink red.

The Emperor is Grand Master, the Crown Prince first Commander. The Knights wear the Order at the button hole, the Commanders have the star upon the left breast, while the Knights of the Grand Cross wear, besides, a broad scarf on which the decoration is suspended.

All these three Orders have, however, lost their religious character in Brazil, owing to her independence of Portugal, and the rejection of the Bull 'Præclara Portugaliæ.' They are now considered as civil Orders, and are presented to native as well as foreign subjects, who have done service to the state (Law 9th September, 1843).

DECORATIONS OF HONOUR.

1. Medal as reward for valour in battle.
2. Medal for the war of Independence (Bahia).
3. Medal of the Division for preservation of good order.
4. The same medal with the inscription 'Constancia e Bravura' (Constancy and valour) for the troops who have kept their post at the bar without assistance.
5. Medal for the campaign to Rio de la Plata.
6. Medal for the campaign in Cis Plata.

BRUNSWICK.

THE ORDER OF HENRY THE LION,

Was founded by the present reigning Duke William on the 25th April, 1834. The object is given in the introductory remark of the patent, 'to reward those who have distinguished themselves in our service, military or civil, in war, or the arts and sciences.' No regard is, therefore, had in the distribution, to birth, rank, or religion, except in the higher classes, when a previous possession of a Knightly cross is required.

The Order consists of four classes, Knights of the Grand Cross, Commanders first and second classes, and Knights. The reigning Dukes of Brunswick are Grand Masters.

The badge consists of a golden octagonal Cross, enamelled bright blue, with gold balls at the points and with a red middle, bearing on the obverse the helmet of the Brunswick Arms so as to allow it to rest upon the lower wing of the Cross, while the crowned pillar with the galloping horse, together with the two sickles, are placed in the centre; the feathers of the peacock are represented upon the right and left wings, and its tail, together with the star, upon the upper wing of the Cross. Above the Cross is a gold lion passant between two laurel branches covered with the Brunswick crown, while between the wings of the Cross is a gold W also covered with the crown. The reverse has in the red centre, the motto of the Order in gold letters, 'Immota Fides' (Immutable faith), encompassed by a golden ring, with the year of the foundation MDCCCXXXIV. The front of the Order is seen Plate 22, Tab. I. No. 3, and the reverse No. 4.

It is worn in different sizes, suspended by a deep red ribbon (of equally different widths) with narrow yellow stripes, by the Knights of the Grand Cross across the left shoulder towards the right hip, by the Commanders round the neck, and by the Knights at the button hole. The first two classes have besides the following insignia, as special distinctions, an octagonal star with silver rays encompassing the golden bright blue enamelled Cross of the decoration, while the centre shows a golden W. covered with the crown, as also a red ring with the motto of the Order in golden letters, which is worn by the Knights of the Grand Cross upon the left breast (Tab. I. No. 1). The Commanders of the first class wear, likewise, upon the left breast an octagonal silver Cross, between the wings of which is the gold W equally covered with the ducal crown (Tab. I. No. 2), while the red centre bears the motto of the Order in gold letters, encompassed by a gold ring with the date of the foundation of the Order in it.

The Knights of the Grand Cross are, moreover, allowed to wear, on high gala days, their decorations round the neck by a gold chain, the links of which consist of three parts; of the escutcheon surrounded by flags with the two fields of Brunswick and Lüneburg, of two golden lions pacing towards the escutcheon, and of the centre of the star of the Knights of the Grand Cross (Tab. I. No. 5).

Equal to this Order and connected with it, was founded the

CROSS OF MERIT,

which is divided into two classes, gold and silver, and is worn suspended by the same ribbon as that of the previous

BRUNSWICK. *Table* I. PLATE 22.

Order, Henry the Lion. Each corner of the gold Cross is filled with a green oaken wreath, but not so the silver. The centre of both contains a W with the crown, and upon the wings are distributed the words, 'Immota Fides' (Tab. I. No. 6). The nomination to the previous Order, precludes the wearing of the present cross.

Besides this Order, Brunswick possesses a variety of decorations and medals of merit, mostly military. We give them here in chronological order of their foundation.

1. *Waterloo Medal* (Plate 23, Tab. II. No. 11) was founded by the Prince Regent of Great Britain, George, as guardian of the minor Princes of Brunswick, on the 11th June, 1818, 'for the perpetual remembrance'—as the patent says—' of the campaign of 1815, and the glorious distinction with which the Brunswick corps has participated in it.' The medal was cast from the captured guns of the enemy, and bears on the front the effigy of Duke Frederick William, who fell at the battle of Quatre Bras on the 16th June, 1815 ; the reverse shows within a laurel oak wreath, the date 1815, with the legend, 'Braunschweig seinen Kriegern—Quatre-Bras und Waterloo' (Brunswick to her warriors—Quatre-Bras and Waterloo). Upon the edge of the medal is engraved the christian and family name, and the character which the owner bore during that campaign, and more especially during the battles of Quatre-Bras and Waterloo. It was presented to all men of the Brunswick corps who had either taken direct part in the campaign, from 15th June to 7th July, 1815, or were present during that period and given assistance to the former, including even field chaplains, &c. Also the heirs of those soldiers who had either fallen in the field or died subsequently, received in memory of the dead this medal, which is worn by all classes suspended by a yellow and blue striped ribbon about six inches long, at the third button hole, or near it upon the left side.

2. *The decoration of Honour for the campaign of the year* 1809, (Tab. II. No. 9), was originally instituted by Duke Charles II. on the 30th October, 1824, for the yet living soldiers in the Brunswick service who had followed the Duke Frederick William in 1809, from Bohemia to England; but was afterwards distributed, also, amongst those of them who were no longer in the Brunswick service.

It consists for officers, of a gold, and for sub-officers and privates of a bronze Cross, surrounded by a laurel and oak wreath. The year 1809 stands in the centre of the front bearing upon the wings the words, 'Für Treue und Tapferkeit' (For loyalty and valour), the reverse shows the Brunswick white steed, and in the centre and upon the wings originally the name, 'Karl Friedrich August Wilhelm,' and since his expulsion, the name of the present reigning Duke. The Cross is worn upon the left breast, suspended by a sky blue watered ribbon.

3. *The medal of Honour for the Spanish-Portuguese Campaign.*— The troops which came over to England with Duke Frederick William in 1809, formed, it is well known, the nucleus of the contingent which England lent to Spain and Portugal in the War of Independence against Napoleon, and which took part in nearly all the battles fought in the Peninsula from 1810 to 1814. Duke Charles II. founded also for these troops (30th October, 1824) a medal of honour (Tab. II. No. 10), for officers in silver, and for sub-officers and men in bronze. It is worn upon the left breast, suspended by a crimson red ribbon; the front shows the word, 'Peninsula,' encompassed by a laurel wreath, while the reverse exhibits within a scutcheon, two C's in monogram (the initial of the founder). As may be supposed, the medal is possessed by nearly all the owners of No. 2.

BRUNSWICK. *Table II.* PLATE 25

Hurst and Blackett, London, 1858.

4. *The Medal of Civil Merit.*—This medal was founded by Duke Charles II. in the first year of his reign, as was, also,

5. *The Medal of Military Merit*, founded by him towards the end of his reign to complete the former. But as the first was presented only to three civil officers, and the latter only to two military officers, both can hardly be ranked amongst the really existing Orders or decorations. Both medals were in silver, and worn at the button-hole suspended by a sky blue watered ribbon with a very narrow white border.

6. *Crosses for twenty to twenty-five years' military service*, (Tab. II. Nos. 7 and 8).—This, together with some other decorations connected with it, were founded by Duke William, 1st April, 1833. Officers and military officials with that rank, who have served honourably twenty-five years or more, receive a gold cross with purple red chevrons, the white centre of which contains on the front a W with the crown, and on the reverse the number twenty-five. It is worn suspended by a royal blue ribbon with similar borders upon the left breast. It can only be claimed by those who are on active service on the nomination day, which is the 25th April of each year. The Brunswick army counts now forty-five owners of this decoration. A similar cross of silver was also founded for sub-officers and soldiers for twenty-five and twenty years' uninterrupted and irreproachable service. The centre of the Cross represents on the front a W with the crown, and the reverse the number twenty-five or twenty; it is likewise worn on the left breast by a royal blue ribbon, but with yellow borders. That for twenty-five years service has its centre surrounded by rays. The first twelve oldest owners of the twenty-five years' cross receive a monthly increase of their pay of one Thaler (3s. 6d.), all the others (not exceeding thirty-six in number) twelve Groschen (1s. 6d.) With the retirement from service the increase ceases.

There are, besides, decorations for fifteen and ten years good service, consisting of silver and iron bolts or buckles, and with the same impressions and ribbons as the former. They are equally worn on the left breast.

7. *The Saving Medal* (Tab. II. No. 12).—It was founded on the 25th April, 1836, and is presented to those who have saved the life of a fellow creature at the risk of their own. The medal is of silver, and contains on the obverse a W upon a scutcheon covered with the ducal crown, borne by lions and surrounded by flags, with the legend, 'Ehrenzeichen, gestiftet am 25th April, 1836' (Decoration of honour, founded on the 25th April, 1836). The reverse shows the Goddess Victoria, pointing with her right to a wreath of stars, and bearing in her left a palm wreath with the legend, 'Müthiger Thaten ehrender Lohn' (Honourable reward for courageous deeds). The medal is worn suspended by a green ribbon.

DENMARK.

THE ORDER OF THE ELEPHANT.

Before entering on the history and statutes of this illustrious institution, it will be as well to give a few prefatory remarks concerning the general principles which regulate the two Danish Orders. Of both, the King is the head, and distributes them at pleasure. The affairs of both are managed under his presidency by a 'Chapter of the royal Orders,' established at Copenhagen on the 28th June, 1808. Its chief business is to watch over the conduct of the members, to report on them, and endeavour to settle their private disputes amicably. The officers of the two Orders consist of a Chancellor, Vice-Chancellor, Bishop, Secretary, Marshall, Treasurer, Master and Vice-Master of ceremonies, Vicar and Historian. The festival days, common to both, are the 28th June, the birthday of King Waldemar, and the respective birthdays of the reigning sovereigns. The Chapter meets on both days; at the Castle of Frederigsborg on the 28th June, and at the Castle of Rosenberg on the birthday of the reigning King.

The Order of the Elephant is one of the most striking proofs that the dignity of an Order is elevated in proportion to the rarity of its bestowal. For, though Denmark only occupies a third rank among European states, the Order of the

Elephant commands as high a respect in public opinion as does the Golden Fleece, or even the Garter. The date of its origin cannot be ascertained with historical accuracy, since even the Danish historians themselves are not agreed on the point. Some would have it founded during the time of the first Crusade, others in the time of Kanut VI. (consequently at the end of the twelfth century), while others refer its creation to the second half of the fifteenth century, under Christian I. The Danish government in its official documents, assumes the date of the foundation to fall in the first half of the fifteenth century, while Christian I., it says, has only renewed the Order in 1458.

That the Order was originally of a religious character is evident, not only from the circumstance that it required the Papal consent (of Pius V. and Sixtus VI. in 1462 and 1464) but also from the name: 'Society and fraternity of the Holy Virgin Maria,' which the fifty Knights, the number as at first fixed, had borne. The surmise is further confirmed by the insignia of the Order, which consisted originally of the figure of the Virgin with the infant Jesus in her arms, as also by the collar of the mantle in the shape of a monk's hood, which the Knights still wear on festival days. It has, however, entirely lost its religious element since the alteration of its statutes by Christian V. on the 1st December, 1693. Since that time it ought only to count thirty Knights, exclusive of the Princes of the blood who are by birth entitled to the Order, though they cannot wear it before the completion of their twentieth year. All the other Knights, if Danes, must have professed the Evangelical religion, for at least thirty years, and be declared by the Board of Enquiry, previous to their nomination, worthy of the Cross of Danneborg. This last regulation is, however, no longer strictly enforced, nor is the number of the Knights now strictly limited to thirty.

The badge of the Order (Plate 24, Tab. I. No. 2) is a white

DENMARK. *Table* 1.   PLATE 24.

Hurst and Blackett, London. 1858.

enamelled elephant with golden tusks, a blue cloth covering, a battlemented tower upon his back, and a negro upon his neck with a spear in his hand. This decoration is worn suspended by a bright blue watered broad ribbon across the left shoulder towards the right hip. On festival days, it is suspended by a golden chain (No. 3) consisting of towers and elephants with blue coverings, upon which is seen the Golden letter D (Dania). The Knights wear, besides, upon the left breast a star, in the centre of which is a small red shield, charged with a cross formed of brilliants and surrounded by a silver laurel wreath (Tab. I. No. 1). The costume of the Knights, on festival days of the Order, consists of a jacket and short breeches of white satin; of a mantle of crimson velvet with a long train, lined with white fur; a collar in the form of a hood; and a black velvet hat with red and white feathers. The King wears, on such occasions, a mantle lined with ermine, and upon the hat a black heron plume and white feathers.

The motto of the Order is: 'Magnanimi Pretium' (Reward of the high minded or magnanimous).

The special festival of the Order which used to be held on Whit-Tuesday, has, since 1808, been transferred to the 1st January.

THE ORDER OF THE DANNEBORG.

A miracle, according to popular belief, was the cause of the foundation of this Order. The tradition relates, that the Knights of the Sword who were introduced into Livonia by Albert III. Bishop of Riga, were, in 1219, so hardly pressed by the heathen Esthonians whom they had subjected, as to induce them to seek assistance at the hands of the King of Denmark, Waldemar II. The latter came, but in the battle which he gave to the combined hordes of Esthonians and Russians, the ranks of his own troops were sadly thinned and dispersed. They had already lost their ensign, and were about to flee, when suddenly a red flag bearing a white cross appeared from the Heavens, the sight of which inspired the Danes with renewed courage. They rallied their ranks, and gallantly vanquished the enemy. The heavenly flag became, to Denmark, what to France was the Oriflamme, whose origin tradition assigns to a similar miracle wrought for Chlodwig. Waldemar II., in commemoration of the event, and at the same time as a reward for his brave warriors, founded the Order of the Danneborg. Thus far tradition. History, however, knows nothing certain about the origin or date of the foundation. The year, 1671, is certainly mentioned as the epoch, but it remains doubtful whether the Order was not renewed rather than founded then, as it may have been lost, or have fallen into decay in consequence of the events of the Reformation. It was Christian V. who most probably revived the Order on the 12th October, 1671, by the advice of his favourite, Count Griffenfeld, who, no doubt, hoped, by this political toy, to indemnify the Danish nobility for their loss of the right to elect a King, the result of the preceding revolution. The statutes of the Order—then reduced to a mere court honour—were published on the 1st October, 1693, and remained in force until 1808. In that last year, King Frederick VI. raised it to an Order of Merit, by a patent of the 28th June, and gave it its present organization.

All native Danes of merit, whether civil or military, are admissible to the Order, without regard to birth or age, nor is the number of the Knights limited. They are divided into four classes, so that no one can enter the higher without having first belonged to the class immediately below it, though the King has the power of making exceptions to the rule.

The Knights of the first class go by the name of Grand Commanders; they are members of the Chapter, bear the

DENMARK Table II. PLATE 25.

Hurst and Blackett, London. 1858.

title of 'Excellency,' are next in rank to Field-Marshals and Admirals, and receive the military honours due to a Lieutenant-General. This degree is considered as a special royal favour.

The Knights of the Grand Cross form the second class. Their rank is that of a Major-General. All those who were in possession of the Order, at the time of its reorganization, were placed in the second class.

The Knights of the third class, the Commanders, have no real rank, but receive the honours due to an officer of the staff, while those of the fourth class receive the honours due to a subaltern officer.

The badge (Plate 25, Tab. II. No. 9) is an oblong golden cross, enamelled white, with red edges, above which is seen the initial of the King under the royal crown, which latter is also found in each of the angles of the cross. The centre of the front contains a crowned 'W' (Waldemar), and upon the four wings of the cross are distributed the words 'Gud og Kongen' (God and the King). The reverse contains the supposed years of the foundation, renewal and reorganization of the Order, 1219, 1671, 1808. The ribbon, by which it is suspended, is white with red stripes at the borders.

The Grand Commanders wear the cross, without the inscription, but with the addition of diamonds (Tab II. Fig. 8) round the neck; and the star (Tab. I. No. 4.) upon the left breast.

The Knights of the Grand Cross wear it (Tab. II. No 9) suspended by a broader ribbon across the right shoulder, towards the left hip, in addition to the star, peculiar to the class, which is worn upon the left breast. Clergymen, or Knights of the 'Order of the Elephant' wear the cross round the neck.

The Commanders wear it likewise (Tab. II. No. 9) round the neck, in addition to an embroidered cross (Tab. I. No. 5.) upon the breast, while, finally, the Knights of the fourth class wear the cross round the neck, without the addition of a star.

The Order celebrates a festival at the Castle of Rosenburg every year, on the 15th of April, the birthday of Christian V. Then, as on all other solemn occasions, the Knights of the two first classes wear a mantle of pale-red velvet, trimmed with white fur, white breeches, white stockings, and white shoes; also a black hat with white and red feathers, while the decoration of the Order is suspended by a chain, the links of which consist alternately of the crowned initials of Christian V. (C. 5.) of Waldemar (W.) and of the cross (Tab. I. No. 6.) The motto of the Order is: 'Pietate et Justitia' (By piety and justice).

Various definitions and derivations are given of the word Danneborg; the most probable deduces it from the old Danish 'Brog,' signifying 'cloth, texture, flag.' Danneborg may, therefore, mean, the flag of the Danes—the standard of Denmark.

As a fifth class of the Danneborg Order may be considered the 'Men of Danneborg.' By two royal patents (28th June, 1808, and 28th January, 1809) the silver cross of the Danneborg Order was likewise conferred upon all Danish citizens who had distinguished themselves in their respective spheres by honest conduct and actions benefitting their fellow-creatures. This decoration is also a sort of stepping-stone to knighthood. The military are bound to shoulder their arms before the wearer, who have also free admittance to the meetings of the Danneborg Knights. There exists also a fund in aid of the necessitous members.

The above silver cross (Tab. II. No. 10) is also worn by the King, Members of the Chapter, and Knights of the Order of the Elephant, while its presentation to Knights of the Order of Danneborg is considered a new proof of royal favour.

DECORATIONS OF HONOUR.

1. *Decoration of the Battle at Copenhagen.*—After this battle, in which the Danes fought bravely (though unsuccessfully), on the 2nd April, 1801, against the English, the King caused a Medal of Honour to be struck for those who had distinguished themselves in the affair. It was presented in gold to officers, and in silver to inferior grades, and was worn suspended by a red ribbon, in which is interwoven the Cross of Danneborg. The obverse exhibits a lion standing upon the forequarters of a man-of-war, holding by one claw the arms of Denmark, with the inscription: ' 2nd April, 1801,' while the reverse shows the royal insignia, crown, sceptre, and sword, with the inscription: ' Kongen Foedrer, Faederlandet Skjönner ' (The King honours, and fatherland is grateful). On the edge is impressed the name and grade of the recipient. The medal is seldom now met with, as but few of the owners are left among the living.

2. *Medal of Merit at the Dockyards.*—It was founded on the 29th January, 1801, by Christian VII, as a reward for the workmen at the royal dockyards, and for the encouragement of those belonging to the fleet. The same medal was subsequently, (4th September, 1814), distributed also amongst the sub-officers of the artillery, and the navy, inspectors of fire-engines and dockyards, and all those engaged in the formation of nautical models. To be entitled to the medal, sailors, artillerymen, cannoneers, ship-carpenters, and other master-mechanics, or their chief clerks, must have completed their twenty-fifth year, while rope-makers, cabinet-makers, and others, must have been full thirty years in the royal service, before they can lay claim to the medal. The obverse of the medal has the inscrip-

tion: 'For ood Tieneste' (For good services), and the reverse the word: 'Fortient' (Merit). (Tab. II. No. 7).

3 and 4. *Decorations for eight and sixteen Years' loyal Service.*—Both (Tab. II. Nos. 11 and 12) were founded on the 23rd August, 1817, for sub-officers, and musicians of the band of the same rank. They are of bronze, and are presented at their re-engagement for another period of eight years. They are worn suspended by a small golden chain, the cross above the medal.

5. *Medal of Merit of* 1771.—This medal which is not allowed to be worn publicly, was founded by Christian VII. It is in gold and in silver. The front shows the effigy of the King, and the reverse two cornucopiæ (horns of plenty), surrounded by a laurel and oaken wreath, and with the inscription: 'Pro Meritis' (For merit).

6. *Medal of Merit of* 1793, was founded by the same King, to reward and encourage inland industry and civil virtues. The front shows the effigy of the King, and the reverse the word: 'Fortient' (Merit), within an oaken wreath. This medal, also, is not intended to be worn in public.

7. *Medal for noble Deeds*, founded in 1793 at the proposal of the College of Finance. The front shows the effigy of the King, and the reverse the inscription: 'For Aedel Daad' (For a noble deed).

8. *Medal for saving from Drowning*, founded in 1812. It differs from the former only in the reverse, which shows within a wreath of water-lilies, the inscription: 'Of Färens Fvaelg ferblomster Prüs og Low' (Praise and reward blossomed forth from danger). As in the preceding case, the name of the recipient of this medal is also engraved on the edge.

Since the 24th July, 1845, a new Medal of Honour for personal merit has existed in Denmark. The obverse represents the effigy of the King with the legend: 'Christian VIII. Rex

Daniæ,' while the reverse shows an oaken or corn wreath, within which is the word 'Fortient' (Merit). On the edge is engraved the name of the recipient. When permission is given to wear it publicly, it is suspended by a red ribbon with a white cross thereon.

In 1854, medals of military distinction were struck for sub-officers, or those bearing that rank. They are of bronze, and are worn suspended by a red ribbon, on which is a white cross. The medal is divided into two classes, each of which enjoys a pension for life of 30 and 15 thalers (90s. and 45s.) The first of which is obtained after sixteen, and the second after eight years' service.

FRANCE.

THE ORDER OF THE LEGION OF HONOUR.

The establishment of this Order, after much discussion and opposition, arising from a feeling that it was contrary to freedom and equality, the watchword of the Revolution, was at last carried (1802) in the Legislative Body by a majority of one hundred and sixty-six to one hundred and ten.

The Legion of Honour was meant to be an institution, at once the safeguard and protection of all republican principles and regulations, of all the laws of equality, and for the abolition of all the differences of rank in society as created directly or indirectly by the nobility.*

The Order was originally divided into three classes:— Legionaries, Grand Officers, and Commanders.

After the coronation of Napoleon (14th July, 1804), the first class of Grand Officers was divided into Knights of the Grand Eagle, (as the highest,) and Grand Officers. In 1810, the first class already exceeded by nineteen thousand the limits fixed by law; while in 1814, the Legion counted about thirty-seven thousand members. This vast number naturally

---

* The real object, however, of the First Consul in creating this Chivalry, to which merit of every social grade was eligible, was to popularize the idea of personal distinction, and pave the way for the establishment of the Empire, and the more exclusive titles of nobility which accompanied it.

FRANCE. *Table* I. PLATE 26.

Hurst and Blackett, London. 1858.

deteriorated much from the value of the decoration. The Restoration, though it retained the Imperial Order of the Legion, by no means resigned the legacy of the old monarchy with regard to orders.

The *Order of the Holy Ghost* was the first rescued from oblivion. The Legion was converted into an Order, and lost its original character and signification. The number of the educational establishments, in connection with the Order, was greatly reduced, the effigy of Napoleon was exchanged for that of Henry IV.; while the Eagle—despite its five wings—was christened 'Cross.' The Knights of the Grand Eagle became Knights of the Grand Ribbon (Grands Cordons), and the Legionaries, became Knights. Moreover, all the nominations which had taken place during the Hundred Days, were nullified by Louis XVIII. on his return to Paris, after the battle of Waterloo. In 1816, the pay of the members was reduced to half, and compensation was only granted in 1820. During the Restoration, sixty-three ribbons of the Holy Ghost, and twelve thousand one hundred and eighty crosses of St. Louis were distributed, while the members of the Legion increased to forty-two thousand.

The present statutes of the Legion provide :—

That the Order is to be conferred by the King as President, for important civil or military services rendered to the state.

That it is to consist, besides the royal family and foreigners, of eighty Knights of the Grand Cross, one hundred and sixty Grand Officers, four hundred Commanders, two thousand officers, and an unlimited number of Knights.*

The candidates, in time of peace, must prove that they have

* In 1843, it counted eighty Knights of the Grand Cross, one hundred and ninety-six Grand Officers, eight hundred and three Commanders, four thousand four hundred and fifty-four Officers, and forty-three thousand eight hundred and eighty-four Knights.

served, with the requisite distinction, for twenty years in some military or civil department.

In time of war, the Order is also awarded for exploits, or severe wounds received in battle.

The first claim to the Order must begin with the lowest degree of Knights, as no degree can be passed over. Promotion requires a standing in the fourth class of four, in the third class of two, in the second class of three, and in the fourth class of five years. There are usually two distributions in the year, on the 1st January, and on St. Philip's day (1st May).

The nomination of military persons takes place on parade; and of civil, at the courts of justice, in the presence of the Grand Chancellor or his deputies.

No ignoble punishment can be inflicted on a member of the Order, so long as he belongs to it.

The decoration consists of a white enamelled star with double rays under a royal crown. The centre represents on the front the effigy of Henry IV., and on the reverse the motto: 'Honneur et Patrie' (Honour and our country), as legend in a golden field with two tri-coloured flags. (Plate 26, Tab. I. No. 2).

The star for the Knights is in silver, and for the other classes in gold.

The Knights and officers wear it at the button-hole; the Commanders round the neck. The Grand Officers wear besides upon the right breast a star embroidered in silver, similar to that of the Grand Crosses, and at the button-hole, a golden star. The Knights of the Grand Cross wear the same golden star, but somewhat larger, suspended by a ribbon across the right shoulder towards the left hip; and, also, on the left breast of the coat or cloak, a star embroidered in silver (Tab. I. No. 1), the centre of which contains the effigy of Henry IV., with the legend: 'Honneur et Patrie.' The intervening spaces of the five wings of that star are filled with golden lances and tri-coloured flags.

The college of the Legion possesses in rentes and shares in the canals of Orleans, Loing and the South, a revenue of 7,103,098 francs, of which sum about 5,829,000 francs are annually spent in the pay of the Legionaries, and in pensions (of 250 francs each) to the sub-officers and soldiers.

Napoleon I. established, at St. Denis and Ecouen, two boarding-schools for six hundred young girls, daughters, sisters, nieces and cousins of the Legionaries, two hundred of whom were educated at the expense of their families, three hundred as half boarders, and one hundred entirely free. Six other establishments for the female orphans of the Legionaries were founded in 1810, while the male orphans were received at the military schools and college. The Restoration only retained the boarding-school of St. Denis, reducing the number to five hundred pupils, four hundred of whom, including the daughters of the members of all Orders in the kingdom, were to enjoy free board and education. The orphan institutions were reduced to two, receiving two hundred pupils free, and being managed by the nuns of the 'Congregation of the Blessed Virgin.' By the law, 19th April, 1832, the decorated of the Hundred Days were admitted to a pension of 250 francs each. On the 16th June, 1837, a new military class was admitted to the decoration of the 'Cross,' together with a pension. In 1845, the Legionaries since 1814, as also the Knights who underwent amputation in consequence of wounds, were ordered to receive 100 francs for life in addition to their regular pay, while to the sub-officers and privates who were in active service at that period, and who, by decree, of the 27th February, 1815, were received into the Legion, was granted a sum of 250 francs each.

From 1831 to 1841, not less than four thousand one hundred and twelve sub-officers and soldiers received the 'Cross,' while on the 30th November, 1845, about fifty thousand two hundred and twenty-seven persons were in possession of it. The amount of pension then paid out was 5,975,000 francs. Since then, the annual distribution of the cross has been reduced to two hundred.

On the 24th May, 1851, it was decreed that until 1860 only one nomination should take place for every two extinct ones, and that the annual pensions are not to exceed 100,000 francs. The Imperial Eagle, which was again placed on the army colours, was also restored to the 'Cross;' and, by a decree, of the 31st January, 1852, the previous imperial form of decoration was generally re-introduced into the realm (Plate 27, Tab. II. Nos. 5 and 6).

The President, Louis Napoleon, decreed, that a part of the property of Louis Philippe, which had been restored to the state, should be set apart as an endowment for the Legion of Honour; he also fixed the pensions of the Legionaries at 250, of Officers at 500, of Commanders at 1000, of Grand Officers at 2000, and of Grand Crosses at 3000 francs each.

On the 1st October, 1853, the Order counted sixty-five Grand Crosses (forty-six with pensions), two hundred and twenty-two Grand Officers (one hundred and twenty-five with pensions), one thousand and thirty-four Commanders (four hundred and fifty-seven with pensions), four thousand seven hundred and fourteen Officers (one thousand four hundred and fifty with pensions), and forty-eight thousand and eighty-five Knights (sixteen thousand eight hundred and thirty-one with pensions).

THE CROSS OF JULY.

On the 9th October, 1830, the Minister of the Interior proposed in the Chamber of Deputies, the foundation of an institution of national reward, for the support and pension of the citizens who had distinguished themselves, or been wounded in the revolution of the preceding July, as also for the widows, orphans, or parents of those who had fallen. According to his account,

FRANCE. *Table II.* PLATE 27.

Hurst and Blackett, London. 1858.

more than five hundred orphans, and a like number of widows resulted from the contest, in which three thousand eight hundred had been wounded. He asked a vote of credit for seven millions francs (£250,000), four millions of which were to be applied to pensions.

The proposal was accepted with a few amendments on the 30th November, and the 'Cross of July' was founded in consequence. It consists of a white-enamelled star with three double rays under a silver mural crown. The similarly-enamelled centre bears in three circles the national colours, and exhibits, on the obverse, the inscription, '27, 28, 29 Juillet, 1830,' in the middle, and 'Donné par le Roi des Français' (Presented by the King of the French) on the edge. The reverse shows the Gallic Cock in gold, and the legend: 'Patrie et Liberté' (Our Country and Liberty). The rays with six points, and with silver balls, are connected by an oak-leaf wreath (No 7). It is worn suspended by a bright blue ribbon (about three and a half inches wide) with a red stripe near each border.

THE MEDAL OF JULY

was also founded for the citizens who had co-operated in the revolution. It is of silver, and shows on the front the Gallic Cock sitting upon a tri-coloured flag, surrounded by an oak wreath, and the words: 'A ses défenseurs la patrie reconnaissante' (A grateful country to its defenders). The reverse exhibits three intertwined laurel-wreaths, between each of which, as also upon the edge, are seen the words: '27, 28, 29 Juillet, 1830. Patrie, liberté.'

THE MILITARY MEDAL

was founded by the President of the Republic (Louis Napoleon), and to it he assigned one of the national castles as an educational establishment for the daughters, or needy orphan girls, of those honoured with it. Each possessor of the medal receives a pension of one hundred francs.

It consists (by decree, 29th February, 1852) of silver of about one inch in diameter. The front shows the effigy of Louis Napoleon inscribed with his name, while the centre of the reverse contains the motto: 'Valeur et Discipline,' and over all is seen an eagle. (Tab. II. Nos. 7 and 8). It is worn upon the left breast suspended by a yellow ribbon with green borders.

The medal is given:

1. To sub-officers, soldiers and sailors on re-entering the service after a discharge or retirement.

2. To all whose names are mentioned in the Army Orders.

3. To those who have received several wounds before the enemy, or on other occasions in the service.

4. To all who have distinguished themselves by courageous deeds as mere officials in the army, without pay or rank, such as military agents, &c.

THE ST. HELENA MEDAL

was instituted by the present Emperor of France, Louis Napoleon III., on the 12th August, 1857, in commemoration of the campaigns from 1792 to 1815, and for the purpose of being conferred on those of the army and navy who were engaged in any, or all, of those campaigns.

The medal (No. 9.) is of bronze, and bears on the obverse the effigy of Napoleon I.; and on the reverse the legend: 'Campagnes de 1792 à 1815—A ses Compagnons de Gloire sa dernière Pensée, 5 May, 1821.' It is worn at the button-hole suspended by a red and green ribbon.

GREAT BRITAIN AND IRELAND.

ORDER OF THE GARTER.

Neither the time when the Order of the Garter was founded, nor the cause of its foundation, can any longer be traced with precision; and, in the absence of all authentic records, fable and tradition have been called in to supply their place. The public muniments afford us no light on this remote topic, and the annals of the Order itself are, for nearly two centuries, exceedingly imperfect. The statutes of EDWARD III. have perished long ago, and the so-called copies of them bear internal marks of having been compiled at a much later period. The Register, usually known as the BLACK BOOK, though treating of the Order from its foundation, was not drawn up in its present form till near the end of Henry the Eighth's reign, when its history begins, for the first time, to assume precision and regularity.

Selden fixes, as the foundation of the GARTER, St. George's Day, in the 18th year of King Edward III. and this statement is corroborated by Froissart. The account given by the old Chronicler is, as is usual with him, so naïve and so vivid that, like a painting, it brings the whole scene at once before our eyes:—" At this time there came into the mind and will of King Edward of England that he would cause to be made and re-erected the Great Castle of Windsor, which King Arthur had formerly made and founded, where first was begun and established the noble 'Round Table,' of which were so many good and valiant men and Knights, who went forth and toiled in arms and in prowess throughout the world. And that the same King would make an Order of Knights of himself and his children, and of the bravest of his land, and that they should be called the KNIGHTS OF THE BLUE GARTER, and that the Feast should be kept from year to year, and should be solemnized at Windsor, the day of St. George." Froissart proceeds to narrate how the King assembled from all his countries, Earls, Barons and Knights, and how he carried out his royal intentions, but our space prohibits our extracting the graphic details.

But even with all these data, there is still a mystery hanging over the subject, which it is in vain to think of solving in the present day; and there is hardly less doubt with respect to the principal ensign, from which the Order has received its name. The popular tradition, derived from Polydore Vergil, is that having a festival at Court a lady chanced to drop her garter, when it was picked up by the King. Observing that the incident made the bye-standers smile significantly, Edward exclaimed in a tone of rebuke: "Honi soit qui mal y pense;" *Dishonoured be he who thinks evil of it*: and to prevent any further inuendos, he tied the Garter round his own knee. This anecdote, it is true, has been characterized by some as an improbable fable: why, we know not. It is strictly in accordance with the romantic habits of an age, when devotion to woman was one of the first duties of Knighthood. A garter has always been united with sentiments of gallantry, and, to wear a lady's favour, her glove, her ribbon, or any thing which belonged to her, was in those days

GREAT BRITAIN. *Table I.* PLATE 28.

Hurst and Blackett, London. 1858.

a common practice, and this token or *Emprize* was regarded with feelings of which we can have no idea.

Camden assigns for the period of the foundation of the Order* the battle of Crecy, at which, says that great antiquary, EDWARD ordered his Garter to be displayed as a signal for the onset. Be the origin of the institution, however, what it may, no Order in Europe is so ancient, none so illustrious, for "it exceeds in majesty, honour, and fame all chivalrous fraternities in the world."

The original statutes of this most noble institution have undergone continuous changes: suffice it to add that by a Statute passed on the 17th January, 1805, the Order is to consist of the SOVEREIGN and twenty-five KNIGHTS COMPANIONS, together with such lineal descendants of GEORGE III, as may be elected, always excepting the Prince of Wales, who is a constituent part of the original institution. Special Statutes have since, at different times, been proclaimed for the admission of Sovereigns and extra Knights, the latter of whom have, however, always become part of the twenty-five Companions, on the occurrence of vacancies.

HABIT AND INSIGNIA.

THE GARTER, of dark blue ribbon edged with gold, bearing the motto "Honi soit qui mal y pense" in golden letters with buckle and pendent of gold richly chased, is worn on the left leg below the knee.

THE MANTLE is of blue velvet, lined with white taffeta; on the left breast the star is embroidered.

---

* The Order being under the especial tutelage of St. George, his Banner continued to be the national ensign of England, until the accession of James I., when, in violation alike of good taste and heraldry, it was mingled with the Banner of St. Andrew.

The Hood is of crimson velvet.

The Surcoat is likewise of crimson velvet, lined with white taffeta.

The Hat is of black velvet lined with white taffeta; the plume of white ostrich feathers, in the centre of which a tuft of black heron's feathers, all fastened to the hat by a band of diamonds.

The Collar, gold, consists of twenty-six pieces, each in the form of a garter, enamelled, azure, and appended thereto.

The George, or figure of St. George on horseback, encountering the dragon. The George is worn to the collar; and the lesser George, pendent to a broad dark blue ribbon over the left shoulder.

The Star, of eight points silver, has upon the centre the Cross of St. George, gules, encircled with the garter.

The Officers of the Order are ;—the *Prelate*, the Bishop of Winchester; the *Chancellor*, the Bishop of Oxford; the *Registrar*, the Dean of Windsor; the *Garter Principal King of Arms*, and the *Usher of the Black Rod*.

Motto—Honi soit qui mal y pense.

THE MOST ANCIENT AND MOST NOBLE ORDER OF THE THISTLE.

Tradition and national partiality have carried up the institution of "the Thistle" to fabulous times, but, leaving conjecture and surmise for fact and reality, we cannot trace the Order as an ORGANIZED KNIGHTLY FRATERNITY, further back than the reign of King James II. of England and VII. of Scotland. Nevertheless, in the Royal Warrant issued by that monarch before the promulgation of the Statutes, reference is made to the fact, that "his Majesty's Royal predecessor, Achaius, King of Scots, did institute the most ancient and most noble Order of the Thistle, under the protection of St.

GREAT BRITAIN. *Table* II. PLATE 29.

Hurst and Blackett, London. 1858.

Andrew, Patron of Scotland, in commemoration of a signal Victory obtained by the said Achaius over Athelstan, King of the Saxons, after a bloody battle, in the time of which there appeared in the heavens a White Cross in the form of that upon which the Apostle Saint Andrew suffered martyrdom."

King James II. may, under any circumstances, be considered the fountain-head from which is derived the present organization of the Order; true it is, that after his abdication, this Knightly institution fell into desuetude, and so remained until the year 1703, when Queen ANNE directed Letters Patent to be passed under the Great Seal of Scotland to revive the Order: the statutes, then authorized by her Majesty, were very similar to those of King James, and are those which are still followed.

THE STAR of this Order, which is worn on the left side of the coat or cloak, consists of a St. Andrew's Cross, of silver embroidery, with rays emanating from between the points of the cross, in the centre of which is a Thistle of green, heighttened with gold, upon a field of gold, surrounded by a circle of green bearing the motto of the Order in golden characters.

THE BADGE OR JEWEL is worn pendent to the collar, or to a dark green ribbon over the left shoulder, and tied under the arm. It consists of a figure of St. Andrew, of gold enamelled, with his gown green, and the surcoat purple, bearing before him the Cross, enamelled white, the whole surrounded by rays of gold in the form of a glory; the cross and feet resting upon the ground, of enamelled green.

THE COLLAR is of Thistles, intermingled with sprigs of rue.

By a Statute passed in May, 1827, the Order is to consist of the Sovereign and sixteen Knights.

Motto—Nemo me impune lacessit.

The Officers of the Order are;—*The Dean, the Secretary, the Lord Lyon King of Arms* and the *Gentleman Usher of the Green Rod.*

THE MOST ILLUSTRIOUS ORDER OF SAINT PATRICK.

KING GEORGE III. wishing to manifest his regard for Ireland by assigning to that kingdom a National Order, was induced to institute, on the 5th February 1783, a Fraternity of Knights formed on the model of "The Garter" and named after the tutelar Saint, St. Patrick. His Majesty was further pleased to assign as insignia the emblems of the country to which the Order was to belong, and gave for "Motto" the words "Quis Separabit MDCCLXXIII," to inculcate that harmony and union which the Royal Founder was anxious to foster throughout his dominions. Thus orignated

THE KNIGHTS OF ST. PATRICK,

a brilliant succession of distinguished men, selected from the most eminent, for birth, rank, or personal achievement, amongst the Irish Peers.

At the present time, the Order consists of THE SOVEREIGN, the Grand Master, twenty-two Knights, and several Officers. By the original statutes, GEORGE III. his heirs and successors, Kings of Great Britain were declared to be the SOVEREIGN, and the Lord Lieutenant General and General Governor of Ireland, Grand Master.

At first, the number of Knights was limited to fifteen, but in the reign of WILLIAM IV. it was increased to twenty-two.

Every person of or above the rank of a Knight is eligible to be admitted, but up to this time, none but Peers have been elected.

The Officers of the Order are THE PRELATE (the Archbishop of Armagh); THE CHANCELLOR (the Archbishop of Dublin); THE REGISTRAR (the Dean of St. Patrick's); THE SECRETARY; THE GENEALOGIST; THE USHER OF THE BLACK ROD; THE ULSTER KING OF ARMS; TWO HERALDS and FOUR PURSUIVANTS.

THE STAR consists of the Cross of St. Patrick gules, on a field argent, surmounted by a trefoil vert, charged with three imperial crowns within a circle of azure containing the motto 'Quis Separabit," and the date " MDCCLXXXIII " in letters of gold, the whole encircled by four greater and two lesser rays of silver.

THE BADGE is of gold, of an oval form, surrounded with a wreath of Shamrock, within which is a circle of sky blue enamel containing the MOTTO, encircling on a field argent the Cross of St. Patrick gu. charged with a trefoil vert, having on each of its leaves an Imperial Crown, or.; in some of the present Badges, however, the field is left open or pierced. The Badge is suspended to the Collar from the neck, but, when the Collar is not used, it is attached to the ribbon and hangs on the left side.

THE COLLAR is of gold, composed of roses and of Harps alternate, tied together with a knot of gold, the roses being enamelled alternately, white leaves within red, and red leaves within white, and in the centre an Imperial Crown, surmounting a harp of gold, from which the Badge hangs. The Collar is worn on all great and solemn feasts, and especially on ST. PATRICK'S DAY, the 17th of March.

THE RIBBON, four inches wide, is light blue, and is worn over the right shoulder.

THE MANTLE is made of rich sky-blue tabinet, lined with white silk, and has on the right shoulder a hood of blue tabinet also lined with white silk. It is fastened by a cordon of blue silk and gold, having a pair of tassels of the same materials. On the left side is placed the Star of the Order. For many years, despite of the injunction of the original statutes that the Knights of St. Patrick should be robed in mantles of Irish manufacture, the dress was invariably made of French satin, but His Excellency, Lord Carlisle, who has always been desirous of promoting Irish industry, restored the original ordinance, and Irish tabinet is now the texture used.

THE MOST HONOURABLE ORDER OF THE BATH.

The present MILITARY ORDER of the BATH, founded by King GEORGE I. in the year 1725, differs so essentially from the Knighthood of the Bath, or the custom of making Knights with various rites and ceremonies, of which one was BATHING, that it may almost be considered a distinct and new fraternity of chivalry. The last Knights of the Bath, made according to the ancient forms, were at the coronation of King CHARLES II; and from that period until the reign of the first GEORGE, the old institution fell into total oblivion.

At the latter epoch, however, it was determined to revive, as it was termed, THE ORDER OF THE BATH, by erecting it "into a regular Military Order;" and on the 25th May, 1725, Letters Patent were issued for that purpose.

By the Statutes then promulgated, the number of Knights, independent of the Sovereign, a Prince of the Blood Royal, and a Great Master, was restricted to thirty-five; but eventually, at the conclusion of the war in 1814, it was found expedient, for the purpose of rewarding the numerous distinguished officers of both services, to extend considerably the limits of the Order of the Bath. In consequence, a complete alteration was effected: and on the 2nd of January, 1815, it was declared that, "for the purpose of commemorating

GREAT BRITAIN. *Table III.* PLATE 50.

the auspicious termination of the long and arduous contest in which this empire has been engaged," the Order should be composed of three classes; and, on the 14th April, 1847, it was further extended by the addition of civil knights commanders and companions, on which occasion new Statutes were promulgated for the government of the Order, and the number of members declared as follow, viz:

First Class—to consist of Knights Grand Cross; number not to exceed, for the military service, fifty, exclusive of the Sovereign and Princes of the blood royal, and such distinguished foreigners as may be nominated honorary Knights Grand Cross; and twenty-five for the civil service.

Second Class—Knights Commanders, number not to exceed, for the military service, one hundred and two, and for the civil service fifty, exclusive of foreign officers who may be admitted as honorary Knights Commanders. In the event of actions of signal distinction, or of future wars, the numbers may be increased of this as well as of the third class. The members of the second class are entitled to the distinctive appellation of knighthood, after being invested with the Insignia; to take precedence of Knights Bachelors; to wear the badge, &c., pendent by a red ribbon round the neck, the star embroidered on the left side.

Third Class—Companions of the Order, to consist, for military service of five hundred and twenty-five, and for the civil service of two hundred; they are to take precedence of esquires, but are not entitled to the appellation, style, &c., of knights bachelors. To wear the badge assigned to the third class, pendent by a narrow red ribbon from the button-hole. No officer can be nominated to the military division of the third class of the Order, unless his services have been marked by special mention of his name in the London Gazette, as having distinguished himself in action against the enemy. This class has never been conferred on any officer below the rank of Major in the army and Commander in the navy.

THE BADGE for the MILITARY CLASSES of the Order is a gold Maltese cross, of eight points, enamelled, argent; in the four angles, a lion passant-guardant, or.; in the centre, the rose, thistle, and shamrock, issuant from a sceptre between three imperial crowns, or within a circle, gules; thereon the MOTTO of the Order, surrounded by two branches of laurel, proper, issuing from an escrol, azure, inscribed ICH DIEN (I serve), in letters of gold. It is worn by the Grand Crosses pendent from a red ribbon across the right shoulder, by the Knights Commanders from the neck, and by the Companions from the button-hole.

THE COLLAR is of gold (weight, thirty ounces Troy weight), and is composed of nine imperial crowns, and eight roses, thistle, and shamrock, issuing from a sceptre, enamelled in their proper colours, tied or linked together with seventeen gold knots, enamelled white, having the badge of the Order pendent therefrom.

THE STAR OF THE MILITARY GRAND CROSSES is formed of rays or flames of silver, thereon a gold Maltese cross, and in the centre, within the motto, branches of laurel, issuant as in the badge.

THE CIVIL KNIGHTS GRAND CROSSES retain the old badge and star of the Order. The Star is of silver, formed with eight points or rays, charged with three imperial crowns, proper, upon a glory of silver rays, surrounded with a red circle, upon which is the motto of the Order. Their badge is of gold, composed of a rose, thistle and shamrock, issuing from a sceptre between three imperial crowns, encircled by the motto. The civil Knights Commanders wear the same badge, of a similar size, round the neck by a red ribbon, and the civil companions the same, but of a still smaller size, from the button-hole, pendent from a red ribbon.

THE STAR OF THE KNIGHTS COMMANDERS is in the form of a cross-patée of silver, having the same centre as the Grand Crosses, but without a gold Maltese Cross thereon. The star of the civil Knights Commanders is of the same form and size, only omitting the laurel wreath round the circle containing the motto, and the escrol with the words, "Ich Dien" underneath.

Motto—Tria juncta in uno.

The Officers of the Order are;—*the Dean; the Genealogist,* and *Blanc Coursier Herald; the Bath King of Arms; the Registrar and Secretary; the Gentleman Usher of the Scarlet Rod and Brunswick Herald; and the Messenger.*

THE MOST DISTINGUISHED ORDER OF SAINT MICHAEL AND SAINT GEORGE.

Not long after the cession of Malta to Great Britain, and the submission of the seven Ionian Isles to the exclusive protection of the same power, it was deemed advisable to institute an Order of Knighthood for the purpose of bestowing marks of Royal favour on the most meritorious of the Ionians and Maltese, as well as on British subjects who may have served with distinction in the Ionian Isles or the Mediterranean Sea.

THE ORDER was founded 27th April, 1818, by letters patent under the Great Seal of the United Kingdom, and a Code of Statutes was promulgated on the 12th August following; but, by its third Sovereign, WILLIAM IV, the Constitution of 'St. Michael and St. George' was so materially changed, and its importance so much enhanced that His Majesty may almost be considered its second Founder. The new Statutes, framed by that Monarch, ordain that the King of the United Kingdom shall for ever be SOVEREIGN OF THE ORDER, that a Prince of the Blood Royal being a descendant of the body of the Princess Sophia, Electress of Hanover, shall be GRAND MASTER, and that there shall be three Classes of Knights, first KNIGHTS GRAND CROSS, second KNIGHTS COMMANDERS and third CAVALIERI or COMPANIONS: the first class to be restricted to fifteen, the second, to twenty, and the third, to twenty-five.

The members of the Order enjoy rank and precedency immediately after the corresponding classes of the Order of the Bath: that is to say, the Knights Grand Cross after Knights Grand Cross of the Bath; The Knights Commanders after the Knights Commanders of the Bath; and the Cavalieri and Companions after the Companions of the Bath. All natives of the Ionian Islands, and of Malta, who receive this third class of the Order are styled 'Cavaliere,' and all natives of Great Britain and Ireland 'Companions.' The Grand Master is the first and principal Knight Grand Cross, and the Lord High Commissioner to the Ionian Isles has precedency of all other Knights Grand Cross. The Knights Grand Cross are entitled to bear supporters and to encircle their arms with the collar, ribbon, and motto of the Order. The Knights Commanders and Cavalieri also encircle their arms with the ribbon and motto; and the Companions suspend the badge of the Order to their arms.

THE STAR of a Knight Grand Cross is composed of seven rays of silver, having a small ray of gold between each of them, and over all the cross of St. George, gules. In the centre is a representation of the Archangel St. Michael encountering Satan, within a blue circle, inscribed with the motto 'Auspicium Melioris Ævi.'

THE COLLAR is formed alternately of lions of England, of Maltese crosses, and of the ciphers S. M. and S. G. having in the centre the imperial crown, over two winged lions, passant-

GREAT BRITAIN. *Table IV.* PLATE 51.

Hurst and Blackett. London. 1858.

guardant, each holding a book, and seven arrows. At the opposite end of the collar are two similar lions. The whole is of gold, except the crosses, which are of white enamels and it is linked together by small gold chains.

THE BADGE is a gold cross of fourteen joints of white enamel, edged with gold, having in the centre, on one side, the Archangel St. Michael encountering Satan, and on the other, St. George on horseback, encountering a dragon within a blue circle, on which the motto of the Order is inscribed. The cross is surmounted by the imperial crown, and is worn by the Knights Grand Cross to the collar, or to a wide Saxon-blue ribbon, with a scarlet stripe from the right shoulder to the left side.

THE MANTLE is of Saxon-blue satin, lined with scarlet silk, tied with cordons of blue and scarlet silk and gold, and has on the left side the star of a Knight Grand Cross.

THE CHAPEAU is of blue satin, lined with scarlet, and surmounted with white and black ostrich feathers.

THE KNIGHTS COMMANDERS wear the badge suspended to a narrow ribbon from the neck, and have on their left side a star composed of four rays, with a small cross of eight points in saltier of silver surmounted by the cross of St. George, gules, and having the same centre as the star of Grand Crosses.

THE CAVALIERI and COMPANIONS wear the small cross of the Order from a still narrower ribbon at the button hole of their coats.

The Officers of the Order are; the Prelate, the Chancellor, the Secretary and the King of Arms.

Motto—Auspicium Melioris Ævi.

MEDALS AND DECORATIONS OF HONOUR.

Medals were, at various times, conferred for great naval actions; for LORD HOWE'S VICTORY of the 1st June, 1794, for CAPE ST. VINCENT, for CAMPERDOWN, for the NILE, for TRAFALGAR, for DUCKWORTH'S capture of the French squadron in 1806, for Captain HOSTE's defeat of the enemy's squadron 1811, &c.

In 1831, a Medal was instituted, to reward the long and faithful services of SEAMEN and MARINES of the Royal Navy, It is of silver, having on one side the words, "For long service and good conduct," and on the other, an "Anchor and Crown." The name of the person to whom the Medal is accorded, is engraved in the centre of the Medal, which is worn to a narrow blue ribbon.

MILITARY MEDALS, CROSSES, and CLASPS, have also been granted to the British army for many glorious actions: for MAIDA; for the brilliant victories of the PENINSULA; for WATERLOO, and for the CRIMEA. In July, 1830, King WILLIAM IV. was pleased to command that a SILVER MEDAL, "for long service and good conduct," should be granted to meritorious soldiers; and regulations for its distribution were then established. The Medal, worn to a narrow crimson ribbon, has upon the obverse, the Royal Arms, with the rank and name of the soldier; and on the reverse, the words, "For long service and good conduct."

For the Battles of ROLIÇA and VIMEIRA, one medal only was given to those officers who were engaged in both or in either.

A Medal was granted for each of the following actions: "Sahagun," "Corunna," "Talavera," "Busaco," "Barrosa,"

GREAT BRITAIN. *Table* V.　　　　　　　　　　　　　PLATE 52.

20

21

22

Hurst and Blackett, London. 1858.

"Fuentes d'Onor," "Albuhera," "Ciudad Rodrigo," "Badajoz," "Salamanca," "Vittoria," "the Pyrenees," "St. Sebastian," "Nivelle," "Nive," "Orthes," and "Toulouse." Medals were also assigned for "the Capture of Martinique," "the Capture of Guadaloupe," "the Capture of Java," "the Capture of Fort Detroit," and "the Defeat of the Americans at Chateauguay," and "Chrystler's Farm."

In consequence, however, of many officers having received several medals, it became inconvenient to wear them; and towards the close of 1812, a new arrangement was adopted. It was determined that no more than one medal should be worn by any individual; that for every other battle wherein he might distinguish himself, he should wear, on the ribbon to which his medal was suspended, a gold clasp, with the name of the event, until the number of such clasps amount to two. In case he should again signalise himself, he was to receive (instead of the Medal and Clasps formerly borne) a Gold Cross, having in each compartment, the name of one of the four battles in which he was present; and for every subsequent affair, a clasp, with the name of the battle or action, was to be issued, which clasps were to be attached to the ribbon above the cross.

THE WATERLOO MEDAL is of silver, nearly an inch and a half in diameter, having on one side the head of the Prince Regent, inscribed, "GEORGE P. REGENT;" and on the other, is Victory, holding a palm branch, and seated on a pedestal, inscribed, "Waterloo," under which is the date, "June 18, 1815;" over the figure of Victory is the name of "Wellington." Round the edge, the name of the officer or soldier to whom the Medal was given, his rank, and the number of his regiment are engraved.

THE MEDAL FOR THE CRIMEAN CAMPAIGN, was instituted on the 15th December, 1854, and was awarded to all the officers, sub-officers, and privates who served in the Crimea. Clasps, with the words, "Alma, Balaklava, and Inkermann," inscribed on them, were also distributed amongst those who were present in those Battles.

A SILVER MEDAL, suspended to a sky-blue ribbon, is also accorded for distinguished service in INDIA.

THE VICTORIA CROSS, (No. 28,)

Was instituted on the 29th January, 1856, by a Royal Warrant, of which the following is a literal copy:—

VICTORIA R.

WHEREAS We, taking into Our Royal consideration that there exists no means of adequately rewarding the individual gallant services either of officers of the lower grades in Our naval and military service, or of warrant and petty officers, seamen, and marines, in Our navy, and non-commissioned officers and soldiers in Our army; and whereas the third class of Our most Honourable Order of the Bath is limited, except in very rare cases, to the higher ranks of both services, and the granting of medals, both in Our navy and army, is only awarded for long service or meritorious conduct, rather than for bravery in action or distinction before an enemy, such cases alone excepted where a general medal is granted for a particular action or campaign, or a clasp added to the medal for some especial engagement, in both of which cases all share equally in the boon, and those who by their valour have particularly signalized themselves remain undistinguished from their comrades: Now, for the purpose of attaining an end so desirable as that of rewarding individual instances of merit and valour, We

GREAT BRITAIN. *Table VI.* PLATE 55.

Hurst and Blackett, London, 1858.

have instituted and created, and by these presents, for Us, Our heirs and successors, institute and create a new naval and military decoration, which We are desirous should be highly prized and eagerly sought after by the officers and men of Our naval and military services, and are graciously pleased to make, ordain, and establish the following rules and ordinances for the government of the same, which shall from henceforth be inviolably observed and kept:

Firstly. It is ordained, that the distinction shall be styled and designated "The Victoria Cross," and shall consist of a Maltese Cross of bronze, with Our Royal Crest in the centre, and underneath which an escroll, bearing this inscription, "For Valour."

Secondly. It is ordained, that the Cross shall be suspended from the left breast, by a blue ribbon for the navy, and by a red ribbon for the army.

Thirdly. It is ordained, that the names of those upon whom We may be pleased to confer the decoration shall be published in the "London Gazette," and a registry thereof kept in the office of Our Secretary of State for War.

Fourthly. It is ordained, that any one who, after having received the Cross, shall again perform an act of bravery, which, if he had not received such Cross, would have entitled him to it, such further act shall be recorded by a Bar attached to the ribbon by which the Cross is suspended, and for every additional act of bravery an additional Bar may be added.

Fifthly. It is ordained, that the Cross shall only be awarded to those officers or men who have served Us in the presence of the enemy, and shall have then performed some signal act of valour, or devotion to their country.

Sixthly. It is ordained, with a view to place all persons on a perfectly equal footing in relation to eligibility for the decoration, that neither rank, nor long service, nor wounds, nor any other circumstance or condition whatsoever, save the merit of conspicuous bravery, shall be held to establish a sufficient claim to the honour.

Seventhly. It is ordained that the decoration may be conferred on the spot where the act to be rewarded by the grant of such decoration has been performed, under the following circumstances:—

>I. When the fleet or army, in which such act has been performed, is under the eye and command of an admiral or general officer commanding the forces.
>
>II. Where the naval or military force is under the eye and command of an admiral or commodore commanding a squadron or detached naval force, or of a general commanding a corps, or division or brigade on a distinct and detached service, when such admiral, commodore, or general officer shall have the power of conferring the decoration on the spot, subject to confirmation by Us.

Eighthly. It is ordained, where such act shall not have been performed in sight of a commanding officer as aforesaid, then the claimant for the honour shall prove the act to the satisfaction of the captain or officer commanding his ship, or to the officer commanding the regiment to which the claimant belongs, and such captain or such commanding officer shall report the same through the usual channel to the admiral or commodore commanding the force employed on the service, or to the officer commanding the forces in the field, who shall call for such description and attestation of the act as he may think requisite, and on approval shall recommend the grant of the decoration.

Ninthly. It is ordained, that every person selected for the Cross, under Rule Seven, shall be publicly decorated before the naval or military force or body to which he belongs, and with which the act of bravery for which he is to be rewarded shall have been performed, and his name shall be recorded in a General Order, together with the cause of his especial distinction.

Tenthly. It is ordained, that every person selected under Rule Eight shall receive his decoration as soon as possible, and his name shall likewise appear in a General Order as above required, such General Order to be issued by the naval or military commander of the forces employed on the service.

Eleventhly. It is ordained, that the General Orders above referred to shall from time to time be transmitted to Our Secretary of State for War, to be laid before Us, and shall be by him registered.

Twelfthly. It is ordained, that as cases may arise not falling within the rules above specified, or in which a claim, though well founded, may not have been established on the spot, We will, on the joint submission of Our Secretary of State for War and of Our Commander-in-chief of Our army, or on that of Our Lord High Admiral or Lords Commissioners of the Admiralty in the case of the navy, confer the decoration, but never without conclusive proof of the performance of the act of bravery for which the claim is made.

Thirteenthly. It is ordained that, in the event of a gallant and daring act having been performed by a squadron, ship's company, a detached body of seamen and marines, not under fifty in number, or by a brigade, regiment, troop, or company, in which the admiral, general, or other officer commanding such forces, may deem that all are equally brave and distinguished, and that no special selection can be made by them: then in such case, the admiral, general, or other officer commanding, may direct, that for any such body of seamen or marines, or for every troop or company of soldiers, one officer shall be selected by the officers engaged for the decoration; and in like manner one petty officer or non-commissioned officer shall be selected by the petty officers and non-commissioned officers engaged; and two seamen or private soldiers or marines shall be selected by the seamen, or private soldiers, or marines engaged respectively for the decoration; and the names of those selected shall be transmitted by the senior officer in command of the naval force, brigade, regiment, troop, or company, to the admiral or general officer commanding, who shall in due manner confer the decoration as if the acts were done under his own eye.

Fourteenthly. It is ordained, that every warrant officer, petty officer, seaman, or marine, or non-commissioned officer or soldier, who shall have received the Cross, shall, from the date of the act by which the decoration has been gained, be entitled to a special pension of Ten Pounds a-year, and each additional Bar conferred under Rule Four on such warrant or petty officers or non-commissioned officers or men, shall carry with it an additional pension of Five Pounds per annum.

Fifteenthly. In order to make such additional provision as shall effectually preserve pure this most honourable distinction, it is ordained, that if any person on whom such distinction shall be conferred, be convicted of treason, cowardice, felony, or of any infamous crime, or if he be accused of any such offence and doth not after a reasonable time surrender himself to be tried for the same, his name shall forthwith be erased from the registry of individuals upon whom the said decoration shall have been conferred by an especial warrant under Our Royal Sign Manual, and the pension conferred under Rule Fourteen shall cease and determine from the date of such warrant. It is hereby further declared that We, Our heirs and successors, shall be the sole judges of the circumstance demanding such expulsion; moreover, We shall at all times have power to restore such persons as may at any time have been expelled, both to the enjoyment of the decoration and pension.

Given at Our Court at Buckingham Palace, this twenty-ninth of January, in the nineteenth year of Our reign, and in the year of our Lord one thousand eight hundred and fifty-six.

By Her Majesty's Command,

PANMURE.

GREECE.

THE ORDER OF THE REDEEMER

Was founded on the 1st June, 1833, by King Otho, in commemoration of the deliverance of Greece. It is conferred both on natives and foreigners who either rendered important services during the War of Independence, or have distinguished themselves in industry, commerce, arms, arts or sciences.

The King is Grand Master, and he alone has the right to confer it. The Order consists of five classes:—Knights Grand Cross, Grand Commanders, Commanders, Knights of the Golden and Knights of the Silver Cross.

The number of the first four classes is limited—the Grand Crosses to twelve, Grand Commanders to twenty, Commanders to thirty, and Knights of the Golden Cross to one hundred and twenty (all exclusive of the Princes of the blood royal, and of foreigners), while the fifth class is unlimited.

Greek subjects cannot enter the higher classes without passing first through the lower. In promotion, only worth and merit are to be considered, without regard to rank, birth, &c.

By Art. 12 of the Statutes, a sufficient sum is annually to be voted in the budget for the Order, to enable the College to pay the annual pensions to the members.

The badge consists of an octagonal white enamelled cross

GREECE. PLATE 54.

beneath a royal crown; the wings of the cross are connected with each other by a wreath of oaken and laurel leaves, while the centre of the obverse contains the arms of the country, surrounded by the words: ΗΔΕΞΙΑ ΣΟΥ ΧΕΙΡ ΔΕΔΟΞΑΣΤΑΙ ΕΝ ΙΣΥΥΙ ('Thy rights, O Lord, are glorified with power). The reverse shows the effigy of King Otho, with the legend: ΟΘΩΝ ΒΑΣΙΛΕΥΣ ΤΗΣ 'ΕΛΛΑΔΟΣ (Otho, King of Greece). (Plate 34, No. 2).

The Order is worn suspended by a blue watered ribbon with white borders; the Knights wear it at the button-hole, the Commanders (both classes) round the neck, and the Grand Crosses across the left shoulder towards the right hip. The Grand Crosses and Grand Commanders wear besides, on the left breast, the star (No. 1.) embroidered in silver; the star of the latter is somewhat larger than that of the former. No member can appear before the King or the Princes of the blood royal, or on public festivals without the decoration of the Order.

MEMENTOS AND DECORATIONS OF HONOUR.

1. *Memento for the Bavarian Auxiliary Corps.*—On the 24th November, 1833, King Otho founded at Nauplia, the cross of cast iron (No. 6.) for the above corps which had accompanied him to Greece. Upon the wings of the cross, which are connected with each other by an oaken and laurel wreath, are the words (in Greek): 'Otho, King of Greece,' and on the reverse, 'To the Royal Bavarian Auxiliary Corps.' It was presented to all the soldiers and officials of the corps, irrespective of rank and standing. It is worn on the left breast, suspended by a bright blue ribbon.

2. *Memento for the Bavarian Volunteers.* (No. 5.)—The form of this cross is exactly the same as that of the former, but the metal is bronze, while the inscription and edge are embossed

bright upon dull ground. The inscription, on the obverse, is the same as on the previous cross, while the reverse contains (in Greek): 'To the Auxiliary Volunteers of Bavaria.' The ribbon is equally bright blue, but with small white borders.

3. *The Cross of Honour.*—Founded by King Otho on the 1st June, 1834, for the Greeks and Philhellens who had contributed to the liberation of Greece (Nos. 3 and 4). The officers received it in silver, the sub-officers in bronze, and the privates in iron. The Greek inscription on the obverse is: 'Otho, King of Greece,' and on the reverse, 'To the heroic combatants of the Fatherland.' It is also worn suspended by a bright blue ribbon.

HAÏTI.

THE ORDERS OF ST. FAUSTIN AND OF THE LEGION OF HONOUR.

These were founded by the President of the Republic, Soulouque, on his ascending the throne as Emperor of Haïti, on the 26th August, 1849. The first is a Military Order (Plate 35. No. 1), and the second a Civil (No. 2.)

HANOVER.

THE ORDER OF ST. GEORGE

Was founded on the 23rd April, 1839, as the 'Order of the House of Hanover.' The statutes appoint the Kings of Hanover Grand Masters, and allow of only one class, called the Knights of St. George.

The sons and brothers of the King are Knights by birth, while the Princes of the royal family have a claim to it. The number of native members is fixed (exclusive of the royal Princes) at sixteen, which cannot be exceeded without some special grounds. With the exception of Dukes and Princes, no member can be admitted before the completion of his thirtieth year of age.

Only noblemen of unblemished reputation are eligible, and those who are already in possession of the Grand Cross of the Guelphic Order.

The badge is an octagonal dark blue enamelled cross, the centre of the obverse representing St. George with lance and dragon, and the reverse the initial of the King. This cross (Plate 37. Tab. IV. No. 11) is worn across the right shoulder by a dark red watered ribbon, about four and a quarter inches wide. Close to it is fastened, on the left breast, a star embroidered in silver. The centre of the star contains likewise St. George on horseback, and the motto: 'Nunquam retrorsum' (Never backward.) (Tab. III. No. 10.)

HAITI—HANOVER. Table I. PLATE 55.

1

HANOVER.

2

17

Hurst and Blackett, London, 1858.

The Knights wear besides, the Cross of the Guelphic Order round the neck, saltire-ways. The members must possess the rank of at least Lieutenant-general; they are allowed to join the insignia to their family crest on seals or otherwise.

THE GUELPHIC ORDER.

King George IV. founded this Order, when Prince Regent of England, in the name of his father George III., on the 12th August, 1815, his birthday, being also the anniversary (101 years), of the accession to the English throne of the Elector, George Louis.

The statutes were revised and modified on the 20th May, 1841; according to these, the dignity and power of the Grand Master is always vested in the Crown of Hanover, and the Order is now divided into four Classes:

1. Knights Grand Cross.
2. Commanders, first and second classes.
3. Knights.
4. Simple Members.

There is, besides, another class of sub-officers and privates who have distinguished themselves in the field by skill and valour, and on whom is conferred a medal. The possession of the medal entitles the owner to a pension of twenty-four thalers (72s). The number of the members is unlimited.

The Grand Cross is conferred on those high military officers who have distinguished themselves by their skill and judgment, when the plan and execution of an expedition has been left to their own discretion and responsibility. It is usually not conferred upon any one below the rank of Lieutenant-general, except in some peculiar cases, when an Ambassador has merited well of his country by his diplomatic skill, or when a Major-general was acting as an independent commander.

The Cross of Commander (first class) is usually not presented to any civilian, or any military individual below the rank of Major-general.

The Cross of Commander (second class), as also the next below it, are bound to no rank whatever.

The presentation of the Order to meritorious subjects of Hanover, usually begins with the lowest, the fourth class, and ends with the first. The Cross of the fourth class is worn by the King himself, as also by the royal Princes.

The badge consists (Plate 36, Tab II.), for the Grand Cross, of a star (No. 1) and a cross, worn by a light blue watered ribbon, four inches wide, across the right shoulder, like a scarf.

The decoration of the Commanders (first class), consists of a similar but smaller cross. It is worn upon the breast, below the neck-tie, saltire-ways, suspended by a broad ribbon (two and a half inches wide), fastened behind, and at the side of it is worn, upon the left side of the coat, a similar cross embroidered in silver, in the form of a star, but without the crown above it (No. 2).

The Commanders (second class), wear a like cross, saltire-ways, but not as a star upon the left side.

The Knights wear the cross, rather small, at the button-hole, suspended by a ribbon about an inch wide, which runs through a ring; the latter is fastened above the crown by the imperial globe.

The badge of the fourth class is a silver cross with the royal initial in it, and is worn in the same manner as the former.

The medal is worn at the button-hole, suspended by a similar ribbon.

The Order is both civil and military, and the difference

HANOVER. *Table II.* PLATE 56.

Hurst and Blackett, London. 1858.

consists only in the star and cross, which contain, for the military, a laurel instead of an oaken wreath, and are, besides, adorned with two swords. The motto of the Order is: 'Nec aspera terrent' (Difficulties do not terrify.)

The Orders of deceased members must be returned to the Commission of the College, except the medal, which may remain in the family.

On gala days, or at festivals of the Order, the ribbon of the Grand Cross is exchanged for a golden neck chain, the links of which consist alternately of the Hanoverian crown, a lion passant guardant with upraised tail (the ancient arms of the Guelphs), and the initials 'G. R.' (Tab. II. No. 5).

The obverse contains, in the red enamelled centre of the cross, the galloping white horse (the crest of the House of Brunswick), and the reverse the initials 'G. R.' beneath the royal crown, and surrounded, with the first class, by the number of the year, when the Order was founded, upon dull golden ground.

Between the wings of the cross, with all classes, is placed the Brunswick lion.

MEDALS AND DECORATIONS OF HONOUR.

1. *The Guelphic Medal* (belonging to the Guelphic Order.) (Tab. II. No. 6).—It is of silver, and of the same size as the next following, Waterloo Medal; it contains, on the front, the effigy of the founder; and on the reverse, the inscription: 'Verdienst und Vaterland' (Merit and fatherland), surrounded by a laurel wreath. Upon the edge are engraved the name and rank of the recipient. It is worn at the button-hole, suspended by the same ribbon as is the Guelphic Order. The pension attached to it has, no doubt, contributed to the observance of strict economy in its distribution.

2. *The Waterloo Medal.*—Was founded in December, 1817,

by the Prince Regent of England, and distributed amongst all the soldiers of his hereditary dominions in Germany (Guelphlands), who were present at that battle, or amongst the heirs of those who had fallen in it. The medal is of silver, and adorned with the effigy of the founder. The obverse and reverse are sketched in Tab. II. No. 9. Upon the edge are engraved the Christian and family names of the owner, as also his rank, and the name of the regiment, battalion or corps to which he belonged. It is worn at the third button-hole on the left side, suspended by a dark red ribbon with bright blue borders. It passes to the family as a token of remembrance after the decease of the recipient.

3 and 4. *The William Cross and William Medal* were founded on the 2nd March, 1837, by King William IV., for the Hanoverian troops, as a reward for long loyal service. The first distribution took place only after his demise.

The Cross (Tab. II. No. 8), is of gold, and has on the obverse the letters: 'W. R. IV.' with the crown above them, and on the reverse the number: '25.' It is presented to all officers (including staff-surgeons and their assistants), commanders, town-majors, and others in active service, who have served in the army, twenty-five years (the years of war counting double).

The medal (Tab. IV. No. 14), is presented to sub-officers, and officers in active service, who have served sixteen years (the years of war also counting double). It is of silver, with the effigy of William IV. on the front, and the inscription: 'Für sechszehnjährige treue Dienste' (For sixteen years' loyal service) on the reverse.

Both cross and medal are worn on the left breast, formerly suspended by a yellow ribbon with white borders, but now by a dark red ribbon with dark blue borders (the ribbon of the English Waterloo Medal).

5. *War Medal for the Volunteers in the Hanoverian Army*

HANOVER. Table III.   PLATE 57.

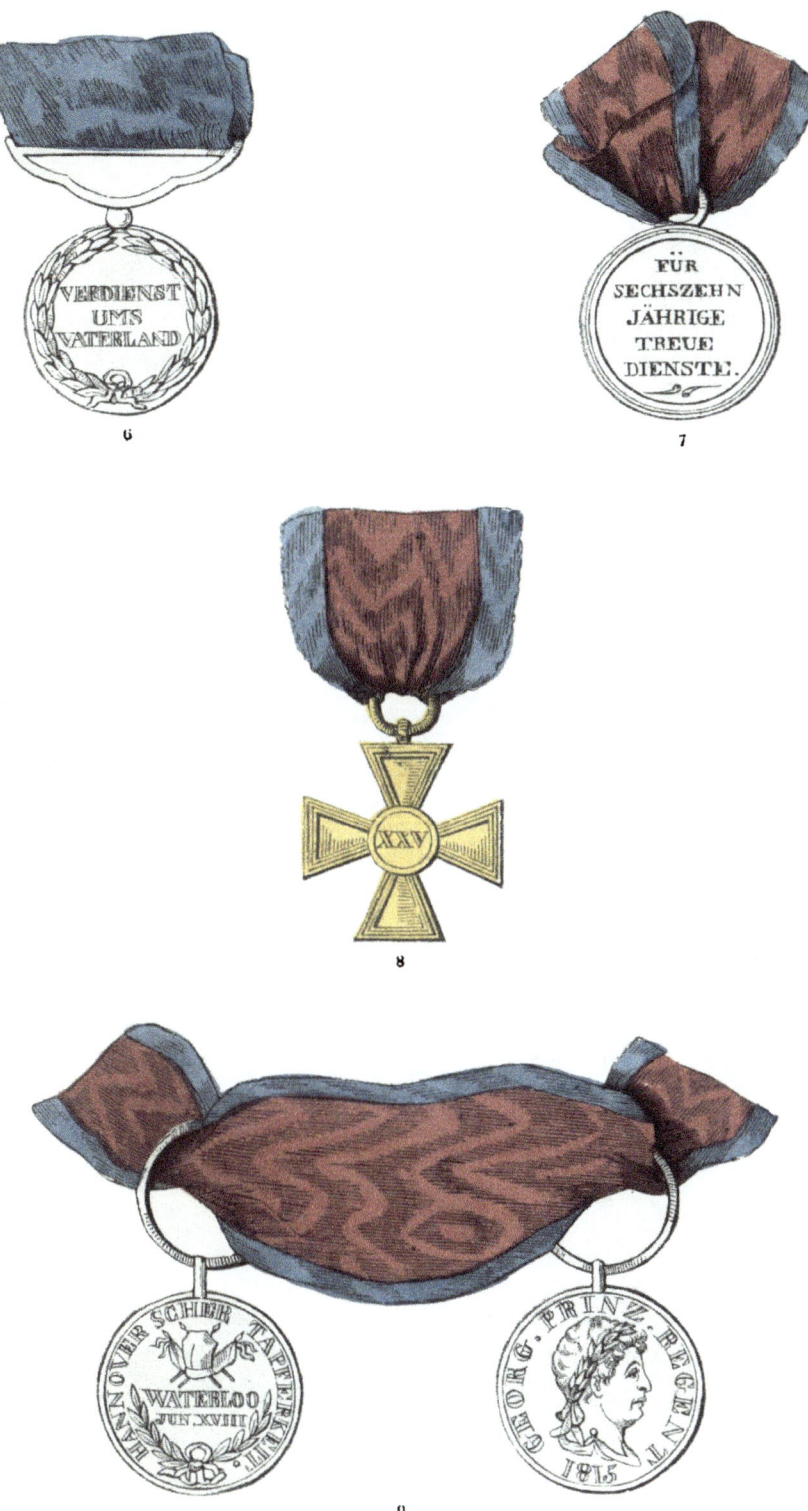

Hurst and Blackett, London, 1858.

in the year 1813.—It was founded by King Ernest Augustus, on the 11th May, 1841, and cast from the guns captured from the enemy at that period. The obverse represents a cross, a royal crown, the initials: 'E. A. R. and (the year) 1813,' while the reverse contains: '1813' within a laurel wreath. (Tab. III. No. 12).

The medal is worn by the still serving military of that period on the left breast, suspended by a white ribbon, with two yellow stripes, and by civilians, *i. e.*, by those who have retired into civil life, at the button-hole.

6. *War Medal for the Volunteers in the British-German Legion, until the conclusion of the Peace at Paris, in* 1814. —The foundation of this medal is coeval with the previous, and was also cast from the captured guns. The front shows a cross beneath a royal crown, with the initials: 'E. A. R.' within its wings, while the reverse contains the words: 'Königlich Deutsche Legion' (Royal German Legion) in the circle, and 'Tapfer und Treu' (Brave and loyal) in the centre, and the whole is surrounded by a laurel wreath. (Tab. III. No. 13.) Like the former, it is worn suspended by a white ribbon with two yellow stripes, by the military on the left breast, and by civilians at the button-hole. It is conferred on military men of all degrees and all nations (including military surgeons), who had entered that legion before the conclusion of peace in 1814, and stood before the enemy in some of the years from 1803 to 1814.

7, 8 and 9. *Medals of Merit in gold and in silver, and General Decoration of Honour*, were founded on the 5th June, 1841. The two medals (gold and silver), bear on the front the effigy of the King, with the legend: 'Ernest August' and the year of his accession to the throne, and on the reverse an oaken wreath, with the inscription: 'Verdienst um's Vaterland' (Merit of the fatherland). Both are worn suspended by a bright blue watered ribbon (the same as that of the Guelph Order).

The *General Decoration of Merit* consists, for Military Merit, of a silver medal (Tab. IV. No. 16), with the initials of the founder on the obverse, and a laurel wreath, with the inscription: 'Krieger Verdienst' (Warrior's merit) on the reverse. It is worn suspended by a white and yellow watered ribbon.

The *Decoration for Civil and other Merits*, consists also of a silver medal (Tab. IV. No. 15), but has within an oaken wreath the inscription: 'Verdienst um's Vaterland' (Merit of the country), and is worn suspended by a tricoloured (black, white and yellow) watered ribbon.

In all the above medals, the name of the recipient is engraved round the edge. They are worn (without a buckle) on the left breast.

The presentation usually begins with the Medal of General Merit, and at further new proofs of merit and distinction, the silver, and next the golden medals are conferred. All medals may be worn together by those who possess them.

DECORATIONS OF HONOUR.

Initials in diamonds are presented for distinguished merit to court ladies. This decoration is worn upon the left shoulder, suspended by the blue commander ribbon of the Guelphic Order, and consists of the letters: 'E. A. F. R.' (Ernest Augustus Frederica, Reges). (Tab. I. No. 17.)

The Ernest Augustus Cross, was founded by King Ernest Augustus on the 9th August, 1845, and was made to form the first class of the above William Cross; it is designated—by the words of the warrant—as "a reward to officers for long faithful service, while it promises, at the same time, a better

HANOVER. *Table IV.*   PLATE 58.

Hurst and Blackett, London. 1858.

HANOVER. *Table* V. PLATE 59.

14

15

16

Hurst and Blackett, London. 1858.

prospect for future promotion than do the William Cross and Medal." It consists of a golden cross, the front of which shows in monogram the initials: 'E. A. R.' beneath a crown, and the reverse, the number '50.' It is worn (without a buckle) on the left breast, suspended by a dark red ribbon with dark blue borders. Only Hanoverian troops of fifty years' active service may claim its possession.

The Medal of Merit for saving from Danger, was founded on the same day with the previous, as a reward for those who have saved, or been the means of saving, the life or property of others at the risk of their own lives. It is of silver, and shows on the obverse the effigy and the name of the King as legend, and on the reverse an oaken wreath, with the inscription: 'Für Rettung und Gefahr' (For saving and danger), while round the edge is engraved the name of the recipient. It is worn on the left breast, suspended by an orange coloured ribbon with bright blue stripes.

HANSE TOWNS.

MEDALS OF WAR AND CROSS OF HONOUR.

In conjunction with the rest of Germany, Hamburg, Lübeck, Bremen, and Frankfort-on-the-Maine hastened to the field, in 1813, against the oppressors of their rights and privileges. The first three (formerly the Hanse Towns), spared no sacrifices in arming a considerable body of regular troops, under the name of, Hanseatic Legion, while Frankfort despatched a voluntary corps to the theatre of war. Both bodies rivalled in valour with their colleagues in arms of other States, and formed, after the peace of Paris, the original stock of the subsequent contingency of the four towns, to the German Bund.

In commemoration, the three Hanse Towns founded afterwards the War Medal (Plate 94, No. 3), and Frankfort, that of No. 4.

Henry XIII., Prince of Reuss-Greiz, founded, besides, in his capacity as Governor of Frankfort-on-the-Maine, the iron Cross of Honour (No. 5). It is octagonal, with golden edges, and contains on the obverse, the initials: 'A. I.' (Alexander I.), 'F. I.' (Francis I.), 'F. W.' (Frederic William), and the year '1814,' with the word, 'Deutschland' (Germany), in the middle. The reverse shows the initials: H. XIII.' (Henry XIII).

THE HAMBURG DISTINCTION OF MILITARY SERVICE.

On the 6th June, 1839, Hamburg founded, as a reward for her regular troops, a decoration of honour for long loyal service. It consists, for privates of the pioneers, and the Bund who have served ten years, of one woollen chevron, fastened upon the left upper arm; for those who have served fifteen years, of two chevrons, with an additional monthly pay of one mark courant (1s. 3d.) The same, but of gold and silver lace, is awarded to sub-officers and sergeants, under the same conditions. For twenty years' service, a silver cross is presented indiscriminately to all ranks. It is worn upon the left breast suspended by a red ribbon with white borders. The owners receive an additional monthly pay of one mark and eight shillings (1s. 8d.) Officers receive, after twenty-five years' service, the same cross of gold (No. 9).

HESSE (ELECTORATE).

THE FAMILY ORDER OF THE GOLDEN LION.

It was founded on the 14th August, 1790, by the Landgrave Frederick II., as a reward for distinguished merit, and placed by him under the patronage of St. Elizabeth of Hungary, one of the ancestors of the Landgrave. The Landgrave had formed only one class, but altered circumstances induced subsequently the Elector William I. to enlarge the statutes on the 1st January, 1818.

The title of the Order has, however, been retained. The reigning Electors are Grand Masters, and bound to contribute, as much as lies in their power, to preserve and increase the dignity and glory of the institution. The members are divided into four classes: Knights Grand Cross, Commanders first and second classes, and Knights. The number is unlimited, and is not confined to any station, military or civil. The Princes of the reigning house are born Knights of the Grand Cross, though they are not decorated until they have reached the age of discretion or reason. The upper degrees cannot be obtained before passing through the lower. Religion is no bar to admission.

The insignia consist for Knights of the Grand Cross, of the decoration (Plate 40, Tab. I. No. 2), worn by a ribbon across the right shoulder towards the left hip, and containing, on the edge of the reverse, the name of the Grand Master; it further consists of

ELECTORAL HESSE. *Table* I. PLATE 40.

a star (No. 1), worn upon the left side of the coat; both badges show the inscription: 'Virtute et Fidelitate' (For virtue and loyalty).

The Commanders (first class) wear the decoration (No. 4) round the neck, and the silver cross (No. 3) on the left side.

The Commanders (second class) wear the same decoration, but without the cross.

The Knights suspend the cross (No. 5) at the button-hole, or on the left side of the breast. Both (Nos. 4 and 5) have, in the centre of the reverse, the letters: 'W. K.' (Kurfürst Wilhelm) beneath a royal crown.

THE MILITARY ORDER OF MERIT.

This Order, which bore, until 22nd October, 1820, the title of: "Ordre pour la Vertu Militaire," was founded on the 25th February, 1769, by Landgrave Frederick II., as a reward of military distinction. In times of peace, it is reserved only for higher officers, while in times of war it can be claimed by all officers, from the rank of General down to that of Lieutenant. It has only one class. The Elector is Grand Master and sole judge of the merits of the candidates.

The badge is an octagonal gold cross, white enamelled, and covered with a crown. The four wings contain (Tab. II. No. 6) the initials of the Elector, and the word: 'Virtuti' (To virtue). In the spaces between the wings is the Hessian lion (crowned and erect). It is worn round the neck by a sky blue ribbon with silver borders.

THE ORDER OF THE IRON HELMET

Was founded by the Elector William I., on the 18th March,

1814, as a reward for military distinction to both officers and men in the war of liberty of 1814.

The decoration consists of an Iron Helmet upon the Brabant Cross; it is divided into two classes, and one Grand Cross. Both classes have the same cross of cast iron, set in silver. The centre of the front shows an open helmet, at the sides of which are the initials 'W. K.' and below, the number '1814' (Tab. II. No. 7). It is worn at the button-hole. The first class wear besides, on the left breast, a cross formed of red ribbon with white borders. The Grand Cross is double the size of the previous, and is worn round the neck. The first class cannot be obtained without previously possessing the second. The Grand Cross is only conferred after a victorious battle, on the commanding officer who has, by skill and courage, contributed to its success, or who has held out a fortress against the besieging foe. In the Iron Helmet, which was distributed in the succeeding year, in 1815, the Brabant Cross was superseded by the German Cross. (Tab. II. No. 8).

MEDALS AND DECORATIONS OF HONOUR.

1. *The Cross of Merit.*—In 1820, the Elector William I. founded a Silver Medal of Merit for both civil and military individuals, who should distinguish themselves by benevolent actions to their fellow citizens, or by special courage in dangers, and other circumstances of national import. In 1831, the medal was exchanged for a cross, without, however, modifying its original statutes. It is divided into two classes, and consists of gold and silver crosses. (Tab. II. No. 9). The inscription within the four wings is: 'Für Verdienst und Treue' (For merit and loyalty), with the initials of the founder in the centre.

ELECTORAL HESSE. Table 11.   PLATE 41.

2. *The Medal of Remembrance and Honour*, was instituted by the Elector William II. on the 14th March, 1821, for the Hessian military of all ranks and stations who had passed the Rhine, and participated in the wars of 1814 and 1815. It was cast of metal from captured guns. (Tab. II. No. 10).

3. *The Cross of Military Distinction for Sub-officers and Soldiers*, was founded on the 19th August, 1835, by the Co-Regent Elector. The statutes say : That the claim thereto is founded on long active service, from and below the rank of sergeant. It is divided into three classes, for twenty, fifteen and ten years' service (the years of war counting double). It is worn upon the regimental uniform, suspended by a crimson red ribbon with blue stripes. (Tab. II. No. 11). The distribution takes place every year, on the 20th August.

HESSE (GRAND DUCHY).

THE ORDER OF LOUIS.

Was founded in 1807, by the Grand Duke Louis I., as a reward for civil and military merit, for all classes, high and low. It was first distributed by him on St. Louis day, (24th August), the namesday of nearly all the members of the Grand Ducal House. But as the founder had published neither its statutes nor its special title, it passed by various names such as: Order of Merit, Order of Louis, &c., until the 14th December, 1831, when the Grand Duke Louis II. thought proper to promulgate the statutes and modify them in one particular point, with regard to the star, which, instead of being as formerly the same with the Commanders of the first class, and the Knights of the Grand Cross, was now superseded for the former class by a silver star with four points, in which is embroidered the cross of the Order.

The Order is now called the 'Order of Louis,' and is divided into five classes; Knights of the Grand Cross, Commanders, first and second classes; and Knights first and second classes. The number of the members in each class is unlimited. In connection with the Order are, also, gold and silver Medals of Merit. The badge consists, for the Grand Cross, of an octagonal black cross set in gold, with red edges and enamel. The centre of the red enamelled obverse contains the letter 'L,' and within the white ring round it are seen the words in golden characters: 'Für Verdienste' (For

GRAND DUCHY HESSE. Table 1. PLATE 42.

Merit). The reverse is a black field, and contains, in golden characters, the words: 'Gott, Ehre, Vaterland' (God, honour, country), surrounded by a laurel and oaken wreath upon white enamelled ground.

The cross, with the crown above it, is worn by the Knights of the Grand Cross across the left shoulder towards the right hip by a black-watered ribbon, three and a quarter inches wide, and with red borders. They wear besides upon the left breast an octagonal silver star, in the black centre of which are seen, surrounded by a laurel and oaken wreath, the above words: 'Gott, Ehre, Vaterland.' (Plate 42. Tab. I. Nos. 1 and 2).

The Commanders' first class, wear the cross, by a ribbon, round the neck, and besides upon the breast, a silver star with four points, in which is embroidered the cross of the Order. (Tab. I. No. 3).

The Commanders' second class wear the same, but without star.

The Knights of the first and second classes wear the same cross upon the left breast suspended by a ribbon of the above colours.

The size of the cross, and the width of the ribbon diminish with the respective inferior classes.

To the first class of Grand Cross are only admitted Princes by birth, or individuals with the title of 'Excellency.'

THE ORDER OF MERIT AND OF THE HOUSE PHILIPPE-LE-BON (THE GOOD).

It was founded on the 1st of May, 1840, by the Grand Duke Louis II., in honour of one of his ancestors, one of the greatest Princes of the House of Hesse. It is divided into four classes: Knights of the Grand Cross, Commanders of the first and second classes, and Knights.

The obverse of the cross shows the effigy of Philippe-le-Bon upon a sky-blue ground, with the legend: 'Si Deus nobiscum, quis contra nos ?' (If God be with us, who is against us?) while the reverse gives the Hessian arms, with the legend: 'Ludovicus II. Magn. Dux Hessiæ instit.' (Founded by Louis II. Grand Duke of Hesse). (Plate 43, Tab. II. No. 7).

The Knights of the Grand Cross wear the decoration by a ribbon across the shoulder, and the star (No. 6) upon the breast.

The Commanders, of both classes, wear it by a narrow ribbon round the neck, but those of the first class wear besides upon the left breast, the embroidered cross. (Tab. II. No. 8). The Knights wear it in smaller size suspended by a ribbon at the button-hole.

Except on solemn occasions, the Knights of the Grand Cross, when they also possess the same degree in the Order of Louis, wear the present cross round the neck by a narrow ribbon.

DECORATIONS OF HONOUR.

1. *Military Service* was founded on the 26th December, 1833; it consists of a cross, for officers, of gold, and for sub-officers and privates of silver. The front shows the letter 'L,' with a crown above it, and the reverse the words: 'XXV. Jahre treuer Dienste' (Twenty-five years' loyal service). (Tab. II. No. 5). It may, therefore, be claimed only after twenty-five years active service. The cross is worn upon the left breast suspended by a red and white ribbon. The years of campaign count double. Since 1839, a similar cross for fifty years' service has been introduced.

2. *Decoration for Field Service* was founded on the 14th of June, 1840, for all military grades; it consists of a medal cast of

GRAND DUCHY HESSE. *Table* II.　　　　　　　　　　PLATE 45.

6

8

7

9

Hurst and Blackett, London. 1858.

heavy or gun metal. The front exhibits the letter 'L,' with a crown above it, and the inscription : 'Gestiftet am 14 Juni, 1840' (Founded on the 14th June, 1840), and the reverse the words : 'Für treuen Dienst im Kriege' (For faithful service in war). (Tab. II. No. 9). It is worn on the left breast suspended by a red ribbon with white borders.

After the decease of the owner, the medal remains in the family.

(PRINCIPALITIES).

HOHENZOLLERN-HECHINGEN AND HOHENZOLLERN-SIGMARINGEN.

DECORATIONS OF HONOUR.

1. *The Cross of Honour*, was founded on the 1st January, 1842, conjointly by the two Princes (Frederick and Charles), of the above Principalities.

They divided it into four classes:

a. Cross of Honour, first class, with the crown. (Plate 44, No. 1).

b. Cross of Honour, second class, without the crown.

c. Medal of Honour of gold, with the crown (No. 2).

d. Silver Medal of Merit (No. 3.)

The badge consists: for the first class, of an octagonal gold cross with black edges, and coated with white enamel. The middle of the cross is white enamelled, and contains the letters in monogram: 'F. and C.' the initials of the founders. The blue enamelled ring round the middle contains, in golden characters, the legend: 'Für Treue und Verdienst' (For loyalty and merit), and is surrounded by a laurel wreath. The reverse shows, on a similar centre, the arms of Hohenzollern. Above the cross is seen the crown in gold.

For the second class, of the same cross, but without the crown.

HOHENZOLLERN. PLATE 44.

For the third and fourth classes, of the medals containing the same impression as does the cross, with the only difference that the gold medal of the third class has, in addition, a gold crown above it.

The insignia of all the four classes are worn at the buttonhole of the left breast, suspended by a white ribbon with black borders. The owners of the first three classes are allowed, on ordinary occasions, to wear the ribbon without the decoration.

All the Princes of the Hohenzollern House are born Knights of the Cross of Honour, but are not allowed to wear it before the completion of the fifteenth year of their age.

The first class Cross is only presented to the higher State and Court functionaries for distinguished merit.

With the second class Cross are honoured, civil officers who possess the rank of Collegiate, Counsellor, or Head-bailiff, while military men must possess, at least, the rank of Captain. The first class is limited (for each Principality) to four, and the second to six members.

The decorations of the third and fourth class are bestowed indiscriminately, on all individuals who have merited well of their country in promotion of the arts, sciences, inventions, useful establishments, &c. The number of foreign members is not strictly limited in some particular instances.

On the 8th April, 1844, another class was added to the former, a sort of an intervening class between the Cross of Honour, second class, and the Golden Medal of Honour. The new class which was then made to form the third, was that of the Silver Cross of Honour, and its members were limited (for each Principality) to eight.

2. *Military Decoration*, was founded on the 25th February, 1841. It consists of a small golden cross (Nos. 4 and 5), and is worn on the left breast by a black ribbon with white borders.

The centre of the obverse contains the crest of the princely house, and the reverse shows the number 'XXV,' alluding to the distinction, which can only be obtained after twenty-five years' active service, the years of war counting double.

After the incorporation of the two Principalities with Prussia in 1850, the Order was received amongst the Prussian Orders, under the name: 'Order of the House Hohenzollern.' The statutes underwent modifications in several points, and the Order now consists of only three classes: Cross of Honour, first, second, and third class, to which are added a Golden Medal of Honour, and a Silver Medal of Merit.

1. *The Cross of Honour, first class*, is a gold octagonal cross, white enamelled, with black edges. In the middle of the cross is a white enamelled field, showing the family crest of the Hohenzollern, quartered white and black, and covered with a crown. Round this field, and within a ring upon blue enamelled ground, is the legend: 'Für Treue und Verdienst.' Between the angles of the Cross are green enamelled wreaths, partly of laurel, and partly of oaken branches, the leaves being adorned with gold edges.

2. *The Cross of Honour, second class*, consists of the same Cross, but of a smaller size. The white enamelled middle of the reverse contains the crowned initials, 'F. and C.' in gold. The ring round it shows in gold, upon blue ground, the day of the foundation of the Order (5th December, 1841).

3. *The Cross of Honour, third class*, is of silver; the arms of the cross are pointed, while the reverse shows the date of the foundation (8th December, 1844). In all other respects, it resembles the Cross of the second class.

4 and 5. *The Golden Medal of Honour*, and *The Silver Medal of Merit*, have the same impression, both on front and reverse, as have the medal and ring of Cross second class.

The Cross of the first class is worn on the left breast; and that of the second and third, as also the two medals at the button-hole, suspended by a white watered ribbon with three black stripes, and about one and a half inches wide. The first class Cross is usually worn by the Prussian Knights of the Black Eagle below the star of that Order.

The Princes of the blood royal have the option of wearing either the first or the second class Cross. In the latter case, the Cross is covered with a crown, consisting of a golden circle, mounted by five leaves and four coronets, above which are joined three rings set with pearls, holding the imperial globe. Between the rings is a red velvet hat, which partially covers the crown.

HOLLAND.

THE MILITARY ORDER OF WILLIAM.

It was the first constitutional Order, founded by King William I., on the 30th April, 1815, and consists of four classes: Knights Grand Cross, Commanders, Knights of the third and fourth classes.

The badge is an octagonal white onamelled cross, with eight knobs, on the points, and with the words distributed upon the wings: 'Voor Moed, Belied, Trouw' (For courage, zeal, and loyalty), while between those wings is the white enamelled Burgundian Cross, and upon the middle of the obverse, the Burgundian Fire-steel, in gold,* and on the reverse, in a blue medal, a 'W' surrounded by a laurel wreath.

The characteristic distinctions for the four classes are:

a. For the Knights of the Grand Cross, an embroidered silver star (Plate 45, Tab. I. No. 1) upon the left side of the coat, and the jewel (No. 3), worn across the right shoulder towards the left hip, by a ribbon about three and a half inches wide.

b. For the Commanders, the Cross (No. 2), embroidered upon the left side of the coat, and a similar one worn round the neck, by a ribbon about two and a half inches wide.

c. For the Knights third class, the jewel (No. 3), worn at the button-hole by a ribbon, about one inch and a half wide.

---

* The Burgundian Cross and Steel are symbols of William the Just, Philip the Good, and the Order of the Golden Fleece.

HOLLAND. Table I. PLATE 45.

Hurst and Blackett, London. 1858.

d. For the Knights' fourth class, the decoration is of a smaller size in silver, and is suspended, also, at the button-hole, by a ribbon about three quarters of an inch wide.

The Knights in the army and navy, below the rank of officers, receive with the first class Order, an addition equal to the half of their pay, which is doubled when promoted to the third class. The scale of the degrees is from the fourth class upwards, so that no intervening class can be passed over.

The festival of the Order is annually held on the 16th January.

CIVIL ORDER OF MERIT OF THE BELGIAN LION,
(Also called the Order of the Netherlands Lion.)

This Order was also founded by King William I. on the 20th September, 1815, for distinguished merit in civil life, patriotism, or eminence in the arts and sciences; foreigners are not excluded from it.

The monarch holds the Grand Mastership, a dignity inseparable from the Dutch crown.

The Order is divided into three classes: Knights of the Grand Cross, Commanders, and simple Knights.

There is also a fourth class, under the name 'Brothers,' for individuals who have merited well, by useful and humane actions towards their fellow-creatures.

The badge is a white enamelled cross, with a gold letter 'W' in each of the angles: the blue enamelled middle of the front contains the inscription in gold, of 'Virtus nobilitat' (Virtue ennobles), and the similar middle of the reverse shows the lion of the national arms. (Plate 46, Tab. II. No. 8). Above the whole is a royal crown. The colour of the ribbon is Nassau blue with two orange coloured stripes.

The distinctive marks of the different classes are:

1. For the Knights Grand Cross, the decoration of the front mounted on a silver star without the crown, and embroidered upon the left side of the coat, (Tab. II. No. 6), while the jewel of the Order, (No. 8), is worn across the right shoulder towards the left hip, by a ribbon about three and a half inches wide.

2. For the Commanders, the same decoration embroidered upon the coat without the star, but with the crown above it. (Tab. II. No. 7). The jewel is worn round the neck by a ribbon about two inches and a half wide.

3. For the simple Knights, the decoration is worn at the button-hole, suspended by a ribbon about two inches and a half wide.

The 'Brothers' wear a silver medal instead of the cross; the front shows the symbol, and the reverse, the motto of the Order. It is worn suspended by a blue ribbon, about one inch and a half wide, with an orange stripe in the middle. (Tab. II. No. 9).

The 'Brothers' receive an annual pension of 200 fl. (about £17), the half of which goes, after death, to their widows.

THE TEUTONIC ORDER.

The history and sketch of this Order is already given under AUSTRIA.

Utrecht, was one of the twelve Bailiwicks, of which the Order consisted in Germany. It originated from a gift bequeathed to the Order, by a nobleman of Munster, a certain

HOLLAND. Table II.   PLATE 46.

Suedre, (of Dingete and Ringenburg), and his wife, Beatrix, of all their estates situated in the diocese of Utrecht.

The first Great Commander of this Bailiwick, was the Chevalier Anthony of Ledersake of Printhagen.

Since 1231, thirteen Commanderies were established, besides that of the Great Commander, eleven of which are still extant, viz: Dieren, Maasland, Tiel, Rhene, Leyden and Katneyk, Schooten, Doesburg, Schaluinen, Middelburg and Schoonhoven.

The Commander of Dieren is always Co-adjutor of the Order and is next in rank to the Great Commander.

Since the 8th September, 1837, there are, in addition to the actual Knights, noblemen who have obtained the expectancy or reversion of a Commandery, and are on that account allowed to wear a small cross.

When the Reformation was introduced into the Netherlands, and the Protestant became the established religion of the country, the Bailiwick of Utrecht was withdrawn from the authority of the then Grand Master, Mergenthein, as were, indeed, all the old church domains then disposed of for the benefit of the towns. The States of Utrecht, however, took in 1580, the Bailiwick under their protection, under the conditions that the Grand Master should follow their instructions, exclude priests from the Order, receive into it those noblemen only who professed the new religion, and enjoin the Commanders to renounce celibacy, in fine, dissolve all ties that might bind the Order to Rome. Of all the vows, there remained, consequently, but one: that of *obedience*.

In course of time, however, the Grand Masters endeavoured to bring the Bailiwick back under their own jurisdiction, and the consequence was, that at the meetings of the General Assembly of the States, the chair of the Grand Master remained vacant, its arms being turned towards the table. Things remained in this state of uncertainty until the war with France, in 1795, when by a decree of Napoleon, (February 27th, 1811), the Bailiwick of Utrecht ceased to exist, as did indeed the Teutonic Order in the whole of Germany, by a similar decree of Napoleon (24th April, 1809).

After the return of the House of Orange-Nassau, King William proposed to the States-General, the restoration of the Bailiwick, which the States consented to, and by a law of the 8th August, 1815, all the previous rights and privileges were restored to it.

The candidates must, previous to their nomination, prove their noble descent, of, at least, two hundred years' standing.

The members are now divided into Great Commanders, Commanders, and Knights, to all of whom the revenues of the Bailiwick belong. They owe obedience and loyalty to the Great Commander, as the representative of the King.

DECORATIONS AND MEDALS OF HONOUR.

1. *Medal for faithful Service;* was founded by King William, on the 19th February, 1825. It is bestowed in bronze for twelve, and in silver for twenty-four years of military service; it is worn at the button-hole, on the left side. (Tab. III. No. 11).

2. *Medal for Courage and Loyalty*, was founded on the 24th January, 1839, for the native troops of the Colonial army, who belong to no European corps. It is of silver and of bronze; the first is conferred for particular distinction, or on those who are already in possession of the latter. It is worn on the left breast, suspended by a blue ribbon. The motto: 'Im Namen des Königs' (In the name of the King), is surrounded by the legend: 'Für Muth und Treue im Holländischen Indien' (For courage and loyalty in Dutch

HOLLAND. Table III. PLATE 47.

India). With the decoration, the pay is increased, by half (with the silver), and by a third (with the bronze).

3. *Medal of the Hague*, was distributed amongst those who had first taken up arms on the 17th November, 1813, to repulse the French, and re-establish the legitimate government. The front shows two swords, with the motto: 'Für das Vaterland und Oranien' (For the Fatherland and Orange); and the reverse, the words: 'XVII November, MDCCCXIII.' while the centre contains an oaken and laurel wreath. It is worn suspended by a ribbon of the colours of the town, blue and yellow.

4. *Medal of Dotrecht* was distributed for a similar circumstance as the previous, amongst the people of the place. The front shows the beak of a ship, and a gun covered by a mural crown, with the words: 'Für unsre Mauern und unsre Wohnungen' (For our walls and dwellings). While the reverse exhibits, within a laurel and oaken garland, the inscription: 'Dotrecht, XXIV November, MDCCCXIII.'

5. *Medal of Naarden*, was presented to the citizens of Amsterdam, who co-operated at the siege of Naarden, occupied by the French. The front shows, within a laurel and orange wreath, the words: 'Belagerung von Naarden, 1814' (Siege of Naarden, 1814). The reverse exhibits, within an oaken wreath, the words: 'Verliehen vom Central-Comité in Amsterdam— N. N.' (Presented by the Central Committee at Amsterdam to ... name of recipient). It is worn suspended by a tri-coloured ribbon, white black and red.

6. *Medal of Java*, was founded on the 27th June, 1831, for the military who were present at the campaigns of Java, from 1825 to 1830. (Tab. III. No. 13).

7. *The Cross of Hasselt*, was cast from the guns taken at the battle of Hasselt, 8th August, 1831, and was distributed amongst the military who participated in that affair. (Tab. III. No. 13).

The same cross, but with the ribbon No. 14, and the inscription: 'Vrywilling' (Volunteer), on the reverse, was distributed amongst the volunteers engaged in the struggle with Belgium, in 1831.

8. *Medal of Antwerp*, was founded on the 31st of May, 1833, for those who had distinguished themselves at the defence of the citadel. (Tab. III. No. 12).

9. *Buckle in bronze*, founded for valour, on the 31st May, 1832.

DECORATION OF HONOUR FOR THE NATIONAL GUARD

Was founded on the 5th December, 1851. It consists, for officers, of a silver buckle, on which is given the number of years of service, within a wreath of olive and oak leaves above two crossed swords, and, for sub-officers and guard-soldiers, of a medal with the words: 'Trouwe Dienst' (Loyal service) above a trophy of standards and weapons, which partly cover the above words; while beneath the trophy is seen within a semi-circle, the word 'Schuttery' (National Guard). The whole is of silver, surrounded by an olive and oak wreath, and covered by a civic crown. The officers fasten it on the left breast, while the sub-officers and privates wear it suspended by an orange coloured watered ribbon. It is conferred on those who have served, irreproachably, in the National Guard for fifteen years. Active service out of the town of domicile, counts double.

LIPPE-SCHAUMBURG (PRINCIPALITY.)

The Military Medal, (Plate 48, Nos. 5 and 6), was founded by Prince George William on the 15th November, 1831, as a reward for the officers and soldiers who have partaken in the campaigns since 1808, and loyally served the Prince and the State. The medal is of silver with the effigy and the usual legend (the name of the founder) on the front, and the words: 'Für Tapferkeit und Treue' (For valour and loyalty), surrounded by a laurel and an oak branch on the reverse.

It is worn at the button-hole suspended by a blue ribbon with white borders. The medal remains in the family after the death of the owner.

LIPPE-DETMOLD (PRINCIPALITY.)

DECORATIONS OF HONOUR.

1. *The Military Medal of Merit*, in bronze, (Nos. 1 and 2), was founded 16th May, 1832, for long military service, or peculiar distinction in war.

2. *The Civil Medal of Merit*, in silver, was founded in 1816 by the same Prince, Paul Alexander Leopold. The obverse contains an oaken branch with the words between the leaves: 'Des Verdienstes Anerkennung' (Acknowledgment of merit), while the reverse shows the Lippe rose, with a forget-me-not garland below, which means: 'The fatherland will never forget merit.' The medal is worn suspended by a crimson ribbon with yellow stripes near the ends.

LIPPE DETMOLD & LIPPE-SCHAUMBURG. PLATE 48.

LUCCA (DUCHY.)

THE MILITARY ORDER OF ST. GEORGE

Was founded by Duke Charles Louis on the 1st June, 1833, under the name: 'Ordine di San Giorgio per il Merito Militare (Order of St. George for Military Merit).

The reigning Duke is Grand Master of the Order, which is divided into three classes, the nomination beginning with the lowest, and advancing gradually to the second and third.

The badge is a cross (Plate 49, No. 1); the middle of the obverse shows the figure of St. George and the Dragon, surrounded by a green enamelled ring with the inscription: 'Al Merito Militare' (To military merit), and that of the reverse, the initial of the founder together with the year '1833.'

The cross for the first class Knights is of gold and enamel, for the second, of silver and enamel, and for the third, of silver without enamel. It is worn by all the classes on the left side of the breast suspended by a red ribbon with white borders, while that of the first class is, in addition, adorned with a rosette. The reigning Duke wears the cross of the first class, accompanied by a star, the middle of which has the same device as that of the front of the cross, with the addition of the year of the foundation as inscribed on the reverse. For extraordinary merit, the cross of the first two classes is adorned with brilliants, (No. 2), or is accompanied by a pension.

The first class cross is usually presented:

a. To the Director General of the armed force, after three years' distinguished management of his department.

b. To officers of the staff, and

c. To officers of any degree for peculiar distinction in a military enterprize that had been left to their own discretion.

The second class is presented to officers of distinction, and the third, even to privates of merit.

THE ORDER OF ST. LOUIS, FOR CIVIL MERIT.

Was founded by Duke Charles Louis on the 22nd December, 1836, and consists of three classes. The badge is a cross, adorned with lillies; the obverse shows the figure of St. Louis in golden armour, and the reverse the Bourbon crest. The cross of the first class is of gold and white enamel; of the second, of silver and the same enamel; and of the third, also of silver, but without enamel. It is worn on the left breast, suspended by a bright blue ribbon with yellow borders. (Plate 49, No. 3). The Chancellor and the Secretary of the Order wear, besides, a cross of peculiar form, characteristic of their respective offices.

DECORATIONS OF HONOUR.

Medal for long Military Service, (Medaglia di Anzianità). —It was founded on the 1st of June, 1833, for officers who had served at least thirty years.

It consists of a cross of gilt metal; the middle of the front shows the initial of the founder, and the reverse the number 'XXX.' It is worn on the left side of the breast suspended by a bright blue ribbon with three yellow stripes. (Nos. 4 and 5).

LUCCA. PLATE 49.

Hurst and Blackett, London. 1858.

LUXEMBURG (GRAND DUCHY.)

THE ORDER OF THE OAKEN-CROWN.

It was founded by King William II. of the Netherlands, on the 29th December, 1841, for all classes of society, for distinguished merit in the army, civil service, or the arts and sciences, and may, in some instances, be also conferred upon foreigners.

The King is Grand Master, and the dignity cannot be separated from the Grand Ducal crown.

The Order consists of four classes: Knights of the Grand Cross, Knights with the star of the Order, Commanders, and (simply) Knights.

The badge (Plate 50, No. 4) is a square silver star with a green enamelled middle which shows a golden 'W' beneath the Grand Ducal crown, with the motto in golden characters: 'Je maintiendrai' (I will maintain), upon red enamelled ground. The motto is encircled by an oaken crown, whence the name of the Order is derived.

The jewel of the Order (No. 5) forms a square cross white enamelled and set in gold, containing upon green enamelled ground in the middle, a golden 'W' beneath the Grand Ducal crown. The ribbon is orange yellow, watered, and with three dark green stripes.

The Knights Grand Cross wear the decoration on the left

side, and the jewel across the right shoulder towards the left hip, suspended by a ribbon about three and a quarter inches wide.

The Knights with the star, wear the decoration as before, and the jewel round the neck suspended by a ribbon about two inches and a half wide.

The Commanders wear the jewel (without the star) as above, while the simple Knights wear it at the button-hole by a ribbon of about one and a half inches wide.

In February, 1850, two decorations were founded for the contingent of the German Bund in that Duchy.

The first is for officers, and others of the same rank, belonging to that contingent, as a reward for long and faithful service, (fifteen years' service under the Dutch flag entitles to the decoration). It consists of a cross, containing on the obverse the initial of the King, and on the reverse the arms of the Grand Duchy; it is worn suspended by an orange-coloured ribbon. (Plate 50, No. 1).

The second is for sub-officers and soldiers of the German contingent, equally for long and faithful service. It consists for ten years' service of a bronze cross, with the royal initial on the front, and the Grand Ducal arms on the reverse; for twenty years' service, of a similar medal in silver, (No. 2). It is worn by an orange coloured ribbon with green borders.

LUXEMBURG. PLATE 50.

MECKLENBURG-SCHWERIN (GRAND-DUCHY.)

MEDALS AND DECORATIONS OF HONOUR.

1. *Military Medal of Merit*, (Plate 11, Nos. 1 and 2), was founded on the 23rd July, 1814, by Duke Frederick Francis, for the troops who had distinguished themselves in that memorable campaign. It is worn at the button-hole suspended by a ribbon of the ducal colours: bright blue with narrow borders of red and yellow, and is divided into two classes—the gold and silver medal. The front exhibits an antique sword in a perpendicular position, entwined by a laurel wreath with the year '1813' at the sides of it; the reverse shows the inscription: 'Mecklenburg's Streitern' (To Mecklenburg's warriors), and the initial of the founder.

2. *Civil Medal of Merit.*—It is rather larger than the previous, and bears on the front the effigy of the founder with the legend: 'Friedrich Franz, Herzog zu Mecklenburg' (Frederick Francis, Duke of Mecklenburg). The reverse shows the words: 'Dem redlichen Manne, und dem guten Bürger' (To the honest man and good citizen). It is presented either in gold or silver, and is worn by a ribbon of the same colour as the previous military medal (No. 3).

3. *The Military Cross of Service*, (Nos. 4 to 8).—It was founded on the 30th April, 1841, by the Grand Duke Paul Frederick, and consists, for officers and officials of the same rank, of a gold cross, bearing in front the initial of the

founder, and on the reverse the number of years of service. For sergeants and under, the decoration has four classes: a cross of silver with a gold middle for the first class: a cross of silver for the second class: a cross of copper with a silver middle for the third class: a cross of copper without middle for the fourth class.

The front shows the initial of the founder, and the reverse, the years of service.

The Military Cross of Service is worn on the left breast suspended by a crimson ribbon with blue and yellow borders.

Officers and officials of a similar grade receive, after twenty-five years' service, the gold cross, while the number on the reverse is altered for every five years' additional active service.

Military sergeants and those of inferior rank, receive, after ten years' active service, the fourth class cross; after fifteen years, the third class cross; after twenty years, the second class; and after twenty-five years the first class cross; also the number of the years on the reverse is altered after every five years' additional service.

4. *The War Medal* was founded on the 30th April, 1841, by the Grand Duke, after the form of the medal of the other German States, for the war of 1814. It is cast from heavy (gun) metal. The obverse shows the initial of the founder, and the year '1841,' and the reverse, the inscription: 'Für treuen Dienst im Kriege' (For faithful service in war). The name of the recipient is engraved on the edge; it was distributed amongst the veterans who had served in the Rhinebund from 1808 to 1812, or made the campaigns of from 1812 to 1815.

5. *The Military Cross of Merit*, was founded on the 5th of August, 1848. It is also cast of heavy gun metal, and

MECKLENBURG. PLATE 51.

Hurst and Blackett, London. 1858.

contains on the front the inscription: 'Für Auszeichnung im Kriege' (For distinction in war), and on the reverse the initial of the founder, and the year '1848.' It is worn on the left breast by a bright blue ribbon with narrow borders of red and yellow.

MEXICO (REPUBLIC.)

ORDER OF THE MADONNA OF GUADALOUPE

Was founded after the model of the old one of the Emperor Iturbide, on the 11th November, 1853. The head of the Mexican government is Grand Master, and nominates twenty-four Knights Grand Cross, one hundred Commanders (exclusive of foreigners), and an unlimited number of Knights.

The Order is worn suspended by a sky blue ribbon with violet borders, and consists of a golden cross, enamelled red green and white, and placed upon palm leaves and an olive branch, with the Mexican eagle above it. The middle of the front shows the figure of the Madonna of Guadaloupe, with the inscription: 'Religion, Independence, Union.' The red middle of the reverse contains the enamelled inscription: 'Heroic Patriotism.' The Order has its chapter, festivals, costume (of satin and taffetas), spiritual and secular officials, salaries and hospitals, all after the model of the old European Orders.

MODENA.

DECORATIONS OF HONOUR.

In addition to the already existing decoration for sub-officers and privates of twelve or eighteen years' service, the Duke (Francis V.) founded on the 16th May, 1852, another Cross for officers who had served the uninterrupted space of twenty-five years, under the standard of the house of Este.

This Cross is of silver, with a golden edge and ring, and is worn on the left breast suspended by a white and blue ribbon. The middle of the obverse contains a small blue enamelled medal, on which is seen the white eagle of Este under a royal crown. The reverse shows the cypher 'XXV' in silver, upon golden ground.

Officers who have completed the fiftieth year of service receive a white enamelled cross, with the cypher '50' on it; in all other respects as just described.

MONTONEGRO (PRINCIPALITY).

In 1837, this government had medals struck to reward the Klephts (Armatols) for their services in the Greek War of Independence; these medals contain the Russian arms, and inscription: 'To loyalty and valour.' Prince Daniel distributed about two hundred of them in 1853.

NASSAU (DUCHY).

MEDALS AND DECORATIONS OF HONOUR.

1. *Military Decoration of Honour.*—This decoration was founded by Duke Frederick Augustus, to save from oblivion —as the patent says—special deeds of valour, such as saving the life of a comrade, &c., performed by a soldier It consists (Plate 52, Nos. 1 and 2) of a medal, gold or silver, and is destined only for sergeants and those of lower rank It is worn at the button-hole of the regimentals, suspended by a dark brown and sulphur-yellow ribbon. The owner of the silver medal receives with it an addition equal to half of his pay, and the owner of the gold medal, an addition equal to his full pay, in time of peace. The addition is retained even after promotion. The owner of the silver medal is not excluded from the additional reward of the gold medal, if subsequent merit entitle him to it.

The medal remains in the family of the recipient after his decease.

2. *The Civil Medal of Merit*, is distributed in gold and in silver to civil officers for long and faithful service. It also remains with the heirs of the deceased owner.

The impression shows, each time, the effigy and name of the reigning Duke.

3. *Military Decoration of Honour, for Service*, was founded on the 25th February, 1834 (Nos. 4 and 5). It consists:

a. For officers, of a golden cross, showing in the middle of the front, a 'W,' and in the arms of the cross: 'XXI. Treue Dienstjahre' (Twenty-one years' faithful service), while the reverse contains in the middle: 'Der 25 Februar, 1834' (25th February, 1834), as the day of the first presentation.

It is worn on the left breast by a blue ribbon (No. 4).

b. For sub-officers, the members of the band, and privates, of a silver cross, with the same inscription as the above, and with the only difference, that the Roman cypher upon the upper arm of the cross is 'XXII., XVI.', X., (No. 5) according to the respective classes.

The ribbon of the first class is blue (like that of the officers); that of the second class the same, but with a gold yellow stripe (No. 6); and that of the third class also the same, but with two stripes (No. 7). The cross is worn, if military, on the left breast of the uniform, and if civil, at the buttonhole.

An increase of pay is granted to sub-officers and soldiers on receiving the silver cross.

4. *The Waterloo Medal* was founded by Duke Frederick on the 23rd December, 1815 (No. 3), for officers and privates who had taken part in that battle, or were at least in active service at that period. It is worn suspended by a dark blue watered ribbon with orange coloured borders.

NASSAU. PLATE 52.

NORWAY.

THE ORDER OF ST. OLAF

Was founded on the 21st August, 1847, by King Oscar. It is the first independent Order the country ever possessed. The name is to commemorate the illustrious monarch who freed (1015) Norway from the sway of Denmark, and introduced Christianity into that realm. To this latter circumstance was owing his canonization (1033).

The Order is designated as a reward for all classes, who distinguish themselves in patriotism, or in the arts and sciences. It consists of an octagonal golden cross, white enamelled, and surmounted with the royal crown. The middle of the obverse is encompassed by a blue and white ribbon, and contains the arms of Norway (a gold lion, crowned), while the reverse shows the motto: 'Ret og Sandhed' (Right and truth). (Plate 53, No. 3). Between each of the arms of the cross is seen a crowned 'O.' It is worn suspended by a red watered ribbon with blue and white borders, by the Knights of the Grand Cross, across the right shoulder; by the Commanders round the neck, and by the Knights at the button-hole. The Knights Grand Cross wear, in addition, a star (Plate 53, No. 1), and the Commanders another (No. 2). The cross of the military has, in addition, two crossed swords beneath the crown.

The first Chapter was held on the 23rd August, 1847, when the King nominated eleven Knights Grand Cross, twenty-two Commanders, and forty-six Knights. Among the first, were the celebrated savans, A. Humboldt, Berzelius, and Oehlenschläger. It may be mentioned, that among the Commanders was the Bishop of Drontheim, the same who refused to anoint the Queen, alleging as a reason, that the fundamental law of the realm only speaks of the coronation of a King, but not of a Queen.

NORWAY. PLATE 53.

1 2

3

OLDENBURG (GRAND DUCHY).

ORDER OF MERIT, AND OF THE DUCAL HOUSE OF PETER FREDERICK LOUIS.

This Order (Plate 54, Nos. 1 to 6) was founded on the 27th November, 1838, by Duke Paul Frederick, in memory of his father, who, the patent says, had himself resolved upon the foundation of a similar Order, as reward to subjects or foreigners for distinguished merit in the arts and sciences, or in the more humble pursuits of domestic and civil life. The reigning Grand Duke is always Grand Master.

The Order consists of Capitulars and Honorary Members. Both divisions are equal in rank, and have four classes: Knights Grand Cross, Great Commanders, Commanders, and Knights Small Cross.

Only natives and citizens of Oldenburg can be received amongst the Capitulars. The Capitular of a lower class may, at the same time, belong to a higher class as Honorary Member. The Princes in direct male line from the Ducal House of Peter Frederick Louis are, by birth, Honorary Members of the Grand Cross. The heir presumptive to the Grand Duchy, bears the title of Grand Prior.

Proofs of valour and distinction in military service entitle to the nomination into the fourth class. The division of Capitulars consists of:

Two Knights Grand Cross with an annual pension of	. .	500 gold thalers		(£75).
Two Great Commanders	,,	400	,,	(£60).
Four Commanders	,,	300	,,	(£45).
Eight Knights Small Cross	,,	200	,,	(£40).

The number of Honorary Members in the Grand Duchy, is, exclusive of the Ducal Princes, limited to four Knights Grand Cross, four Great Commanders, eight Commanders, and sixteen Knights Small Cross. In time of war, the latter class may be augmented as regards the military.

The insignia consist, for the first class, of a star worn on the left breast, and of a cross worn across the right shoulder towards the left hip by a dark blue watered ribbon, with a narrow red stripe near each border (Nos. 1 and 2). For the second class, of a star worn on the right breast, and of a small cross worn round the neck by a similar ribbon about two inches wide.

For the third class, of a small cross also worn round the neck by a similar ribbon about one inch and a half wide.

For the fourth class, of a small cross, worn at the buttonhole of the left side, and suspended by a similar ribbon about one inch and a half wide.

Military persons who have received the small cross in war, wear, in addition, upon the ribbon of the Order, a round cockade formed of the same ribbon.

The Capitulars wear, besides, a particular decoration, varying with every class (Nos. 3 to 6).

The Chapter is usually held on the 17th January, the birthday of Duke Peter Frederick Louis.

The middle of the star and obverse of the cross contain the initials of the Duke Peter Ferderick Louis.

The inscriptions upon the four white enamelled wings of the

OLDENBURG. PLATE 54.

cross indicate the birth-day (17th January, 1755), the date of the accession to the throne (6th July, 1785), and of the death (2nd May, 1829) of that Duke, as also the day when the Order was founded (27th November, 1838).

The additional special decoration of the Capitulars consists of a medal surrounded by an oaken wreath. It is for the first class, of gold, and adorned with a golden crown; for the second class, of silver, with a silver crown; for the third class, of gold, without a crown; and for the fourth class, of silver, also without a crown. It is worn, suspended by a ribbon, round the neck.

MEDALS AND DECORATIONS OF HONOUR.

1. *The Medal of Honour*, was founded on the 30th April, 1815, at the suggestion of Field-Marshal Blücher, who bore testimony to the gallant conduct of the Oldenburg regiment in the war with France. The decoration was accordingly distributed amongst those officers and men who took part in any one of the battles. It consists of a medal (No. 7), and is worn on the left side of the breast suspended by a dark blue ribbon with two red stripes.

2. *The gold and silver Crosses of Honour, for twenty-five years faithful Military Service* (No. 8).—It was founded on the 24th December, 1838, as a reward for long military service as above. The decoration consists of a cross, the obverse of which contains the number 'XXV.' in Roman cyphers, and the reverse, the initials 'P. F. L.' (Peter Frederick Louis) in gothic characters, and surmounted by a crown. It is worn on the left breast, suspended by a red ribbon with narrow blue borders.

For officers, the cross is of gold, and for sub-officers and privates of silver. Non-combatants in the army, such as military surgeons, mechanics, secretaries, and other officials, may claim the decoration, if present, at least, in one campaign. Lieutenants receive with the decoration a monthly addition to their pay of 10 gulden (£1), and sub-officers and those under, an increase amounting to the half of their pay.

The day of distribution of the decoration, is the 24th December of each year.

PAPAL STATES.

ORDER OF SAINT GREGORY THE GREAT.

This Order was founded by Pope Gregory XVI., on the 1st September, 1831, as a reward for zeal and devotion displayed in the cause of the Roman Catholic religion, and Apostolic authority, in an age of religious opposition and indifference.

In 1834, the original statutes were in some parts modified, the classes were reduced from four to three, and their respective numbers, as regards Roman subjects, limited to thirty, seventy, and three hundred.

The badge consists of an octagonal golden cross, chased and enamelled red. The blue middle contains on the obverse the effigy of Saint Gregory, and on the reverse the words: 'Pro Deo et Principe' (For God and the Chief), both accompanied by the legend: 'S. Gregorius Magnus' (Plate 55, Tab. I. No. 2). It is worn suspended by a red ribbon with yellow borders by the Knights of the Grand Cross, across the right shoulder towards the left hip, together with the star (No. 1), on the left breast; by the Commanders round the neck, without the star; and by the Knights in a smaller form at the button-hole. For civil service, the Cross is appended to a green enamelled olive branch (No. 2), and for military service, it is adorned with golden trophies (No. 3), and sometimes, by special favour, with brilliants. There is no particular costume in connection with the Order.

THE ORDER OF CHRIST.

As this is, properly speaking, a Portuguese Order, its history will be detailed among the Orders of Portugal, and we shall, therefore, confine our remarks here to a few principal particulars.

Pope Clement V., it is well known, abolished, in 1312, the Order of the Templars. The measure was then objected to by King Dionysius of Portugal, who allowed the Order to exist in his dominions, with all its rights, privileges and possessions. It naturally led to misunderstandings between the two courts, until Pope XXII. (successor of Clement), compromised the matter by consenting, in 1319, to the existence of the Order in Portugal under a new name: 'The Knights of Christ,' but reserved to himself, and his successors, the right of creating a similar Order also in the Papal States, of which right his successors avail themselves to this day, by conferring this Order, as a distinction of merit on both native and foreign Catholics.

The Roman Order of Christ has only one class.

The decoration consists of a red enamelled gold cross, with another white cross in the middle, surmounted by a crown. (Tab. I. No. 5). To this cross is appended, above the crown, when for military merit, some golden trophies (No. 6). It is worn round the neck by a red ribbon, accompanied by the star (No. 4) upon the breast. The Cross in the middle of the star is adorned with precious stones or pearls. Formerly, the Order was worn suspended by a gold chain. The candidates of the Roman Order are not obliged, like those of the Portuguese, to prove their noble descent; nor is there any particular costume for the Roman Order.

PAPAL STATES. Table I.   PLATE 55.

ORDER OF THE GOLDEN SPURS.

This Order of the Golden Militia, but better known as the Order of the Golden Spurs, claims prior antiquity to all other knightly Orders. The presumption that it was founded by Constantine, and confirmed by Pope Sylvester, at whose hands the Emperor even received the insignia, rests upon the testimony of several not unimportant writers, though it seems more probable, as some other authors affirm, that its origin falls in the reign of Paul III. or his successor, Pius IV. (in 1559). Its existence previous to the reign of Paul III. is, at all events, not historically evidenced.

The Knights, who formerly bore in the patent the title of 'Lateran Court Palatines,' possessed, at one time, numerous rights and privileges, and had even precedence in rank to the Maltese and Teutonic Knights, and the Order therefore commanded then a very high position in public opinion.

In process of time, however, the various alterations effected in the statutes, added to the lavish distribution of the Order, greatly detracted from its value and respect, while the words in the nomination patent: "That the new Knights were to partake of all the advantages and privileges peculiar to the Order," became an empty form. The Order was confined to no rank or station, and was usually conferred by the Popes, on the anniversaries of their accession, during their procession from the Vatican to the Lateran, on their pages and other attendants of their household.

The right of nomination was even vested on certain prelates and Cardinals, while the Ducal house Sforza-Besarini professed to be in possession of a power granted by Pope Paul III.

(1539), (which the succeeding Popes seemed to have confirmed) to invest with the Order any one whom they should deem worthy of it.

That, under such circumstances, the Order gradually became depreciated in public esteem may easily be imagined from the vast extent to which the distribution was carried; and no wonder that it fell so low, that no one coveted its possession, until Pope Gregory XVI. again succeeded in imparting to it a dignified character, by the new regulations he made in 1840 respecting its distribution.

He decreed that henceforth the Order should be granted, as a public acknowledgment, only to those who had really distinguished themselves, either in their zeal for the Catholic religion and the Holy Chair, or in civil virtues, or in the arts and sciences. He, moreover, divided the Order into two classes: Commanders and Knights. He retained the form of the insignia as prescribed by Pope Benedict XIV., and the only innovation he introduced consisted in the Cross: he ordered that in the round blue and white enamelled middle of its obverse, the effigy of Sylvester was to be exhibited, while the reverse should show the words: 'Gregorius XVI. restituit' (Restored by Gregory XVI). The Order is now worn suspended by a black ribbon with white stripes by the Commanders round the neck, and by the Knights upon the left breast. (Tab. III. No. 12).

The number of the first class he fixed at one hundred and fifty; and of the second class at three hundred (both, exclusive of foreigners). Every nomination that does not emanate direct from the Pope is considered null and void.

The costume of the Order consists of a red military coat, white breeches, sword and spurs.

PAPAL STATES. *Table* II.   PLATE 56.

Hurst and Blackett, London. 1858.

PAPAL STATES. Table III. PLATE 57.

Hurst and Blackett, London. 1858.

DECORATIONS OF HONOUR.

1. *The Military Medal of Merit* was founded by Pope Gregory XVI. in 1832, of gold for subaltern officers, and of silver for sub-officers. The front shows the effigy of the Pope, and the reverse, the inscription ' Bene Merenti.' It is appended to a tiara and keys, and suspended by a white and yellow ribbon. (Tab. III. No. 16). It is sometimes encompassed by a green enamelled laurel wreath. (Tab. III. No. 15).

2. A somewhat large medal, founded by Pope Pius VII., and each time adorned with the effigy of the reigning Pope. It is rather profusely distributed in bronze amongst the soldiers, and in silver amongst the officers. (Tab. III. No. 13).

3. The same Pope founded also another medal (Tab. II. No. 11) in 1816, for the troops who had distinguished themselves in the Crusade against the robbers of the State. It is of gilt silver, white enamelled, and with the inscription 'Latronibus Fugatis Securitas Restituta' (Safety restored by the expulsion of robbers). It was also distributed in bronze amongst the sub-officers and soldiers for lesser distinction and merit.

4. *The Decoration of Honour* ' Ordine del Moreto' presented each time to the President of the Academy of St. Luke, who may wear it even after his retirement. (Tab. III. No. 14).

THE ORDER OF PIUS

Was founded on the 17th June, 1847. It is divided into two classes, hereditary and personal nobility.

The decoration is an hexagonal blue star. The white enamelled obverse contains in the middle, in golden characters,

'Pius IX.,' while in the circle round it are the words: 'Virtuti et Merito.' The reverse shows the inscription 'Anno MDCCCXLVII.' (Tab. IV. No. 18).

The Knights of the second class wear the Order upon the right side of the breast, suspended by a dark blue ribbon with red borders, while the Knights of the first class who formerly carried it by a ribbon round the neck, and, by special permission, accompanied by a star (No. 17) upon the left breast; are now, by a Bull issued at Gaeta on the 17th June, 1849, enjoined to wear the badge across the right shoulder towards the left hip, suspended by a broad ribbon, and accompanied by the star, which may, by permission, also be adorned with precious stones. The costume for both classes, is a blue coat with red facings, and gold embroidery.

THE ORDER OF ST. JOHN OF JERUSALEM.

After the fall of Napoleon, Pope Pius VII. having restored this Order, and the deputy Grand Master having established his head-quarters at Rome in 1831, a considerable portion of its previous possessions at Parma, Lucca, Tuscany, Piedmont, and in the Lombardo-Venetian kingdom, was restored to the Order in 1839, as we have already mentioned under the head of Austria; and we will here only allude to the Bull of Pope Pius IX. of the 28th July, 1854, in which he in so far altered the statutes, by introducing a sort of noviceship in the Order for the space of ten years, during which time the candidate may alter his mind and resign the Order, which binds him to vows of chastity, poverty and obedience. The candidate makes, in the first instance, only a simple vow of poverty and obedience, but not of perpetual chastity, which is reserved for the solemn procession, after the lapse of ten years' probation.

17

18

This simple vow is as follows: "I N. N. vow to God "Almighty, to his immaculate mother, and to John the "Baptist, poverty, mercy, and obedience, towards all superiors "of the Order, in the sense as given by his Holiness "Pope Pius IX., in his Bull beginning 'Militarem Ordinem "equitum.'"

DECORATIONS OF HONOUR.

During his residence at Gaeta, Pius IX. founded two medals, one for the foreign military who had given assistance to his government, and another with the inscription 'Alla Fedeltà,' for papal subjects of all classes, as an acknowledgment of their devotion in the cause. Both are worn suspended by a ribbon of the papal colours, but no privileges are attached to them.

The following is a list of the Orders which were founded by those Popes who have sanctioned and confirmed the ancient secular Orders, as established by Christian Princes.

1. The Order of St. Peter, founded by Pope Leo X. for the victorious campaign against the Turks.

2. The Order of St. Paul, by Pope Paul III.

3. The Order of the Knights of St. George, by Pope Alexander IV.

4. The Order of the Knights of St. John of the Lateran, by Pope Pius IV. in 1560.

All these Orders, even the last, may now be considered as extinct or dormant, since no nomination has taken place in them during the present century, though some of the Knights who wore the Cross as given Tab. II. No. 10, are still alive, and the abolition has, moreover, never been publicly or officially announced.

There still exists at Rome a knighthood, the members of which generally pass by the name, 'Merciful Brethren of the Holy Ghost.' Both priests and laymen belonging to it, make vows of chastity, poverty, and obedience, and engage themselves, besides, to nurse and assist the sick, even in times of pestilence. Since the Pontificate of Innocent III., under whose reign the Knights of the Order came over to Rome from France, they have had the sole management of the hospital of Santo Spirito, at Sassia, near the Vatican.

The badge is a white Cross, embroidered upon the coat, or suspended round the neck.

PARMA (GRAND DUCHY).

ORDER OF ST. CONSTANTINE,

(ALSO CALLED, AFTER ITS FOUNDER, 'ORDER OF ST. ANGELICUS,' AND SOMETIMES 'ORDER OF ST. GEORGE.')

This Order lays claim to the earliest antiquity. Tradition asserts that it was instituted under Constantine the Great, while sober history curtails 800 years from its pretended age, and assigns its origin to the year 1190, giving, as its founder, the Eastern Emperor, Isaac Angelas Comnenas, who lent to it the name of Constantine, (the Comnenas race professed to derive their descent from him), and also that of St. George, it's Patron Saint.

The rules were formed after those of St. Basilius, and the Order rapidly acquired so many members, that it was found necessary to establish in all parts of Christendom Vicar-Generals to manage its concerns and possessions which increased from day to day, by the legacies of 100 crowns, which every Knight was bound to bequeath to it.

The members were divided into secular and spiritual, and these again into officials and dignitaries (Grand Priors, Priors, &c.) and into Knights. The candidates were originally bound to prove their noble descent through four generations; but after the repulse of the Comneni by the Turks, they began to traffic with the Order for pecuniary purposes, granting it to any one who was able to pay for it without regard to birth, rank, or station, until 1699, when the last scion of the race, who lived at Parma, and was childless, sold the dignity of Grand Master to Duke Francis I. of Parma, of the house of Farnese.

The purchased title was confirmed by Popes Innocent XV. and Clement XI., and the new Grand Master again brought the Order into respect by the scruples he observed in its distribution, as also by the large domains he conferred on it, among others, the richly endowed church of the Madonna della Steccata, at Parma.

After the extinction of the Farnese family, in 1731, the Infante Don Carlos, heir of the Duchy of Parma, declared himself Grand Master of the Constantine Order, and transferred, three years afterwards, its seat to his new residence, at Naples which he obtained by force of arms. Having taken with him the Archives, he introduced, renewed and established the Order in his new kingdom, despite the declamations of the Infante Don Philip, who had succeeded his brother upon the throne of Parma. The Order thus remained in full force until 1806, when Joseph Bonaparte abolished it, together with all the Orders of the kingdom.

The Order then followed the expelled King to Sicily, where it remained until after the Peace of Paris in 1814, when the Empress Marie Louise became heiress to the dominions of the Farnese. On the 13th February, 1816, she declared herself, solemnly and formally, its Grand Mistress, resting her claim on the circumstance, that her mother, Maria Theresa of Sicily, had descended from the Farnese family, in whose possession the Order had existed for upwards of one hundred years.

PARMA. PLATE 59.

As no compromise or negotiations had taken place on the subject, both sovereigns, the Bourbon King of Naples, and the Archduchess of Parma, considered themselves its legitimate heads. In the article 'Sicily,' the reader will find the regulations now existing at Naples with regard to it. As for Parma, the Order has been divided into: Senators of the Grand Cross, Commanders, Knights, Serving Brothers, and Squires or Shield-bearers.

The Costume of the first three classes consists: of a sky blue coat after the French fashion, with white collar, and gold embroidery upon the breast and the edges, which have the double width in that of the first class. The members of the latter class wear, besides, gold epaulettes with large tassels, the Commanders, the same with smaller tassels, and the Knights with pearls. The hat is worn after the French fashion, cocked, and with golden cords: it is, moreover, adorned with white feathers for the first class, and with black feathers for the second and third classes. The boots, gold spurs, and weapons are the same for the three classes. The Serving Brothers wear the sky blue uniform without epaulettes, and with simple embroidery on the collar, and the hat adorned with black feathers.

The insignia consist of a cross (No. 4), beneath which is appended, for the Grand Master and the first class, the figure of St. George (No. 3). In this form the Grand Master wears it on a collar (necklace) of fifteen links (No. 5), and the Grand Cross Senators, across the right shoulder towards the left hip, suspended by a ribbon. Both are accompanied by a star (No. 1) upon the left side of the coat, where also the Commanders wear the crosses (Nos. 2 and 4) suspended by a sky blue ribbon. The Knights wear the cross (No. 4) in a diminished form at the button-hole, and that (No. 2), also in a smaller size on the left side of the coat.

The Serving Brothers wear the badge in the same manner

as do the Knights, except that the cross, which is worn by them as a star, has no upper point, nor does it contain, as in that of the other classes, the initials : 'I. H. S. V.' These letters signify : 'In hoc signo vinces' (In this sign thou shalt conquer), while two Greek letters A (Alpha, the first), and Ω (Omega, the last of the Greek alphabet) in the centre, together with a cross, resting upon the letter 'P.' are to represent: 'God and Jesus Christ' (Father and son), the beginning and end of all things.

The Grand Prior, chief of the spiritual part of the Order, wears the costume of a bishop : a long blue mantle with red lining, and a blue and red coat. He officiates in the church of the Order, Santa Maria della Steccata, and possesses numerous privileges granted to him by the Popes, among others the right to issue dimissory letters to fourteen persons.

The Chapter is usually held on the 11th December.

THE ORDER OF ST. LOUIS

Was revised on the 11th August, 1849, by Duke Charles III., as an Order of Merit, both civil and military. It had been founded by his father, Duke Charles II., in the year when he abdicated the throne.

The Dukes of Parma are always Grand Masters.

The Order is divided into Grand Cross Knights, Commanders, Knights, first and second classes, and Members decorated with the fifth class cross.

The number of the Knights Grand Cross is fixed at twenty, of the Commanders at thirty, of the first class Knights at sixty, of the second class Knights at eighty, and of the fifth class members at one hundred; exclusive of reigning princes, and distinguished foreigners.

The Order is limited to Roman Catholics, though exceptions may be made in favour of Protestants if they possess the other qualifications which entitle them to the honour.

When the Grand or Commander Cross is conferred on a citizen or civilian, he receives with it a free patent of hereditary nobility of the State. The degree of first and second class Knights confers *personal* nobility, or nobility only for life.

The claim to the Order is *Merit* generally, whether in civil or military spheres of life.

The badge consists of a Greek cross, composed of four lilies, joined together by their leaves, the middle of the obverse containing upon a sky blue ground, three golden lilies, and the reverse, the motto as legend, 'Deus et Dies.' The figure of St. Louis of the Grand Cross, Commanders, and first class Knights, is of gold and enamel, surmounted by a golden crown; of the second class Knights, of enamelled silver and with a silver crown; and of the fifth class members, of enamelled silver without a crown. The first two classes wear besides a gold enamelled star. The ribbon is blue and yellow. The *secular* Knights of the Grand Cross wear the cross across the right shoulder, and the star on the left breast, while the Spiritual wear it round the neck, and the star on the left side of the mantle. The Commanders wear the cross round the neck, and the star on the left side, while all the other classes wear the decoration on the left breast. The Grand Master, alone, has the right to adorn his Order, without special permission, with precious stones.

PERSIA.

THE ORDER OF THE LION AND THE SUN. (Plate 60.)

But little or nothing is known of this Order, and we must, therefore, content ourselves with an extract from F. von Hammer's work: 'Fundgruben des Orientes' (Mines of the East). He says:

"The Sultan Selim III., among other innovations, created "towards, the end of the past century, the 'Order of the "Crescent,' which he divided into two classes. The great "one, which is worn as a star, represents the Crescent and "the Tuyra (Initials) of the Sultan in brilliants; the smaller "one is a mere medal with the above sketches, and is worn "suspended by a fire-coloured ribbon. An imitation of that Order "—the Turkish Order of the Crescent, presented exclusively to "Europeans—was that of the Order of the Sun, founded by Feth "Ali Shah, (in 1808), and which was equally divided into two "classes; a star and a medal, which Gardane, and other members "of the French Legation, received in Persia, and which was sub-"sequently transformed into 'The Order of the Lion and the Sun.' "The badge represents the Sun rising upon the back of the Lion, "or the Sun in Leo, i. e., the Sun in its fullest power in the zodiac."

The form of the curious Eastern diploma is as follows:

"The Emperor by the spirit of enterprise and high merciful "look, which always sees the truth by the solar life of his mind,

PERSIA. PLATE 60.

1

2

"has resolved to distinguish the servants of his ever-happy
"empire, and the *confidants* of his eternal excellence, with the
"head ornament of glory, and the girdle of service, as also to
"raise, and specially to favour with a gracious look, those
"among their equals, who walk the straight path of the senti-
"ments *without a head of their own.* In conformity with
"these principles, the highly esteemed and loyal N. N., who
"bears as an amulet upon the neck of the soul and spirit, the
"cross of true sentiments, and good-will of the eternal court,
"and has shewn himself by long honesty, worthy of the mild
"sunny look of imperial favour, has been covered with the impe-
"rial decoration of honour of the Sun and Lion, and distin-
"guished and glorified amongst his equals, by the super-
"abundant grace of the Emperor.

"We therefore command, that the same should in perfect
"good hope, give every day additional proofs of his good
"sentiments, and will in the service of our glorious court, and
"thus show himself worthy of the imperial favour and grace,
"which may be showered upon him. We have resolved,
"that the inhabitants of the empire, and of our imperial well-
"preserved dominions, the inhabitants of the Islam town,
"Teheran, and other towns of the empire, shall acknowledge the
"above-named N. N., as possessor of the decoration of the
"Sun and Lion, and make it their duty, continually to honour
"and respect him. The high functionaries and dignitaries of the
"Court, the experienced counsellors and *confidants* of the
"*Chakeva*; the chamber Presidents of the Sublime Divan, the
"well-meaning Secretaries of the Exchequer, should register this
"diploma in their books and act accordingly.

"Given in the year 1823 (1811)."

PORTUGAL.

The three first orders of Portugal, those of Christ, St. James, and of Aviz, were originally spiritual Orders, but were secularized in 1789. Though the Kings of Portugal were Grand Masters of all the three, they used, nevertheless, to wear only the insignia of the Order of Christ. At present the usage is different, and that there may be no show of preference, the three decorations are now united into one medal, and divided into three equal spaces (Plate 61, Tab. I. No. 1). The medal is worn suspended by a three coloured ribbon, green, red and violet.

On solemn occasions, the Knights of all the three Orders wear a white mantle, kept together at the breast by a long cord in the form of a rosette. On the left side of the mantle is embroidered the star. (Tab. I. No. 2). A red cap, sword, morocco boots, and golden spurs, complete the costume; and in this costume the Knights are also buried.

The red enamelled heart which is appended above the decorations of the two first classes, was instituted by Queen Maria in token of reverence of the Holy Heart of Christ under whose protection she placed the Orders of the kingdom.

The management and superintendence of the Orders are entrusted to the care of a particular court, called the 'Tribunal of Conscience and Orders.'

PORTUGAL. *Table I.* PLATE 61.

Hurst and Blackett, London. 1858.

THE MILITARY ORDER OF ST. BENEDICT OF AVIZ.

(FORMERLY CALLED 'ORDER OF EVORA.')

In the reign of the first King of Portugal, Alphonso I. in the year 1143 or 1147, several noble Portuguese formed themselves into a military fraternity, which they named the 'New Knighthood,' having for its object the subjection of the Moors. Sanctioned by the King, and presented with the Castle Mafra, which they had conquered, the knighthood existed for a long time without solemn vows, and almost without any statutes, until 1162, when it was converted into a spiritual Order, and received from John of Cirita, the Papal Legate, a series of statutes, which bound the Knights to solemn vows of chastity and mercy, to the defence of the Catholic religion, to the observance of the rules of the Benedictine and Cistercian monks, and to the wearing of a costume consisting of a white military coat, with a black hood above it, to which was fastened a narrow black scapulary reaching below the sword belt, but without mountings of precious stones or gold on either weapon, spurs or apparel.

In 1188, when Sancho I., son of Alphonso I., had availed himself of the presence of James of Avesnes, who, with an army of Crusaders, had been thrown by a gale upon the Portuguese coast, to reconquer a few provinces of his kingdom, he transferred to the new order of knighthood the reconquered town of Evora, and, by the name of Knights of Evora, they were subsequently known, until the reign of Alphonso II., the successor of Sancho I., (1211—1223), who put them into possession of the frontier fortress, Aviz, in Alemtejo, a designation they thenceforth adopted.

In 1213, Rodrigo Garcia de Aça, seventh Grand Master of the Order of Calatrava, ceded several important places and domains which his Order possessed in Portugal to the Knights of Aviz, who, in return, adopted the rules, statutes, and authority of Calatrava; the union was, however, broken off in 1385, and as neither the efforts of the Kings, nor even the decision of the Council of Basle were able to prevent the complete solution of the union, the Order stood, since 1550, with a few interruptions during the reign of Philip II., under an Administrator, and the independent authority of the Kings of Portugal, who are Grand Masters of the same.

In 1789, Queen Mary converted it into an Order of Merit, and divided it into three classes: six Knights of the Grand Cross, (who wear the decoration (Tab. I. No. 4) across the right shoulder towards the left hip by a broad green ribbon); forty-nine Commanders (who wear the same decoration round the neck) and an unfixed number of Knights (who wear the decoration (No. 5) fastened at the button-hole.) The first two classes wear, besides, on the left side of the breast the star (No. 3).

At that period, the Order was in possession of eighteen villages, and forty-nine prebends, or benefices, while its annual revenue exceeded 80,000 ducats.

THE MILITARY ORDER OF ST. JAMES OF COMPOSTELLA, OR THE SWORD.

This Order originated in Spain. After Henry of Burgundy had captured the province of Portugal from the infidels, and made it an independent state, his son, Alphonso Henriquez, who completed the conquests of his father, thought it advisable to withdraw the Portuguese Knights of the Order from the authority of the Spanish Grand Masters. The separation from Spain was confirmed by Popes Nicolaus VI. and John XXII.

PORTUGAL. Table II.   PLATE 62.

under the reign of King Dionysius, but the statutes remained the same in both countries. Afterwards, the Order shared the fate of those of Christ and Aviz, it came under the administration of James II., and finally under the perpetual Grand Mastership of the Crown. In 1789, it was secularized by Queen Mary, who divided it into three classes: six Knights Grand Cross, one hundred and fifty Commanders, and an unlimited number of Knights.

The Order had its head-quarters at Palmella, and possessed forty-seven villages and boroughs, one hundred and fifty prebends, and four cloisters and convents in Santos, which enjoyed the same rights as did the cloister of Barcelona.

The decoration (Plate 62, Tab. II. No. 7) is worn by the Knights Grand Cross across the right shoulder towards the left hip, by the Commanders round the neck, and by the Knights at the button-hole.

The first two classes wear, besides, the star (No. 6) on the left breast.

THE ORDER OF CHRIST.

The Order of the Templars having been abolished in France by Philip le Bel, its property confiscated, and the members persecuted and expelled with the sanction and authority of Pope Clemens V; it was revived in Portugal, where it flourished under the name of the 'Knighthood of Our Lord Jesus Christ.' The extreme persecutions which the Templars were subjected to in France, apparently for the mere sake of seizing hold of their property, under the pretext of their conspiring against the state, roused universal sympathy with the sufferers, while the Portuguese government needing, in addition, their support and valour, as a bulwark against the Spanish Moors at Algravia, King

Dionysius devised a means of giving an asylum to the Knights and their Order in Portugal, without openly violating the decision of the Pope. He transferred (1317), the castles and vassals, as also the statutes of the Order of the Templars, to a new Order which he founded under a different name, and for which he received, after two years' negotiations, the sanction of Pope John XXII.

Nor was Dionysius deceived in his expectations. With grateful feelings, the Knights of the Order of Christ joined the Portuguese Kings in their crusades against the infidels, and accompanied them in their adventurous campaigns to Africa and India, while the Kings, on their part, acknowledged the important services of the Knights, by increasing their possessions with the increase of their own conquests, and procured for the Grand Prior of the Order, from Pope Calextus III., an investment of power, equal to that of a Bishop. As an encouragement to further conquests and discoveries, they were finally promised, also, the independent possession (under, however, Portuguese protection), of all the countries which they might happen to discover.

Under such favourable circumstances, the new Order grew in power and wealth to such an extent, as to raise the fears of the subsequent Kings of Portugal, who began to endeavour to limit and curtail the concessions made by their predecessor, especially as regarded the *eventual* discoveries made by the Order, which instead of, as originally stipulated, being its own independent property, were now to be marked Crown domains; leaving to the Knights only, the civil jurisdiction, and a certain military preponderance in them. Nor was the limitation confined to the future conquests of the Order alone; even the territories which were already in their possession, the Pope thought fit to include in the new contract, when laid before him for sanction. Subsequently, King John III. even procured from Pope Adrian VI. (1522), an edict by which the functions of Administrator and Grand-Master of the Order were exclusively transferred to the Portuguese Crown.

The principal seat of the Order was originally Castro-Marino, in the Diocese of Faro, but in 1366, it was transferred to Tomer (seven leagues from Santarem), where a fine cloister is still to be seen.

No one could present himself as candidate who was not able to prove his noble descent, and a three years' military noviceship in the wars against the infidels. The members were originally bound to make the three vows of chastity, poverty, and obedience; but Pope Alexander VI. released them from the two first, on condition that they should apply the third part of their revenues to the building and support of the Tomar Cloister, the priests of which he bound to the whole of the three vows. It serves now, together with the Seminary at Coimbra, as a theological institution for the priests of the Order, as an immediate fief of the Crown.

The Order possesses twenty-six villages and farms, and four hundred and thirty-four prebends.

Since 1789, the members consist (besides the Grand Master and Great Commander) of six Knights of the Grand Cross, four hundred and fifty Commanders, and an unlimited number of Knights.

Foreigners are exempt from the rules, but, at the same time, are excluded from the participation in the revenues of the Order.

Catholics, only, of noble descent can be admitted to the Order.

The Knights Grand Cross wear the decoration (Tab. II. No. 9) across the right shoulder towards the left side, by a broad red ribbon, while the left side of the breast is adorned with the star (No. 8).

The Commanders wear the same cross and star round the

neck, and the Knights have the cross (Tab. III. No. 12) suspended at the button-hole, though when in uniform they wear it now also round the neck.

Members are allowed to adorn the badge with precious stones.

THE ANCIENT AND MOST NOBLE ORDER OF THE TOWER AND SWORD.

To solemnize his arrival at Brazil, the Prince Regent renewed, on the 3rd May, 1808, the Order of the Sword, which had been founded in 1459, by Alphonso V.

The same Order was thoroughly renovated and reformed on the 28th July, 1832, by the Duke of Braganza, who gave it the name of 'the Tower and Sword,' and thus classified it: the Grand Master into Grand Officers, Knights Grand Cross, Commanders, Officers and Knights. The number of the last four classes is unlimited.

The Sovereign or Regent is always Grand Master of the Order. The Grand Officers consist of the Great Commanders, Claveyro (treasurer), Great Ensign, and Great Chancellor.

There are, besides, seven other Officers, viz., a King of Arms, (called Tower and Sword) who is always to be a Knight of the Order, two Heralds and four Pursuivants.

The claim to the Order is Merit in the most extended sense of the term, distinction in military career, in civil life, or in literature of any description, without regard to birth, religion or country.

The badge of the Order is a Medal (Tab. III. No. 11) containing in the blue middle of the obverse, a sword resting upon an oak wreath, with the legend: 'Valor, Lealdade e Merito' (Valour, Devotion and Merit). The reverse shows an open book, on one page of which are the Portuguese

PORTUGAL. Table III. PLATE 65.

10

13

11

12

Arms, and on the other the words 'Carta Constitutional da Monarquia' (Constitutional Charter of the Monarchy), and the legend, 'Pelo rei e pela lei' (for the King and the Law). The other part of the medal consists of a pentagonal white enamelled cross, resting upon an oaken wreath, and of a Tower to which the ring of the badge is fastened. For the Knights, the decoration is of silver; and for the other classes, of gold. The Knights of the Grand Cross, and the Commanders wear, besides, a star (Tab. III. No. 10) embroidered on the left side of the coat.

Usually the decoration is worn suspended by a dark blue ribbon; but at Court and on gala days, the Knights append it to a silver, and the officers to a golden chain, in the form of a collar, while the other classes append it to a collar composed of swords and towers.

The Knights enjoy the rank of Captain, the Officers that of Lieutenant-Colonel, the Commanders that of Colonel, the Knights Grand Cross that of Major General, and the Grand Officers that of Field Marshal.

In the States'-budget, a sum of money is annually demanded for the support of the orphans and children of needy members of the Order, for the pensions of such members, and for the maintenance of an asylum for the poor invalids of the Order; as also for the rent of a building where the archives are kept, the Chapter meets, and the festivals are celebrated. The festival day is the 29th April.

THE ORDER OF OUR LADY OF THE CONCEPTION, OF VILLA VICOSA.

This Order was founded on the 6th Feburary, 1818, by King John VI. and received its statutes on the 10th September, 1819.

It consists of the King as Grand Master, the Princes and Princesses of the royal house as Knights of the Grand Cross, twelve Honorary Grand Cross Knights, forty Commanders, one hundred Knights, and sixty Servant-Brothers, besides the Dean of the Royal Chapel at Villa Viçosa, (who ranks among the Commanders), and the Canons, Priors, and Prebendaries of that Church who belong to the class of Knights.

Only noblemen of high title are admitted to the Order. Its principal seats are the Chapel of the Madonna of Conception, at Villa Viçosa in Alemejo, and the Chapel of the royal residence, where festivals are celebrated every year in honour of the Patroness of the Order; in the first, on Conception day; and in the other, on the succeeding day. The badge (Tab. IV. No. 15) consists of a nine-pointed white enamelled star surrounded by golden rays, upon which are placed nine little stars of white enamel. Above the star is a gold crown, while the middle contains, on a dull ground of gold, the letters in monogram 'M. A.' of polished gold, surrounded by a bright blue enamelled ring, with the legend: 'Padroeira do Reino,' (Patroness of the realm).

This star is worn in different sizes by the various classes, suspended by a bright blue ribbon with two white stripes; by the Knights of the Grand Cross, across the right shoulder towards the left hip; by the Commanders round the neck, and by the Knights and Servant-Brothers at the button-hole. The first two classes wear, besides, the star (No. 14) embroidered on the left side of the coat.

THE ORDER OF ST. ISABELLA.

This Order, designed for ladies only, was founded on the 4th November, 1801, by the Prince Regent, who authorized, on

PORTUGAL. *Table* IV   PLATE 64.

Hurst and Blackett, London, 1858.

the 17th December following, his Consort to frame the statutes, which were promulgated on the 25th April, 1804.

The badge is a Gold Medal, (Tab. IV. No. 16) of which the obverse contains the figure of St. Isabella of Portugal with the subscription, 'Pauperum solatio.' (Comforter of the poor), and the reverse 'Real Orden do Santa Isabel.' (Royal Order of St. Isabella). On gala and festival days, the decoration is worn suspended by a broad rose coloured ribbon with white stripes in the form of a scarf; but on ordinary occasions, it is fastened at the left side by a bow of a similar but narrower ribbon. The Order is limited to twenty six ladies (besides the Princesses of the royal family, and of foreign reigning houses), married, or not younger than twenty-six years.

On St. Isabella's day, the Grand Mistress, accompanied by the members, visit, after Divine Service, the Foundling Hospital, while the Orphan Asylum is inspected by them once every week.

The insignia must be returned by the heirs after the decease of a member.

MEDALS AND DECORATIONS OF HONOUR.

1. *Cross for the Peninsular War*, was instituted by King John VI. on the 26th July, 1816. The war in the Peninsula having consisted of six campaigns, the officers who were present at all of them, wear on the left side of the breast a Roman cross of gold with six laurel branches, and the number six in the middle, suspended by a blue and red ribbon. Those who were present at only some of them, have the same cross of silver. The reverse contains the inscription, 'War of the Peninsula.' On the same day was also instituted the

2. *Commander's Cross.*—It consists of as many stars as the

number of battles participated in by the commander of a regiment or battalion. The edge contains the name of the owner. It is worn in the same manner and by the same ribbon as the previous cross.

3. *Cross of Loyalty*, was instituted after the Revolution of 1823, on the 24th July.

a. For all the officers under Count Amarant, (afterwards Marquis of Chaves), who first declared himself by force of arms against the Constitution of 1822, and in favour of Absolutism. The obverse contains the effigy of the King, and the reverse the inscription, 'Heroïca fidelidade trans-montana.' It is worn suspended by a green and white ribbon.

b. For all who accompanied the King from the 30th May to the 5th June, 1823, to Villa Franca, as also for the military who had followed Don Miguel to Santarem. The obverse shows the effigy of the King, and the reverse the inscription 'Heroïca fidelidade ao rey e patria,' and is worn suspended by a tri-coloured ribbon, red green and white.

4. *Cross of Emigration* of 1826-1828, was instituted in September, 1828, by the Infante Don Miguel, whose effigy it bears on the obverse. The reverse shows the year of Emigration, and the number of battles participated in by the wearer, from the promulgation of Don Pedro's Constitution until the 7th March, 1827. It is worn by a ribbon, partly red and partly white.

5. *Medal of the Belgian Sharp-shooters*, was instituted on the 24th December, 1835, by Queen Maria, for the sub-officers and soldiers who had greatly contributed to the Restoration of her throne. The obverse shows the effigy of the Queen with the legend, 'Amor et Obedientia Spes publica,' and the reverse, the Portuguese Arms, and the words on the edge, 'Rainha, Patria, Liberdade.' It is worn suspended by a ribbon of the national colours, bright blue, and white.

PRUSSIA.

In 1810, a new system was introduced in Prussia, with regard to Orders and Decorations.

They are now divided into two heads: civil and military. To the first belong: the Orders of the Black and Red Eagles, first, second, and third classes; as also the gold and silver Medals of Merit, worn suspended by the ribbon of the Red Eagle decoration.

The Cross of the first class of the Red Eagle is now in so far altered, that it has neither points nor gold mountings. It is white enamelled, and bears, in the round middle of the obverse, the Red Eagle, and of the reverse the initials: 'F. W.'

The second class, which has been introduced since 1810, has the same cross but a little smaller, and is, moreover, worn round the neck by a narrow ribbon of the same colour as that of the first class.

The new third class suspends the same cross at the button-hole, but neither of the new classes are accompanied by a star on the breast.

The general Medal of Merit, both the gold and silver, is worn at the button-hole suspended by the same ribbon as the former, which is white watered with an orange stripe at each border.

Each of the medals forms an exclusive category in itself, so that the gold naturally excludes, and renders superfluous the silver. To the second division belong, the old Order 'Pour le Mérite,' and the gold and silver Medals which are worn suspended by a black ribbon with a white stripe near each border.

The Order 'Pour le Mérite' as also the medals, are now strictly military decorations for merit in battle.

THE ORDER OF THE BLACK EAGLE.

The close of the seventeenth century was distinguished by an advance in the several ranks of the reigning houses in Europe. Brunswick was elevated to an Electorate, a Prince of Orange mounted the throne of England, the Elector of Saxony assumed the title of King of Poland, and the Elector of Brandenburg, that of King of Prussia, under the name of Frederick I. This last named monarch founded, on the day of his coronation, (17th January, 1791), the Order of the Black Eagle, the insignia of which are sketched (Plate 65, Tab. I. Nos. 1 to 3.)

The number of the Knights, exclusive of the Princes of the royal family, is limited by the statutes to thirty, who must, at their nomination, have reached the age of, at least, thirty years.

The candidates have to prove their noble descent through four generations by both parents.

The Chapter is held twice a year, on the 18th January, and the 12th July.

The insignia consist of an octagonal cross, blue enamelled, with the initials in monogram: 'F. R.' (Fredericus Rex), in the middle of the obverse, and a Black Eagle, with expanded wings, between each of the arms of the cross. The cross is

PRUSSIA. *Table 1.*   PLATE 65.

worn across the left shoulder towards the right hip, by a broad ribbon of orange colour, accompanied by an embroidered silver star, fastened at the left side of the breast. The centre of the star represents a black flying eagle, holding in one claw a laurel wreath, and in the other, a thunderbolt, with the legend: 'Suum Cuique' (To every one his due).

Every new member has to pay a nomination fee, fifty ducats, for the support of the Orphan Asylum at Königsberg, while he receives, gratis, the costume and insignia of the Order. The costume consists of an undergarment of blue velvet, and over it a velvet mantle of flesh colour, lined with sky-blue watered silk; the mantle has a train, long in that of the Crown Prince, but short in that of the other Knights, and is fastened in the front by long cords with tassels at the ends. Above is fastened round the shoulders a large chain or collar, which is composed alternately of the initials of the founder, and the Eagle with the thunderbolt in his claws, while to the front link of the same, is appended the real blue cross of the Order. On the left side of the mantle is fastened the silver embroidered star, and the whole costume is completed by a black velvet hat with a white plume.

No member, with the exception of foreign princes, and the Knights of St. John, is allowed to wear any other Order at the side of the Black Eagle; nor is he allowed to travel from home a distance of more than twenty German miles (about one hundred English), without due notice to the King.

The seal of the Order bears on the obverse, the royal arms, surrounded by the chain of the Order, and on the reverse, the motto: 'Suum Cuique,' and the legend: 'Magnum Sigillum Nobillissimi Ordinis Aquillæ Borussicæ.'

Time and circumstances have wrought various alterations in the statutes. The number of the members is no longer limited, nor is the costume any more in use, except at a funeral of one of the royal family, when the chain is allowed to be exhibited.

The Knights of the Black Eagle are, at the same time, also, Knights of the Red Eagle, first class, the badge of which they wear round the neck, suspended by a narrow ribbon.

THE ORDER OF THE RED EAGLE.

In 1705, George William, the hereditary Prince of Anspach and Baireuth, founded the 'Ordre de la Sincerité:' consisting of a gold cross set in diamonds, with wide edges. The middle contained the initials, 'C. E.' (afterwards 'G. W.') with a palm branch beneath a prince's coronet, while in the four corners of the cross were seen golden rays, richly mounted with diamonds. The Chapel of the Order was always to belong to the Evangelical Church of the original Augsburg Confession.

This Order was re-organized on the 13th July, 1734, by the Margrave, George Frederick Charles, under the name, 'The Brandenburg Red Eagle.' The number of the members was limited to thirty, who could show their noble descent through eight generations, by both parents, while the nomination fee was fixed at twenty ducats. In 1759, the same Margrave added to the Order a first class of the Grand Cross. In 1777, the number of the members was increased to fifty, and the nomination fee to 500 fl., Rhenish, while the candidates were, previous to their nomination, to bear the title of 'Excellency.'

In 1791, Frederick William II. raised the Red Eagle to be the second in point of rank of the Orders of his house, and he changed the decoration into a golden white enamelled Maltese Cross, surmounted by a royal crown, with the Brandenburg Eagle in the corners, and the letters, 'F. W. R.' in the middle. It was worn across the left shoulder towards the left hip, by a white ribbon with two orange-coloured stripes.

The embroidered silver star (Tab. I., No. 4), which still exists, contains in the centre, the Brandenburg Eagle, with the Hohenzollern Arms on its breast, a green garland in its claws, and the legend: 'Sincere et Constanter' (Sincerely and with Constancy).

All the Knights of the Black Eagle were received into this Order, the badge of which they wear round the neck; and to limit the number still more, it was latterly decreed that only those who are already decorated with the Red Eagle, can be received into the Black Eagle. The entrance fees were fixed at thirty Frederics d'or.

The Order, as we mentioned in the Introduction, was re-organized in 1810, in the form as given (Tab. I., No. 6) while two more classes were added to it.

The first class, it was enacted, was to continue to wear the badge across the left shoulder by a white ribbon with orange-coloured stripes.

The Knights of the second class, who had advanced from the third, were to append to the ring on which the cross hangs, three golden oak leaves (Tab I., No. 8), while those of the first class, who had advanced from the two previous classes, were to have, also, this additional decoration appended to the upper part of the star (Tab. I. No. 4).

In 1830, the second class was subdivided into two. The first division were allowed to wear at the side of the Order also a square star (Tab. I. No. 5) representing the cross of the Order with the middle of the star of the first class. The two divisions now pass by the name, second class with the star, and second class without it.

By the same decree of 1830 (18th January), the insignia of the first class, Decoration of Merit, were made to be those of the first class of the Red Eagle, consisting of a silver cross with an eagle in relief, and worn at the button-hole suspended by the ribbon of the third class.

An ordinance of the 22nd January, 1832, provides that the Knights raised from the fourth to the third class, shall have attached to the ring, a rosette or a bow (No. 7), instead of an oaken leaf, as is the case for the first and second classes; the same decree also provides that no one is admissible to the latter classes with the oaken leaf, without being already in possession of the bow or rosette.

THE ORDER OF MERIT.

(Tab. III. No. 13).

Prince Charles Emil founded, in 1665, an 'Order de la Générosité,' conferring the Grand Mastership on his brother, the Elector Frederick III. The Order came, however, officially into force only in 1685. The decoration consisted of an octagonal cross enamelled sky blue, with small golden balls on the points, and with the golden letter F within the upper wing, surmounted by an Electorate hat, but this Frederick I. afterwards converted into a crown, while in the three other wings was distributed the word 'Générosité.' The corners of the cross were filled out by gold eagles with expanded wings; the reverse was simply blue, and the ribbon on which the cross was suspended, was black and watered.

On his accession, in 1740, Frederick II. converted the Order into that of 'Pour le Mérite,' leaving the decoration, however, entirely unaltered, and allowing the possessors of the old cross to wear it for life. The Order consisted of only one class, both civil and military, until 1810, when it was reduced to one strictly military. It is now worn round

PRUSSIA. Table II. PLATE 66.

Hurst and Blackett, London. 1858.

PRUSSIA. *Table III.* PLATE 67.

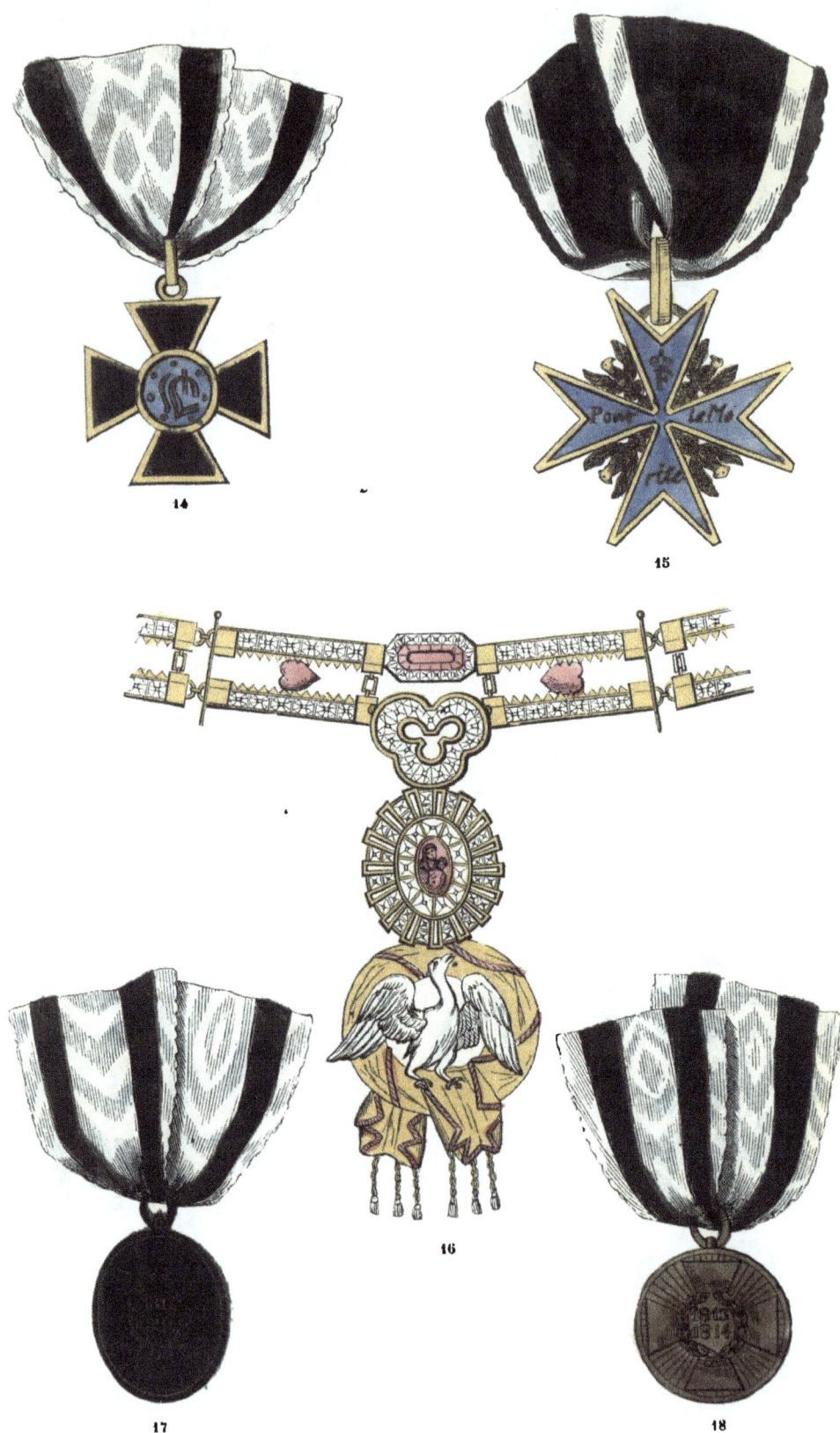

the neck, suspended by a black watered ribbon with a narrow silver stripe near the borders.

In 1813, an ornament for special and distinguished merit was added to the decorations, in the form of three golden oak leaves.

In 1819, the Order counted two thousand four hundred and sixty members.

By decree of the 31st May, 1840, the Order of Merit was again extended to civil merit, viz. to the arts and sciences, for which, however, a new class was created. The number of that new class was limited to thirty members of German extraction. The decoration remained unaltered, with the exception of the form of the middle (Tab. II. No. 9), which contains in its round golden centre, the Prussian eagle, and in the ring round it two reversed 'F. II.' four times repeated. The motto of the Order in golden letters is seen in the blue enamelled circle which encompasses the whole, and connects the crown with the initials. It is worn as usual round the neck, by the same ribbon as the above for the military. Distinguished foreigners may become honorary members of the Order.

The days fixed for nomination are the accession to the throne, or the birthday of the reigning monarch, or the anniversary of the death of Frederick II.

The following members of European celebrity, were nominated at the first foundation of the new cross:

1. Germans.

a. Literary and scientific men: W. Bessel, F. Bopp, L. von Buch, F. Diffenbach, F. Enke, F. Gauss, J. Grimm, A. von Humboldt, F. Jacobi, Prince Clemens Metternich Winneburg, E. Mitscherlich, J. Müller, C. Ritter, F. Rückert, C. von Savigny, J. von Schelling, W. von Schlegel, L. Schönlein, L. Tieck.

b. Artists: P. von Cornelius, F. Lessing. F. Mendelsohn

Bartholdy, J. Meyerbeer, C. Rauch, G. Schadow, J. Schnorr, von Carolsfeld, M. Schwanthaler.

2. Foreigners.

a. Literary and Scientific men: Arago, Avellino, Berzelius, Count Borghese, R. Brown, Châteaubriand, Faraday, Count Fossombroni, Gay-Lussac, J. Herschel, W. von Jukoffsky, Kopitar, B. v. Krusenstern, Letronne, Melloni, T. Moore, Oerstedt.

b. Artists: Daguerre, Fontaine, Ingres, F. Liszt, Rossini, Thorwaldsen, Toschi, Horace Vernet.

THE ORDER OF THE IRON CROSS,

Was instituted on the 10th March, 1813, by Frederick William III. for peculiar military or civil distinction in the war then being carried on. The possessors of the decorations are, with the exception of the Knights of the Grand Cross, divided into two classes, though the cross is of the same form and character in both, being composed of cast iron with silver mounting, and bearing no inscription on the reverse (Tab. II. No. 11). The upper wing of the obverse contains the initials F. W. with a crown, while the middle is adorned with three oak leaves, below which is seen the cypher '1813.' It is worn at the button-hole, suspended either by a black ribbon with white borders, when given as a reward for military distinction, or by a white ribbon with black borders when presented for civil merit in that war of liberty. The first class wear, besides, upon the left breast instead of a star, a similar cross (Tab. II. No. 10). The decoration of the Grand Cross is double the size of the former, and is worn round the neck by a black ribbon with white borders.

The Grand Cross was presented exclusively for the gaining of a decisive battle, the conquest of an important position or place, or the brave defence of a fortress.

By a royal order of the 5th May, 1813, the names of the heroes who had fallen in the war, and were consequently deprived of the reward of the cross, were to be inscribed on tables adorned with the decoration, and hung up for public show and honour in the chapel or church of the regiment to which they belonged.

By a decree of the 3rd August, 1841, a pension for life was granted to a portion of the surviving owners of the Iron Cross, with the black ribbon, namely :

Of the first class, to twelve seniors of the rank of officers, and to a similar number of the seniors of the rank of sergeants, and under, 150 thalers each (£22 10s.); of the second class, to thirty-six seniors of the rank of officers, and to a similar number of the rank of sergeants and under, 50 thalers each (£7 10s.).

THE ORDER OF ST. JOHN.

The general outlines of the history of that Order, and the sketches of its insignia are given under AUSTRIA, and we may add here its history and position as regards Germany in particular.

The Grand Prior of Germany, availing himself of a schism in the Order, in 1319, asserted the independence of his sixty-seven Commanderies, and declared himself their independent Prince. His successors were, in 1546, nominated German Princes of the Empire, with seat and vote in the Council of the Diet, and made sovereigns of their Principality, Heitersheim, with the towns, Ginglingen, Bremgarten, Griesheim and Schlart, under the immediate protection of

Austria. For the losses they had subsequently sustained on the left bank of the Rhine, they were amply compensated at the Diet of 1803. But the peace of Pressburg deprived them of all their possessions in favour of the German Princes, by which the Grand Priorate of the Order ceased to exist in Germany, and it was Austria alone that suffered its existence in Bohemia, with a few Commanderies in Austria, Moravia and Silesia.

The Grand Bailiwick or Commandry of Brandenburg had already, in 1319, separated from the Order, and elected a Grand Master of its own, but submitted, in 1382, to the principle of having the election of Grand Master each time sanctioned and confirmed by the Grand Prior of Germany. In this state it remained until the Reformation : that great movement joined by the greatest portion of the Knights of St. John, while the Elector of Brandenburg declared himself as the "Summus Patronus et Protector Ordinis." The Knights, however, though they had, in the peace of Westphalia, effected their release from the Order of Malta, by a ransom of 2,500 gold florins, did not entirely separate from that fraternity, but re-united themselves, on the contrary, under their Bailiff, Prince Ferdinand, brother of Frederick II., once more with Malta, and even paid, of their own good-will, the responsions to the Order, without being prevented from the act by Frederick who had himself proposed, in 1775, a plan for an union with the Order of Malta, provided the latter would accept the principle of tolerance then adopted by all the German Knights, and content itself with the general form of an oath which bound the Knights to union and mutual defence. His plan was, however, rejected.

The chief place of the Commander of Brandenburg was Sonnenburg. The Commander having sworn allegiance to the Elector (afterwards King), enjoyed the rank of first Prelate of the State, with a revenue of 40,000 thalers. The Knights were to be both Germans and Protestants, and count eight noble ancestors of both parents.

On the 30th October, 1810, a royal edict abolished the Commandry of Brandenburg, and incorporated all the estates of the Order with the crown dominions. By way of compensation, Frederick William III. founded, on the 23rd May, 1812, a new Order of St. John, having, in common with its powerful predecessor, only the name and a part of the insignia. This new Order now bears the name of

THE ROYAL PRUSSIAN ORDER OF ST. JOHN.

The King is Sovereign Protector, and sole dispenser of the Order.

Prince Ferdinand was appointed by the King, first Grand Master, and after him, Prince Henry (brother to the King).

All the Knights belonging to the old, were invested with the insignia of the new Order, though new nominations also took place.

The badge of the Order is a gold octagonal white enamelled cross, but without a crown over it. The four angles are filled with the Prussian Black Eagles, surmounted by gold crowns, and the whole is worn round the neck suspended by a black ribbon, and accompanied by a white star fastened to the left side of the coat (Tab. II. Nos. 13 and 12).

The costume of the Knights consists of a red coat with golden epaulettes, and with white collar, facings, and lining, as also of a white waistcoat and trousers. The collar and facings are trimmed with golden lace. The buttons are yellow, and have the cross of the Order stamped on them. The nomination fee was fixed at six Frederics d'or.

On the 15th October, 1852, King Frederick William IV. gave it a new constitution. The Commandry of Brandenburg was thereby re-established, without, however, restoring to it the estates of which it was deprived in 1810. The new members have now to pay an annual contribution of, at least, 12 thalers, besides the entrance fee, which is fixed at 100 thalers. The sums, thus received, are to be employed for the support of the sick, and the establishment of an hospital of the Order, at its former castle at Sonnenburg, as soon as they are sufficient to cover the required outlay.

THE ROYAL ORDER OF THE HOUSE HOHENZOLLERN.

This Order, which originally belonged to the Principalities, Hohenzollern, was incorporated with the Prussian Orders by a royal decree of the 23rd August, 1851. It is now divided into two sections: the Order of the Royal House of Prussia, and that of the princely House of Hohenzollern. The first was founded in commemoration of the origin and progress of Prussia, which now extends from the rocks of Hohenzollern to the Baltic, and across the rivers of the Northern Sea. In keeping with that political progress, is the motto of the Order: 'Vom Fels zum Meer' (From the rock to the sea). The decoration contains both the Hohenzollern Arms and the Prussian Eagle, while the chain is additionally adorned with the Burgrave Arms of Nüremberg, and the Electorate sceptre of an Archchamberlain of the German Empire. It is bestowed in the form of a cross, as a reward for military merit and devotion to Fatherland, and divided into three classes, **Grand Commanders, Commanders, and Knights.**

The same Order in the form of an Eagle, and also divided into three classes, is conferred as a reward for civil merit, for distinction in the arts and sciences, in literature and more especially in the department of education, for which latter purpose certain funds are to be handed over to the Treasury to establish schools and seminaries, and appoint teachers in every province of the kingdom.

The badge of the Order for Military distinction is a gold cross, with white and black enamel. The azure blue circle round the middle of the obverse, contains the legend: 'Vom Fels zum Meer,' the motto of the Order, while in the centre is seen the royal Eagle bearing upon its breast the arms of Hohenzollern. The azure blue circle of the reverse contains: 'Der 18 Januar, 1851,' the day of the foundation; while in the white centre are seen the royal initials. The space between the arms of the cross is filled with a golden green enamelled wreath of partly (to the right side) oaken leaves, and partly (to the left side) laurel leaves. The cross is surmounted by the royal crown.

This cross is worn by the Grand Commanders round the neck, suspended by the silver chain of the Order, adorned with the arms of Hohenzollern and Nüremberg, as also with the electorate sceptre of an Arch-Chamberlain of the Empire.

The Commanders wear the same cross round the neck by a broad white and watered ribbon, with three black stripes.

The Knights wear it by the same ribbon in a smaller form and size at the button-hole, or upon the breast.

The badge of the Order for Civil Merit consists of the Royal Eagle in gold, with black enamel, and the Hohenzollern arms upon its breast. The motto of the Order is inserted within a blue circle round the head of the eagle. The distinct marks of the three classes are the same as in the former, except that the Knights of this section have the Eagle in silver instead of gold.

An additional decoration of a medal (Plate 50, Nos. 3 and 4) was founded for the officers, sub-officers and soldiers who had taken part in the engagements of 1848 and 1849. The medal is cast of cannon metal. Its obverse shows the obverse of the Cross, and the reverse the inscription: 'Friedrich Wilhelm,' with 1848 above, and 1849 below it, in separate segments. The circle round the medal contains the legend: 'Seinen bis in den Tod getruen Kriegern,' (to his warriors, faithful unto death).

The Princes of the Royal House of Prussia, or of the Hohenzollern family have, by virtue of their birth, the right to wear the badge of the Grand Commanders' Cross. The Presidency in the Chapter is vested in the Crown, who may appoint as a deputy any of the Royal Princes.

THE ORDER OF LOUISA.

This Order was founded on the 3rd August, 1814, and is a decoration for services rendered by women in the hospitals, and otherwise to the wounded and sick military in the war of 1813 and 1814. The badge is a small gold cross with black enamel. The middle of both sides is enamelled sky blue, and contains on the obverse the letter L. with a wreath of stars round it, and on the reverse the cyphers: '1813, and 1814.' The Order is worn upon the left breast, suspended by the white ribbon of the Iron cross, and fastened by a bow (Tab. III. No. 14). It was presented equally to single or married females, Prussians by birth or naturalization The number was limited to one hundred. The chapter was composed of four ladies, the Countess Arnim, the wives of General Buguslowsky, and of Welper (merchant) and finally of the widow of the Statuary Eben, under the presidency of the Queen.

THE ORDER OF THE SWAN.

This is the oldest of all the Prussian Orders. It existed in the fifteenth century, under various names, such as: 'The Society of the Madonna of the Swan,' 'The Society for the honour of the Holy Mother of Christ,' 'Order of the Blessed Mary,' 'Order of the wearers of the chain of St. Mary,' 'Order of the Swan,' &c., and had its seat in the Saint Maria Church near Brandenburg.

This church was, most probably, built towards the year 1140 by the Vandal Prince Pribislaw, and was presented by the Prince of the House Ascania, to the Canons of the Castle of Brandenburg, in 1166. It stood in great repute for sanctity, and drew for a long time a number of pilgrims from various quarters, enriching thereby the revenue of the Canons. This source of income soon, however, ceased with the rise of a new church in the village Nykamer, which by its miraculous workings eclipsed the glory of the former, and drew the stream of pilgrims to its own walls.

To restore the ancient glory of the St. Maria Church, the Elector Frederick I. added to it, in 1435, a cloister, instituting therein a chapter consisting of a Dean, Prior and four Priests, which he richly endowed, while his successor Frederick II. founded, in continuation of his father's work, on the 29th September, 1449, a corporation, consisting (besides the Prince himself) of thirty noblemen and seven ladies, who were bound to say daily, in honour of the Blessed Virgin, seven Paternosters and Ave-Marias, or distribute in default seven pfennige daily amongst the poor. They were, however, to prepare themselves by fast and prayer for the solemn celebration of the festival of the Virgin, and pay four groschen to the Canons on every quarter day, in return for which the latter were to read mass on the same days for the departed souls of the members, whose names were read over aloud on that occasion.

The badge which the members were bound to wear daily by fine of eight pfennige for the poor, consisted of a neck chain of thirteen links, joined together by rings, and each of which represented (a martyr-instrument), two saws and a red heart between them, the figure of the Blessed Virgin, with the infant Jesus in the moon, surrounded by rays in oval form appended to that chain, and of a swan with expanded wings placed in a towel tied in the form of a bow, the two ends of which were adorned with small golden chains and fastened under the figure of the Virgin.

The statutes explain the symbolic insignia as follows: the chain with the bleeding heart between, signifies contrition, true repentance, confession, penance, and chastisement. The towel is the symbol of unspotted purity and innocence; the small golden chains or fringes point to good works. The free unconquered swan, ' called Frank,' reminds us that the founders of the Order had, at the period, ruled as free and noble Francs; while the Madonna with the Child constitute the principal symbols, and the moon and sun-beams are the heralds of their glory.

At the death of a member, the chain was returned to the St. Maria Church, where a funeral procession took place.

After the lapse of three years, new statutes were published in consequence, as it appears, of complaints made, by the monks about the scanty and insufficient income derived from the endowment and other sources. The new statutes did not limit the number of the members; but required the proof of four generations of noble descent. At their nomination, the members paid to the Provost of the church, or cathedral, who handed them over the insignia, eleven florins, Rhenish; the wives of the members could also be admitted to the Order on the payment of one florin entrance fee, while single women were subject to the full amount.

At the death of a member, all other members were bound to attend in person, or by proxies the funeral mass at the St. Maria Church, or pay in default a fine of eight ounces of silver to the church.

If a member were, in his travels, attacked or taken prisoner, the Order was obliged to demand satisfaction of his assailants, or effect his release. A member falling into needy circumstances, was, by promise of the Elector, to be received at court, or at one of his castles, as an inmate for life.

The son, or next heir of a deceased member, might claim the right of taking his place in the Order on payment of eight ounces of silver and one florin.

The Canons were bound to attend, daily, divine service, and pray for the welfare of the members, while the officiating priest prayed for the union of Christendom, for the Elector, for the living and dead members of the Order and their families. Upon the members was, on the other hand, the duty imposed to protect the rights, liberties, revenues and reputation of the Canons.

A tribunal of arbitration was also instituted by way of election, for the maintenance of the statutes and the settlement of disputes among the members. The Elector had the casting vote in the decisions.

Pope Nicolaus V. confirmed these statutes. The Order counted, at that period, forty-nine members in Brandenburg, twenty in Brunswick, Anhalt, Mecklenburg and Lusatia, and thirty-four in Upper Germany. The number of the unmarried female members was twenty-three.

In 1450, the Knights in Franconia having represented to the Margrave Albert, brother of the Elector Frederick II., that the distance of their homes from the seat of the Order was too great for them to attend regularly the meetings of the society, it was arranged, by sanction of the Elector and of Pope Pius II., that the Chapel of St. George in the Cathedral of Anspach, should be declared a branch church, where all the Knights in the countries beyond the Thuringian Forest were to attend on festival days, though the nomination remained as before the privilege of the principal church.

The Grand Master of the Teutonic Order, Albert of Brandenburg, intended to introduce the Order of the Swan in the Baltic provinces; he, in consequence, contrived to procure from Pope Leo X., the permission of using his own private chapel as the second branch church of the Order. Albert's conversion to Protestantism, however, soon put an end to the scheme, and, with the progress of Luther, the Order entirely dis-disappeared from Northern Germany, where it had existed for upwards of a hundred years, and its estates fell to the crown.

At the date of its extinction, the Order numbered three hundred and thirty-one members, among whom were twenty-four Princes, twenty-one Counts, eight Barons, nineteen Knights, and two hundred and twenty-nine nobles of both sexes.

The fall of the Order caused the decline of the Chapter in Brandenburg. In 1539, they were forbidden to supply the ranks by new members, and the consequence was, that, shortly afterwards, the only inmate of the deserted cloister, was the Provost of the Church, who at last died in the equally deserted cloister of the Franciscan monks. Though stripped of all its monuments, the Church of St. Mary was still in existence in 1722, but the adjoining cloister had long previously become a heap of ruins.

The Church of St. Gumbertus, at Anspach, yet remains. Several of the monuments of St. George's Chapel have been transferred to the chancel.

The Order of the Swan was in connection with many religious societies, and more especially with the Convent of the 'Madonna Congregation,' at Chatelleraut. As late as the beginning of the past century, the nuns of that community used officially to report to the members of the Order of St. Mary, the death of any of their sisterhood, for whose souls they requested mass to be said. Well might they have been under the impression of the continued existence of the Order, since it had never been formally dissolved.

In recent times, the Order was revived by the King of Prussia, on the 24th December, 1843, exactly four hundred years after it was first founded by the Elector Frederick II.

The following is a literal translation of the decree concerning its revival.

"We, Frederick William, by the Grace of God, King of Prussia, &c., &c., &c.

"Of the many gratifying things produced by our time, under "the blessings of a long peace, may Heaven preserve it to us, "nothing deserves greater acknowledgment and consideration, "than the far spread efforts of societies to alleviate, by educa- "tion and civilization, the physical and moral sufferings of "mankind. These efforts are one of the proofs which evidence "Christianity, not in theological controversies, or outward "manifestations, but in truth and in spirit, by life and by action. "Impressed with the conviction, that many of those respectable

"societies can only arrive at the full and perfect extent of the
"operations of which they are capable, by being closely united
"round a guiding and animating central point, we have resolved
"to revive and re-model, according to the requirements of the
"age, the oldest Order of our House, 'The Society of the
"Order of the Swan,' which was founded exactly four hundred
"years back, by one of our glorious ancestors, the Arch-Cham-
"berlain and Elector Frederick II., but was never formally
"abrogated. Even the sense in which the statutes of the
"Order were composed, in 1443, is no other than the
"'Acknowledgment of Christian truth by action.' We have
"given orders for the construction of new statutes, and the
"formation of a managing Board of the Order, divided into
"various sections. Our first care to promote the practical
"activity of the Society of the Order of the Swan, will be the
"establishment of an evangelical head institution at Berlin, for
"the attending on, and nursing of the sick in the large
"hospitals.

"We have wrought such modifications in the original
"insignia of the Order, as we deemed more in harmony
"with present circumstances. The members who are imme-
"diately engaged in the labours of the Order, such as: the
"male and female attendants on sufferers, fallen penitents,
"punished criminals, &c., as also the spiritual members of the
"Order, who are entrusted with the immediate conduct and
"management of the establishments of the Society, and the
"salvation and care of the souls of their inmates, are not to
"wear the decoration.

"With the exception of the golden chain, which is presented
"as a mark of honour only to crowned heads, the insignia of the
"Order of the Swan are not intended to be like those of other
"Orders, an ornament of merit, a mark of distinction, but a mere
"sign of recognition, a mark of connection with the society, the

"entrance into and departing from which is entirely left to the
" discretion of the members, without entailing any dishonour to
" those who, feeling themselves incapable of performing the task
" before them, think proper to leave the Order. The various
" officers and ranks of the Order only point to the sphere of ope-
" ration allotted to the individual members, and the distance of
" their removal from the central point of activity. Individuals
" of both sexes, and all creeds, may be received into the Order,
" if they bind themselves to undergo the labours of the
" Society.

" We, ourselves, in conjunction with our Consort, Her
" Majesty the Queen, have taken upon us, as did our ancestors,
" the office of Grand Mastership of the Order, and therewith the
" head management of its concerns. We thought of deeply
" acknowledging the virtue, which at the side of valour is the
" finest ornament of our people, by intruding our personal
" efforts into the sanctuary of silent benevolence peculiar to the
" glorious Order. Our only object is to produce, by united
" powers, great results upon the productive field of humanity.
" Everything depends on the blessing of the Almighty. We
" beseech his help upon this our work, that the renewed society
" of the Order may grow up and flourish for the alleviation
" and healing of manifold sufferings, and that men and women
" of all creeds, ranks and descent among our subjects, may show
" by numerous associations and most noble emulation, that they
" have at heart the words of our Lord : ' By their fruit ye shall
" know them.' In the conviction that the object for which we
" have restored the ' Order of the Swan ' is good, being chiefly di-
" rected towards the removal of many defects, and the promotion
" of salutary establishments, we commend our Institution con-
" fidently and joyfully to the King of Kings. Under his
" blessing, a truly noble host will gather, conceive, and on
" the one hand energetically accomplish all that is great

"salutary and effective in all directions of our present age, and "on the other, remove and remedy chivalrously all that is evil "and obnoxious in society, not by means of the sword and "combat, not by secret workings, but solely by those means "in which all Christian confessions might and should unite, "by active exercise of the will of God, in the consciousness of "success and divine love.

"The motto of the Order is to be: 'Gott mit uns' (God with us).

"FREDERICK WILLIAM.

"Berlin, Christmas Eve, 1843."

MEDALS AND DECORATIONS OF HONOUR.

1. *Medal for* 1813 *and* 1814.—This bronze medal was instituted on the 24th December, 1813, at Frankfort-on-the-Maine, by King Frederick William III. It was presented to all the military who were present at any one of the battles or sieges during the war in 1813 and 1814. The obverse shows beneath the crown the initials of the founder, with the inscription: 'Preussen's tapfern Kriegern' (To Prussia's brave warriors), surrounded by the legend: 'Gott war mit uns, ihm sei die Ehre' (God was with us, to him the honour). The reverse exhibits a cross upon rays, and in the middle surrounded by a laurel wreath, are the years: '1813 or 1814,' or both, according to the share the recipient has had in either or both of those campaigns. On the edge is the legend: 'Aus feindlichem Geschütze' (From the enemy's guns). (Tab. III. No. 18).

2. A similar medal of iron, containing the inscription 'Für Pflichttreue' (For faithful duty), was instituted for the civil officers who had taken part in the above campaigns. (Tab. III. No. 17).

PRUSSIA. Table IV. PLATE 68.

3. and 4. *Distinction in Service.*—On the 18th June, (the anniversary of the battle of Waterloo), 1825, King Frederick William III. founded:

a. A golden cross for officers who had served twenty-five years, bearing on the obverse the crowned initials: 'F. W. III.' and on the reverse the number 'XXV.' It is worn on the left breast suspended by a blue ribbon. (Tab. IV. No. 23).

b. Buckles with the initials 'F. W. III.' worn on the left breast by sub-officers and privates, suspended by a blue ribbon with yellow borders, for twenty-one years' service. (Tab. IV., No. 24), by a blue ribbon with white and blue borders for fifteen years' service, (Tab. IV. No. 25), and by a blue ribbon with black borders for nine years' service. (Tab. IV. No. 26). Years of war count double.

5. *Medal for Military Merit in* 1793, was founded on the 14th of June, 1793, by Frederick William II. for the military who had distinguished themselves in that campaign. It is of gold for officers, and of silver for sub-officers and privates. The obverse shows the initials of the King with a crown above, and the year '1793' below, and the reverse, the inscription within a laurel wreath: 'Verdienst um den Staat' (Merit of the State). It is worn suspended by a black ribbon. (Tab. IV. No. 20).

6. *The Silver Medal of Military Merit,* or *the Military Decoration, second class.* — King Frederick William III. founded on the 30th September, 1806, a gold and silver medal as a military decoration of honour for the soldiers who might distinguish themselves by valour in the pending war. The first distinction was to be rewarded by the silver, and the second by the gold medal. By a government ordinance, however, of the 27th March, 1807, it was determined that he who should capture a General, a cannon, or a standard, should receive the gold Medal of Merit, with the additional

pay, though he should not be in possession of the silver medal.

The obverse of the medal contains the initials: 'F. W. R. III. beneath a crown, and the reverse the inscription within a laurel wreath: 'Verdienst um den Staat' (Merit of the State). It is worn suspended by a black watered ribbon with white stripes. (Tab. IV. No. 21).

The gold medal has been discontinued since the 30th September, 1814, and replaced by a silver cross in the form of the Red Eagle fourth class, under the name:

7. *Military Decoration of Honour, first class.*

8. *General Decoration of Honour, first class.*—By the same decree of 30th September, 1814, the golden medal of Civil Merit instituted in 1810, was substituted by a silver cross under the above name, and worn by the ribbon of the Red Eagle, while the silver medal of Civil Merit, also instituted in 1810, is now worn as:

9. *General Medal of Merit.* (Tab. IV. No. 22).

10. *The Decoration of Merit for saving from Danger*, was founded by Frederick William III. on the 1st February, 1833, as a brilliant mark of public acknowledgment. It consists of a silver medal, and shows on the obverse the effigy of the King, and on the reverse the inscription within an oaken wreath: 'Für Rettung von Gefahr' (For saving from danger). Unlike a similar medal instituted in 1802, for a similar purpose, which the owner was not allowed to wear publicly, this new one is worn at the button-hole suspended by an orange coloured ribbon with two narrow white stripes. (Tab. IV. No. 19).

11. *Medal of Neufchatel.*—This silver medal was founded on the 18th January, 1832, by King Frederick William III. as sovereign Prince of Neufchatel and Valangin, as a reward for those who had taken part in the military operations of 1831.

The obverse shows the initials of the founder, and the inscription: 'Treue gegen Pflicht und Vaterland' (Faithfulness to duty and fatherland); and the reverse, the arms of the principality, Neufchatel and Valangin. It is worn at the button-hole, suspended by a ribbon of the Prussian and Neufchatel colours.

12. *Decoration for dutiful service in the Landwehr.*—The patent says:

1. "This decoration consists of a blue hyacinth or blue-"bottle coloured ribbon, in which is worked with yellow silk "thread the initials 'F. W. IV.' It is worn upon the left "breast by an iron clasp.

2. "It is the same for officers, sub-officers or privates.

3. "The claim thereto is founded on the correct fulfilment "of the duties in the two arrière-bans of the Landwehr, after "having accomplished the prescribed term of service in the "standing army.

4. "The decoration is usually bestowed at the discharge "from the second arrière-ban in the autumn of every year, "beginning with those who were discharged in the autumn of "1842.

5. "It is required from candidate officers, that they should "have strictly fulfilled their duties through all the above "stations (§ 3), and most punctually attended the exercises "to which they were summoned, as also the target-shootings "and control-assemblies, and never been punished by a court-"martial, &c., &c., &c."

Medal for Agriculture was founded in 1847, by King Frederick William IV., for the agriculturists who may distinguish themselves in their calling by inventions, writings, or any other act tending to improve agriculture and husbandry. It consists of three degrees; the nomination to the first is reserved to the King himself for the higher classes, while that to the two others is left to the decision of the Commission for Agriculture for the lower classes. The obverse of the decoration contains the effigy of the King, and the reverse the name of the recipient, with the inscription: 'Für Verdienst um den Ackerbau' (For merit in agriculture).

REUSS (PRINCIPALITIES).

CROSS OF HONOUR FOR THE CAMPAIGNS OF 1814 AND 1815

Was founded by the united Princes (Henvys) of the lines Reuss-Lohenstein, and Reuss-Ebersdorf, to whose memory the cyphers: XIII, LI, LIV, XLII upon the four arms of the cross are devoted. It is worn between the first and second button-hole on the breast, by sub-officers and civilians in a plain and simple way, and by officers, appended to a small bow. It was presented as a reward for devotion in the cause of German liberty, during that stormy period. The owner does not lose the decoration on retiring from military service, but forfeits it by desertion, insubordination, or degradation of rank, by crimes, such as theft, perjury, &c., though not without due judgment pronounced by the Military Tribunal or Court Martial. Civilians forfeit the decoration by betraying sentiments against German liberty, or agitating against the laws of the land, though also not without a judgment pronounced against them by the competent authorities.

The Iron Cross of Henry XIII. is given Plate 94.

RUSSIA.

GENERAL REMARKS.

The Emperor is Grand Master of all the Russian Orders, with the exception of that of St. Catherine, which is an Order for ladies. The Grand Dukes become, at their baptism, Knights of the Orders of St. Andrew, Alexander Newsky, the White Eagle, and St. Anne. The other Imperial Princes receive them on attaining majority. In like manner do the Grand Duchesses receive, at their baptism, the Order of St. Catharine, while the Princesses receive it only when of age.

The administration of all the Orders belongs to a Chapter, consisting of a Chancellor (elected from the Knights of the Order of St. Andrew), a treasurer, and the Master of Ceremonies of the Imperial Court. Every Order has, however, a Master of Ceremonies, a secretary and two heralds, as also a peculiar costume of its own. The Chapter is in possession of funds to the amount of 200,000 roubles, for the education of the daughters of poor Knights, who are received into the educational Institution at St. Petersburg, established for the children of noble families, under the patronage of the Empress.

The nomination to an order confers nobility upon the member, which becomes hereditary, if the latter is not born a serf. Bashkeers obtain personal nobility, with the Order, and Russian merchants (since 10th April, 1832), hereditary honorary freedom of a citizen.

Pensioned members is the only class, the number of which is limited. Every member has to pay an entrance fee at his nomination, according to the Order and class of his reception. The sums thus received pass into the Exchequer, established for invalid officers. Foreigners, Circassians, and all those who receive the decoration adorned with brilliants, are exempt from the tax.

St. Michael's day (8th November), is fixed for the general festival of the Orders. On this day, all the Knights domiciled at St. Petersburg and Moscow, elect six members of every Order to serve in the managing committee of the charitable institutions existing in the two capitals.

With the exception of active service in Siberia and Circassia or some peculiar merit of distinction, when the term of service is shortend by five years, no Order is conferred on any one who has not been fifteen years in the army. Every Order confers a certain rank, and imposes certain duties on the member.

The decorations are classified in degrees, so that no one can be favoured with a higher Order without first possessing the inferior ones. Deviations from this rule are, however, of frequent occurrence. By deeds of crime or disgrace, the owner forfeits the decoration. Degraded officers or suspended clergymen can only resume the decoration with the resumption of their degree or office.

The Academy of Science at St. Petersburg is bound to publish every five years, a complete list of the members of all the Orders.

Besides the Orders and medals, there exists in Russia a variety of other decorations, or badges of honour. For the last forty-seven years, military distinction of officers and generals was not unfrequently rewarded with swords mounted with gold, or adorned with brilliants, and bearing the usual inscription:

'To courage,' and sometimes even a statement of the special service rendered.

The ladies-in-waiting on the Empress wear her portrait set in diamonds, and the court ladies generally a medal with her initials equally adorned with diamonds, and suspended by a blue watered ribbon.

By an imperial ukase of March, 1834, the pensions attached to the respective Orders, were divided into the following scales: The Knights of

1. St. Andrew receive from . . 800 to 1000 roubles.
2. St. Catherine first class „ 350 „ 460 „
3. „ second class „ 90 to 130 or 200 „
4. St. Alexander Newsky „ 500 to 700 „
5. St. George from 150, 200, 400 or 1000 „
6. St. Vladimir „ 100, 150, 300 or 600 „
7. St. Ann first class from . . 200 to 350 „
8. „ second „ „ 120 „ 150 „
9. „ third „ „ 90 „ 100 „
10. „ fourth „ „ 40 „ 50 „
11. St. Stanislaus „ 86, 115 or 143 „

Foreigners not in the Russian service, receive the decorations without pension. The number of the pensioned Knights of the Vladimir Order, is fixed at sixty. The total amount of the pensions is 158,660 R.S. (about £26,444).

THE ORDER OF ST. ANDREW

Was founded on the 20th December, 1698, by Peter the Great, to initiate his own court in the refinement of the civilized courts of Europe, as also to encourage his nobility in the pending war with Turkey. The first who obtained the Order was the Chancellor, Field-Marshal and Great Admiral Golovin, who, in his turn, performed the same

RUSSIA. Table I. PLATE 69.

Hurst and Blackett, London. 1858.

ceremonies of investiture with regard to the Czar himself after his naval victory over the Swedes. The next who received it were the officers who had distinguished themselves at the siege of Azoff. Still later, when the Czar formed an alliance with King Augustus of Saxony against Charles XII., he rewarded with it the Generals of Augustus who had been stationed in Livonia and Poland.

St. Andrew is the patron saint of the empire, who, according to Muscovite traditions, first preached the gospel to the Slavonians in Novogorod. He was, therefore, chosen as the patron of the Order, the highest in Russia, which is only bestowed by special favour of the Emperor. It is usually confined to members of the imperial family, foreign princes, or individuals who are already in possession of the other Orders. With the Order, the nominee receives, also, the Alexander Newsky, St. Ann, and St. Stanilaus decorations.

Every Knight pays 240 silver roubles (£40) entrance fee. Twelve of the members (inclusive of three spiritual members) divide among themselves the annual pension of 6092 roubles (about £1000).

The decoration has undergone manifold alterations, and consits now (Plate 69, Tab. I. No. 2) of the blue enamelled figure of St. Andrew on the cross, bearing on each arm the initials S. A. P. R. (Sanctus Andreas Protector Russiæ), and resting upon the Eagle of the Empire with three crowns. It is worn across the right shoulder towards the left hip, by a sky blue ribbon.

The costume of the Knights, at festivals, consists of a long cloak of green velvet, lined with white taffetas, and with silver facings, cords and shoulder belt, of a white jacket and black velvet hat adorned with a red feather. The badge is appended to a collar (Tab. I. No. 6), the links of which now represent alternately the cross of the Order, (an Andrew cross with red and golden flames in the angles), and the initials of Peter I. upon a bright blue field surrounded by trophies.

The star (Tab. I. No. 1) which is fastened to the left side of the coat, shows in the golden centre the double Eagle of the Empire, round which a dark serpent is winding itself. This centre is encompassed by a bright blue ring, containing the legend (in Russian) 'For Faith and Loyalty.'

The Knights present at St. Petersburg are bound by fine of 50 roubles, to attend in costume the annual festival of the Order, usually held on the 30th November.

As a mark of special favour or particular distinction, the decoration is presented adorned with diamonds.

ORDER OF ST. CATHARINE.

It is a well known fact, that a certain Martha Rabe, a young Livonian woman, after having been married to a Swedish dragoon, and after living subsequently as mistress alternately under the protection of the Generals Bauer, Sheremetoff, and Menshikoff, inspired, at last, the Czar Peter with such intense affection for herself as to induce him to make her Empress of Russia, under the name of Catharine I. In raising her to the throne, the Czar declared that he owed her that reward, for the great services she had rendered him in various dangers, and more especially at the battle near the Pruth (1711), where his army had been reduced to twenty-two thousand men. He had, however, already at a much earlier date, shown his gratitude by the foundation of the Order of St. Catharine, on the 25th November, (7th December), 1714.

Originally, men were received into the Order, though Catharine herself was the first who was decorated with it, and had, moreover, the privilege of bestowing it on any of her sex whom she might deem worthy of it. At a later period, however, the decoration was strictly confined to ladies, and the Empress was instituted Grand Mistress of the Order.

It is divided into two classes. The Grand Cross (Tab. I. No. 4) adorned with diamonds, exhibits in the middle the figure of St. Catharine, and is worn across the right shoulder towards the left side, by a broad (formerly blue) now poppy red ribbon with silver stripes, and with the silver embroidered inscription (in Russian) ' For love and fatherland.'

The reverse shows an airie on the top of an old tower, at the foot of which two eagles, with serpents in their beaks, are seen in the act of carrying them up as food to their young. Above are the words: 'Aequat munia comparis' (She is equal to the duties of a consort).*

The number of the members of the Grand Cross is limited, besides the Princesses of the Imperial family, to twelve noble ladies of the highest Russian aristocracy.

In the second class may also be received, foreigners of high rank, though that class consists chiefly of the Court ladies of the Imperial household, to the number of about ninety-four members. The decoration of the second class (Tab. I. No. 5) chiefly differs from that of the first class, by its size and number of diamonds, and is worn on the left breast appended to a bow.

The silver octagonal star (Tab. I. No. 3) has in its red

* The inscription is probably in allusion to the services rendered by the young Catharine to the much older Peter, and is composed after the following verse of Horace. (Ode 5, II).

> " Nondum subacta ferre jugum valet
> Cervice, nondum munia comparis
> Aequare."

—*Note by the Translator.*

middle an Imperial diadem, surrounded by the motto of the Order, and is equally worn on the left breast.

The costume consists of silver stuff with gold embroidery, and of hat and bow of green velvet.

The members are, by the statutes, bound to render daily thanks to God for the deliverance of Peter I., and pray for the health of the reigning Czar and his family, to say every Sunday three paternosters, to try to convert infidels to the Greek Church, to free, at their own expense, Christians from the hands of barbarians, and to serve in the Committee of Management of the St. Catharine institution, into which every member of the Grand Cross is free to place one pupil.

The annual festival of the Order is celebrated on the 25th November.

ORDER OF ALEXANDER NEWSKY.

Novogorod was once under the rule of Alexander, son of Yaroslaw, one of the numerous Princes of Russia.

The town was then (1240) at war with the Tshudi, the Finns, the Swedes, and the Livonian and German Knights. The Swedes, who had forced their way as far as the Neva, were beaten by Alexander, whence he received the surname Newsky. Peter I., after having established his new capital on the Neva, resolved to found an Order in commemoration and under the patronage of that great warrior and national saint. He died, however, before he had carried out his intention. It was realized by Catharine, who invested with the decoration, her intimate friend, Menshikoff, on the 8th April, 1725.

The insignia consist of an octagonal red enamelled cross, showing in its corners, the Imperial Eagle in gold, and in the white enamelled middle, the figure of St. Alexander on horseback (Tab. II. No. 8). It is worn across the right shoulder towards the left hip, by a flame-coloured ribbon. The silver star (No. 8) is worn on the left breast, and contains the initials, 'S. A.' (Saint Alexander), beneath an Imperial crown. In the red ring round the initials, is seen the motto of the Order (in the Russian language): "For Merit of the Fatherland.'

The Order is both civil and military, and consists of only one class. The rank of the candidate must, at least, be that of Major-General.

The Knights of St. Andrew wear, usually, the present cross round the neck suspended by a narrow ribbon, but on solemn occasions, they must carry it by the large ribbon, and must also dress in the costume of the Order, which consists of a mantle of red velvet with white facings, of a jacket of silver stuff, and of a black hat with a white feather.

Twelve Knights, including five spiritual members, divide among themselves the annual pension of 7014 roubles, and 8 copecks (£1169).

Every member pays 180 roubles entrance fee.

The annual festival of the Order is held on the 30th September (old style).

The decoration, set in diamonds, is a high mark of honour, granted by the Emperor only for peculiar services or distinction.

THE ORDER OF ST. ANN.

This Order belonged originally to the House of Holstein-Sleswig, and was founded on the 14th February, 1735, at Kiel, by Duke Charles Frederick, in memory of the Empress Ann, and in honour of the Duchess Ann Petrowna, daughter of Peter III. It consisted of only one class, of fifteen Knights, and was brought to Russia by the son of the founder, the Emperor Peter III. Under the reign of the Empress Catharine II., the dispenser of that Order was the Grand Duke, afterwards Emperor Paul I., who, after his accession to the throne, in 1796, declared it a Russian Order, and divided it into three classes, indiscriminately for natives and foreigners, decreeing that the Knights of St. Andrew should also wear the decoration of St. Ann.

In 1815, the Emperor Alexander added to it a fourth class, exclusively for the military, and ordered that the members of that fourth class should wear the enamelled decoration upon the hilt of the sword.

The annual festival of the Order is celebrated on the $\frac{13\text{th}}{14\text{th}}$ February.

The decoration (Tab. II. No. 10) is worn by the Knights of the first class, across the left shoulder towards the right hip, by a broad bright red ribbon, with small yellow borders, accompanied by a star (No. 9) on the breast. The Knights of the second class wear the cross round the neck suspended by a similar, but narrower ribbon, and those of the third class at the button-hole. The middle of the cross contains the initials of St. Ann, and that of the star, the inscription: 'Amant. just. piet. fidem' (To the friends of the fear of God, justice and fidelity).

The Emperor Nicholas frequently presented, for special merit, this decoration of the first and second classes set in rubies, and the corners adorned with brilliants, or with the imperial crown of white enamel.

Of all the Russian Orders, 'St. Ann' is mostly conferred on foreigners who are not in the service of the country. In 1818, the Order counted (by the Court Almanack) one thousand and twenty Knights of the first class, five thousand four hundred

RUSSIA. Table II. PLATE 70.

Hurst and Blackett, London. 1858.

and ten of the second, thirty-one of the third, and ten thousand two hundred and twenty of the fourth classes.

It may, by the statutes, be conferred:

1. On every ecclesiastic who has converted, at least, one hundred infidels, or heretics, to the Greek Church; who has brought back to loyal obedience some revolted peasants, or given important assistance to the soldiery. Also on those ecclesiastics, who have built cloisters or churches from other than Crown or State resources, who have served the State without pay for at least five years, or who have distinguished themselves in the arts and sciences.

2. On Military Commanders of a corps (stronger than a company or squadron), or of one thousand recruits, though in various divisions. To entitle the Commander to the decoration, the corps under his command must have occupied a distinguished position in the army for, at least, three years, and the number of its sick, or of the soldiers dismissed from service for bad conduct, ought not to have exceeded one in one hundred.

3. On persons in the Civil Service, who have managed to settle amicably, within three years, ten pending law-suits; on justices of peace who have arranged all the disputes before them; on those who have secured the future subsistence of widows, orphans, or the poor; who have procured to government an unexpected important advantage; have risked their life or property for public good; or have conducted satisfactorily an educational establishment for, at least, ten years, without any support from government.

The deliberations on the merits of the proposed candidates take place with closed doors, and are secretly voted in the Chapter of twelve Knights, composed of the eldest of each class residing in St. Petersburg. In war, the General-in-chief has the right to confer, at discretion, the decorations of the three lower classes.

The entrance-fee of the Knights of the first class is 60, of of the second 30, of the third 18, and of the fourth 9 roubles.

The Emperor Nicholas instituted a yellow medal (Tab. II. No. 11) for long and faithful service in the army, which may be considered as the fifth class of the Order.

The obverse shows a red cross within a ring of the same colour, and with the name of the possessor. The Emperor distributed it also amongst foreigners, and more especially amongst the whole company of the sub-officers of the Royal Guard at Berlin. The cross thus distributed had a crown above it.

THE MILITARY ORDER OF ST. GEORGE.

This Order was founded by Catharine II. on the 26th Nov. (7th Dec.) 1769, as a reward for Officers of the army and navy. The biographer, Castera, says: "It cannot be denied that the hope of this reward has greatly contributed to the many victories of Russia during that period, and no one knew better than that Empress the great power which vanity exercises on the actions of men."

Emperor Paul I. who was dreaming and planing great reforms in his empire, never thought of distributing the Order amongst his soldiers, and it was only restored to practice by an ukase of his son Alexander I. on the 12th December, 1801. In gratitude, the Chapter offered the same insignia to the Czar the restorer of the Order, which the latter, however, modestly, refused to accept until after the campaign of 1805, when he accepted the Cross of the lowest, the fourth class. Whatever the cause of hesitation may really have been, there can be no doubt that the circumstance of the modest refusal, greatly enhanced the value of that Order in public opinion.

RUSSIA. Table III.   PLATE 71.

Hurst and Blackett, London. 1858.

Two colleges, selected from the army and navy, prepare after every campaign, the list of officers who deserve the cross.

The Order is divided into four classes. The members of the first two, have the rank of Major-Generals; and those of the last two, the rank of Colonels.

It is conferred, for the taking of a fortress, for the defence of a place in the empire, for the capture of vessels, cannons and standards, or for the capturing high officers, such as generals, &c. It is also bestowed on those by whose counsel a victory has been gained, or who had forced their way through the lines of the foe, as also on those who have served in the army or navy twenty-five years,* or have shared the dangers of twenty campaigns on land, or eighteen at sea. In the two latter cases, the cause of the honour thus conferred is inscribed on the cross. Despite, however, these severe conditions, the number of the members exceeds now ten thousand.

The Field-marshals and Generals-in-chief, possess the discretionary power of conferring the decoration of the fourth and fifth classes in times of war. The decoration of the two first classes, however, must be presented by the Emperor himself.

There is no entrance fee for this Order. The whole of the pensions attached to it, amounts to ten thousand nine hundred and seventy-one roubles.

The festival of the Order is solemnized on the anniversary of its foundation. The Generals are bound to appear at that festival in uniform without its embroidery, while the other members may attend as they like.

The St. George Cross (Tab. III. No. 13) can never be adorned with diamonds, and is worn by the Knights of the first class across the right shoulder towards the left side, by

* Since 1855, military services of twenty-five years are rewarded with the Vladimir decoration, fourth class, adorned with a bow, and containing in golden letters the number of years of service.

a broad orange coloured ribbon with three black stripes, and by the second class round the neck.

The cross of the third and fourth classes is of smaller size, and is worn by the former round the neck, and by the latter at the button-hole.

The Knights of the first two classes have besides, fastened to the left side of the coat, a star (No. 12), bearing in its middle the initial of St. George, and in the Russian language, the motto of the Order: 'For military merit and valour.'

As a fifth class, may be considered the Silver Cross of St. George (Tab. III. No. 14), instituted in 1807 by the Emperor Alexander, as a reward for the sub-officers and men who had distinguished themselves in those warlike times. An additional pay of one third accompanied the grant of the cross.

By a decree of the 22nd October 1814, the Russian crosses which had been distributed amongst the Prussian soldiers, after the campaigns of 1813 and 1814, were to be transferred, after the death of the first recipients, to those who stood next on the list of proposed candidates.

THE ORDER OF SAINT VLADIMIR.

Was founded on the 22nd September, (4th October,) 1782, by the Empress Catharine II. on the anniversary of her coronation, to the memory of the Great Vladimir, who introduced, in 976, Christianity into his States, and received from his people the prefix of Apostle.

Paul I. suffered this Order also to fall into disuse, while his son Alexander renewed it together with that of St. George.

It is an Order of general merit in Military or Civil life, in literary, artistical or scientific spheres of study. It consists of four independent classes, (as the entrance into the higher class does not necessarily require the passing through the lower.) The claims of the candidates are investigated by the Chapter, held for the purpose once every year.

The decoration of the first class, (Tab. III. No. 16.) is worn across the right shoulder, towards the left hip by a broad ribbon with crimson red and black stripes. If the Knight is not yet in possession of another higher Order, the ribbon is thrown over the dress coat, otherwise across the waistcoat.

The Knights of the second class wear the same cross round the neck, while those of the third class have it in a smaller size, also suspended round the neck, and those of the fourth class at the button hole. For Military merit, the ribbon is besides adorned with a bow. The Order is never presented adorned with diamonds.

The reverse of the cross shows (in Russian language) the date of the foundation of the Order.

In addition to the Cross, the Knights of the two first classes wear a Star (No. 15) on the right breast. The four Russian letters in the middle, 'S. R. K. W.' signify: 'St. Vladimir the Apostle,' while the Russian motto in the ring round the middle, means : ' Utility, honour, glory.'

The annual festival of the Order is held on the 27th September. The claim to the Order, besides the services rendered to the Emperor personally, rests on the following merits :

1. Removal of abuses in any department of the administration.

2. Encouragement and preparation for State services.

3. Amicable settlement or prevention of law-suits.

4. Saving ten persons from danger.

5. Assistance rendered to a place visited by famine, or any other calamity.

6. Co-operation for the increase of National wealth, by agricultural invention or otherwise.

7. Any scheme which enriched the public Treasury, by at least 3000 roubles.

8. Any work of classical distinction.

9. Thirty-five years active and faithful civil service, (in the trans-Caucasian provinces, only twenty-five years). Every demonstration of high satisfaction, shortens the period by one year.

Also physicians who have vaccinated in one year, three thousand children, are entitled to the decoration, as are also noblemen who have three times been elected, or filled the functions of Chancellor of a College or University, deputy-chairman, or secretary, &c.

In time of war, the General-in-Chief is authorized to confer the fourth class at discretion.

The entrance fee of the first class is 180, of the second 60, of the third 30, and of the fourth 9 roubles.

Candidates for thirty-five years service, are exempt from the tax.

The widow of a Knight receives the full pension for one year after the death of her husband.

THE ORDER OF SAINT JOHN.

The general outlines of the history of this Order will be found under AUSTRIA.

The two Russian Grand Priorates still preserve the appearance of the old Constitution and form, under the protection and patronage of the Emperor, who is head of the Chapter. Its connection with the Chapter at Rome is of a very loose character.

The Grand Priorate of Poland, established in 1776, was for a long time connected with the English and Bavarian branches, and was composed of twenty Commanderies, which brought to the Grand Master an annual revenue of 15,000 thalers, while under Paul I. the revenues were even increased to 300,000 florins. At present, it is united with the Russian Priorates, and the whole is now divided into two Grand Priorates, for the Knights of the Greek and those of the Roman Catholic confession. The former now counts ninety-eight Commanders, while previously it had three hundred and ninety-three Commanders, and thirty-two Knights of the Grand Cross.

There are also Grand and small crosses for female members.

ORDER OF THE WHITE EAGLE.

In the time of Vladimir IV., one of the Princes of that period, when the nobility had already consolidated their own power, and the Kings found it, in consequence, advisable to introduce for the safety of their thrones an aristocracy in the ranks of the nobility, George Ossilinsky, Great Chancellor of the Republic (Poland), having inherited the Seignory of Teneczin, assumed the title of Count, which he thought was attached to his new estates. He, at the same time, solicited the Emperor and the Pope to bestow upon him the dignity of *Prince*, which he no sooner obtained, than he projected the foundation of a new Order, of 'the Immaculate Virgin,' and the statutes of which Pope Urban VIII. confirmed in 1634.

Public opinion was, however, against such innovations, and it was therefore an easy task for the more ancient family of the Radzivils to agitate the nobility against this act of presumption.

In 1638, the States passed a law, that every distinction nd decoration should amount to an offence against the equality of Knighthood; and they accordingly issued a direct prohibition for any one to accept any foreign title, decoration, escutcheon, or any marks whatsoever of honour, declaring at the same time all titles as null and void, except those which the Union of Lublin had in 1569 conferred on the Princes of Lithuania and Russia. The consequence was, that the new Order of Ossilinsky was soon condemned to extinction, while those who were already in possession of the decoration, dared no longer wear it in public.

In 1703, when Augustus II. was obliged to flee from the Polish provinces, which were then occupied by the Swedes, he distributed amongst a number of high personages who had remained true to him, a medal appended to a narrow blue ribbon, and which bore on the obverse a white eagle, with the legend: 'Pro Fide, Rege, Lege' (For Religion, King and Law), and on the reverse, the initials, 'A. R.'

The real foundation or rather constitution of the Order, however, only dates from the year 1713.

To obviate the necessity of repealing the prohibitive law of innovation, it was alleged that the new Order was only the revived one of the 'Immaculate Virgin,' which was supposed to have been founded as early as 1325, by Wladislaw the Short, on the occasion of the marriage of his son Casimir with Ann, a Princess of Lithuania.

The decoration, not unlike that of the Maltese Cross, consisted of a cross containing upon its face the White Eagle with expanded wings, and gold flames in the corners. It was worn suspended by a light blue ribbon. The King was to receive it with the crown as Grand Master. The number of the Knights (divided into four classes) was limited to seventy-two.

During the reigns of the Saxon Kings, however, the party opposed to the Order, was yet too strong to be trifled with, and the Kings dared not accept the decoration at their public coronation, without defying public opinion, and the strong party of the ancient nobility; the decoration was indeed more seen abroad

RUSSIA. Table IV. PLATE 72.

17.

19.

18.

20.

Hurst and Blackett, London. 1858.

than at home; it shone at foreign courts, but was hardly ever exhibited at Warsaw, and throughout the whole extent of the kingdom. It was only under the reign of Stanislaus Poniatowsky, that the Order apparently received a more solid footing, when it had only to contend against the antipathy of the old aristocracy, while the lavish and scandalous abuse in the distribution of the decoration was but ill calculated to weaken the prejudice against it.

After the division of Poland, in 1795, the Order like the kingdom itself, was nigh extinction, none of the three conquerors having thought proper to accept it with their respective shares of the territory. In this passive state, it remained until 1807, when the Constitutional decree of the Duchy of Warsaw, which was issued on the 21st July, proclaimed the restoration, at the same time, of the ancient Orders of Poland. Frederick Augustus, King of Saxony, declared himself Grand Master, but was subsequently superseded in that dignity, by the Emperor Alexander of Russia.

The Revolution of 1831 having annihilated the last vestige of Poland's independence and constitution, her Orders were united with those of Russia, and the 'White Eagle' with altered insignia (Tab. IV. Nos. 17 and 18), occupies now the rank next to the 'Alexander Newsky.' It has at present only one class.

The diploma of presentation is always signed by the Czar himself, and written for Russians in the Russian language, and for Poles in both Polish and Russian. But as all the Russian Orders are placed under the patronage of saints, the White Eagle is usually conferred on non-christians, such as the Shah of Persia, and other eastern Princes.

An ukase of the 29th March, 1835, ordered, that all those Knights who are in possession of the decorations of Alexander Newsky, White Eagle, St. Stanislaus, and St. Ann first class, should wear round the neck the Polish cross, at the side of the Russian.

The entrance fee of the Order is 150 roubles.

THE ORDER OF SAINT STANISLAUS

Was founded on the 7th May, 1765, by Stanislaus Augustus Poniatowsky, to procure friends and adherents to his throne. He placed it under the patronage of St. Stanislaus, the patron saint of his country, as also of his own name.

The number of Knights was fixed at one hundred, exclusive of foreigners. The badge was a red enamelled cross, attached to a poppy red ribbon with white borders, worn across the right shoulder towards the left side: the middle of the cross, rested upon the Polish White Eagle, and on the obverse appeared a representation of the patron saint of the Order clad in the episcopalian ornaments, with the initials 'S. S.' (St. Stanislaus) at the side, while the reverse showed the initials of the King. The star which the Knights wore on the left side of the breast, was of silver, and exhibited in the middle the red initials of the King twisted round a lancet, and in the red ring, with golden edges, the legend: 'Præmiando incitat' (Encouraged by reward).

The lavishness, however, with which the Order was distributed, soon lost it all due respect, while the division of Poland brought it into entire oblivion, though it reappeared on the stage for a while on the restoration of the other Polish Orders in 1807.

When the Duchy of Warsaw, subsequently, united her ill fate with that of France, the Emperor Alexander, as King of Poland, confirmed the Order on the 1st December, 1815, but wrought various modifications in it; he divided into four classes, and imposed upon the Knights (16th December, 1816) the annual tax of 4, 3, 2 and 1 ducats (according to the respective four classes), in support of the Foundling Hospital at Warsaw, a contribution that had indeed been instituted already at the first foundation of the Order.

After the Revolution of 1831, the Emperor Nicholas united the Order of St. Stanislaus (on the 29th November, 1831) with the Russian ones, placed it next in rank to St. Ann, first class, and made various alterations in the insignia.

Eight years afterwards, the Order was limited to three classes.

With the third class decoration, are rewarded all those who have sacrificed their property for the good of the country, or have served the state gratuitously for a whole year in some function or other. It is also presented to the trustees of private institutions under the same conditions, and with the same privileges as the Order of St. Anne; useful works or inventions, as also detection of serious abuses, or crime, equally entitle individuals to the decoration.

The Commander of an active army has the right to bestow the second and third class decorations for deeds of valour.

The entrance fee is 90, 30 or 15 roubles, according to the respective classes. The money thus collected, is applied to certain useful objects suggested by the Emperor. Those who have been invested with the Order since 1831, become thereby hereditary nobles. Previously, that favour was confined to members of the first class alone.

Russian priests are excluded from the Order, and it is unnecessary to add that the nobility thus conferred on Roman Catholic priests cannot become hereditary.

Thirty members of the first class, sixty of the second, and ninety of the third class receive respectively annual pensions of 142, 114 and 85 roubles. Those who advance to a higher class lose their previous pensions, and must wait until their turn comes in the new class. Members who turn monks lose their pensions. Widows receive the full pensions of their husbands during the first year of their widowhood.

In case of death, the insignia must be returned, or the value paid in money.

The annual festival of the Order is held on the 23rd April (7th May).

The sketch of the cross will be found in Tab. IV. No. 20, and that of the star, first class, under No. 19.

ORDER OF MILITARY MERIT.

The new constitution proclaimed in Poland, on the 3rd May, 1791, met the approval of Prussia, Saxony and other foreign courts, and was received with unfeigned applause by the nation at large. Its opponents, however, whose selfish discontent with the new arrangements fully met the ambitious views of the Empress Catharine II., concluded with her Majesty on the 24th May, 1792, the secret convention of Targowitz which induced the Empress to send her troops across the frontier of Poland. The Poles courageously accepted the challenge, and investing Stanislaus Augustus with the chief command, provided from their own resources all the necessary means for the defence of the state. Stanislaus then founded the Order of Miltary Merit, but having at the head of the troops transferred the chief command to his nephew Joseph Poniatowsky, he ordered him to retire before the Russians.

Soon afterwards (25th August) he acceded, himself, to the Targowitz convention, subscribed to all its conditions, annulled the constitution, and even abolished the Order of his own creation, instructing the Knights who were in possession of it, to return the insignia to the treasury.

The establishment, however, of the Duchy of Warsaw, in 1807, restored the ephemeral existence of the Order, under the Grand Mastership of King Frederick Augustus of Saxony.

The Emperor Alexander did not interfere with the Order, even after his having taken possession of Poland; it thus dragged on its

RUSSIA. *Table V.* PLATE 75.

21

24

22

23

nominally independent existence until 1831, when it shared the fate of all the other Polish Orders. The Emperor Nicholas gave it a new form, placed it in the third rank of the Russian Orders, and, having divided it into five classes, decreed the discontinuance of new distributions, thus condemning it, as it were, to a slow extinction.

The badge of the first class consists of a star (Tab. V. No. 21) worn upon the left side of the breast, and of the decoration (No. 22), appended to a ribbon thrown under the uniform across the right shoulder towards the left side. The Knights of the second class wear the same cross suspended by a ribbon round the neck, while those of the three other classes wear it at the button-hole, the only distinction consisting in the appearance of the cross, which is in the third class, of enamelled gold, in the fourth class, of gold with enamel, and in the fifth class of silver (Tab. V. No. 23 .

MEDALS AND DECORATIONS OF HONOUR.

1. *The Maria Medal*, was founded on the 14th October, 1828, in memory of Maria Feodorowna, by her son, the Emperor Nicholas. It is a decoration reserved solely for ladies of unblemished character, for faithful service. It consists of two classes. The decoration of the first is worn on a scarf across the shoulder, and the second on the breast. The badge of the first class consists of a gold blue enamelled cross, the middle of which contains the name 'Maria' and a laurel branch with the number (in Roman cyphers) of the years of service, while that of the second class consists of a blue medal, also with the name and number on it. The ribbon is that of the Vladimir Order. The decoration is usually conferred

on the directresses and inspectresses of the institutions under the immediate management of the Empress Maria.

The first class decoration is bestowed on ladies who have acted in the above capacities for twenty-five years and upwards, and the second class for fifteen years' service. The claims of the candidates are examined by a board of the charitable institutions, and submitted to the Emperor for approval. The possessors cannot, under any circumstances, be deprived of the Order.

2. *The Ismail Cross* was founded by the Empress Catharine II. The Russian inscription signifies: 'Ismail taken on the 2nd December, 1790' (Tab. V. No. 24).

3. *The Gold Medal* was founded by the Emperor Alexander, as a reward for officers. It is worn at the button-hole, suspended by the St. George's ribbon (Tab. VII. No. 30), and counts for three years, as regards the title to pension, or to the St. George's Cross.

4. *Medal for* 1807, is of gold for officers, and of silver for the militia (dissolved in September of that year), who took part in any one of the battles of that period. It is worn suspended by the St. George's ribbon. To officers who were not present at any battle, it was presented with the St. Vladimir ribbon.

5. *Cross of Bazardjick*, was also founded by the Emperor Alexander, and worn by the St. George's ribbon. It bears on the obverse, the inscription (in Russian): 'For the storming and taking of Bazardjick, on the 22nd May, 1810,' and on the reverse, 'For distinguished Merit' (Plate 74, Tab. VI. No. 25).

6. *Medal of* 1812, was distributed amongst the Russian troops who shared in the campaign of 1812. It is of silver for the officers, and copper for the men; it is worn by the military, suspended by the Vladimir ribbon, and by

RUSSIA. *Table VI.* PLATE 74.

RUSSIA. Table VII. PLATE 75.

31

32

30

33

34

Hurst and Blackett, London. 1858.

civilians (surgeons, &c.) by a blue ribbon. It bears the inscription (in Russian) 'Not to us, but to thy name, O Lord, are praise, honour and thanks due' (Tab. VI. Nos. 26 and 27).

7. *Medal of* 1814, is of silver, and worn by a ribbon, partly blue, and partly of the colour of the St. George's ribbon. The obverse contains the Russian inscription: 'For the taking of Paris, on the 19th March, 1814,' the reverse is sketched in Tab. VI. No. 28.

8. *Medal for the Persian campaign*, is also of silver, and worn by a ribbon composed of the colours of St. Vladimir and St. George. It was founded by the Emperor Nicholas as a reward for the troops who made that campaign. The obverse exhibits the eye (Omnipresence) of God, and two laurel branches, between which are placed the years: 1826, 1827, and 1828 (Tab. VI. No. 29), and the reverse shows the words: 'For the Persian War.'

9. *Medal for the Turkish campaign*, is equally of silver, and shows on the obverse, a radiant cross over a half-moon or crescent, and the years: '1828, 1829,' and on the reverse, the words: 'For the Turkish War' (Tab. VII. No. 31).

10. *Medal for the taking of Warsaw*. It is of silver, and was distributed amongst the troops who were present at the storming of that city. The obverse shows the Imperial Eagle, with the inscription: 'For the taking of Warsaw on the 26th September, 1831.' The reverse contains the words: 'Utility, Honour, and Glory.' It is worn suspended by a blue ribbon with black borders (Tab. VII. No. 32).

11. *Decorations of Service*. The Emperor Nicholas instituted decorations of honour for long and faithful service, of, at least, fifteen years. It shows the years of service 'XV.' in Roman cyphers, and is worn fastened to the left side of

the breast, by military persons suspended by the St. George's ribbon (Plate 75, Tab. VII. No. 33), and by civilians, by the St. Vladimir ribbon (No. 34).

Merchants are presented, for various services, with a gold medal of moderate size, which bears on the obverse the portrait of the Emperor, and on the reverse the words 'For zealous services' or 'For utility,' the former words are inscribed on the medals of those who have distinguished themselves in their civic or government functions, and the latter on the medals of those who have effected much in manufactures and industry. These medals are worn round the neck by ribbons of the advancing degrees of the following Orders, viz. St. Ann, Alexander Newsky, St. Vladimir and St. Andrew. For those who are already in possession of all these ribbons the inscription is further adorned with diamonds. Even mechanics and country people are not, with the exception of the diamond adornment, excluded from the medal, or any of the ribbons.

Mahometans in civil or military service, are presented, if they have served against the enemy, with a gold or silver medal, which bears the inscription 'for valour,' and is worn round the neck attached to the St. George's ribbon.

For saving from fire or drowning, noblemen, functionaries and merchants receive a gold medal with the inscription 'For saving the emperilled,' while sub-officers, privates, mechanics and peasants receive the same medal in silver. It is worn at the button-hole, suspended by either the St. Ann or St. Vladimir ribbon.

The latter decorations, when obtained for deeds of humanity towards fellow-creatures, are subject to no fee whatever, while all the other medals are to be paid for, according to the ribbon by which they are suspended, with a sum varying from seven to a hundred and fifty roubles.

Persons in possession of any of the medals worn round the neck, are exempt from military service, while the owners of any of the other medals are, at least, exempt from corporal punishment.

There are besides various decorations of cloth, velvet or damask, chiefly given as rewards to country people or rural labourers.

SARDINIA.

THE ORDER OF THE ANNUNCIATION.

Historians, though they seem to agree that this Order was founded by Count Amadeus VI. of Savoy, under the name of: 'the Order of the neck-chain or collar,' are yet at variance about the cause of its foundation; some attribute it to an act of gallantry, and others to a sentiment of piety. Possibly it owed its origin to both causes combined, since the spirit of that age usually blended together the two feelings of love and religion.

Count Amadeus ordered in his will the establishment of a cloister at Pièrre Castle in Bugey, where fifteen Carthusian Priors were to read mass daily in honour of the fifteen Joys of the Blessed Virgin, and for the welfare of fifteen Knights.

The Cloister was finished in 1392, and the fickle Amadeus VIII. first Duke of Savoy, who first exchanged the crown for the tiara, and then again resigned the chair of St. Peter to enjoy the pleasures of Rippaille (at the Geneva Lake), held in the latter place, 1410, the first Chapter of the Order, and proclaimed its first statutes.

The Order which was placed under the Grand Mastership of the Dukes of Savoy, was only accessible to the high and ancient nobility of unblemished repute in virtue and honour, nor was it allowed to to be worn with any other decoration.

SARDINIA. *Table I.* PLATE 76.

The chief duties of the Knighs were:

1. To assist the Dukes of Savoy by word and deed on every occasion, and at any time they should stand in need of that assistance.

2. To protect the oppressed.

3. To submit their own disputes to the judgment of the Chapter.

4. To wear constantly the collar or chain of the Order, which is composed alternally of love-knots and the old-fashioned letters: 'F. E. R. T.'*

5. To present the Church of Pièrre Castel with a chalice, a surplice and all the other articles requisite for the celebration of Mass.

6. To bequeath, at their death, 100 livres for the support of that Church, and to enjoin their heirs to have read one hundred masses.

At funerals of members, the whole fraternity used to be present, dressed originally in white, and subsequently in black cloaks, which they abandoned, after the ceremony, to the Carthusian monks. On all other occasions, the colour of the cloak or mantle was crimson, trimmed with fringes and embroidered with love-knots.

Charles III. of Savoy, proclaimed, on the 11th September, 1518, new statutes, and, at the same time, he gave to the Order, a new name: that 'of the Holy Annunciation;' he also added, round the motto of the collar, fifteen roses, (seven white, seven red, and one of both colours), and to the fifteen Knights, five Officers: a Chan-

---

* They have reference to an old motto of the Counts of Savoy, and supposed to be the initials of: 'Fortitudo ejus Rhodum tenuit' (Rhodes was kept by his bravery), in allusion to the exploits of Amadeus V. against the Turks.

cellor, Secretary, Master of Ceremonies, Treasurer and Herald.

The statutes received further modifications under Emanuel Philibert (on the 18th October, 1577), and under Charles Emanuel.

The latter having in 1620 ceded to Henry IV., Bresse and Bugey in exchange for the Marquisate of Saluzzo, transferred the Chapter, first to the St. Dominican Church at Montmeillan, and thence to the hermitage of the Camaldali Monks upon the Turin mountain.

The costume under Emanuel Philibert consisted of a sky blue mantle, lined with white taffetas, and trimmed with rich gold embroidery. Since 1627, however, the colour of the mantle is amaranth, lined with blue silk, and embroidered with silver.

Victor Amadeus on becoming, by the peace of Utrecht, ruler of Sicily, which he was, however, afterwards obliged to restore in exchange for Sardinia, placed upon his own head the royal crown, raised the 'Order of the Annunciation' to the first rank of the Orders in his kingdom, abolished the limitation in the number of Knights, accorded to the latter, the title of "Excellency," and decreed that they should be chosen from amongst the Knights of St. Lazarus and Mauritius, as also from the ancient pure nobility.

The Order has only one class. The decoration (Plate 76, Tab. I. No. 2), is a gold medal, on which is represented the Annunciation, surrounded by love-knots. It is usually worn suspended by a simple gold chain, except on the nomination and the two following days, on the great festivals of the year, the Corpus Christi, the festivals of the Blessed Virgin, the Circumcision, the festival of St. Maurice, (the patron of Savoy), as also on the day when the Knights take the sacrament, and on the eve of a battle, when the Knights are wont to assemble round a standard, and lastly at the meeting of the Chapter, on all which occasions it is worn appended to the gold collar, which, however, can never be adorned with precious stones or pearls.

Since 1680, the Knights wear, on the left side of the breast, a star (No. 1). embroidered in gold.

The costume has been frequently altered. At present it consists of a garment of white taffetas, with golden embroidery, of a sword, of a cap edged with fur, and with a long flap of sky blue velvet, and finally of a mantle over the whole.

Three months after the death of a member, the decoration, costume, and the volume of the statutes must be returned to the Chapter by his heirs.

The Abbots of St. Gallen were always exempted from that rule, their successors being the legitimate inheritors of the collar and rank of the Order.

The four supreme officers of the Order: the Chancellor, (who must always be a Bishop or Archbishop), the Secretary, (usually the Minister of Foreign Affairs), the Almoner, (usually first Almoner of the King), and the Treasurer, wear the decoration round the neck, suspended by a sky blue ribbon, accompanied by a star on the left side of the breast.

The Herald, usually the first brigadier of the royal guard, wears a cross, exhibiting the Annunciation, at the button-hole, suspended by a sky blue ribbon.

All the officers of the Order have separate costumes of their own.

The annual festival is held on Annunciation Day (25th March).

ORDER OF SAINT MAURICE AND LAZARUS.

When the Reformation had crossed the German frontier, and began to find adherents in the South of Europe, the Roman

Church, and the Catholic Princes attached to her, saw the necessity of increasing their means of defence. To arrest the progress of the Calvinistic doctrines in Savoy, the Duke Emanuel Philibert founded in 1572, the Order of St. Maurice, imposing upon the Knights, the duty of defending the Catholic religion. The Order was confirmed by a Bull of the 14th September of the same year, by Pope Gregory XIII., and to increase still more the strength and power of this new chivalrous militia, the Pope united with it a part of the Order of St. Lazarus, transferring to the new Order the Commanderies, which the latter had possessed in Spain and Italy. The Grand Mastership he vested in the crown of Savoy; while, in the new decoration, were also inserted the white cross of St. Maurice, and the green one of St. Lazarus.

In this form, the Order existed until the incorporation of Piedmont with France, but was subsequently reinstituted anew with the restoration of the old monarchy, though only in the character of a mere Order of Merit, indiscriminately for all subjects. This new organisation as proclaimed by Victor Emanuel, on the 27th December, 1816, was somewhat modified by Charles Albert, and was by a later decree of the 9th December, 1831, divided into three classes: Knights, Commanders, and Knights Grand Cross.

The Knights are subdivided into Cavalieri di Giustizia, (Knights by right), and Cavalieri di Grazia (Knights by favour).

The former must undergo the strict probations prescribed by the statutes, and receive the diploma on payment of entrance fee.

The latter receive it as a reward for long military service, in the grade of Lieutenant-Colonel; it is also granted to civilians, who have rendered important services to charitable institutions by rich donations, establishment of benefices, or voluntary official service. The honorary, or members by favour, are not subject to any fee, or vow, except on receiving a pension from the King. The diploma is the same as with the former. All members indiscriminately may aspire to the highest degrees of the Order.

The badge consists of a green ribbon. The smaller cross is sketched in Plate 76, Tab. I. No. 4, and that of the Commanders in No. 5. The latter is somewhat larger, and is worn round the neck. The number of the Commanders is fixed at fifty, who receive the cross after having made the necessary vow of the Order, which must be done within six months after their nomination, if not already made by them as simple Knights.

The number of the Knights Grand Cross is limited to thirty. Their cross is surmounted by a crown, and is worn across the right shoulder towards the left side by a broad ribbon, and accompanied by a star on the left side of the breast, embroidered in gold and silver (Nos. 1 to 3). They may make use of the small cross when not wearing the insignia of their proper class.

The Royal Princes, Knights of the Annunciation Order and Foreigners, are not included in the number fixed for the two first classes.

The Grand Dignitaries of the Order are: the Grand Prior, Grand Hospitaller, Grand Guardian or Conservator, Grand Chancellor, and Grand Treasurer.

Their respective tasks are defined by the statutes of 1816, while the oldest of them usually occupies the chair. Only Knights of the Grand Cross can aspire to any of these dignities. The Council is composed of the above five dignitaries, of the Auditor-General, of the first Secretary, of the Grand Master, and of the Secretary appointed by the Council. With the exception of the five Dignitaries, the members of the Council, must, at least, belong to the class of Commander.

In each of the provinces of the Kingdom: in Turin, Coni, Alessandria, Novara, Aosta, Savoy, Genoa, and Nizza, a Knight Grand Cross or Commander, bearing the title of Provincial Chief, is entrusted with the management or superintendence of the estates of the Order.

When a member shows himself, by some action, unworthy of the Order, the Provincial Chief reports the circumstance to the first Secretary, and the Council, empowered by the Grand Master, pronounce sentence upon the accused.

The aspirants to the Order, or those who wish either to found or enjoy a prebendary, by family right, must apply to the Provincial Chief by petition, which is forwarded to the first Secretary, whose duty it is to prevent the admission of unworthy individuals.

The Knights and other officials who are entrusted by the Grand Master with the direction of hospitals, independent of the Order, receive a proportionate remuneration.

With the exception of a sum of 30,000 lire, the revenues of the Order are divided into five parts.

1. Costs of building and administration.
2. Gratuities for real or honorary Knights.
3. Funds derived from nomination fees, &c. applied for the institution of new pensions.
4. Sums for the maintenance of the hospitals of the Order, &c.
5. Reserve fund for miscellaneous outlays, and accidents.

A commission is appointed by the King to review occasionally the Administration of the Order with a view, possibly, to diminish the expenses on the one hand, and increase the reserve fund on the other.

The sum fixed for the Commanderies and pensions, amounts to 200,000 lire, which are divided as follow: five Commanderies at 4000, six at 3000, ten at 2500, twenty-five at 1000, and one hundred and twenty pensions at 600 each. The reserve fund receives 20,000 lire.

The officers of the Order are remunerated by the Grand Master with either Commanderies or pensions.

The entrance fee is fixed at 1500 francs.

No alteration can be made in the administration of the estates of the Order in Sardinia.

ROYAL MILITARY ORDER OF SAVOY.

This Order was founded by King Victor Emanuel. The warrant is dated Genoa, 14th August, 1815, in which the Order is described as a purely military one, given as a reward for prudent valour upon the field of battle or elsewhere.

The King and his presumptive successor is chief, or Grand Master.

The decoration consists of a red enamelled cross of gold, or silver, resting upon a green enamelled garland, upon which is placed another white enamelled cross. The reverse is not enamelled, and shows the crowned initials of the King, 'V. E.' Above the cross is a crown, and the whole is worn by a blue ribbon. (Plate 77. Tab. II. No. 7).

The Order is divided into four classes.

The first class, that of the Grand Cross, wear the decoration across the right shoulder towards the left side by a broad ribbon about two inches and a half wide, and have a star on the left side of the breast. (Tab. II. No. 6).

Except on solemn occasions, the ribbon is worn under the coat.

If already a Knight of the Order of the Annunciation, the new star is fastened below that of the latter.

The second class, or the Commanders, wear the decoration

of one inch in diameter round the neck suspended by a ribbon about one inch three quarters wide.

The third class, or Knights, suspend the decoration of three quarters of an inch in diameter, at the button-hole by a ribbon about one inch wide.

The decoration of the fourth class, or privates, is of silver, three quarters of an inch in diameter, and is worn by a ribbon about one inch wide without bow or rosette.

The Order has three functionaries, a Chancellor, a Treasurer, and a Secretary. The two first must be Commanders, the third is chosen from amongst the Knights. The salary of the Chancellor is 2000, of the Treasurer 1500, and of the Secretary 1800 lire. There is also a Herald with a salary of 800 lire.

With the exception of the Crown Prince, who may without further ceremony be nominated by the King, provided he has been present in one or more campaigns of the country, no one can be admitted to the Order without first submitting to the following formalities:

The candidates must apply direct, or through their superiors, to the War Chancellory, which then communicates the request to the Secretary. This functionary submits the petition to a tribunal composed of two members of each class, always chosen by the Grand Master from the resident Knights of the place. The oldest member of the first class is invariably President of the Tribunal. Having examined the merits of the petition, and found them well founded, the tribunal reports the case to the Grand Master, and proposes the class to which the candidate ought to be admitted in conformity with the following principle.

To the fourth class, for a deed of personal valour.

To the third class, for personal valour and skilful guidance displayed on occasions wherein the candidate commanded a detachment.

SARDINIA. Table II.   PLATE 77.

To the first and second classes, for distinguished merit in those entrusted with the command of a regiment, division, or army.

Should the Grand Master approve of the proposal, the candidate receives from the tribunal the diploma or patent, while he is decorated with the insignia by a Knight specially commissioned by the Grand Master for the purpose, in the presence of the troops, after having had read to him the following oath:

"You swear that you will live and die true to the King and to "honour, that you will never bear arms in foreign service, nor "ever belong, without royal permission, to any sect or associa- "tion, contrary to the loyalty you have sworn to your King, or "in opposition to the laws of the land."

Whereupon the candidate laying his hand upon his heart, answers: "I swear it."

The nomination of a new Knight is made known to all regiments, and to the public at large by the public press, in which the merits of the claim are given in full detail.

Knights, who are not officers by rank, receive an annual pension of 120 lire.

The claim to the Order is not confined to Catholics alone. Christians of any denomination may aspire to it.

All Knights are allowed to adorn the decoration with their own crests.

The annual festival is held on St. Amadeus' day.

CIVIL ORDER OF SAVOY

Was founded by King Charles Albert, at Turin, on the 30th October, 1831. The statutes say:

"The history of past ages, as also the events of recent

" and the present times, have incontestably shown, that rewards
" of Merit, when impartially granted, lead to emulation, and,
" thereby, to the rapid promotion of the glory and welfare of
" states, by imparting to all talents and capacities, a precise
" direction towards all and everything that is useful, grand,
" and beautiful.

" Our predecessor, King Victor Emanuel, of glorious
" memory, founded, in 1815, the Order of Savoy, to
" reward brilliant military merit, by honourable distinction.
" We are of opinion, that it behoves us to imitate his
" example, and complete his work, by bestowing another
" decoration on those of our subjects who have chosen a
" different, but not less useful, career in life, than the military,
" and have become the ornaments of our country, to which
" they have rendered important services by long study, and
" great efforts of mind. Our attention has particularly been
" drawn to those who have devoted themselves to education,
" and produced great results, on which we place the more
" value, as we are convinced that the well-being of indi-
" viduals, of families, and of the whole nation, depends chiefly
" on the good education of youth.

" Our intention is, therefore, that the rewards which we
" have resolved to institute for Civil Merit, should be granted
" only, after a strict and careful examination of the claims
" thereto, for which purpose we have entrusted the task to
" those who are mostly interested in the preservation of our
" institutions. The decoration, we are sure, will the more
" command respect, the more it is confined exclusively
" to individuals of known merit, and unsullied name, in
" principle and practical life; as, also, to those who are attached
" to our person, and devoted to our laws. We therefore
" decree that:

" 1. In founding for ever the Civil Order of Savoy, we

" declare ourselves Grand Master of the same, which dignity
" shall pass, after us, to the successor and heir of our throne.

" 2. There shall be only one class of Knights in the Order,
" consisting of natives, or resident foreigners.

" 3. The Knights shall wear a blue enamelled cross,
" the round middle of which shall bear on the obverse,
" the initial of the founder, and on the reverse, the words:
" 'Al Merito Civile, 1831' (Plate 77. Tab. II. Nos. 8
" and 9).

" 4. This cross shall be worn on the left side of the breast,
" suspended by a blue ribbon with two white stripes.

" 5. The decoration shall be conferred:

" *a.* On the higher functionaries of our government, for zeal
" displayed in their respective departments. *b.* On literary men
" and authors, who shall have published at home, or (with our
" permission) abroad, some important work of literary merit.
" *c.* On engineers, builders, and artists of distinguished merit.
" *d.* On those who have discovered a new useful invention, or
" wrought important improvements in the old. *e.* On professors
" who have effected much good in education, and acquired a
" great name by their knowledge and writings on subjects
" connected with it.

" 6. The candidates for the Order shall submit to us their
" request, accompanied by the necessary testimonials, through
" our Secretary of the Interior. The petition shall then be for-
" warded by us to the Council, composed of seven Knights,
" and a President appointed by ourselves.

" 7. The Council shall take proper information of the
" social position, merits, and principles, both moral and political,
" of the aspirant.

" 8. This done, a secret vote is to be taken, and report
" made of the result of the votes.

" 9. Our Minister of the Interior shall then communicate to

"us the decision of the Council in all the details, which we may
"sanction or not, according to our view of the case.

"10. The same Minister shall lay before us, for signature,
"the diploma of the approved candidate, who is to take the
"oath in his presence, binding himself to be true to us, to
"obey our laws, not to violate morals and decency in his
"works, and not to teach anything that may clash with the
"Roman Catholic creed, or with the principles of our
"monarchy.

"11. The Knights of the Civil Order of Savoy shall be
"admitted to Court, and the same marks of honour shall
"be shown to them as to the Knights of St. Maurice,
"St. Lazarus, or of the Military Order of Savoy.

"12. The following pensions shall be attached to the
"Order, namely: 1000 lire to ten Knights, 800 to ten, and
"600 to twenty, making a total of forty members, enjoying
"pensions amounting in all to 30,000 lire."

DECORATIONS OF HONOUR.

1. *Cross of Loyalty.*—It was founded in 1814, by Victor Emanuel, for those of his subjects who gave proofs of loyalty and devotion to him during the French occupation of the country.

2. *Military Medal.*—As the rigour and strict limitation of the statutes frequently interfered with the bestowal of the Military Cross for noble and heroic deeds, which had proved of important benefit to the country and the army, King Charles Albert instituted, on the 26th March, 1833, for the army and navy, a decoration consisting of a gold and silver medal, (Plate 77. Tab. II. Nos. 10 and 11), of which the obverse shows a cross beneath a crown, with the legend: 'Al valore militare,'

and the reverse two laurel branches, with the name of the recipient engraved between them. On the edge is stated the deed for which, and the day on which, it was bestowed.

The medal may be claimed by any military person in active service, and the recipient is entitled to the same rights and display of honour as are the possessors of the 'Military Order of Savoy.' In addition, a pension is attached to the possession of the medal, viz.: 100 lire to the owner of the gold, and 50 lire to the possessor of the silver medal. Both medal and pension pass to the widow of the deceased owner, so long as she remains single, or to his children until they pass the fifteenth year of their age.

SAXONY.

ORDER OF THE RUE CROWN.

Napoleon having raised Saxony to a kingdom, the new King, Frederick Augustus, yielded to the general wish and founded a separate Order for his monarchy. The suggestion, in fact, emanated from Napoleon himself, whose portrait adorned the original decoration. In the warrant, dated 20th July, 1807, the King says: "that it was his intention to bequeath to his successors a remembrance of the time when Providence showed itself so favourable to Saxony, and his own house; and to furnish them, moreover, with the means of rewarding in a brilliant manner those of their subjects who might distinguish themselves in devotion to fatherland."

The King is Grand Master, and his sons and nephews are born Knights of the Order.

To the King, is reserved the exclusive right to admit into it other Princes of his house, as well as foreign Princes and grandees.

The obverse of the decoration (Plate 78. Tab. I. No. 2) shows the initials F. A. surmounted by the royal crown, and the reverse, the motto: 'Providentiæ memor,' (Mindful of Providence). It is worn across the right shoulder, towards the left hip by a broad green watered ribbon.

In the octagonal radiant star which the Knights wear on the left side of the breast, is a medal surrounded by the

SAXONY. Table I.

PLATE 78.

lozenge crown, and containing, upon golden ground, the motto of the Order. (Tab. I. No. 1.)

It has no statutes.

THE MILITARY ORDER OF SAINT HENRY.

This Order, destined as a reward for distinguished merit upon the battle field, was originated by Augustus III. King of Poland, and Elector of Saxony, who decorated with it, on his fortieth birth-day (7th October, 1739), at Hubertsburgh, himself, the Crown Prince and several of his Generals. At that time the Order consisted of only one class, while the badge was a red enamelled cross, with the Polish white eagle in the angles, and the figure of St. Henry in the middle, It was worn upon the breast suspended by a dark red ribbon with white borders.

In this state and form, it remained until the 4th September, 1768, when Prince Xavier, administrator of the Electorate, divided the Knights into three classes, altering at the same time the shape and form of the decoration. No further distribution took place until 1796, when seven more Knights were decorated with the Order. In 1807, however, numerous distributions were made in all the three classes.

On the 23rd December, 1829, King Antony added a new class to the former, that of second class Commanders, and proclaimed also the following statutes:

1. The Order is to bear the name of the Saxon Emperor St. Henry.

2. The Grand Mastership to be vested in the Crown of Saxony.

3. The Military Members to be divided into four classes: Knights, Grand Cross Commanders, first and second classes,

and Knights. The number is unlimited, while the Commanders previously nominated are to belong to the first class.

4. The badge to consist of a gold octagonal cross, with wide edges enamelled white. The middle, to show a round yellow enamelled scutcheon, containing the portrait of the Emperor Henry in armour and full imperial state robes, as also the name 'St. Henricus,' beneath it. The blue ring round it, to exhibit the legend: 'Frederick Augustus.' D. G. Rex Saxoniæ instauravit.'

The reverse of the cross to be blue enamelled, and to show the royal Saxon arms, with the inscription 'Virtuti in Bello.' The four angles round the middle to be filled out with green branches of the Saxon rue wreath. This decoration is to be of three different sizes, for three different classes.

5. The Knights of the Grand Cross, to wear the decoration of the largest size across the right shoulder, towards the left hip, by a wide (three inches wide) sky blue ribbon, with citron coloured stripes near the borders, and accompanied by an octagonal radiant star, embroidered in gold, and fastened to the coat on the left side, and measuring four inches from point to point. The middle of the obverse to show the above motto: 'Virtuti in Bello.'

The Commanders, of both classes, to wear the cross of middle size round the neck suspended by a similar ribbon three inches wide, and those of the first class to have, in addition, fastened to the left side of the coat the above star of smaller size, measuring only three inches from point to point.

The Knights to wear the small cross at the second buttonhole suspended by a similar ribbon of only two inches wide.

These decorations are to be constantly worn by the members.

6. With the exception of the monarch as Grand Master, and the royal Prince, no member to be allowed, without special permission, to adorn the decoration with precious stones.

7. The right of nomination is vested in the Crown of Saxony, though the opinion and recommendation of the commanding Generals is each time taken into consideration on the subject.

This military Order is instituted solely for superior officers in the Saxon service, without regard to religious persuasion, birth, or length of service. Its sole claim rests on merit, or distinction in the field, added to loyalty to the King and devotion to the country: no officer is allowed to petition for it.

In promotions, the Knights Grand Cross are selected from the class of Commanders, and the latter from that of the Knights, so that no one can be admitted to a higher class without having first belonged to the inferior. Promotion, as stated above, depends solely on renewed distinction, without regard to seniority in years or service. The Grand Cross is, however, strictly limited to Lieutenant-Generals who have commanded a corps in the field, while the Commander-Cross, first class, is confined to Lieutenant-Generals, or Major-Generals who have commanded a brigade in the field, and that of the second class Commanders is reserved for staff-officers who have acted as such in a campaign.

With this Order, are connected as a fifth class, the gold and silver medals of military merit, which were first instituted on the 17th of March, 1796, for sub-officers and men. They are usually distributed on the field of battle, on the recommendation of the Commander-in-Chief.

These medals bear on the obverse the portrait of the founder with the usual inscription, and on the reverse a garland adorned with arms, and within it the words: 'Verdienst um das Vaterland' (Merit of the fatherland). They are worn at the second button-hole, suspended by a blue ribbon with yellow stripes at the borders, but narrower by one-third than that of the Order of St. Henry. The gold medal can only be granted to those who are already in possession of the silver, in which case the latter is returned, and the owner receives for it a gratuity of 25 thalers.

After the death of the owner, the medal is restored to the War Chancellory, and the widow, children or parents of the deceased, receive in return a gratuity of 100 thalers for the gold, and 25 thalers for the silver medal.

ORDER OF MERIT.

After the battle of Leipsic, King Frederick Augustus remained for twenty months a prisoner in the hands of the allied powers, while Saxony was, during that period, governed partly by Russia and partly by Prussia. He was at last, on the 7th of June, 1815, allowed to return to his capital, and resume the independent government of his now greatly curtailed kingdom. On the same day, he founded the Order of Merit, the first distribution of which took place on the 23rd December in that year.

Representations of the cross are given in Plate 79, Tab. II., Nos. 6 and 7, and that of the medal of the fourth class, either gold (weighing 8 ducats) or silver, will be found in No. 8 of that Table. If the cross is presented to foreigners, it bears the simple inscription: 'Dem Verdienst' (To merit).

The right of conferring the Order, belongs exclusively to the King.

Every subject who has rendered useful services to the state, or otherwise distinguished himself by civil virtues may aspire to the Order. Nor are foreigners who have claims on the acknowledgment of the King or state, excluded.

The Order consists of three classes: Knights of the Grand

SAXONY. *Table* II. PLATE 79.

Cross, Commanders, and Knights. The fourth class comprises the recipients of the civil medal.

The badge of the Order is: a gold octagonal cross enamelled white. The round white middle has a gold ring, and shows on the obverse the Saxon arms, and the legend: 'Friedrich August, König von Sachsen, den 7ten Juni, 1815,' and on the reverse an oaken wreath, in which are intertwined the words: 'Für Verdienst und Treue' (For merit and loyalty).

The civil medal exhibits, on the obverse, the royal effigy with the above legend, while the reverse is precisely the same as that of the Order.

The 7th June is generally fixed for the distribution of the decoration, and promotions in the Order.

The Knights of the Grand Cross wear the badge across the right shoulder, by a broad white watered ribbon (four inches wide), with two grass-green stripes, and accompanied by a silver sextuple and radiant star on the left side of the breast, containing the oaken wreath and inscription as above.

The commanders wear the same cross round the neck by a similar ribbon three inches wide, while the Knights have the cross in smaller size, fastened to the second button-hole by a bow of the same ribbon, two inches wide.

By a decree of the 24th September, 1849, the Order of Civil Merit was extended to Military and other distinctions, and it passes now by the simple name: Order of Merit. It has undergone the following alterations:

1. It now consists without the medal, of five classes: Knights Grand Cross, Commanders, first and second classes, and Knights, first and second classes.

2. The medal is also divided into two classes for the gold and silver ones.

3. The Commanders first class, wear now in addition, on

the left side of the breast a square silver star, similar to that of the Grand Cross.

4. The small cross is of silver, with the white enamelled middle of the cross of the Knights.

THE ORDER OF ALBERT.

It is represented in Plate 78. No. 2, and was founded on the 31st December, 1850, by King Frederick Augustus, in memory of the founder of the Albert line, of the House of Saxony, Duke Albert the Bold.

The claim to this Order is founded on merit in general, civil, military, literary or scientific.

It consists of five classes: Grand Cross Knights, Commanders, first and second classes, Knights, first and second classes.

The decoration for the first four classes consists of an oblong gold cross, enamelled white, with the lower arm much larger than the others. It has small mountings of gold, and a white enamelled middle, the obverse of which exhibits, within a blue enamelled centre, the effigy of Duke Albert in gold relief, while the circle round it contains the legend: 'Albertus animosus.' The reverse shows the Saxon arms, and within a blue ring, the year '1850.' The cross is, moreover, placed on a green enamelled oaken wreath worked in relief.

The decoration of the first three classes is of the same size, and surmounted by a gold crown, which is omitted in the somewhat smaller crosses of the two other classes.

The small cross is of silver. Its obverse shows the effigy of Duke Albert, and the engraved words: 'Albertus animosus,' while the reverse exhibits the Saxon arms and the year of the foundation of the Order.

The Knights of the Grand Cross wear the decoration across the right shoulder by a green watered ribbon, three and a half inches wide, and with two white stripes across the whole length. They have also, by an octagonal radiant silver star, fastened to the left side of the breast, and containing, on its white enamelled middle, the effigy of the Duke in gold, surrounded by a blue enamelled ring with the words 'Albertus animosus.'

The Commanders, first class, wear the same decoration round the neck by a similar ribbon, two and a half inches wide, and accompanied by a rather smaller square star fastened to the left side of the breast, as described above.

The Commanders, second class, wear the same decoration, but without the star.

The Knights of both classes wear the cross of a smaller size, at one of the left button-holes, suspended by the ribbon of the Order, about one inch and a half wide.

Several medals are conferred in Saxony under various titles and for various merits, but as they are not allowed to be worn in public as a decoration, they do not belong to the category of insignia.

GRAND DUCHIES OF THE SAXE-GOTHA BRANCH OF THE ERNESTINE LINE.

(COBURG-GOTHA, ALTENBURG, MEININGEN-HILDBURGS-HAUSEN.)

THE FAMILY ORDER OF SAXE-ERNEST.

This Order (Plate 80. Tab. I. Nos. 1, 2, 3) was restored conjointly by the Dukes Frederick, Ernest, and Freund of the Saxe-Duchies, in remembrance of the line of Saxe-Coburg Altenburg which became extinct in 1825, as well as in honour of the common ancestor of their illustrious houses, Duke Ernest, the Pious. The Order was originally founded as a reward for the distinguished services of high State functionaries by Frederick I. Duke of Saxe-Gotha and Altenburg, eldest son of Duke Ernest, in 1690, under the name of the 'Order of German Integrity,' and with the motto: 'Fideliter et constanter.' In 1825, as just stated, it was renewed under its present name, and the statutes then underwent various modifications.

The Order now consists of four classes, Knights Grand Cross, Commanders, first and second classes, and Knights.

In connection with it are the decorations of the Cross and Medal of Merit.

All the Princes of the Ducal line, as given at the head of the article, are born members of this family Order, though they are not actually received as Knights of the Grand Cross before the completion of their eighteenth year, when they are, in

DUCHIES OF SAXE. Table I.   PLATE 80.

due form proposed by the head of the House to which they belong.

Distinguished State functionaries of, at least, the rank of Privy Counsellor, are admissible to the first class.

Each of the three Ducal Courts is allowed to distribute three Grand Crosses only to their respective high functionaries.

If a commoner is honoured with the Grand Cross, he enters into all the rights and privileges peculiar to the hereditary nobility.

The total number of native Commanders, first class, is limited to twelve, that of the second class, to eighteen, and that of the Knights, to thirty-six. Of this total, each of the three courts can nominate one third for each class.

The number of members of the Cross and Medal of Honour is unlimited.

The decoration of first class Commanders ought by right to be presented only to functionaries of the rank of privy counsellor, or to members of the cabinet.

The decoration of the second class Commanders is bestowed on civil functionaries of the rank of President, Director of the Board, &c., and to military persons of, at least, the rank of Colonel or Lieutenant-Colonel.

The claim to the decoration of first class Commander is founded on fifteen years' faithful and distinguished service, and that to the second class Commander, on ten years' similar service. Exceptions in rank and term of service are usually made in favour of persons of special merits, or of those who have rendered peculiar services to the state or the King.

Foreign functionaries who enter inland service, may include the years of their service abroad, in the term required for the decoration.

The number of foreign members is unlimited, though the

nomination of a foreigner requires the unanimous consent of the three courts.

The three reigning Dukes are Superintendents of the Order; they usually meet, for the transaction of business, once in every two or three years, by rotation in their respective capitals.

The badge of the Order consists:

a. For the Knights of the Grand Cross, of an octagonal white enamelled cross encased in gold, and with small gold balls at the points. The angles of the cross are filled out with gold lions, two of which are red, and the other two black. The round middle of the obverse contains the effigy of Ernest the Pious, in gold, surrounded by a blue enamelled ring with the legend in gold: 'Fideliter et Constanter.' The ring is, in its turn, encircled by a green oaken wreath, intertwined with golden ribbons. The middle of the reverse contains the Saxe family crest of the rue garland, surrounded by a blue enamelled ring, indicating in golden letters the date, '25th December, 1833.' This ring is also in its turn encompassed by a green oaken wreath, intertwined with golden ribbons. Above the two upper points of the cross is a gold crown. Within the upper arm of the cross is inscribed, in golden letters, the name of the founder, in whose line and state the decoration is each time conferred.

In the crosses presented to foreigners, the oaken wreath round the blue ring is omitted, while in those presented to military persons for distinguished valour, &c., the laurel wreath is now substituted for the oak, and the space between the pales of the cross is filled with two crossed swords.

The badge is worn across the right shoulder towards the left hip, by a red watered ribbon about three inches wide, with a green stripe near the borders.

The Knights of the Grand Cross carry, besides, on the

left side of the breast, an octagonal star partly of gold and partly of silver. Upon this star is placed the white cross with gold mountings and balls, while the round gold middle exhibits a green rue crown. This scutcheon is encompassed by a blue ring with the golden inscription: 'Fideliter et constanter,' and is, in its turn, surrounded by a green oaken wreath, intertwined with golden ribbons; this wreath is omitted in the stars presented to foreigners.

b. For the Commanders first class, the badge is the same cross as the former, and is worn round the neck suspended by a similar ribbon, about one and a half inches wide, while the cross on the left side of the breast is deficient of the star.

c. For the Commanders second class, the badge is the same cross and ribbon round the neck, but without the cross on the breast.

d. For the Knights, the same cross, but of smaller size, worn at the button-hole, or on the left side of the breast, by a ribbon about one inch wide.

The silver *Cross of Merit*, contains on the obverse, the effigy of Ernest the Pious, and, on the reverse, the arms and motto of the Order.

The silver *Medal of Merit* shows upon the obverse the effigy of the founder of the line, by which it is distributed, while the reverse exhibits the cross and legend of the Order.

MEDALS AND DECORATIONS OF HONOUR.

1. *Cross of distinguished Service*, for officers of the Saxe-Altenburg troops, was instituted by Joseph Frederick Ernest, on the 1st Januury, 1836, for twenty-five years' service (years of war counting double, and those on leave

of absence, only half). It is distributed twice a year, on the 1st January, and 27th August, and consists of a silver cross with gold encasement, bearing in the middle of the obverse, the cypher 'XXV.' and of the reverse, the initial of the founder in gilt relief. It is worn upon the uniform, between the first and second button-hole, suspended by a green ribbon with silver stripes at the border (Plate 81. Tab. II. No. 6).

2. *Medal for the Campaign of* 1814, was instituted in 1816, by Duke Ernest, at Coburg-Saalfeld, by Duke Frederick at Altenburg, and by the Duchess Louise Eleonore, at Meiningen, and distributed amongst the troops of those Duchies who had participated in the campaign of 1814. It is of silver, and bears, on the obverse, the Maltese Cross, surrounded by an oaken wreath, and on the reverse, the inscription: 'Dem Vertheidiger des Vaterlandes, 1814' (To the defender of the Fatherland), round which are the words: 'Ernst, H. z. S. C. S.,' or 'Friedrich, H. z. S. H.' or 'Louisa Eleonora, H. z. S. O. V. u. L. R.' (Plate 81. Tab. II. No. 7).

3. *The War Medal of the Duchy Saxe-Gotha-Altenburg*, was instituted, in 1816, by Duke Emilius Leopold Augustus, for the troops who were engaged in the campaigns of 1814 and 1815. For the private soldiers, it was entirely of bronze, and for the officers of bronze plated with gold. The obverse contains the Altenburg rose; and the reverse, a ducal crown with the legend, in old German characters: 'Im Kampfe für das Recht' (In the struggle for right). Round the edge are the words: 'Herzogthum Gotha und Altenburg, MDCCCXIV and MDCCCXV' (No. 9)

4. *Medal of Military Merit*, was instituted in 1814, by Duke Ernest of Saxe-Coburg-Saalfeld, for the troops then under his own command (as General of the 5th German

DUCHIES OF SAXE. *Table* II.   PLATE 81.

Hurst and Blackett, London. 1858.

corps) who had distinguished themselves in that campaign (No. 10).

5. *The Iron Medal*, was founded by the same Duke, for the volunteers under his command. The obverse shows a bundle of arrows tied together by a laurel wreath, and the legend: 'Einigkeit macht stark, Vaterlands-Liebe unüberwindlich' (Union makes strength, and patriotism invincibility). The reverse contains the inscription: 'Den freiwilligen Vaterlandsvertheidigern des 5. Deutschen Armee corps, von ihrem commandirenden General E. H. z. S.' (To the voluntary defenders of the Fatherland, from their commanding General of the 5th German army corps). (No. 8).

SAXE-COBURG GOTHA.

Cross for the Battle of Eckern-förde, was founded in 1851, for the troops of that Duchy who had taken part in the Sleswig-Holstein campaign. It consists of a cross of bronze for privates, and of silver for officers. The obverse shows a crowned 'E,' and below it the word: 'Eckern-förde,' and the reverse: '5th April, 1849.' It is worn on the left side of the breast, by a tri-coloured ribbon (orange, green and black).

(GRAND DUCHY) OF SAXE-WEIMAR EISENACH.

ORDER OF THE WHITE FALCON; OR, OF VIGILANCE.

This Order was founded by Ernest Augustus, Duke of Saxe-Weimar and Eisenach, commanding General of the whole imperial Cavalry, on the 2nd August, 1732, and was bestowed on twenty-four exalted personages—princes and chevaliers—who were in charge of some high functions in the civil or military service. The duties imposed upon the members were: " To be true to God : to practice virtue and avoid vice ; " to promote as much as lay in their power, his Majesty's glory " and interest, and to be ready to sacrifice for the Emperor, " life and property, if called upon by circumstances to do so ; " to live with the other Knights of the Order in union, love " and perfect confidence, without deceit and falsehood, " and to assist them in their emergencies and necessities, " as also to afford relief to the poor and oppressed generally, " but, more especially, to poor officers and soldiers."

The decoration underwent but little alteration in process of time, except that it was originally adorned with four diamonds, and worn by a ribbon drawn through a ring set in diamonds, across the jacket. The ribbon was of poppy-red colour, with double golden stripes near the border. " The " reason," say the statutes, " that the Falcon has been chosen " for the insignia of the Order, is because the illustrious founder "directed his own look towards the eagle, the Imperial "escutcheon, and, in the same way as the falcons follow in "the track and flight of the eagle, in like manner are the "wishes of the members of the Order directed towards his "Majesty, to approach him by loyal service and willing "obedience. The whiteness of the falcon indicates sincerity "which the members are bound to show to the illustrious "founder, and to each other on all occasions. As regards "the name and symbol, it has been chosen from the circum- "stance that the falcon is by instinct, a very watchful "and attentive bird; and that it, therefore, behoves every "Christian and honest man to watch over himself, lest he "should fall into vice, suffer injury in his honour and "good name: or fail in the duties of his office and station."

On the 18th October, 1815, the statutes of the Order were remodelled by the Grand Duke Charles Augustus.

The following are the principal provisions of the new statutes.

1. The name and symbol of the Order remain the same.

2. The Orders constitute the only one existing in the Duchy.

3. It consists of three classes. The first is formed of the Grand Master, the reigning Grand Duke of Saxe-Weimar, or the princes of the house, and twelve Knights of the Grand Cross.

4. The recipient of the Grand Cross must possess the rank of privy Counsellor or Major-General.

5. The second class consists of twenty-five Commanders, who must bear the title of honorary Privy Counsellors, or possess the rank of Major in Military service. The third class consists of fifty Knights. The principal duties of the members of the Order are:

1. Loyalty and devotion to the common fatherland, Germany, as also to the supreme legitimate authority of the nation.

SAXE WEIMAR. PLATE 82.

Hurst and Blackett, London. 1858.

2. To contribute as much as lies in their power to the development of the German spirit, of the arts and sciences, as also to the improvement and perfection of the social Institutions, Political Constitution and Legislative Administration of the fatherland, and not less to the diffusion of truth and light, worthy of the sober character of the German nation:

3. To assist their needy brethren who had suffered by the calamities of the war, but more especially those who were wounded in the defence of their country, or the widows and orphans of the warriors who fell in the struggle.

The badge of the Order is now, a golden white enamelled falcon, with gold legs and claws, and placed upon a gold octagonal star, enamelled green. Between this star and the falcon is another red square star of smaller size, and with white enamelled points. At the side of the star is seen a gold Royal Crown. The reverse exhibits the same octagonal star, but in white colours, as also the square one, but enamelled green. The blue enamelled middle contains a motto: 'Vigilando ascendimus.' The same is mounted with a golden laurel wreath, (for the military, with an armature), and surmounted by a gold Royal Crown, (Plate 82, Tab. I. Nos. 3 and 4). The silver star (No. 1) belongs to this decoration, and is worn on the left side of the breast. The middle exhibits a flying white falcon, upon a gold ground, and is surrounded by the motto of the Order in blue enamel. The gold ring round it rests upon the green enamelled star, and the latter, in its turn, upon the larger silver star of the Order.

This decoration is worn by the first class, Knights Grand Cross, across the right shoulder, by a broad bright red watered ribbon, accompanied by the star fastened to the left side of the breast.

The second class Commanders wear it round the neck, suspended by a narrow red ribbon which reaches down to the breast.

The third class Knights suspend it in smaller size at the button-hole, by a similar ribbon.

The annual festival of the Order is now celebrated on the 18th October, which is also the national festival day of the liberation of the country from foreign rule.

A subscription is then made for the widows and orphans of fallen soldiers, as mentioned in § 3 as one of the duties imposed upon the members.

On the 16th February, 1840, Duke Charles Frederick introduced the following modifications in the statutes:

1. As a mark of special distinction, the Commanders may sometimes be favoured with a star (No. 2) to be worn on the left side of the breast.

2. Those specially favoured must occupy the rank (in civil service) of a privy counsellor, president, &c., and, in military service, of, at least, a Colonel.

3. The third class Knights are divided into two sections. The decoration of the first section remains unaltered, while that of the second now consists of a cross of honour, the middle of the obverse exhibiting a white falcon, and that of the reverse the initial of the reigning Grand Duke and dispenser of the Order. The cross is to be fastened to the button-hole by a narrow red ribbon (No. 5).

No. 6 represents the collar of the Order.

MEDALS AND DECORATIONS OF HONOUR.

1. *Cross of Distinction.*—It was instituted by the Grand Duke as reward for military service and discipline.

The following are the principal provisions of the statutes:

a. The decoration for officers, sub-officers, and privates to consist of a black cross, the middle of the obverse to exhibit the initials in monogram of his royal highness the Grand Duke, and above it the royal crown, while the reverse is to contain within an oaken wreath the number of years service.

b. The cross to be divided into two classes, the first having for distinction a silver edge. Both are to be worn fastened to the left side of the breast by a ribbon of the national colour.

c. The claim to the first class is founded on twenty years' and to the second on ten years' service, and good conduct.

On receiving the cross of the first class, that of the second must be returned. For officers, the years served as sub-officers or privates count in the term required for the decoration. Years of campaign count double.

2 *Medal for Faithful Warriors.*—It was founded by the Grand Duke Charles Augustus, on the 4th December, 1815, for the troops who had distinguished themselves in the campaigns from 1809 down to that period.

After the death of the possessors, the medals are ordered to be suspended in the churches of their respective birthplaces.

3. *Civil Medal of Merit.*—During his stay at Paris in 1815, the Grand Duke Charles Augustus had a medal struck, the obverse of which represented his effigy, and the reverse exhibited the words: 'Carolus Augustus Magnus Dux Saxoniæ,' or 'Mitescunt Aspera Sæcula' (The severity of the times is ameliorated). The medal was either of bronze, silver, or gold, and was allowed to be appended to the red ribbon of the Falcon decoration.

At the same time with the above, was also struck at Paris a smaller medal, the obverse showing the effigy of the Grand Duke, and the reverse the words: 'Doctarum frontium præmia'

(The reward of cultivated intellect.)* It was distributed in gold among literary men.

The same Grand Duke instituted, besides the above, another small medal with the inscription on the reverse 'Meritis nobilis' (Ennobled by merit) surrounded by an oaken wreath. It was to be appended to the ribbon of the Falcon Order. Since 1329, however, the medal forms an independent decoration; is distributed in gold and in silver, and is worn at the button-hole, by a ribbon of the national colour.

Each of the above medals remains, after the decease of the person decorated, the property of his family, who are, however, not allowed to dispose of it except to government, for which they receive the intrinsic value of the metal.

The Grand Duke Charles Frederick likewise instituted gold, silver, and bronze medals, which show on the obverse his effigy, and on the reverse the words: 'Dem Verdienste' (To merit), surrounded by an oaken wreath. They are equally worn at the button-hole, suspended by a ribbon of the national colour.

* Hor. Ode I. l. 29.

SCHWARZBURG-RUDOLSTADT.
(PRINCIPALITY.)

MILITARY DECORATION OF HONOUR.

It was founded in 1816 for the troops who participated in the campaigns of 1814 and 1815. It consists of a simple cross of dull or unpolished silver, placed upon an oaken wreath; the obverse shows the inscription: 'Schwarzburg's braven Kriegern für Deutschland's Befreiung' (To Schwarzburg's brave warriors, for the liberation of Germany), and the reverse, the years '1814 and 1815.' It is worn suspended by a bright blue watered ribbon with white borders (Plate 83, No. 1).

SCHWARZBURG-SONDERSHAUSEN (PRINCIPALITY).

MEDALS AND DECORATIONS OF HONOUR.

1. *Cross and decoration for distinguished service* were instituted on the 22nd May, 1838, by Prince Günther, for long military service.

Years of war for the Principality count double, while those spent in active service, among the troops, of other German states, are included in the term required for the decoration. This latter consists for officers of a gold cross, showing on the obverse the initial of the Prince, surmounted by the coronet, and on the reverse the No. XX. (Plate 83, No. 2). It is worn at the left side of the breast, by a blue and white ribbon, after twenty years faithful service and irreproachable conduct, and passes by the name of the Cross of distinguished service.

The decoration for privates or sub-officers, is a buckle with the initials of the Prince on it, and is worn in the same manner as the previous (No. 3). It passes by the name of 'Distinction of Service,' and is divided into two classes, for fifteen and ten years' service (No. 3).

The decoration of the first class is of gold, and that of the second, of silver.

2. *Medal of War;* was instituted for the campaigns of 1814 and 1815, and distributed amongst all the military of the line, as also volunteers and militia, who shared in them. It bears on the obverse the inscription: Schwarzburg-Sondershausen (as legend), 'Im Deutschen Freiheit's Kriege, 1814 und 1815' (In the German War of Liberty, 1814 and 1815), while the reverse shows the initials of the Prince in monogram (No. 4).

SCHWARZBURG-RUDOLSTADT & SONDERSHAUSEN — PLATE 85.

1

2

4

3

Hurst and Blackett, London. 1858.

THE TWO SICILIES.

ORDER OF ST. JANUARIUS.

This Order was founded by King Charles of Sicily (afterwards King Charles III. of Spain), on the 6th July, 1738, on the occasion of his marriage with the Princess Amelia, daughter of King Augustus III. of Poland.

The reigning Kings of Sicily are Grand Masters of the Order, which consists of only one class; and he nominates the Knights, whose number is now unlimited, though it was originally fixed at sixty.

After the invasion of Naples by the French in 1806, the Order was abolished in that kingdom, though it continued to flourish in Sicily, whither Ferdinand had fled; and it was re-introduced into both countries, on the return of the fugitive Prince in 1814.

The badge of the Order is a gold octagonal white and red enamelled cross (Plate 84, Tab. I. No. 2), with golden lilies in the upper and side angles. The obverse represents the patron saint of the Order, St. Januarius, in episcopal garments, and with an open book in the left hand. The round middle of the reverse shows a golden open book and two phials partly filled with blood.

This cross is worn across the right shoulder, towards the left hip, by a broad poppy red ribbon, accompanied on the left

TWO SICILIES. *Table I.* PLATE 84.

Hurst and Blackett, London. 1858.

Sicily, where it continued its circumscribed existence until 1814, when it was again extended to Naples.

The Order was originally composed of only two classes: Knights of the Grand Cross, and Commanders. In 1810, however, a third class was added, that of Knights, consisting chiefly of Officers of all degrees who had distinguished themselves by valour, wise conduct or in any other way.

The reigning monarch is always Grand Master of the Order, and in him alone is vested the power of nomination. The number of the first class, is, by the statutes, limited to twenty-four, including the royal family; while that of the two other classes is unlimited.

The badge of the Order is a star formed of six bundles of golden rays, of six Bourbon lilies in the intervening angles, and a royal crown above it. The obverse shows upon a gold ground, the figure of St. Ferdinand in regal robe and mantle, with the crown upon his head, and holding a naked sword in his right, and a laurel crown in his left, hand. Round it, within a dark blue circle are in golden characters, the words: 'Fidei et Merito' (to fidelity and merit). The reverse of gold, contains the inscription: 'Fed. IV. inst. Anno 1800,' (Plate 84, Table 1. No. 4).

With the exception of the size which decreases with each inferior class, the star is the same with all the three classes. It is worn, by the first class, across the right shoulder towards the left hip, by a dark blue ribbon with red borders (the colours of the royal house), accompanied upon the left side of the breast by a star, the contents of which being, with the exception of the colours, the same as those of the obverse of the Order (No. 3).

The costume consists, for novices or honorary members, of a coat, waistcoat and breeches, of drap d'or (cloth of gold,) of white silk stockings with golden lilies, and of a round hat with upturned flap, trimmed with gold and adorned with a red silk cockade and three large feathers, two red and one blue in the middle. The actual or professed members wear besides a mantle, neck-chain and sash. The mantle is of blue watered silk interspersed alternately with embroideries of golden lilies, and the initials of the founder: 'F. Q.' (F. within a Q); it is lined with white taffetas and ermine stripes, and tied at the front of the neck by two long cords of gold and blue and white silk. The sash above the coat is of blue watered silk with red stripes near the borders, embroidered like the mantle:

The neck-chain (Plate 86, Tab. III. No. 15) is composed of crowns, lilies, mural-towers, and the letter 'F.' with flags at the back.

With this chain, the Grand Cross Knights adorn their shields of arms. They receive the title 'Excellency,' have free access to the King, like the officiating Chamberlains, take on solemn occasions their place on the right side, close to the steps of the throne, and have the privilege of the Spanish Grandees of the first class, to stand covered, in the presence of the King, on all occasions. A general who has gained a complete victory in a battle is, *de jure*, entitled to the Grand Cross.

The Commanders wear the decoration round the neck, without the star on the breast. On solemn occasions they occupy a place next to the Knights of the Grand Cross, and are by the statutes entitled to pensions. The claims to that class rest on the merits of having so vigorously maintained the defence of a place as to compel the enemy to raise the siege, or, vice versâ, of having taken a place, despite the obstinate defence of the garrison.

The Knights suspend the decoration at the button hole, and place themselves, on solemn occasions, next to the Commanders.

TWO SICILIES. *Table* II.   PLATE 85.

TWO SICILIES. *Table III.*   PLATE 86.

Hurst and Blackett, London. 1858.

The principal duties of the members are: the defence of the Catholic religion, and loyalty and obedience to the Grand Master.

By a decree of the 25th July, 1810, King Ferdinand IV. added to the Order a subdivision, consisting of a gold medal and a silver medal (Plate 85, Tab. II. No. 10). The first to be bestowed on Aide-de-Camps, sword-bearing ensigns, graduated mates and head sailors, and the other, on sub-officers and privates of distinguished service.

THE ORDER OF CONSTANTINE.

The historical description of this Order, has already appeared under 'Parma,' from which place it was transplanted, in 1734, to Sicily, but has, since 1816, been re-introduced into the former state.

Together with the other Sicilian Orders, that of Constantine was abolished by Joseph Bonaparte in Naples, but it followed the Neapolitan monarch to Sicily, whence it was again brought back, in 1814, to Naples, with the King, who restored to it all its previous rights and privileges.

The King is Grand Master of the Order in the kingdom of the Two Sicilies. It is divided into three classes: Knights of the Grand Cross, simple Knights, and serving companions or brethren.

The two latter are subdivided into various sections: into Cavalieri di Giustizia, or Donatori, (*i. e.*, members who make a present to the institution at their nomination) Cavalieri di Grazia, (Honorary Members), Cavalieri Capellani (Chaplains), and Cavalieri Scuderi (Shield-bearers).

The badge has already been described and sketched under 'Parma.' The Knights of the Grand Cross wear it round the neck, or embroidered upon the left side of the coat, while the Knights suspend it at the button-hole. Another distinction between the two classes, consists in the addition of the figure of St. George, which is appended to the lower point of the cross, worn by the Knights of the Grand Cross. The chain for the latter is described under 'Parma,' while that of the Knights is simply of gold, to which they append the decoration, when in full costume.

The costume consists of a mantle of sky blue silk, lined with white taffetas, and held together by long white and blue cords; of a white robe, and sky blue waistcoat and breeches; of white stockings, similar shoes with blue ribbons; of a sash of crimson velvet; of a red velvet hat with feathers and white silk flaps, and with, in the front, the golden letters in monogram: 'I. H. S. V.' (In hoc signo vinces).

The Cavalieri Capellani wear under the mantle a blue surplice trimmed with white lace.

The conditions required for the admission to the first class, are: ancient, true nobility, the profession of the Catholic religion, a certain degree of wealth, and an age not under sixteen years.

The Cavalieri di Giustizia (Knights by right), must prove their noble descent through four generations. The Cavalieri di Grazia (Knights by favour), have only to prove their merits of the State or King.

The duties imposed upon the Superior Knights are: to practice virtue, to follow the Grand Master in war, to maintain two soldiers at their own expense, to appear always with their swords at the side, not to play any game of hazard, or to engage in any mercantile speculation and trade.

ORDER OF SAINT GEORGE OF THE REUNION.

Joseph Bonaparte founded on the 24th February, 1808, an Order which he named 'the Order of the two Sicilies,' though he was then master of only one of the two States, but it was done no doubt to increase his adherents, and fortify himself upon the throne of Naples. The Order was divided into three classes, Dignitaries, Commanders, and Knights, and their respective numbers limited to fifty, one hundred, and six hundred. The Knights took, at their nomination, an oath to defend the throne and the state with their blood and property, and they received in return a pension derived from the revenues of the Orders which Joseph had abolished in Naples. His successor on the throne of Naples, Joachim Murat, retained the Order, in its integrity, with a few slight modifications in its statutes, and, in that state, it existed until the return of Ferdinand from Sicily in 1815. It was then generally believed that he would deal with the Order created by the French, in the same manner as they did with the Sicilian Orders, eight years previously; owing, however, to some political considerations, Ferdinand thought proper to retain and array it among the other Sicilian Orders, though he gave to it a new shape, form and character, as decreed in the new statutes which were promulgated on the 1st January, 1819. The Order then received its present name, in commemoration of the reunion of the two kingdoms, and in requital of military distinction and loyalty.

Besides the Grand Master (the King), the Great Constable (the Duke of Calabria), and the Great Marshal, the members are divided into six classes.

1. Knights of the Grand Cross (Plate 85. Tab. II. No. 7, and the star No. 6).

2. Commanders (decoration No. 8).

3. Cavalieri di dritto (decoration No. 8).

4. Cavalieri di Grazia (decoration No. 9).

5. Gold medal (No. 14), and,

6. Silver medal.

The decoration, together with the ribbon, decreases in size with each lower degree. It is worn by the first two classes round the neck, and by the Knights, at the button-hole.

The decoration of the first three classes is considered as a distinction of valour, and is conferred upon officers and generals for some exploit in war, in the same way as the gold medal is bestowed upon sub-officers and privates.

The degree of a Cavaliere di Grazia and the silver medal are rewards of merit for brave conduct in war, or for forty years service, during which at least two campaigns must have been shared in by the candidates. Sub-officers and privates are only entitled to the silver medal.

ORDER OF FRANCIS I.

Was founded on the 28th September, 1829, by King Francis I., as reward for civil merit in public offices, the arts, sciences, agriculture, industry, and commerce. Nor are military persons precluded from receiving the decoration on the above claims.

The monarch is chief and Grand Master, which is divided into five classes.

1. Knights of the Grand Cross (Plate 86, No. 12, and the cross No. 11, embroidered upon the coat).

2. and 3. Commanders and Knights, wearing the same cross, but smaller in size, and the Knights without the cross as a star.

4. and 5. Members wearing the gold or silver medal (No. 13).

The badge is a gold cross of four broad points, enamelled white, the angles being filled with gold lilies. In the centre, on a gold field, is the initial of the founder, F. I., surmounted by a crown, and surrounded with a laurel wreath, and on a second circle upon a blue ground is the motto: 'Optime merito de Rege' in gold characters, the whole being surmounted by a royal crown. It is worn by the Knights Grand Cross round the neck by a deep red ribbon with blue borders. The star, which is a silver cross of four points, presents the obverse of the badge, and is worn at the left breast.

The cross of the Commanders is a little smaller, and is worn round the neck.

That of the Knights is yet smaller, and is worn from the left button-hole.

The gold and silver medals are also worn from the button-holes.

SPAIN.

ORDER OF SAINT JOHN.

Since 1530, when the Emperor Charles V. (*vide* "Austria)" ceded to the Knights of St. John of Jerusalem the islands of Malta and Gozzo, together with Tripolis, the 'Order of St. John' has continued under the suzerainty of Spain, the Knights having engaged themselves, by oath, on taking possession of those islands, among other things, never to abuse their authority there to the prejudice of Spain, to consider the King of Spain as the patron of the Malta diocese, to restore the island to Spain in the event of the Knights re-conquering Rhodes, or settling at some other place; and, finally, to despatch annually, by two Knights, a tribute of one falcon to the Viceroy of Naples, as a token of acknowledgment of Spanish suzerainty. Subsequently, when Sicily ceased to be a Spanish province, that tribute was regularly discharged and sent direct to the King of Spain.

After the Peace of Amiens, in 1802, the Portuguese and Spanish languages (Aragon and Castile) separated from the Order, and formed a college of their own, under the supreme authority of their respective monarchs, who, in consequence, exercised essential influence in all matters connected with nominations, benefices, &c., the Grand Mastership being thus, in effect, though not by right, vested in the Crown.

A description of the insignia of the Order will be found under PAPAL STATES, Plate 56, Tab. II. Nos. 7, 8 and 9.

SPAIN. *Table* I.   PLATE 87.

Hurst and Blackett. London. 1858.

The spiritual elements and ecclesiastical possessions of the Order are nearly annihilated in Spain and Portugal by the political events of the present century.

MILITARY ORDER OF ST. JAMES OF COMPOSTELLA.

Spain cherished, in early times, a lively reverence for the relics of St. James the elder, which were preserved at Compostella. She had adopted him as her patron saint after the victory of Clavijo, while the marvels, connected with those relics, continually drew vast numbers of pilgrims from distant parts to Galicia, long before the beginning of the twelfth century. To support these pious wanderers in their journey, the canons of St. Eloy established hospitals under their own management. The high roads being subsequently rendered unsafe by the vicinity of the Moors, thirteen noblemen united their strength and wealth for the protection of the Christian pilgrims, and, in accord with the canons, resolved to found an Order similar to that of the 'Hospitalers' or 'Templars.' For that purpose, they delegated a deputation to Rome to seek the Papal consent.

Pedro Hernandez de Fuentes, head of the deputation, returned with the desired Bull, dated 5th July, 1175, in which the statutes were framed in seventy-one paragraphs, himself instituted Grand Master of the Order, and the possessions and conquests of the Order guaranteed to it by the Holy Chair. A council of thirteen Knights was instituted with authority, not only to elect a Grand Master, but even, with the consent of the Prior and the Chapter, to depose him, should he be found guilty of mismanagemant or neglect of duty. The inspection of the hospitals was confided to four visiting members, who had full power to remedy all sorts of abuses and evils in the establishments, or to report them to the General Chapter, which was to meet annually on All Saints' Day. The Order obtained many spiritual privileges, and was entirely independent of the Bishops.

At their nomination, the Knights made vows of poverty, obedience, celibacy, protection and support of poor travellers, and belief in the Immaculate Conception of the Blessed Virgin. They also promised not to listen, in their combats with the Saracens, to the voice of ambition, glory, covetousness, or bloodshed, but to have only one single object in view, the protection of Christians, and the conversion of infidels.

The candidates were bound to prove that they had descended from a purely Christian race, without any intermixture of Moorish, Jewish or infidel blood, and they were, besides, obliged to undergo a six month's probation or noviciate, to learn the rules of the Order. The Canons of the Order were subject to the rule of St. Augustin, and were bound to prove at the nomination, that none of their ancestors, either paternal and maternal were, through four generations, engaged in any mercantile trade, or even acted as agents, brokers, money-changers, &c., and that none were condemned by the Holy Inquisition as Jews or infidels.

The Order soon proved exceedingly useful to the State, and acquired much reputation abroad. The members were indefatigable in their warfare against the Moors, and the red cross of the Order shone at the side of the royal standard in all the engagements, and great battles which Christendom fought against the professors of Islam, or Europe against Africa. Nor did the grateful piety of the Kings and nations, added to the conquests made by the Order itself, less contribute to increase its power, for it counted, towards the end of the fifteenth century, besides the three large Commanderies of Leon, Castille and Montalvan, nearly two hundred other

Commanderies, comprising more than two hundred priories, fiefs, cloisters, hospitals, castles, boroughs, two towns, and one hundred and seventy-eight villages, exclusive of its possessions in Portugal. The extent, however, of such power and wealth (the revenue of the Grand Master alone amounted to 15,000 pistoles) naturally roused the envy and fear of the Kings, and more especially, when they (the Kings) considered the important part which the Order had played during the internal disturbances in Spain in the fourteenth and fifteenth centuries, as also in the disputes between the crowns of Leon and Castille. Nor was the reluctance evinced by the members to accommodate themselves to the new order of things, as introduced by the preponderate power of the monarchs into all the political and civil affairs of the State and society, more calculated to allay those fears and suspicions. The consequence was, that the Order had recourse to cabals and intrigues to maintain its own authority and power, especially after the Moors had been expelled from Spain, when its existence had become less necessary, and when its practical utility for the State was almost nugatory. At last, after the death of the forty-third Grand Master, Don Alfonzo de Cardenas, in 1493, Ferdinand and Isabella assumed the administration of the Order on the strength of a Bull of Pope Alexander VI.—which was but a prelude to that of Pope Hadrian VI., of the 12th May, 1522—in which the Grand Mastership was for ever vested in the crown of Spain.

In consequence of the latter Bull, the Emperor Charles V. established a council, composed of a President and six Knights, to manage and conduct all the affairs of the Order, and with full power to appoint ecclesiastical commissioners in all matters purely spiritual. The only appeal from the tribunal was to the Holy Chair at Rome.

The Order, having thus become dependent on, and subject to the arbitrary power of a secular sovereign, rapidly decreased in respect and importance. In 1652, many of the previous severe provisions in the statutes were abolished, while others were, by some means or other, evaded. It was, on the other hand, required that the candidates should in future prove their noble descent through four generations, on both parental sides. The Order having thus gradually assumed a worldly, or rather courtly character, though under a religious guise, finally degenerated into a mere decoration of military merit.

The costume consists of a white mantle, upon the left side of which is fastened a cross of red cloth, in the form of a sword, with lilies carved on the hilt (Plate 87, Tab. I. No. 1), and of a shield (No. 2) worn round the neck by a treble chain of gold. Without the costume, the decoration is suspended at the button-hole by a red ribbon.

The escutcheon of the Order is the same cross on a gold field, and with a gold shell upon it.

The flag was yellow, and adorned with the same cross and shell, in addition to the four golden shells at the angles.

Since 1312, the Order had been increased by an institution for ladies, through the bounty of Pelago Perez and his wife Maria Mendez, who instituted seven canonesses for each of the seven convents, the inmates of which were divided into professed and lay sisters, dressing in black, and wearing the same decoration as the male Knights. Their duty was, to give shelter and food to all the pilgrims journeying to St. Iago de Campostella. They were formerly allowed to marry or leave the institution; but since 1480, they have been forced to make the vows of poverty, chastity and obedience. Those in the two convents of Barcelona and Santos (Portugal), however, retained their original more liberal constitution.

ORDER OF CALATRAVA,

(FOR A LONG TIME KNOWN AS: 'ORDER OF SALVATIERRA.')

One single campaign had, in 711, reduced the whole of the Pyrenean peninsula under the power of the Moors. In 718, however, Pelagius once more raised the banner of the Goths; and after an uninterrupted warfare of three hundred years, Catalonia, Navarre, Aragon, Castile, Leon, Galicia and Portugal were once more ruled by Christian Princes, while numerous dynasties, internal dissensions, and civil and religious wars gradually undermined the power of Islam. In 1130, Alphonso Raimond advanced the devastated frontiers of Castile, as far as Sierra Morena, imposed tribute upon Cordova, and attacked the kingdoms of Murcia and Jaën. Calatrava, which covered the frontier of Andalusia, fell into his power in 1147, and he confided its custody to the brave and valorous Templars. Subsequently, however, when the invincible Emir Almohade, the ruler of a great part of Northern Africa, led his ever victorious army into Spain, and subjugated (in 1157) Cordova, Jaën, Grenada and Almedia, the intimidated Templars restored Calatrava to Don Sancho III., son and successor of Alphonso Raimond, who was at first unable to find any one bold enough to venture upon the defence of a place which had been despaired of by the renowned warriors who had abandoned it. At that time, two Cistercian monks, Don Raimond, Abbot of Fitero in Navarre, and Don Diego Belasquez, were staying at Toledo, on some business of their community. The latter, an old soldier of Alphonso, roused the enthusiasm of his colleague the Abbot, whom he persuaded to accept the offer of the King, to give Calatrava to whatever valiant soldiers would undertake its defence. The Archbishop of Toledo, in whose diocese the town was situated, supplied the adventurer with money, and summoned, in an open assembly, all men, high and low, to support the efforts of the Abbot, and arm themselves in behalf of the Christian religion and their native land. Roused patriotism, and a delay in the arrival of Almohade, whom important matters retained for a while in Africa, greatly contributed to promote the rapid and complete organization of the measures of defence, the town was saved; and Calatrava with its vast but desolate district, soon after received a colony of nearly twenty thousand inhabitants from Fitero, whom Raimond helped to settle on a solid footing, and amongst whom he created a new religious Order. This Order received statutes from the Chapter-General of the Cistercian monks, which were sanctioned by the Archbishop of Toledo (1164), and subsequently also by Pope Alexander III. Numerous privileges, civil and religious, were gradually added, such as the undisturbed possession of all the provinces and districts taken from the Moors, exemption from taxes and royal jurisdiction, and permission for the cattle belonging to the Order to pasture everywhere in the kingdom, and for their herdsmen or shepherds, to fell wood for their own use wherever they might please, &c.

After the death of Raimond (1163), those Knights who were unwilling to obey any longer the commands of an Abbot, separated themselves from the Cistercian monks, and elected Don Garcias de Redon, as Grand Master. Subsequently, they again reunited, and even more closely than before, with the Cistercian Order, and received in 1187 new statutes from the Abbot Guy, after they had acquired many rich possessions in Spain and Portugal, the result of their victories over the Moors.

When Castille had fallen into anarchy, after the death of Sancho, and the other kingdoms of Spain were weakening themselves by incessant feuds amongst themselves, the war of religion was almost exclusively carried on by the Knights of Calatrava alone. To protect his European subjects against the continual pillages of these knightly warriors, Emir Jacub ben Yuseff crossed the strait with an African army, and met the Castilians near Fort Alarcos. Alphonso IX. would have acted wisely had he delayed the battle until the arrival of the troops from Leon and Navarre, which kingdoms had likewise armed themselves against the common enemy, but, in his eagerness to obtain the glory of victory for himself, he hastened to the field, and was completely routed. Nearly all the Knights who were present, and the best soldiers of Alphonso fell in the battle, and Calatrava was soon after occupied by the Moors. The Knights then transferred their seat to the Castle of Salvatierra, and under that name they passed for a long time afterwards.

The peace of twelve years, which was concluded after this fatal battle, terminated in 1208, when the Christians again began to prepare for a renewal of the national war. The Knights of Calatrava opened the campaign by the invasion of the kingdom of Valencia; and the victory they gained over the enemy on the 16th July, 1212, near Las Navas de Tolosa, fearfully avenged the defeat of Alarcos. According to the account of Archbishop Rodriguez, the Moors lost thirty-five thousand horse, and one hundred and seventy thousand foot soldiers, while the loss of the Spaniards barely amounted to one hundred and thirty-five men. During two resting days which followed the battle, the conquerors are said to have maintained the bivouac fires, with the lances and arrows left on the battle field by the enemy.

The Knights again returned to Calatrava, which had been reconquered already in 1210, whence they soon, however, transferred their seat to the new town of the same name. Despite the vast conquests made by the Knights, the Order was never in possession of the great wealth and riches, for which the Knights of St. James of Compostella were so famous. Its moderate income was probably owing to the circumstance that it had ceded a part of its conquests to the Orders of Alcantara and Aviz. The Order of Calatrava possessed only sixteen Priories and-fifty six Commanderies, the largest of which yielded no more thak 10,500 ducats of revenue, and the others of no more than 7000 to 9000. Notwithstanding, however, these scanty resources, the Grand Masters, whose incomes amounted to about 40,000 gold thalers, became very powerful and influential, chiefly owing to their having been elected from the highest Spanish families, by which means they exercised great influence on the public affairs of the country, though they frequently paid for it with their lives. Two of them died on the scaffold, accused of high treason, while after the death of the thirtieth Grand Master Garcia Lopez de Padilla, when the Chapter was about to elect a successor in 1489, Ferdinand and Isabella, produced a Bull of Pope Innocent VIII., by which he transferred for ever the administration of the Order to the King and his heirs, alleging that he was led to the measure by the conviction that the Order was, in its existing constitution, entirely incompatible with the power and unity of the State, and that it continually acted in opposition to the will and intention of the monarch, retarding thereby the growing welfare of the nation at large, and lending support and encouragement to the usurping and ambitious aristocracy. Ferdinand accordingly reserved to the Crown the right of appointing a Grand Master, and became himself the manager of the property of the Order, with the view—as the Jesuit Mariana said—to apply the revenues of the Commanderies to the honourable support of brave soldiers in their old age.

Afterwards, when the Emperor Charles V., as Administrator of the Order, held in 1523, the first general Chapter of the Order, Pope Hadrian VI. he vested for ever in the Spanish

Crown, the Grand Mastership of the three Orders: Calatrava, Alcantara, and St. James of Compostella, thus putting an end to the independence of those Orders, even as regarded the nomination of members, &c. which thenceforth became a mere matter of Court favour, irrespective of merit or distinction. By way of compensation, Pope Paul III. granted, in 1540, permission to the Knights to renounce celibacy, and to marry once, though they were still bound to make vows of poverty, obedience and conjugal chastity, and after the year 1652, to profess belief in the Immaculate Conception of the Blessed Virgin.

Until 1397, when the Anti-pope Benedict XIII. granted them the permission to wear, in battle, a civil apparel, instead of the cumbersome dress of the Order, their costume consisted of a white coat-of-mail with a white scapulary, and of a black cap, with a pilgrim's hood. The present costume is a white mantle with a red cross cut out in the form of lilies, upon the left side of the breast. (Plate 87, Tab. I. No. 3), while the Cross of the Order has the same symbol upon silver ground (No. 4).

The Grand Master Don Martin Fernandez, who built the new town, Calatrava, about thirty-five English miles distant from the old one, and who transferred to it the seat of the Order, intended to have added a convent for nuns, but, his death intervening, the plan was carried into effect, in 1219, by his successor Don Gonzalvo Yanes. The cloister Barrios at St. Felix, near Amaya, was the first residence assigned to the nuns, who were, however, afterwards transferred to Burgos. A second convent was established in 1479, in the cloister of St. Salvador at Pinilla, but the most magnificent one was founded by the Grand Master Walter of Padilla, in the cloister of 'the Assumption of the Holy Virgin,' at Almagra.

The nuns, who, like the Knights, must, before their

admission, prove their noble descent, pass by the name of 'Female Commanders,' and are apparelled like the Cistercian nuns, with the addition only of the Cross of the Order, which they wear on the left side of the capoch, fastened to the Scapulary. They are, or rather were, richly endowed.

ORDER OF ALCANTARA,

(PREVIOUSLY OF ST. JULIAN.)

The Order of Calatrava was, as we have seen, mainly founded with a view to protect Castille against the Moors, and the Knights of St. James of Compostella rendered Estramadura secure against the same inveterate opponents, by their first settlement in Carrcerès and Alharilla. But when Ferdinand, King of Leon and Galizia, compelled them to emigrate to Ucles, they turned their arms chiefly against the infidels in La Mancha. To fill up the chasm which was created in Estramadura by their absence, Ferdinand favoured and patronized a society of Knights, which had been formed by the brothers Don Suero and Don Gomez Barriento, in the small town of St. Julian de Pereiro (St. Julian of the pear tree) near Ciudad Rodrigo, as a barrier against Moorish inroads. In 1177, Pope Alexander III. raised this society to a Knightly Order, and Pope Lucius, in 1183, confirmed the Papal decree. Pope Alexander framed statutes for it, which were those of St. Benedict in a rather modified and milder form, and which were followed also by the Knights of Calatrava, while Pope Lucius granted, in addition, considerable privileges, at the same time that he submitted the Order to the jurisdiction of the Holy Chair.

The defence of the Christian religion, and continued war against the Moors were the principal duties of the Knights.

The original costume consisted of a white coat-of-mail with a black pilgrim hood over it, and of a capoch and black scapulary (three inches wide) reaching down to the girdle.

The Knights were not only continually engaged in war with the infidels, in which they fought bravely for the cause of religion and the fatherland, but they frequently took part (against the express laws in their statutes), in the feuds of the Christians amongst themselves, by which means the Order acquired great power, authority and wealth.

Alphonso IX. having wisely availed himself of the despondency of the Moors, after their defeat in the battle of Las Navas de Tolosa, invaded in his turn their own territory, and took possession of the town of Alcantara on the Tagus, which he ceded in 1213 to the Order of Calatrava. The latter unable to defend alone so many places, and so distantly scattered frontiers, yielded the new conquest to the Knights of St. Julian, who transferred their seat to Alcantara, by which name they were thenceforth known. From a sense of gratitude, they submitted to the superintending authority of the Calatrava Knights, which they soon, however, found irksome to bear, and which consequently led to various disputes, until Pope Julius II. absolved them from it. Nor was the Order itself free from internal dissensions which, at last, assumed so violent a character as to lead, at a later period, to bloody feuds amongst the various parties who respectively elected Grand Masters of their own, and even presumed to interfere in the affairs of the State, and meddle with the concerns of the various Monarchs of the Spanish kingdoms. At last, in 1495, King Ferdinand V. obtained the consent of Pope Innocence VIII. to vest the Grand Mastership of the Order in the Spanish crown, by which means he increased his own revenue by 150,000 ducats, the Order being at that time in possession of ten thousand five hundred large, and thirty-two smaller, Commanderies, some of which yielded an annual income averaging from 6000 to 7000 ducats. By way of compensation, the Grand Master, Don Juan de Zuniga was enfeoffed with an Archbishopric, and received a reversionary patent of a Cardinal's hat.

The Cross of the Order of Alcantara, which was substituted in 1441, for the previous black collar and scapulary, and which is worn by a green ribbon, is the same as that of the Order of Calatrava, with the exception of the colour, which is green (Plate 87, Tab. I. Nos. 5 and 6). The costume is, likewise, with the exception of the colour of the lily wreath, the same. The crest of the Order is a pear tree.

In 1540, the Knights obtained permission to marry, though they remained still bound to the vows of poverty, conjugal chastity and obedience, as also to the defence of the doctrine of the Immaculate Conception of the Blessed Virgin. At their nomination they are obliged to prove their noble descent through four generations.

ORDER OF OUR LADY OF MONTESA.

The long and protracted wars with the Moors involved the Spanish monarchs in difficulties of various kinds, and necessitated the creation of new resources, and the adoption of extraordinary measures, more especially as the clergy, who possessed a great portion of the national property, as well as the towns and nobility in the enjoyment of extensive privileges and exemptions, did not always show themselves ready to lend the necessary support and assistance in cases of emergency. These peculiar resources, the princes found in the chi-

SPAIN. *Table II.* PLATE 88.

valrous spirit and religious enthusiasm of the knightly Orders, who appeared everywhere as brave, indefatigable, and energetic champions, and as strong bulwarks on the Moorish frontiers. They were, at that period, almost indispensable institutions for the political power of Spain and Portugal, and they proved, indeed, the chief promoters of Christianity, and the most efficacious organs to stimulate patriotism and national spirit in those countries.

The abrogation of the Order of the Templars which was pronounced at the Council of Vienne, in 1312, by the contrivances of the designing Philip-le-Bel, could not, therefore, be a matter of indifference to those countries whose interests were so deeply involved in the existence of that and similar institutions. The history of Spain shows, indeed, that warm and well-founded demonstrations were made in various quarters against the injustice of the measure, and more especially so by King James II. of Aragon and Valencia, who most urgently pressed Pope Clement V. to allow him to employ all the estates of the Templars, situated in his dominions, for the foundation of a new knightly Order, so indispensably necessary for his kingdom. His request was, however, only granted in 1316 by Pope John XXII., who yielded to him all the estates of the Templars, and of the Knights of St. John, situated in Valencia. Provided with these funds, King James founded, in 1317, a new Order, that of our Lady of Montesa, after the Fortress Montesa, which he assigned as its head-quarters.

The Order received the rules of the Benedictines, and the statutes of the Knights of Calatrava, who were intrusted with the super-inspection of the new institution.

Pope Benedict XII. united with it, in 1399, the Order of St. George of Alfama.

King Philip II. procured for the Crown the supreme administration of the Order, and after the death of the fourteenth

Grand Master, the dignity was transferred, in 1587, to the Kings of Spain. Fifteen years previously, Pope Paul had allowed the Knights to marry and make their wills. The Order possessed at that time thirteen Commanderies.

At present, the badge is merely a mark of royal favour, though in the distribution, the provisions of the statutes are still nominally consulted.

The insignia are sketched in (Plate 88, Tab. II. No. 8). The costume, on gala days, consists of a long white woollen mantle, tied at the neck by very long white cords, while a cross (No. 7) adorns the left side of the breast.

ORDER OF THE GOLDEN FLEECE.

The history of this Order is given under AUSTRIA. In Spain, Princes, Grandees, and other high personages of peculiar merit and distinction are alone admissible to it.

The decoration (Tab. II. No. 9) differs in some points from the Austrian, and is worn on a collar (No. 10), or suspended round the neck by a red ribbon.

By a decree of the present Queen of Spain, the decoration of the Grand Cross can only be conferred at the recommendation of the Cabinet Council.

ROYAL AND DISTINGUISHED ORDER OF CHARLES III.

The Order was founded, in 1771, by King Charles III., on the occasion of the birth of his grandson, Charles Clement, and was confirmed by a Bull of Pope Clement XIV., dated the 21st February, 1772, who also granted to it various spiritual privileges.

The statutes now in force date from the 12th January, 1804, as promulgated by King Charles IV.

The Order shared the fate of all other Spanish orders, which were abolished in 1808 by Joseph Bonaparte, but were restored in 1814. It is devoted 'to the pure Conception of the Virgin,' and destined to reward marked zeal displayed by the nobility for the interests of the Crown.

The King is Chief and Grand Master: he nominates the members and dignitaries, and has also the right to make alterations in the rules and statutes.

The members form two classes: Knights of the Grand Cross, and simple Knights. The first class is limited to sixty members (exclusive of the King and the royal Princes) among whom are four Prelates. Two hundred members of the second class enjoy a pension of 1000 reales (£10) each. Those who are without it, pass as supernumeraries, and form as it were a separate class of their own.

The candidates for the first or the second pensioned class, must not be less than twenty-five years, and those for the supernumerary class not less than fourteen years, of age. The rule does not, however, apply to the members of the royal family, or to foreign princes. The candidates must, in addition, prove their noble descent through four generations by both parents. The badge may be worn at the side of the Golden Fleece, but the Knights of the Grand Cross are not allowed to wear the ribbon of St. Januarius, or the Grand Cross of St. John, nor any foreign decoration, without special permission from the Grand Master. The simple Knights are forbidden to enter any of the four military orders, or the St. John, or any foreign order, though the members of all these orders may retain their previous decorations on receiving the Grand Cross of the Order of Charles III.

The Knights of the Grand Cross may possess or administer a

military Commandery without prejudice to their decoration; but, when a simple Knight comes into possession of such a Commandery, he must resign the Cross and pension.

A Knight Grand Cross is styled 'Excellency,' has free access to the royal palace, and is saluted with all the honours attached to the title.

The Knights enjoy the same rights and privileges as do the members of the four military orders, or of the Order of St. John, but are not allowed to marry, without the consent of the Council.

At the nomination, the Knight must swear to live and die in the established religion of the country, to defend the mysterious doctrine of the Immaculate Conception, to be true to the throne, to defend the rights of the crown and the nation, to protect loyal subjects, and to assist the sick and the poor, especially those of the Order. Foreigners only swear to live and die in the Catholic religion, to defend the doctrine of the Conception, and acknowledge the Sovereign, as the head of the Order.

The other duties of the members are: to take the sacrament on Conception day, or on the following Sunday, to say daily the prescribed prayers, and to possess a copy of the statutes.

The management of the Order is conducted by a committee, consisting of a Grand Chancellor, Deputy Chairman (in the name of the monarch), four Knights of the Grand Cross, Secretary, Treasurer, Master of Ceremonies, Attorney-General and four pensioned Knights. The council is to meet at least once every month in the royal castle, in the office occupied by the Grand Chancellor, who is the head manager of the affairs of the Order, and is always one of the most eminent Prelates of the kingdom.

The expenses are usually defrayed from a part of the revenues derived from the vacant Commanderies of the four military Orders, from a portion of the income of the metropolitan churches and cathedrals, and from a few other benefices at the disposal of the Crown, and also from the entrance fees of 8500 reales paid by the Knights of the Grand Cross, of 4000 reales paid by the pensioned Knights, and of 3750 reales paid by the supernumerary Knights. In passing from a lower to a higher class, only the difference of the fees is paid.

The decoration consists of an octagonal gold cross with buttons on the points, and appended to a laurel wreath. The arms of the cross are bright blue, edged with white enamel, and connected with each other by golden lilies. The middle of the obverse is enamelled yellow, partly bright and partly dark, and is encircled by a blue ring. It exhibits the figure of the Blessed Virgin standing upon a silver crescent, and clad in a tunic, and in a bright blue mantle interspersed with silver stars. The reverse shows the initials of the founder within a laurel wreath, and the legend: 'Virtuti et Merito' (Plate 88, Tab. II. No. 13). The decoration is, with the exception of the size, the same for both classes, and is worn, by the first class, across the right shoulder by a ribbon, white in the middle and blue at the borders, and by the second, suspended at the button-hole.

The Knights of the Grand Cross wear, besides, the same cross embroidered in silver, (the middle in silk), on the left side of the breast. The initials of the founder and the motto of the Order, are placed beneath the crescent. (No. 4). On gala days this cross may be adorned with brilliants, and the collar (Plate 89, No. 19) is added to it.

Ecclesiastics, when in their official dress, wear the decoration round the neck, otherwise they have the cross embroidered on the coat or cloak. Since the time of Ferdinand VII. the second class Knights are also allowed to wear upon the breast an embroidered cross, representing the reverse of the decoration (Plate 88, Tab. II. No. 12).

The costume consists of a blue silk mantle interspersed with silver stars, of a blue silk coat with white and blue fringes, of a white and blue sash, black silk breeches, blue velvet hat *à la Henri IV.* with white feathers for the Grand Cross Knights, with blue feathers for the pensioned Knights, and with a blue plume for the supernumerary Knights. The secular officials of the Order have the same costume as the first class Knights, but wear the decoration like the spiritual Knights round the neck.

It may not be uninteresting to know that amongst the Knights of the Grand Cross, created within the last forty-five years, is St. Ignatius Loyola, the founder of the Order of Jesuits. It was customary in Spain during the wars with the Moors, to honour Saints with such decorations, and even nominate them Field-Marshals in some peculiar expeditions. The above worldly honour was conferred on St. Ignatius in 1847.

By a decree of the 26th July, 1847, the Order of Charles III. was divided into four classes: Knights of the Grand Cross, Commanders first and second class, and Knights. The Knights wear the decoration at the button-hole, and the Commanders round the neck. The Commanders, first class, wear besides a star upon the coat, the form of which differs with the Knights of the Grand Cross, who possess the title 'Excellency.' The latter wear on solemn occasions the chain of the Order.

Exclusive of foreign members, the number of Knights Grand Cross is not to exceed one hundred and twenty, and that of the Commanders, first class, three hundred, while that of the two last classes is unlimited.

THE ROYAL ORDER OF MARIA LOUISA.

Was founded on the 19th March, 1792, by King Carlos IV.

to afford the much beloved Queen, as the Warrant says, an additional opportunity of testifying her gratification and good wishes to those noble ladies who distinguish themselves by their loyal services, sincere attachment and noble virtues."

The Order stands under the patronage of St. Ferdinand.

The Queen nominates the lady members, who are bound to visit once a month, one of the hospitals for females or some other similar institution, and also order mass to be read in their presence once a year, for the deceased souls of departed members.

The cross (Plate 89, Tab. III. No. 14) represents on the obverse the figure of St. Ferdinand, and on the reverse the initials of Maria Louisa, with the legend: 'Rl. Ordo dla, Reina Maria Luisa.' It is worn across the right shoulder towards the left side, by a broad violet ribbon, with white stripes in the middle.

This Order, by decree of the present Queen, can only be conferred on individuals recommended by the Cabinet Council.

THE MILITARY ORDER OF ST. HERMENGILDE.

This Order was founded on the 28th November, 1814, by Ferdinand VII., for officers of the Spanish army and navy, as a reward for long service.

The King is Chief and Grand Master of the Order, which is divided into three classes.

To the first class, or Knights of the cross, belong Captain-Generals and Generals, who have possessed the rank of officers for forty years. With the nomination, they receive the title 'Excellency.'

The second class comprises officers of the degree of Brigadier and under, who have also occupied the rank of officers for forty years.

The claim to the third class, is founded on twenty-five years' service, with the rank of officer for at least ten years.

The King has the right to waive the condition of the number of years, in favour of candidates who have specially distinguished themselves in a battle or siege.

Officers who are still on active service, ten years after their nomination, are entitled to a pension, amounting, in the first class, to 10,000 reales (£100), in the second class to 4800 R. (£48), and in the third class to 2400 R. (£24).

The badge consists of a white enamelled cross, surmounted by a gold crown. The round middle is enamelled blue, and represents on the obverse the figure of St. Hermengilde on horseback, holding in her right hand a palm branch, and the legend: 'Premio á la constancia militar' (Reward for military perseverance). The reverse exhibits the initial 'F. VII.' (Plate 90, Tab. IV. No. 21).

The Knights of the Grand Cross wear the decoration across the right shoulder towards the left side, by a broad ribbon with three stripes, crimson in the middle and white at the sides, and are entitled to a star (No. 20) of gold and silver upon the left side of the breast.

The Knights of the second class wear the same star, but suspend the cross at the button-hole.

The Knights of the third class, wear, likewise, the cross at the button-hole, but have no star.

The Chapter meets once a year under the presidency of the Monarch or the Captain-General of the province.

MILITARY ORDER OF ST. FERDINAND.

The foundation of this Order took place in 1811.

SPAIN. *Table* IV.   PLATE 90.

20

22

21

24

23

Hurst and Blackett, London. 1858.

Despite the stanch conservative principles adhered to by the Cortes, that august assembly thought it advisable to yield in this instance, at least, to public opinion. The old monopolies of the nobility, their exclusive possession of all the superior places in the army, navy and military schools, had already been abolished at an early period, while the old knightly orders were about to become so, owing to the extreme unpopularity of the nobility who were the sole owners of those decorations. The creation of new military rewards came then under the serious consideration of the Assembly. Government was resolved to substitute her new military decorations founded on real merit, love of independence and patriotism, for the old ones, which had become mercenary and were an article of traffic in the hands of the generals and local authorities. The new military Order of Merit was then founded and named after St. Ferdinand; it was made accessible to all military persons, whose real distinction and merit were testified by a Commission of Enquiry which was instituted for the purpose.

The badge consisted of a Grand Cross for Generals, a gold cross for officers, and a silver one for sub-officers and privates, the latter exchanging the silver for the gold, on promotion to epaulettes. Certain demonstrations of honour were connected with the Order, as also some pecuniary reward for repeated acts of distinction.

King Ferdinand VII., immediately after his return to his kingdom, declared himself head of the Order, and promulgated on the 10th July, 1815, the following regulations: The King is Chief and Grand Master of the Order: he alone nominates the Knights, who are divided into five classes. The first consists of officers up to the rank of Colonel, the second of officers of the same grade, who have distinguished themselves by heroic deeds; the third comprises Generals; the fourth Generals of prominent distinction; and the fifth, Generals, who, in their capacity of Commanders-in-chief, have done their duty with peculiar skill and success. These last named bear the titles of 'Excellency' and Grand Cross Knights. It is prohibited to petition for nomination into this class.

Knights of repeated and new acts of distinction and merit, receive pensions, viz. a Division-General 15,000, a Brigadier-General 12,000, a Colonel 10,000, a Captain 6000, a subaltern-officer 1095, and a private 750 reales.

For a third exploit or distinction, the pension becomes hereditary, and passes after death, to the widow, or (if single) to the father of the Knight.

Every year, on St. Ferdinand's day, a solemn high mass is said in the presence of all the Knights, and on the following day, for the departed souls of the deceased members.

Plate 89, Tab. III. No. 17, represents the decoration of the first and third classes, and No. 18 of the second and fourth classes, which is worn at the button-hole. No. 16 exhibits the middle of the third, and No. 15 that of the fourth class.

The Knights of the Grand Cross wear besides, a broad ribbon in the form of a scarf across the right shoulder towards the left side.

Sub-officers receive the decoration of the first or second class in silver.

ROYAL AMERICAN ORDER OF ISABELLA THE CATHOLIC.

This Order was founded by Ferdinand VII. on the 24th March, 1815, and placed under the patronage of St. Isabella of Portugal. It was originally destined as a reward of loyalty to the Royal House, and for the defence of the Spanish possessions in America. At present it serves as a distinction of honour for all kinds of merit. The King is head of the Order, which is divided into three classes, Knights of the Grand Cross, Commanders, and Knights.

Nomination to the Order confers personal nobility, and the Grand Cross, the title of 'Excellency.'

The decoration (Plate 90, Tab. IV. No. 23) is worn by the Knights of the first class by a ribbon across the right shoulder towards the left side, (if ecclesiastics, round the neck); by those of the second class round the neck, and by those of the third class at the button-hole; the latter, if ecclesiastics, wear it round the neck by a black ribbon.

The decoration for the Indians is a gold medal with the effigy of the King, and is worn on the breast by a violet ribbon.

The first class have, besides, fastened to the left side of their dress, the star No. 22.

The costume, on gala days, consists of a mantle of yellow velvet, of a tunic of white velvet trimmed with gold embroidery, of white shoes with golden bows, and of a Spanish hat with white and yellow feathers. The decoration is then appended to a collar, and may be adorned with precious stones.

ORDER OF MARIA ISABELLA LOUISA.

It was founded by Ferdinand VII., for the army and navy, on their having taken the oath of allegiance to the Infanta Maria Isabella Louisa, the presumptive heiress to the throne.

It is of gold for officers, and of silver for privates (Plate 90, No. 24).

MEDALS AND DECORATIONS OF HONOUR.

Their number is very great, as in recent times many have

been struck and instituted for special events, purposes, and even individuals.

We shall arrange them, to the best of our knowledge, in chronological order.

1. Medal for the Andalusian army under General Castaños who, on the 19th July, 1808, compelled the French General, Dupont, and his division to surrender at Baylen. It was instituted, in 1808, by the Junta of Seville in the name of the King.

2. Cross for the troops of General La Romana, instituted on the 23rd March, 1809.

3. Cross for the zeal and patriotism displayed by the Junta of Catalonia, instituted by the Central Junta on the 15th January, 1810, and confirmed by the King on the 12th May, 1815.

4. Medal for the eldest son of Count Casa-Roxas, Don José, for his distinguished patriotism and exemplary disinterestedness in the sacrifices made by him during the French invasion. It was founded in 1810.

5. Cross for the defence of Gerona in 1809, founded on the 14th September, 1810.

6. Cross for the generals and officers who were present at the battle of Talavera, on the 28th July, 1809. It was founded on the 8th December, 1810.

7. Cross for the carabine batallion which defended the town of Lerin, on the 25th, 26th and 27th September, 1808. It was founded on the 23rd July, 1811.

8. Cross for the Spaniards who accompanied the King to Valencey. It was founded on the 23rd August, 1814.

9. Cross for the military who distinguished themselves at the siege of Saragossa. It was instituted on the 30th August, 1814, of gold for generals and officers, and of copper, for privates.

10. Cross for the military who were present at the battle of St. Marcial, near Bidassoa, on the 30th August, 1813. It was founded on the 24th October, 1814, of gold, for generals and officers, and of copper, for common soldiers.

11. Medal for the military who were prisoners in France. It was founded on the 6th November, 1814, of gold, for superior officers, and of silver, for privates. A decree of the 26th July, 1815, admits civilians also to this medal.

12. Cross for the individuals who incurred the disgrace and persecution of the Prince of the Peace by their adherence and loyalty to the King, at and after his arrest in the Escurial. It was founded on the 5th December, 1814.

13. Cross of gold for the officers, and of silver for the privates of the garrison of Ciudad-Rodrigo, who distinguished themselves at the sorties on the 10th July, 1810. It was instituted on the 6th December, 1819.

14. Cross of gold, for the guards and officers, and of copper for the men, of the Andalusian corps, who distinguished themselves in the campaign of 1813, and more especially at the taking of Pancorbo, and the engagements of Soraura in the Pyrenees and Nivelle. It was founded on the 28th December, 1814.

15. Cross for the Generals and officers of the 4th army, who were present at the battle of Toulouse on the 10th April, 1814. It was founded on the 30th January, 1815.

16. Cross for the troops who were present at the battle of Chiclana, on the 5th March, 1811. It was founded on the 13th February, 1815.

17. Cross for the Generals, officers, and men of the army of Estremadura, who distinguished themselves at the battle of Albufera, won by the Generals Castaños and Blake, on the 16th March, 1811. It was founded on the 1st March, 1815.

18. Cross founded on the 17th March, 1815, in com-

memoration of the recapture of Seville on the 27th August, 1812. It is of gold for officers, and of bronze for privates.

19. Cross for the brave soldiers of the first army who distinguished themselves in the war of independence, especially in Catalonia. It was founded on the 31st March, 1815.

20. Cross, founded on the 31st March, 1815, for the troops of the second army, who had distinguished themselves in Murcia.

21. Cross for the third army, commanded by the Duke Albuquerque, in the island of Léon, and at the defence of Cadiz. It was also founded on the 31st March, 1815.

22. Cross, instituted on the 2nd April, 1815, in commemoration of the Battle of Vittoria, on the 21st June, 1813, won by the divisions of the 4th Corps of the Army, under the command of the Captain-General, the Duke of Ciudad Rodrigo (Wellington), and Field-Marshal, D. Francisco Thomas de Longa.

23. Cross of merit for the Artillery Corps, for the defence of the castle San Lorenzo del Puntal, in the environs of Cadiz, in 1814. It was founded on the 10th April, 1815.

24. Cross founded on the same day in commemoration of the defence of Astorza against the Corps-d'armée of Junot.

25. Cross founded on the 27th April, 1815, in commemoration of the Battle of Valls, in Catalonia, on the 25th February, 1809, which was won by General Reding.

26. Cross conferred on a Grenadier column (second Army Corps, third division) for the sanguinary battle near Ordal, in Catalonia, on the night of the 12th September, 1813.

27. Cross founded on the 14th May, 1815, for the troops under Don Juan Senen de Contreras, who succeeded in prolonging for two months the defence of Tarragona.

28. Cross founded on the same day for the soldiers of the small Army Corps of Arragon, under the command of Don Joachim Blake, who had distinguished themselves at the

Battle of Alcaniz, on the 23rd May, 1809, against Marshal Suchet.

29. Cross for the Generals, officers and soldiers of the Galician Army (6th army, or left wing), who had distinguished themselves in the sanguinary mountain engagements of Rio-Seco, Sornaza, Gueces, Espinosa, &c. It was founded on the 14th May, and 12th and 25th of June, 1815.

30. Cross founded on the 29th May, 1815, for the troops of the 7th army, in the War of Independence, in the towns of Castille, Astoria, Arragon and Navarre, as also in the Basque provinces, under General Don Gabriel de Mendizabal.

31. Cross founded on the 3rd June, 1815, in gold for officers, and in silver for privates, who had distinguished themselves on the 7th June, 1808, near the bridge of Alcolea, against General Dupont.

32. Cross founded on the 4th May, 1815, in gold, for the officers, and in silver, for the men of the 4th army, and of the navy, who had distinguished themselves at the defence of Tariffa, in December, 1811.

33. Cross founded on the 4th June, 1815, for civilians, who, true to the King and the legitimate cause, preferred incarceration in the prisons of France, to the recognition of the government of Napoleon.

34. Cross founded on the 4th June, 1815, for the Army Corps, which defended Asturia against Marshal Ney, and the Generals Kellerman and Bonnet.

35. Cross founded on the 5th June, 1815, for the Army Corps of Estramadura, under the Duke Albuquerque, which covered the retreat of the government to the island of Leon, in the year 1810.

36. Medal instituted on the 12th June, 1815, of gold, for the officers, of silver, for the sub-officers, and of copper, for the men of the van-guard of the centre, commanded by General

Don Franciscus Xaverus de Venegas, for the engagement of Tarancon, on the 25th December, 1808.

37. Cross founded on the 14th June, 1815, of gold for the Generals, officers and soldiers, who were present at the sieges of Pampeluna and Bayonne, in 1813 and 1814, under the command of General España.

38. Medal (of the 2nd July), for the troops present at the battle of Tamames, on the 18th October, 1809.

39. Medal (of the same date) for the troops who were engaged in the battle of Medina del Campo, on the 23rd November, 1809.

40. Cross (of the 9th July, 1815), for the Cabinet-couriers employed in active service during the War of Independence.

41. Cross, founded on the 2nd July, 1815, for the Spanish divisions, who forsook the French army in Portugal, in 1808, on the War of Independence breaking out, and who joined the patriotic levies which were fighting for their King and country.

42. Cross founded on the 27th October, 1815, for the widows' children and near relations of those who fell at the rising of Madrid, against the French, on the 2nd May, 1808.

43. Cross of gold and enamel for the officers, and of gilt silver, for the sub-officers and men of the army and navy, who had taken part in the siege of Cartagena de las Indias, in America, under the command of Lieutenant-General Morillo. It was founded on the 1st of April, 1816.

44. Cross founded on the 18th April, 1816, for the troops of the 1st Division, under General Reding, in the engagement of Menjibar, on the 16th July, 1808.

45—47. Crosses founded on the 30th May, 1816, for the officers and men who were present at the Battles of Bubierca (29th November, 1808), of Aranjuez (5th August, 1809), and of Almonacid (11th August, 1809).

48. Decoration of honour, founded on the 31st May, 1816

for the members of the council of the Mesta (a privileged corporation of the owners of migratory flocks of sheep), who had taken part in the sittings of the 26th April, and 3rd May, 1816, under the presidency of the King.

49. Cross (of the 27th June, 1816), for all the military who formed the division of Majorca, during the War of Independence, under Lieutenant-General Wittingham.

50. Cross (of the above date) for the troops of the division of Malloria, who were present at the battle of Castella, against Marshal Suchet, on the 13th April, 1813.

51. Cross founded on the 22nd September, 1816, for the Chefs, officers, and other individuals of the royal navy, who had contributed to the success of the War of Independence. For officers it is of gold and enamel, and for the lower ranks, of silver.

52. Medal purposely struck on the 23rd October, 1816, for Don Fernando Ramirez de Luque, Don Antonio Ortiz Repiso, Don Francisco Polo Valenzuela, and Don Francisco d'Assis de la Carrera, as a reward for their services rendered on the 25th September, 1810, in Lucena, at the risk of their own lives.

53. Cross founded on the 13th May, 1807, for the troops of the Galician army who took an active part, under the command of General Don Nicolas Mahy, at the re-capture of Villafranca del Vierzo, as also in the engagements of the 18th and 19th May, 1809, near Lago. It is of gold for officers, and of bronze for the lower degrees.

54. Cross founded at the same date, for the inhabitants of Madrid, who so stoutly resisted the entrance of the French in the first three days of December, 1808. The claims to this decoration were rigidly examined, and refused to those who had directly or indirectly purchased, or were engaged in the sale of any of the national property at that period; and none

were admitted who had accepted places or served in the National Guard during the unlawful government of the French.

55. Medal bestowed on the 19th October, 1823, on twenty-seven inhabitants of Villar de Ciervos, who had distinguished themselves on the 27th August of that year, in the engagement against the constitutional band of Don Alonzo Martin, Lieutenant-Colonel of the regiment of Algarbia, and brother of the notorious Empecinado.

56. *Scutcheon of loyalty*, founded on the 14th December, 1823, for the Spaniards who, in the years 1820 and 1823, quitted their herds and flocks and fought with courage, perseverance, and inviolable faith for the cause of their King, religion and country. It is worn on the left side of the breast, embroidered, for sub-officers, with silk, and for privates, with wool, and has the inscription: 'El Rey á la fidelidad' (The King to loyalty).

57. *Cross for Military Loyalty*, was founded on the 9th August, 1824, as a reward for the royal troops who resolutely and bravely defended, in the years 1820 and 1823, the sovereignty of the King. It is of gold for the higher grades, of silver for subaltern officers, and of copper for privates. The obverse bears the inscription: 'El Rey á la Fidelidad Militar,' and the reverse, the royal crest with the legend: 'Fernando VII. á los defensores de la religion y del trono en grado heroico y eminente' (Ferdinand VII. to those who defended in a most heroic and eminent manner the religion and the throne). For those who merited the reward in the time from the 7th March, 1820, to the 30th June, 1822, the cross is additionally adorned with a laurel branch. The period is divided into two parts, from the 7th March, 1820, to the 30th June, 1822, and again from the latter date to the 1st March, 1823. Those who have taken part in the

campaigns of either of the two periods, wear the decoration at the button-hole, while those who were engaged in both periods suspend it round the neck.

58. Queen Maria Christina founded, in her capacity of Regent, on the 10th October, 1832, a decoration of honour under the name: 'Constancia Militar' (Military constancy.) It is divided into four classes: the first is conferred for ten years' service, and is accompanied by an additional pay of 4 reales per month, the second for fifteen years' service with an addition of 10 R., the third for twenty years' service with an addition of 20 R., and the fourth for twenty-five years' service with an addition of 30 reales.

SWEDEN AND NORWAY.

GENERAL REMARKS.

The King is the head and Grand Master of all the Swedish Orders, but has not the right to abolish any of them.

As a mark of special favour, he may confer the decoration set in diamonds.

The entrance fees paid by foreigners go to the treasury of the Hospital at Stockholm.

He who wears a decoration unlawfully, is liable to a fine of 333 rixthalers and 16 skillings (about £23).

In 1783, King Gustavus III. ordered, that a collection of the portraits of all the Knights, in copper-plate engravings, should be published, accompanied by a brief biography, written by the Court historiographer. The work had actually been begun, and a considerable number of the portraits been worked off by the celebrated J. F. Martin, when the war put an end to the undertaking.

No Swedish subject can accept a foreign Order without special permission from the King.

The decorations are not hereditary, and must be returned after the decease of the owners.

BP/GP

Stockholm, December 28, 1966.

William Reid, Esq.
The Armouries
H.M. Tower of London
London, E.C.3.

Dear Mr. Reid,

Unfortunately, I must tell you that the Order of Amaranth was founded by Queen Christina and has no older origin. It was founded by the Queen in connection with a festival in 1653 arranged in honour of the Portuguese Ambassador Pimentelli. He was viz. born in the town of Amarante in the north of Portugal. The Queen personated on that occasion the shepherdess Amaranta. The order became never an order of the State but was to a certain extension used by the Queen during the short time to her abdication in 1654. Thereafter it came to an end.

The existing social Order, The big Order of Amaranthe was founded in 1760 and has no direct connection with Queen Christina's order, though, they try to maintain it. Thus the existing device, Memoria Dulcis, is related to the original one, Dolce nella memoria. The monogram is directly imitated and ought to be two A, one of them upside down, not AV. The symbol in Christina's order was surrounded by a laurel wreath, the latter has a Maltese wreath.

Yours sincerely,

SWEDEN *Table* I. PLATE 91.

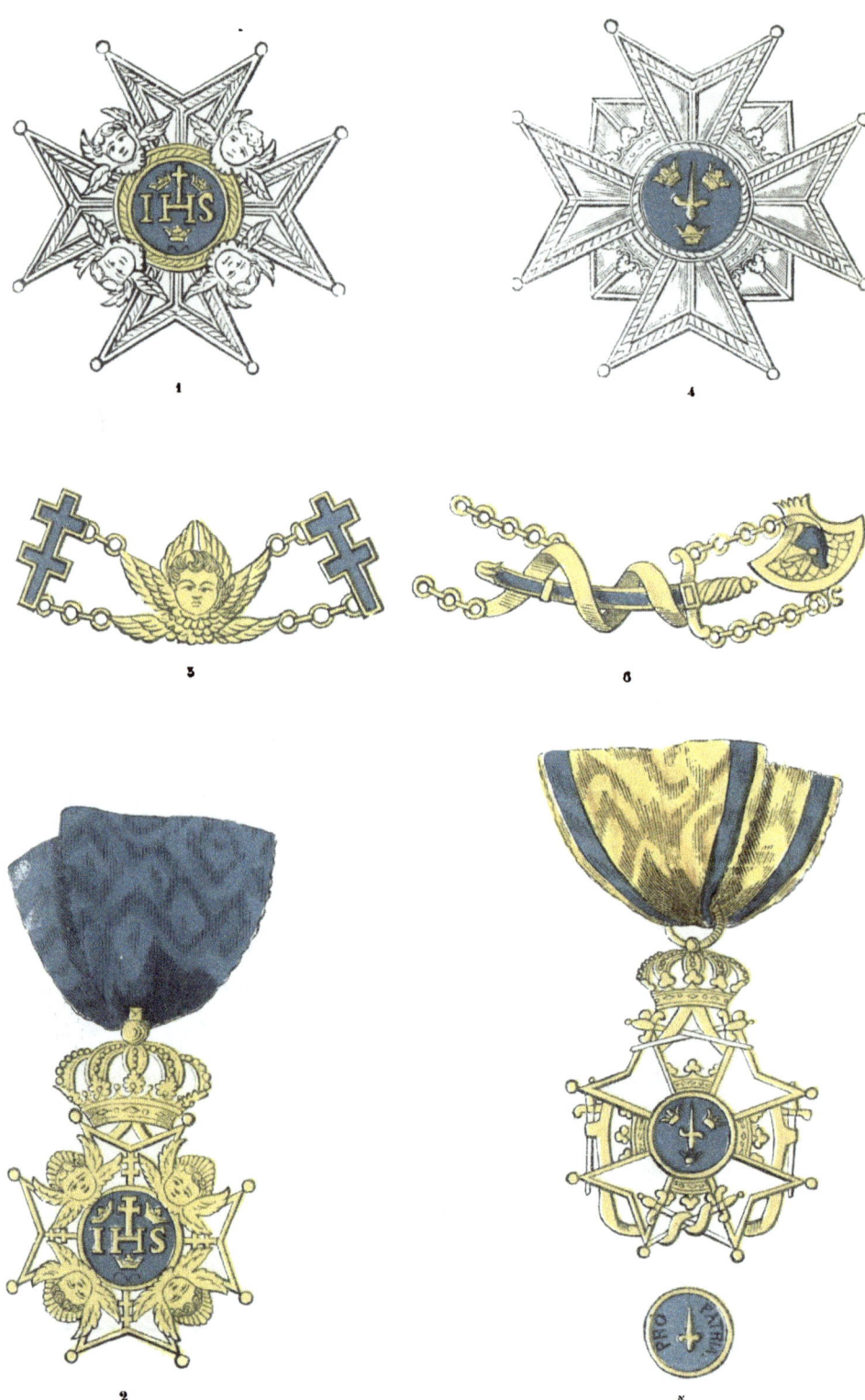

Hurst and Blackett, London. 1858.

THE ORDER OF THE SERAPHIM, OR THE "BLUE RIBBON."

There is no doubt whatever of the antiquity of this Order, yet it is very difficult to arrive at the exact date of the foundation. General opinion, though without positive proof, ascribes its origin, about the year 1280, to King Magnus I., who is said to have instituted it at the persuasion of the Maltese Knights. Another account ascribes the foundation to Magnus's grandson, Magnus Erichson. This presumption is somewhat supported by the historical fact, that Erichson had, at his coronation, in 1336, dubbed several persons Knights of the Order of the Seraphim. From this bare fact, however, we would rather be inclined to infer that the Order had already been in existence at the time of his accession to the throne.

Quite as uncertain are the form of the insignia, and the provisions of the statutes in ancient times. We only know, that on grand occasions, a certain number of individuals were knighted and created members of the Order, while the earliest form of the badge is only known to us historically by a description of the time of Charles IX., who abolished the Order on the introduction of Lutheranism in Sweden. At that time, the decoration consisted of an oval medal, enamelled blue, with the name 'Jesus' in gold, and with four small white and black enamelled nails at the narrow edges, in allusion to the passion of Christ. This medal was then worn appended to a gold neck-chain, composed of red enamelled cherubims, and patriarchal crosses without enamel.

King Frederick I. revived the Order, as also those of the Sword and North Star, on the 28th April, 1748 (his seventy-second birthday). He also promulgated new statutes, which King Charles XIII. afterwards modified in many points.

The principal provisions of the new statutes are:

That the Order is to consist of only one class, comprising twenty-four Swedish and eight foreign Knights (the number has, however, of late been greatly exceeded), exclusive of the King and the royal princes, who are considered born Knights, as also of the reigning monarchs and princes abroad, and their eldest sons, who may be admitted to the Order.

The candidates to possess the rank of, at least, Lieutenant-General.

The nomination of new members to take place once a-year in the Chapter, usually on the Monday after Advent, to remind the Knights that faith is due to the King of Zion. The actual reception into the Order, however, is fixed at the 28th April, the birthday of King Frederick I. of glorious memory. In the interval between the nomination and reception, the newly elected member can only wear the star, but not the cross with the ribbon.

The reception takes place at Stockholm in the Knightly Holm Church, or in the royal chapel in the Castle, in the presence of all the Knights and functionaries of the Order, as also of the Commanders of all the other Orders.

The ceremonies are as follow:

The King is seated under a canopy to the right of the altar, and the Knights assembled occupy benches to the right and the left, while the newly elected member is placed in front of the altar between two senior members, who act, as it were, as sponsors. After the hymn, "Come, Holy Spirit" is chanted, the chief preacher of the Court briefly addresses the meeting on the duties of the subjects towards God, the King, and the country. The Chancellor, who stands to the left of the sovereign, then explains in a few words the object of the Order, the honour attached to it, and the reasons which have induced

His Majesty to elect the new Knight. The two sponsors, thereupon, conduct the postulant before the King, where he kneels down, and replies affirmatively, with a simple "Yes," to all the following questions: Does he promise before God and the King:

1. To honour, defend and preserve the laws and statutes of the Order?

2. To be ready to shed his blood for the Evangelical Lutheran religion, and for the welfare of the country?

3. To assist, by his courage, to sustain the ancient glory of the Swedish name?

4. To contribute, to the best of his power, to a life of peace and union amongst the Knights of the Order?

5. To watch over the honours and privileges now granted to him?

6. To do good to the poor, and protect widows and orphans?

On these questions being answered, the King hands the diploma to the Secretary from whom the Chancellor receives the document and reads it aloud to the assembly, after which the new Knight swears to defend with his life and property the Christian religion, to remain true to the King and the State, to protect the poor, widows and orphans, and to promote their welfare to the best of his power.

The King then takes from the Treasurer the chain of the Order, hangs it round the neck of the new Knight, and, dubbing him with the coronation sword, says: "We . . . . "King of Sweden, Gothia and Vandalia, receive thee as a "brave and honourable Swedish and Gothian Knight of our " Order of the Seraphim. Be worthy of it," and embracing him amid the sound of drums and trumpets, he concludes with the words: " May the Lord protect thee !" The Knight, thus elected, then thanks His Majesty, kisses his hand, and embraces all his new colleagues, whereupon each of them repeats the words:

"May the Lord protect thee!" With this, the ceremony terminates.

The spiritual functions of the Order are managed by the chaplain of the Court, who is also an ecclesiastical member of the Order, and in that capacity wears a small seraphim cross appended to a gold chain.

No Swede can obtain this Order without already possessing either that of the 'Sword' or the 'North Star.' On receiving the 'Order of the Seraphim' he becomes a Commander of the previous Order or Orders.

The new member pays entrance fees of 200 ducats for the treasury of the Order, 25 rixthaler, stamp duties, 5 rixthaler, chancery dues, and 1 thaler and 16 skillings, for every year of his age. The annual subscription is only 8 skillings to defray the necessary expenses of the Order.

The entrance fees of foreigners go—as mentioned above— to the treasury of the Hospital of Stockholm.

No member can accept a foreign decoration without special permission from the Chapter.

In 1784, Gustavus III. appointed a Bishop for the Order, to supervise the ecclesiastics placed in the hospitals and schools of the Order.

At festivals, the costume of the Knights consists of a garment of white satin, after the national fashion, with black cuffs, facings, buttons and cords; of white shoes, with heels of black velvet, and with bows instead of buckles; of a round hat of black velvet, with a white ribbon and five feathers, (four white and one black), at the left side; and of a mantle of black satin and white lining, and collar, with the star of the Order (Plate 91, Tab. I. No. 1) on the left side. This latter is also embroidered, in a smaller size, upon the doublet. The cross of the Order is appended to the neck-chain, consisting of seraphim heads and patriarchal crosses (No. 3). On festival days, the Knights dine at the royal table with their hats on their heads.

The cross (Tab. I. No. 2) is usually worn across the right shoulder, towards the left side, by a blue ribbon. The letters I. H. S. upon the star and the cross, are the initials of the words: 'Jesus hominum salvator.' The reverse of the cross contains the initials: 'F. R. S.' (Fredericus Rex Sueciae).

The high officials of the Order, the Treasurer, the Secretary, and the Master of Ceremonies wear the star on the left side of the breast, and the cross round the neck, by a ribbon about two and a half inches wide. The inferior officers have a small cross at the button-hole, suspended by a ribbon about one and a half inches wide.

Above the seat of each Knight in the Holm church, at Stockholm, are engraved on a copper table his arms, name, motto, and the day of his nomination. There exists, also, a Register office of the Order, in which the armorial bearings of the Knights are recorded, and for which registration 8 rixthalers must be paid in every instance.

THE ORDER OF THE SWORD, OR OF THE YELLOW RIBBON.

The foundation of this Order is ascribed to King Gustavus Vasa, and was originally designed as a reward for military courage and useful service in the army. After a long interval of desuetude, it was revived by King Frederick I. on the 28th April, 1748, together with the Orders of the Seraphim and North-Star. The same monarch gave it statutes, which were, with a trifling modification, confirmed by his successor, Adolphus Frederick. King Gustavus III. added, 1772, a fourth class, now marked as the first, to the three former ones. The present statutes were promulgated by Gustavus IV., on the 28th November, 1798, while Charles XIII. added to them, on the 9th July, 1814, supplementary bye-laws.

The Order consists of:
1. Commanders with the Grand Cross.
2. Commanders.
3. Knights of the Grand Cross, first class, and
4. Knights.

The first class, that of Commander of the Grand Cross, is only conferred in time of war, for some signal victory gained by land or sea. Not even the King himself can obtain this cross without the unanimous approval of the army—an instance of which happened with Gustavus in 1789.

To be eligible for commanders, the rank of, at least, a general is required. To this class belong the royal princes by birth.

No one below the rank of Major-General is admissible to the third class. The candidate must have commanded a division or a corps at a siege, or in a battle, or been employed against the enemy in the capacity of a Division-General.

To be admitted to the fourth class, the rank of Captain and a service of twenty years are required.

The reception of the Knights takes place without religious ceremonies in the royal apartments, in the presence of the Grand Cross members of the Order, of the Knights of the Seraphim, and the Commanders of all the other Swedish Orders. By the oath, the Knight binds himself "to defend with life and property the Evangelico-Lutheran religion, to serve faithfully the King and the country, and to combat courageously against the foes of the country." When a foreigner is elected Knight of the Grand Cross, the insignia are sent to him abroad, while he, in his turn, transmits to the Archives of the Order a statement of the services rendered by him.

The revenues of the Order are applied to pensions granted by the Chapter to the Commanders and Knights.

The entrance-fee of a Commander is 12 rixthalers, 12 skillings, stamp duty, and 2 rixthalers, Chancery dues: that of Knight of the Grand Cross, 20 rixthalers banco, or 5 ducats in gold, and that of the Knights is 2 rixthalers and 24 skillings stamp duty, and 2 rixthalers Chancery dues.

The badge is a gold octagonal white-enamelled cross, surmounted by a gold crown (Plate 91, Tab. I. No 5). Between the angles are gold crowns, and above them crossed swords, entwined by their appendages. Upon the blue middle are exhibited, on the obverse, three gold crowns with a gold sword in the centre, and, on the reverse, a similar sword, with a laurel wreath upon its point, surrounded by the words: 'Pro patriâ.' The first class wear the badge across the left shoulder, towards the right side, by a yellow ribbon with blue borders, accompanied by a star (No. 4), embroidered in silver upon the left breast.

The second class wear it, of a smaller size, round the neck, by a somewhat narrower ribbon, accompanied by a sword of silver, or embroidered in silver upon, the left breast. Those who have entered the second class, from the third, are distinguished by two crossed swords on the breast, while those who pass from the second class into the Order of the Seraphim, or are nominated commander of some other Order, wear the sword below the star of the Seraphim or other Order. The third class wear the Grand Cross by a still narrower ribbon round the neck. The cross of that class has the two crossed swords only between the two upper arms. The same cross is also worn by the fourth class at the button-hole, suspended by a very narrow ribbon.

The costume of the Order, bright blue and white, is the old national colour. When worn with this costume, the decoration is appended to a chain (No. 6), consisting of swords and appendages, and eleven blue helmets upon golden shields.

The two heralds wear, by a blue and yellow silken cord, an oval shield with the Swedish arms. The centre contains a blue sword, and above it the inscription: 'Pro patriâ.' Their costume is that of the first two classes, except that they wear, instead of the mantle, a camail, trimmed with cords and golden fringes. Upon the breast and back of the camail is a sword, embroidered in gold, and upon the shoulders the motto of the Order (Pro patriâ).

ORDER OF THE POLAR STAR, OR "THE BLACK RIBBON."

The existence of this Order, previous to the 28th April, 1748, is, like that of the two former, extremely uncertain. It is usually conferred for civil virtues, for zeal in the promotion of public good and useful institutions; nor are foreigners excluded from it. The symbol of the Order, the Polar Star, is to remind the Knights never to allow the glory of the Swedish name to set.

The Order has three classes, Commanders of the Grand Cross, Commanders, and Knights. The Princes of the blood royal are, by birth, members of the first class, and the reception of a Knight of this Order into the Seraphim creates him a Commander of the Polar Star. No one can be admitted to the Commander class who does not already possess another decoration, and has besides a civil rank, which entitles him to the predicate of 'Tro Man' (Trusty and well beloved), or to episcopal dignity in the Church.

The number of the members is unlimited, though by the decree of Gustavus III. the clergy were to have eight crosses of Commanders, and twelve of Knights. A Swede cannot become a Commander without previously possessing the Knight's cross.

The entrance fee of a Commander is 12 rixthalers, and

SWEDEN. Table II.   PLATE 92.

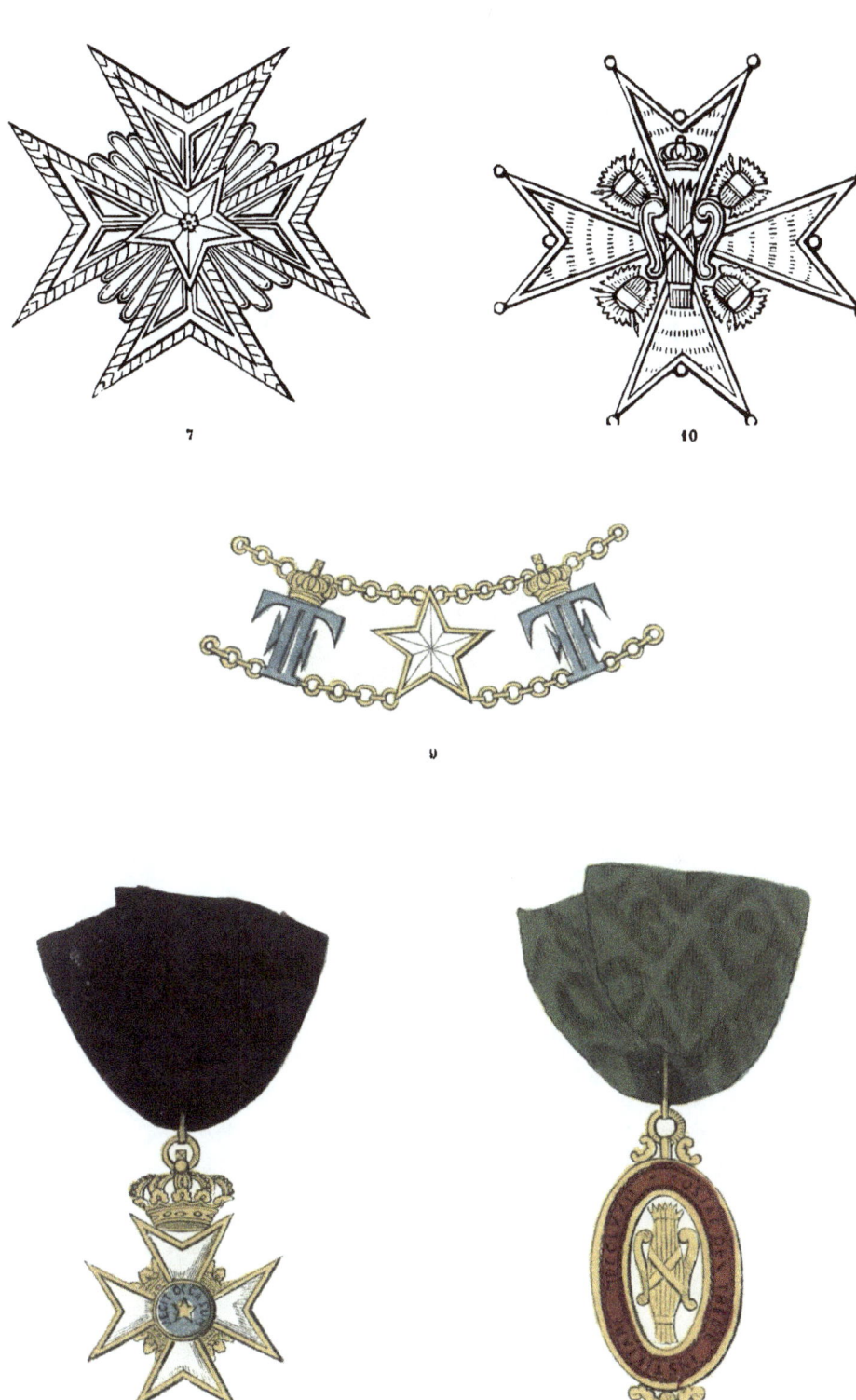

24 skillings stamp, and 2 rix thaler Chancery dues. The Knights pay only half of the stamp duty, and 2 rix thaler, Chancery dues.

The decoration is an octagonal gold cross, enamelled white, and with gold crowns in the angles. Upon the blue middle is a pentagonal star, with the legend: 'Nescit Occasum' (It knows of no setting or going down,) (Plate 92, Tab. II. No. 8).

This cross is worn by the Commanders of the Grand Cross across the right shoulder towards the left hip by a large black cord, accompanied upon the breast by the silver star (Tab. II. No. 7) with the North Star in the middle.

The Commanders wear it round the neck by a black ribbon, without the star upon the breast, while the Knights suspend it, in smaller size, at the button-hole.

On solemn occasions, the cross is worn appended to the neck chain (Tab. II. No. 9), the links of which represent the North Star, and a blue double 'F' (Frederick), while the Commanders then appear in red velvet and white satin breeches.

THE ORDER OF VASA.

This Order was founded by Gustavus III. on the 26th May, 1776, on the day of his coronation, to reward therewith individuals who render important service to the nation, by their writings, or by practical improvements in agriculture, mining or commerce.

It is divided into three classes, Commanders of the Grand Cross, Commanders, and Knights. The number is unlimited and includes foreigners.

The right of nomination is vested in the crown; and the King himself, if he be not already a Knight of the Order, receives the insignia, at his coronation, from the hands of the Bishop who performs the ceremony.

The badge, an oval gold escutcheon, contains the Vasa crest, surrounded by a red enamelled stripe with golden edges, and with the legend: 'Gustaf den Tredie instiktare MDCCLXXII,' (Gustavus III. instituted 1772), (Tab. II. No. 11). It is worn by a broad green ribbon, by the Grand Cross Commanders across the shoulder, and by the Commanders round the neck. Both are accompanied by the star No. 10.

The Knights who were nominated previous to the 14th October, 1844, wear the decoration equally round the neck but without the star, while those, elected since, suspend it at the button-hole, surmonted by the royal crown.

On festival days, the decoration is appended to a chain (Plate 93, Tab. III. No. 14), the links of which represent alternately, gold sheaves, and shields with the Swedish arms, surrounded by the attributes of commerce, the arts and agriculture, and the arms of Holstein. On such days, also, the Commanders appear in the national costume, in green velvet, and white satin breeches, and a green velvet mantle with white lining.

The nomination ceremonies are the same as those of the Order of the Sword, and so is, in substance, the oath. The fees of the Commanders are 18 rix thalers and 36 skillings, stamp duty, and 2 rix thalers, Chancery dues. The Knights pay only 6 rix thalers and 12 skillings, stamp duty while the Chancery dues are the same (2 rix thalers).

ORDER OF CHARLES XIII.

This Order was founded by the King, whose name it bears, on the 17th May, 1811, as a badge of honour for the Swedish

SWEDEN. Table III.   PLATE 93.

Freemasons of the higher degrees. It has only one class. The King, the presumptive heir to the throne, and the Princes of the royal family, can never divest themselves of the insignia.

The decoration (Tab. III. No. 13) is worn round the neck, and the cross (No. 12) of red cloth or enamel, upon the breast. The middle of the cross shows on the obverse the number XIII. between two C's in monogram, and on the reverse a G within a triangle, the mysterious sense of which is only known to the fraternity.

MEDALS AND BADGES OF HONOUR.

1. *Medal for Valour in the Field,* is of gold for officers, and of silver for sub-officers and privates, with the inscription: 'För Tapperhet i Fält' (For valour in the field); it is worn upon the left side of the breast. There are some with the effigy of Gustavus III., others, with that of Gustavus Adolph, and again others, with that of Charles John (Tab. III. No. 16.)

2. *Medal of Svenksund,* of gold, weighing from five to ten ducats. It was instituted in commemoration of the naval victory gained in the reign of Gustavus III. over the Russian fleet on the 8th July, 1790, which brought about the peace of the 14th August, of the same year (Tab. III. No. 15).

3. *The Seraphim Medal, or Medal for Charitable Institutions.*—It is of gold, weighing five ducats, and is bestowed upon those who distinguish themselves by zeal and care for the poor. The obverse bears the portrait of the King with the inscription: 'Fredericus D. G. Rex Sueciae,' and the reverse shows the words: 'Ordo eq. Seraphin. restauratus natali regis

LXXIII' (The Order of the Seraphim restored on the seventy-third birth-day of the King), surrounded by a collar of the same Order, with the legend: 'Proceres cum rege nectit, 1748.' (It unites the Peers with the King).

4. *Medal of* 1772, in commemoration of the Revolution. It is of gold, weighing eight ducats.

SWITZERLAND.

MEDALS.

1. *Medal of* 1815.—Under the Bourbons, the Republic, the Directory and the Consulate of France, a number of Swiss troops served as volunteers in the French army, and in 1812 a Swiss contingency was promised to the French empire by a formal convention. After the abdication of Napoleon, the four Swiss regiments, which he had retained, remained in France, and passed over to the restored monarchy. It was not so, however, when Napoleon returned from Elba; most of the Swiss officers and soldiers refused to change masters, and preferred going back to their own country, where, moreover, a call for their assistance had been made by the Swiss Confederacy. In acknowledgment of this proof of patriotism, the Swiss government resolved, on the 20th April, 1815, to issue a badge of honour for them. It consists of a silver medal, representing, on the obverse, the old Confederate banner, with the inscription: 'Schweizerische Eidgenossenschaft, 1815,' (Swiss Confederacy, 1815), and on the reverse an oak wreath, with the inscription: 'Treue und Ehre' (Faith and Honour), and is worn at the button-hole by a red and white ribbon (Plate 94, No 1).

By a decree of the 24th August of that year, the company of one hundred Swiss, who had joined Louis XVIII. at Ghent, was allowed to partake of the distinction. The distribution took place at Iverdun, on the 15th October, 1815, with great solemnities.

2. *Medal of the 10th August.*—On the 7th August, 1817, the Swiss government resolved to confer a medal of cast iron on all the survivors of the Swiss Guard, who had defended the Tuileries on the 10th August, 1792. The obverse represents the Confederacy Cross, and the words: 'Treue und Ehre,' and the reverse contains the inscription: 'August, MDCCXCII.' It is worn upon the left breast by a red and white ribbon (No. 2). A list of those who had died previously, was deposited in the Archives of the Confederation.

SWITZERLAND AND HANSE TOWNS.

PLATE 94.

TUNIS. PLATE 95.

TUNIS.

THE NICHAN.

The historical data about this Order (Plate 95, No. 3) are imperfect. It is worn round the neck, and its degree seems to be estimated by the number and value of the precious stones with which it is adorned.

On the Bey's visit to France in 1846, he distributed several, of the value averaging from 10,000 to 30,000 francs.

TURKEY.

ORDER OF THE CRESCENT.

MEDAL WITH PORTRAIT OF MAHMUD.

The Sultan Selim III., under the impression that radical reforms could alone save his tottering empire from utter ruin, resolved to introduce into Turkey various useful customs and regulations prevailing in the civilized states of Europe, and amongst others, the creation of decorations. He accordingly founded in 1799, the Order of the Crescent; but, owing to national prejudices, he was obliged to confine its distribution to foreigners. Nelson was the first who received it, for his victory of Abukir, and General Sebastiani, the next, for his defence of Constantinople against the English fleet, in 1807. The insurrection of the Janissaries suspended all further attempts at reform, until the accession of Mahmud, who resumed the schemes of progress commenced by his uncle.

After the annihilation of the Janissaries, Mahmud resolved (1827) to re-organize his troops, and introduce, at the same time, military distinctions of merit and honour. He instituted, accordingly, a gold medal, set in diamonds, bearing his initial, and conferred it on several of his officers. He next instituted a medal with his portrait, also set in diamonds (Plate 96, No. 3), which he presented to many great dignitaries of state, and to a few foreign Ambassadors; still later, on the 19th August, 1831, he founded the Badge of Glory, or the decoration of

TURKEY. PLATE 96.

Hurst and Blackett, London. 1858.

NICHANI-IFTIHAR,

a gold medal with or without brilliants, and with the *tughra* (initial) of the founder.

This Order has, properly speaking, no particular classes, though the difference in the styles of the diplomas, as also in the number of the brilliants with which the badge is adorned, would almost lead to the belief that there are higher and lower degrees in it. The medal with brilliants is usually bestowed on persons of rank and eminence; but, as there are no regulations concerning the adornment of the decorations, the recipients can do with it whatever they like. The badge is meant to be worn round the neck, and so it is actually worn by the Sultan, the high functionaries, and most of the foreigners. Some, however, fasten it to the breast.

Neither is the colour of the ribbon clearly defined. Most of the Turks append the decoration to a chain or cord of various colours, or fasten it by a buckle, while Europeans usually suspend it by a red ribbon, with or without a green stripe near the borders. In recent times, the ribbon, with green borders, seems to have become the fashion (No. 1 and 2).

Since the accession of the present Sultan (Abdul Medjid), the badges conferred on foreigners are nearly all of the same form, and only differ in the size and number of the diamonds, as also in the style and expressions of the diplomas.

THE ORDER OF THE MEDJIDIE,

Was founded in 1852, as reward for distinguished services in the various departments of the administration. The principal provisions of the statutes are as follow:

The Order (Plate 96, No. 6) is under the special patronage of the Sultan, and has five classes, the number of the respective native members being limited to fifty, one hundred and fifty, eight hundred, three thousand, and six thousand.

The badge consists of a silver sun with seven rays or points, between which are inserted the Turkish arms, star and crescent. The middle shield, which rests upon the sun, and is for the first four classes, of gold, bears upon red enamelled ground the legend, in the vernacular tongue: 'Zeal, decoration, loyalty,' and also '1268' (1852) the year of the foundation of the Order, and in the centre, the name of the Sultan. The size of the decoration, though it diminishes with every descending class, is, nevertheless, rather smaller with the second than with the third class, owing no doubt, to the additional star which is worn upon the right breast by the latter class, in the same way as it is worn by the first class upon the left breast in a larger size. This star is almost similar to the badge. The first three classes suspend the decoration round the neck by a red ribbon with green borders, and the two inferior classes wear it upon the left side of the breast by a similar ribbon.

No one can be proposed as a candidate who has not eminently served the state, for at least twenty years, either in the army, the law (Ulema), or some civil department. Military service in time of war does not require that long term of years, nor are very distinguished services bound by it. The entrance into the Order begins with the lowest class, and the gradual promotion depends on new services, and only after an interval of two years in the fifth class, three years in the third and fourth classes, and four years in the second class.

The board or council, which meets once a month for despatch of business, consists of a president elected from the first class, and six members, (two from each of the three next classes).

The entrance fee of the first class is 2500 piasters (£25), or the second 1500 (£15), of the third 750 (£7 10s.), and of the fourth and fifth classes 200 (£2). Foreigners and the military are exempt from these fees.

MEDAL.

In 1833, when Mehemet Ali was rapidly advancing with his victorious army under Ibrahim Pasha, upon Constantinople, which was only saved from falling into his hands by the arrival of a Russian army at Unkiar Silesia, by which a more favourable turn was given to the Sultan's prospects in the East, the latter distributed, amongst the Czar's troops, medals of gold, set round with diamonds to the Generals and Admirals, as also to the Ambassador of Russia; of gold, in different sizes to the officers; and of silver, to the military of inferior degrees.

All these medals represent, on the obverse, the initial of Mahmud between two laurel branches, and below it, the year 1249 of the Hegira, in Turkish characters and cyphers, while the reverse shows the crescent between laurel branches, with the year (1833) of the Christian Era.

ORDER OF THE HOLY SEPULCHRE.

We are led to introduce this Christian Order here, from the circumstance that it has now no other seat than Jerusalem which belongs to Turkey.

This Order may justly rival in antiquity that of St. Lazarus, credible authors dating its origin as early as the year 69, when St. James, the first Bishop of Jerusalem, entrusted the guardianship of the Holy Sepulchre to a number of men, distinguished for piety and high birth. Some writers, however, consider that it originated with the Canons regular, whom St. Helena, mother of Constantine the Great, introduced into her new church of Mount Calvary; while others again assert that the Knights of the Holy Sepulchre arose in the time of Godfrey de Bouillon, or his successor Baldwin, and that by the latter the Patriarch of Jerusalem was nominated first Grand Master. But the most probable date may, with some historical truth, be fixed at a much later period, in the year 1496, during the papacy of Alexander VI. His Holiness sought, in fact, to be considered as the founder of the Order—by means of which he intended to stimulate zeal for religion and for pilgrimages.

The Grand Mastership, and the right of nominating Knights were originally vested in the Holy See, though the Pope ceded subsequently those rights to the Guardian Father of the sacred tomb. Noble descent was one of the conditions of the reception. The duties of the Knights were to hear mass daily; combat, live and die for the Christian religion; to procure substitutes in the war with the infidels, in case their own presence should be prevented by unavoidable circumstances, to grant constant protection to the servants of the Church; to prevent all sorts of unjust feuds, quarrels, disputes, and usury; to favour peace amongst Christians; protect widows and orphans; to abstain from swearing and cursing; and to guard carefully against intemperance, lewdness, &c., &c. These heavy and severe duties were amply compensated for, by the extraordinary privileges granted to the Knights, by the Pope or the Guardian; so extraordinary, indeed, that we can hardly conceive how or by what means they could be secured or guaranteed to the Knights. Among those privileges was the right conceded to members of the Order to legitimatize bastards, change their names, grant escutcheons, possess church property though married, to be exempt from taxes on salt, wine, beer, &c., and to cut down and bury the bodies of those who were executed on the gallows.

This Order, formerly spread throughout France and the rest of Europe, was reconstructed by Louis XVIII. on the 19th August, 1814, as a royal institution, and also in Poland. In the latter country, it expired at the Revolution of 1830, but it is still extant within a very small circle of Knights, elected by the Guardian from the most respectable pilgrims who come to Jerusalem.

The badge (No. 2) is worn round the neck, or at the buttonhole, by a black watered ribbon, while the star (No. 1) is only allowed to those Knights who have visited Jerusalem.

The collar consists of small red enamelled crosses joined together by gold rings.

When, in 1847, a Latin Patriarch was once more established at Jerusalem, the Roman Propaganda transferred to him the right of conferring the Order of the Holy Sepulchre.

TUSCANY.

ORDER OF ST. STEPHEN.

Cosmos of Medicis, first Grand Duke of Tuscany, founded, in 1562, this Order at Pisa, in commemoration of the victory gained by him on the 2nd August, 1554 (St. Stephen's day) over the French, under command of Marshal Strozzi, by which his safe possession of Tuscany was secured.

The Order is subject to the rule of St. Benedict, and had its seat originally at Pisa, where the founder erected for it two splendid cloisters, one for the Grand Prior and the Knights, and the other for the Prior who wore the Grand Cross and the episcopal robe in his clerical functions. The church service was performed by the chaplains, who took the vows of chastity, poverty and obedience.

The statutes, confirmed by Pope Pius IV., were formed after those of the 'Order of St. John,' as were also the insignia and costume of the Order. The Knights, however, were neither bound by the vow of chastity, nor by that of poverty, being allowed to marry, and also to possess private property and beneficcs.

The object of the institution was the defence of the Catholic Church, and the destruction of the pirates who rendered the navigation of the Mediterranean unsafe, and threatened the ruin of the Tuscan trade and commerce.

In the year 1563, the Knights commenced their operations,

TUSCANY. PLATE 97.

enterprizes and victories by which they freed, on the one hand, about six thousand Christians from slavery, and altogether more than fifteen thousand human beings, while they took, on the other hand, an equal number of Turkish prisoners.

The Order shared, at last, the fate of the feudal system, and was suffered to remain in oblivion until 22nd December, 1817, when it was resuscitated by the Grand Duke Ferdinand III. who, at the same time, promulgated the statutes and decreed that:

Every Catholic nobleman, native or foreign, who can show noble descent through eight generations, and an annual income of 300 scudi, may become a real Knight (Knight by right).

The decoration is given under Plate 97, No. 2. The Grand Crosses (class 1) wear it over the shoulder; the Priors (class 2), and Baillies (class 3), round the neck; and the Knights (class 4), at the button-hole. All classes carry, besides, the star (No. 1) on the left breast.

The costume on procession days, and in the Chapter, consists of a long robe of white camlet, lined with red silk, and an over garment of the same stuff and lining.

The military costume is royal blue, with facing and collar of scarlet cloth, and with gold embroidery; the breeches are trimmed with gold lace, the epaulettes have thick tassels, and the buttons sword-guard, spurs, and hat-cord are of gold.

The Knights wear besides a military State uniform, the same as the above, except that the colour is white instead of blue.

The Dignitaries of the Order are: the Grand Commander, the Great Constable, the Admiral, the Grand Prior, the Treasurer, and the Prior of the Church.

ORDER OF ST. JOSEPH.

The Grand Duke Ferdinand III. founded this Order on the 19th March, 1807, being then only Grand Duke of Würzburg. After Tuscany was restored to him in 1814, he carried the Order with him, and renewed it in 1817. It since forms the second Order of Knighthood in Tuscany.

As an Order of Merit, in the fullest acceptation of the term, it is conferred indiscriminately on ecclesiastics and laymen, military and civil, natives and foreigners, though care is usually taken that the recipient should belong to the Catholic Church.

The number of the first class (Grand Crosses) is, exclusive of foreigners, limited to two hundred, who must all belong to high families. The second class (Commanders) is fixed at thirty; they receive hereditary nobility with the decoration, while the third class (Knights) is limited to sixty members, who receive personal nobility with the Order.

The reigning Duke is always Grand Master.

The badge (No. 4) represents, in the middle of the obverse, the figure of St. Joseph, with the legend: 'Ubique similis' (Everywhere the same), and of the reverse the letters: 'S. J. F.' (Sancto Josepho Ferdinandus) (dedicated by Ferdinand to Saint Joseph), and the year '1807.' It is worn, by the first class, by a broad ribbon across the right shoulder towards the left side, accompanied by the star, (No. 3) on the left breast. Ecclesiastics of the first class wear it by a narrower ribbon round the neck. The second class suspend it also round the neck, while the third class wear it by a much narrower ribbon at the button-hole.

The Grand Master and the hereditary Prince alone are privileged to adorn the decoration with precious stones.

The affairs of the Order are managed by a Chancellor elected from the first class, a Secretary, taken from the second class, and an Archivist, who is not necessarily bound to be a member of the Order.

ORDER OF THE WHITE CROSS,

Was founded by the Grand-Duke Ferdinand III., in 1814, after his restoration to Tuscany. This, an exclusively military decoration of merit, is named from the colour of the cross: it is not infrequently styled the *Cross of Loyalty*.

ORDER OF MILITARY MERIT.

On the 19th of December, 1850, the Grand-Duke Leopold instituted, for officers of all degrees, a long service decoration for thirty years' uninterrupted duty, intimating at the same time his intention of founding, at some future period, a similar badge of distinction for officers who might distinguish themselves by signal acts of merit for the good of their country. Three years afterwards (19 December, 1853,), this promise was fulfilled by the creation of the Order of military merit. It has three classes. The first and second consist usually of officers, and the third, of sub-officers and privates. If a commoner be honoured with the first class decoration, he receives, with it, hereditary nobility designated from some locality near his place of nativity or domicile. The sub-officers and privates, who obtain the third class decoration, have a right to an increase of 100 lire per annum until their promotion to the grade of officer. Should they quit the service from bodily infirmities or advanced age, the increased pay is not withdrawn, and they retain it, independently of the pensions to which they may have claim.

The badge is a pentagonal radiating star, the round middle of which contains, on the obverse, the initials 'L. II.,' and is surrounded by the words 'Merito Militare,' while the reverse shows the year '1853.' The star of the first two classes has a gold edge, and is surmounted by a gold crown, while that of the third class has only a silver crown. It is worn suspended by a red and black ribbon, by the first class round the neck, and by the two others, upon the left breast.

MEDAL OF MILITARY MERIT,

Was founded by a decree of the 19th May, 1841, and is to be worn by the same ribbon as described in the preceding Order, Third Class.

It bears the inscription 'Fedeltà e Valore.'

MEDALS AND DECORATIONS OF HONOUR.

1. *Medal of Merit*, of gold, value 50 ducats, instituted in 1816, by Ferdinand III., as a reward of virtue, for those who distinguish themselves by noble deeds and humane actions.

2. *Military Medal* of silver, instituted in 1815, for distinguished sub-officers and privates. No. 5 contains the obverse, while the reverse exhibits the inscription, 'Ai Prodi e Fedeli Toscani, 1815,' (To the brave and faithful Tuscans).

3. *The Long Service Military Medal*, of copper, bestowed on soldiers after twenty-five years' active duty. It is connected with a pension of 3 lire per month. The obverse is represented

in No. 6, while the reverse shows the inscription: 'Al lungo e fedel servizio,' (For long and faithful service). After ten years' service, the sub-officers and privates receive a *chevron*, and one lira monthly; after fifteen years, another *chevron* and an additional half lira; and after twenty years, a third *chevron* and one lira more.

WÜRTEMBERG.

ORDER OF THE CROWN OF WÜRTEMBERG.

In 1702, Duke Frederick Charles of Würtemberg founded the Order of the Golden Eagle, also called the Chase-Horn or Bugle, from the circumstance that the Dukes of Würtemberg bore the title of Imperial Masters of the Hunt. This Order which was subsequently renewed by Duke Charles Alexander, was, on the 6th March, 1807, entirely remodelled by Frederick I., on his assuming the royal dignity, after having already, on the 6th November, 1806, founded the Order of Civil Merit. These two Orders were, on the 23rd September, 1818, united with that of the crown of Würtemburg, by King William, who promulgated new statutes, and formed three classes: Knights of the Grand Cross, Commanders and Knights. The number of the Knights of each class is not fixed, though care is taken to keep it as much as possible within the limits prescribed by the statutes of the Order of Civil Merit.

In connection with the Order, are gold and silver medals for civil merit.

The badge of the Order is an octagonal gold cross, coated with white enamel, and having in the four angles the royal escutcheon with the gold leopard-lions. The round white-enamelled centre in the middle of the cross contains, on the obverse, the crowned cypher of the King, surrounded by a crimson red border, with the legend in golden characters:

WURTEMBERG. Table I. PLATE 98.

" Furchtlos und trew' (Intrepid and true). The reverse shows a similar border, with the royal crown of gold upon white ground in the centre. Above the cross is the royal crown connected by golden wings. (Plate 99, Tab. II. No. 6).

The badge is worn by a crimson red ribbon, three inches wide, across the right shoulder, towards the left hip, accompanied by an octagonal silver star, which the Knights of the Grand Cross wear upon the left breast: the middle of the Star contains the obverse of the cross with the royal crown on a white-enamelled ground (Plate 98, Tab. I. No. 1).

The Commanders and Knights wear the cross suspended by a narrower ribbon, the former, round the neck, and the latter, at the button-hole.

The gold and silver medals are worn at the button-hole, suspended by the same ribbon.

Civilians receive with the Order personal nobility, and access to Court, but nothing more.

The right of nominating Knights is vested solely in the crown, even to the exclusion of the Regency, during the minority of the King.

The sons of the King receive the Grand Cross on the completion of their seventh year, and the princes of the blood royal, at fourteen. The King is, however, empowered to make exceptions to the rule.

The nomination is free from all sorts of fees and charges.

Neither festivals, oaths nor vows are customary in the Order.

The Chapter only meets by special convocation of the sovereign.

The Chapter now consists under the presidency of the Chancellor of the Order, of:

Two Knights of the Grand Cross,

Two Commanders, and
Four Knights.

THE ORDER OF FREDERICK.

This Order was founded by King William, as reward for military and civil services.

The Order has only one class, that of Knights.

The badge is a gold, white-enamelled cross, with rays of bright gold in the angles. The middle of the obverse shows a round field of dull gold, and within it, in relief, the effigy of King Frederick. Around this middle is a ring, of dull gold and enamelled blue, with the legend: 'Friedrich König von Würtemberg,' in golden letters. The middle of the reverse shows, upon white-enamelled ground, the words: 'Dem Verdienste' (To merit), while the blue-enamelled ring round it contains the motto of King Frederick: 'Gott und mein Recht' (God and my right) (Plate 98, Tab. I. No. 4).

The cross is accompanied by an octagonal star, the four main rays being embroidered in silver, and the intervening rays, in gold. The middle is of dull gold, with the effigy of King Frederick, surrounded by a blue-enamelled ring, with the above motto: 'Gott und mein Recht.'

The colour of the ribbon is royal blue.

The cross is worn by a broad ribbon, across the right shoulder, towards the left hip, and the star upon the left breast.

The Order confers personal nobility, and gives free access to Court, but nothing more.

As in the previous Order, the nomination of Knights rests solely with the King.

THE MILITARY ORDER OF MERIT.

This Order was founded by Duke Charles Eugene, of Würtemberg, on the 11th February, 1759, as a reward for officers who had distinguished themselves in the seven years' war just then terminated. He gave it the name of the Military Order of St. Charles. It was renewed in November, 1799, by the Elector, afterwards King Frederick I. (who died in 1816), and was, by him, entirely re-modelled and re-named in 1806, when the electorate was raised to a kingdom. By the new statutes, the Order was designated as a reward for merit in war, or for twenty-five years' faithful service in time of peace. The King nominated the Knights at the recommendation of the Chapter, and the members were divided into four classes, of unfixed number, several of whom were to be in the receipt of considerable pensions, viz., twenty of the first class, of 2000 florins each (£200), four of the second class, of 1200 florins, twelve of the third class, at 1000 florins (£100), and fifty-two of the fourth class, of 300 florins each (£30). Until 1817, the pensions, paid from the funds of the Maltese commanderies, (amounting to 24,000 fl.) were fixed at 1200, 800, 600 and 300 fl. respectively.

In 1818, the Order was once more re-modelled, when it received new statutes, by which it was provided:

1. That henceforth it shall count only three classes: Knights of the Grand Cross, Commanders and Knights.

2. That two more classes shall be added to it, the decoration of which is to consist of gold and silver medals of military merit.

3. The badge to consist, for the first and second classes, of

an octagonal gold cross, enamelled white, the middle to contain, on the obverse, a green laurel wreath, within a blue border, the latter to show, in golden letters, the motto of the Order (' Furchtlos und trew'), and the reverse to exhibit the initial of the King, in a white field, surrounded by a blue circle with the above legend in it (Tab. I. No. 2).

The cross is worn by the Knights of the Grand Cross and Commanders, round the neck by a dark blue ribbon, accompanied, for the former, by a white octagonal star, embroidered in silver, the middle of which shows the contents of the enamelled obverse of the cross (No. 1). With both classes, the ribbon is appended to the cross by a crown.

The Knights wear the same cross in smaller size at the button-hole.

The gold and silver medals of merit are suspended at the button-hole by a similar ribbon (Tab. II. No. 7). The candidates of the first class must occupy the rank of at least Major-General; of the second class, that of staff-officer, and of the third class, that of officer.

No one can be received into a higher class without having previously belonged to the immediate lower class, nor can any one be received into even the lowest—the third class, without previously possessing the Military Medal of Merit.

The gold medal is conferred on officers down to corporals, and the silver on those below.

The King alone has the right to nominate the Knights, whose reception into the Order is free of all costs, fees and charges.

Civilians receive, with the badge, personal nobility, and the entrée at Court.

The Chapter consists of the Knights of the Grand Cross, the two oldest Commanders, and the four oldest Knights. It only meets by the special convocation of the King.

WURTEMBERG Table II.   PLATE 99.

5

8

6

7

Hurst and Blackett, London. 1858.

WURTEMBERG Table III.   PLATE 100.

MEDALS AND DECORATIONS OF HONOUR.

1. *Cross of Military Merit.*—It was founded by King William, on the 9th September, 1833, and remodelled on the 27th May, 1839, as a reward for twenty-five years loyal service for officers, and for twenty years, for sub-officers and privates (Tab. II. No. 8).

The cross for officers is yellow, and for the second class white. Both are worn upon the left breast by a red ribbon with blue borders. Years of campaign count double.

2. *War Medal for Faithful Service in Campaigns.*—This medal (Tab. III. No. 9) is cast of gun metal, and bears upon the obverse a W, with a crown and laurel wreath. It was founded on the 1st January, 1840, by King William. All military persons who have participated in a campaign, or crossed the enemy's frontier, may lay claim to the medal. Each of the years from 1793 to 1815 (except 1797, 1798, and 1810) is counted as a campaign.

3. *Military Medal of Merit.*—It appertains to the Military Order of Merit, described above, and illustrated Tab. II. No. 7.

4. *The Civil Medal of Merit.*—It belongs to the Order of the Crown of Würtemberg, and is also described above.

5—7. *Decorations of Honour for the Campaign of* 1814. King Frederick I. founded on the 8th February and 16th August, 1814, three medals:

a. For the victory of Brienne, with the inscription: 'König und Vaterland dem Tapfern' (The King and the country to the brave), on the obverse, while the reverse shows the words: 'Für den Sieg am 1sten Februar, 1814' (For the victory of the 1st February 1814), and the crowned initials 'F. R.' within a laurel wreath (Plate 100, Tab. III. No. 10).

b. For the victory of *La Fère Champenoise*, with the inscription: 'Für den Sieg am 25 März, 1814.' All the other contents are the same as given in *a* (Tab. III. No. 11).

c. For Paris, with the inscription: 'Für Paris, den 30 März, 1814.' The reveree is the same as in *a* (Tab. III. No. 12).

These three medals were bestowed, in gold, upon the officers who participated in the respective campaigns, and in silver upon sub-officers and men who had distinguished themselves in them. They are worn at the button-hole by a poppy coloured ribbon.

8. The same King instituted also on the 3rd July, 1815, a Decoration of Honour for the Campaign of 1815, consisting of a gold cross (No. 13), of a silver cross, and of a silver medal.

The gold cross was distributed as a reward for distinction amongst superior officers, the silver cross, similarly formed, amongst subaltern officers, and the medal (in the form of the Military Medal of Merit) amongst sub-officers and privates. All the three classes wear the decoration by a tri-coloured ribbon, red, yellow, and black.

APPENDIX.

THE MOST NOBLE ORDER OF THE GARTER.

Instituted by King Edward III. about August, 1348.

(K. G.)

THE SOVEREIGN.

THE PRINCE OF WALES.

H. R. H. The Prince Consort	Duke of Sutherland
King of Hanover	Duke of Buckingham and Chandos
Duke of Cambridge	Marquess of Salisbury
King of the Belgians	Duke of Cleveland
King of Wurtemburg	Earl De Grey
King of Prussia	Marquess of Abercorn
Prince Frederick of Prussia	Marquess Camden
Emperor of the French	Marquess of Hertford
King of Sardinia	Duke of Bedford
The Sultan	Earl of Clarendon
Reigning Duke of Saxe Meiningen	Marquess of Normanby
Reigning Duke of Brunswick	Duke of Northumberlannd
Reigning Duke of Saxe Coburg and Gotha	Earl of Carlisle
	Earl of Aberdeen
Marquess of Exeter	Earl Fortescue
Duke of Richmond	Viscount Palmerston
Duke of Buccleuch	Earl Granville
Marquess of Lansdowne	Marquess of Westminster

OFFICERS OF THE ORDER.

Prelate—Bishop of Winchester (Dr. Sumner).
Chancellor—Bishop of Oxford (Dr. Wilberforce).
Registrar—Dean of Windsor (The Hon. and Very Rev. Gerald Wellesley).
Garter principal King-of-Arms—Sir Charles George Young, Knt.
Usher of the Black Rod—Sir Augustus W. I. Clifford, Bart., C.B.

THE MOST ANCIENT AND MOST NOBLE ORDER OF THE THISTLE.

Revived by King James II. in 1687. *Re-established by Queen Anne,* 31*st December,* 1703.

(K.T.)

THE SOVEREIGN.

H. R. H. The Prince Consort	Marquess of Dalhousie
Earl of Aberdeen	Earl of Camperdown
Marquess of Tweeddale	Earl of Eglinton and Winton
Marquess of Breadalbane	Earl of Haddington
Duke of Roxburghe	Duke of Athole
Earl of Rosebery	Lord Panmure
Earl of Mansfield	Duke of Argyll
Duke of Montrose	Lord Kinnaird
Earl of Elgin	

OFFICERS OF THE ORDER.

Dean—William Muir, D.D.
Secretary—Sir John Stewart Richardson, Bart.
Deputy—Albert William Woods, Esq.
Lord Lyon King-of-Arms—Earl of Kinnoull.
Gentleman Usher of the Green Rod—Frederic Peel Round, Esq.

THE MOST ILLUSTRIOUS ORDER OF ST. PATRICK.

Instituted by King George III. February 5th, 1783.

(K.P.)

Consisting of the Sovereign, a Grand Master, and twenty-two Knights. The Lord-Lieutenant of Ireland for the time being is Grand Master.

THE SOVEREIGN.

GRAND MASTER,

His Excellency the Lord-Lieutenant of Ireland.

H. R. H. The Prince Consort	Earl of Rosse
Duke of Cambridge	Marquess of Waterford
Earl of Roden	Lord Farnham
Marquess of Clanricarde	Earl of Fingall
Earl of Charlemont	Viscount Masserene and Ferrard
Marquess Conyngham	Lord Cremorne
Earl of Howth	Earl of Gosford
Viscount Southwell	Marquess of Londonderry
Marquess of Headfort	Earl of Granard
Earl of Milltown	Viscount Gough
Earl of Arran	Marquess of Donegall
Earl of Wicklow	

OFFICERS OF THE ORDER.

Prelate—Archbishop of Armagh.
Chancellor—Archbishop of Dublin.
Registrar—Dean of St. Patrick's (the Hon. and Very Rev. Henry Pakenham.)
Secretary—Lowry-Vesey Townley-Balfour, Esq.
Genealogist—Sir William Edward Leeson, Knt.
Usher of the Black Rod—Colonel Sir George Morris, Knt.
Ulster King-of-Arms—Sir Bernard Burke, Knt.

THE MOST HONOURABLE ORDER OF THE BATH.

Instituted in 1399. *Revived in* 1725. *Enlarged in* 1815 *and* 1847.

THE SOVEREIGN.

FIRST AND PRINCIPAL KNIGHT GRAND CROSS AND GREAT MASTER, HIS ROYAL HIGHNESS THE PRINCE CONSORT, K.G.

MILITARY KNIGHTS GRAND CROSS.
(G.C.B.)

The King of the Belgians
H.R.H. the Duke of Cambridge
Blakeney, Right Hon. Sir Edward
Brisbane, Sir T. M. Bart.
Brown, Sir George
Burgoyne, Sir John Fox, Bart.
Caldwell, Sir James L.
Campbell, Sir Colin
Combermere, Viscount
Cotton, Sir Willoughby
Dundas, Sir James Whitley-Deans
Dundonald, Earl of
England, Sir Richard
Evans, Sir De Lacy
Gordon, Sir James Alexander
Gough, Viscount
Halkett, Sir Colin
Hamond, Sir Graham Eden, Bart.
Lushington, Sir James Law
Lyons, Lord
Outram, Sir James
Parker, Sir William, Bart.
Pollock, Sir George
Ross, Sir Hugh Dalrymple
Seaton, Lord
Simpson, Sir James
Smith, Sir Henry Geo. Wakelyn, Bart.
Strafford, Earl of
Thackwell, Sir Joseph
Woodford, Sir Alexander

CIVIL KNIGHTS GRAND CROSS.

Aston, Sir Arthur
Broughton, Lord
Bulwer, Right Honourable Sir Henry Lytton
Clarendon, Earl of
Cowley, Earl
Douglas, Sir Howard, Bart.
Ellenborough, Earl of
Graham, Right Hon. Sir James R. G. Bart.
Grey, Right Hon. Sir George, Bart.
Heytesbury, Lord
Howard de Walden, Lord
Lawrence, Sir John Laird Mair
Lyons, Lord
MacNeill, Right Hon. Sir John
Minto, Earl of
Normanby, Marquess of
Palmerston, Viscount
Panmure, Lord
St. Germans, Earl of
Seymour, Right Hon. Sir George H.
Stratford de Redcliffe, Viscount
Westmoreland, Earl of
Wood, Right Hon. Sir Charles, Bart.

HONORARY KNIGHTS GRAND CROSS.

Bosquet, Marshal
Canrobert, Marshal
De Salles, General
De MacMahon, General
Esterhazy, his Highness Prince
Hamelin, Admiral
Hohenlohe, the Prince of
La Marmora, General
Morris, General
Napoleon, H.I.H. the Prince
Pacha, his Highness Omar Lutfi
Pélissier, Marshal, Duke de Malakoff
Prussia, H.R.H. the Prince of
Regnault de St. Jean d'Angély, General
Saxe Weimar, Duke Bernard of
Strelitz, Hereditary Grand Duke of Mecklenburgh
Valliant, Count, Marshal
Victoria (Espartero), Duke de la
Walmoden, Count
Wurtemberg, his Majesty the King of

SECOND CLASS.

MILITARY KNIGHTS COMMANDERS.

(K.C.B.)

Airey, Sir Richard
Auchmuty, Sir Samuel B.
Austen, Sir Frances W.
Aylmer, Lord
Bell, Sir John
Bentinck, Sir Henry J. W.
Berkeley, Rt. Hon. Sir Maurice, F. F.
Bowles, Sir George
Brotherton, Sir Thomas William
Buller, Sir George
Bunbury, Sir H. Edward, Bart.
Burnett, Sir William, M.D.
Cardigan, the Earl of
Carroll, Sir William F.
Cathcart, Earl of
Chads, Sir Henry Ducie
Cheape, Sir John
Clifton, Sir Arthur B.
Cochrane, Sir Thomas
Codrington, Sir William John
Coode, Sir John
Dacres, Sir Richard James
Douglas, Sir James
Downes, Lord
Dundas, Hon. Sir Richard Saunders
Eyre, Sir William
Fergusson, Sir James
Fitzgerald, Sir John F.
Fremantle, Sir Charles Howe
Gardiner, Sir Robert William
Garratt, Sir Robert
Gomm, Sir William M.
Grant, Sir Patrick
Grant, Sir James Hope
Grey, Hon. Sir Frederick Wm.
Guise, Sir John W., Bart.
Hearsey, Sir John Bennett
Herbert, Sir Thomas
Hope, Sir Henry
Hope, Sir James A.
Hornby, Sir Phipps
Inglis, Sir John Eardley Wilmot
Houston, Sir Robert
Jackson, Sir James
Jones, Sir Harry D.
Keppel, Hon. Henry
Lambert, Sir George Robert
Leighton, Sir David
Leith, Sir Alexander
Love, Sir James Frederick
Lovell, Sir Lovell B.
Lucan, Earl of

Lugard, Sir Edward
Lushington, Sir Stephen
Maclaine, Sir Archibald
Maclean, Sir George
M'Grigor, Sir James, Bart., M.D.
M'Mahon, Sir Thomas, Bart.
Maitland, Hon. Sir Anthony
Martin, Sir Henry Biam
Melville, Viscount
Moore, Sir William G.
Moresby, Sir Fairfax
Mundy, Sir George
Napier, Sir William F. P.
Napier, Sir Charles
Nicolls, Sir Edward
Pasley, Sir Charles W.
Pennefather, Sir John L.
Peel, Sir William
Plumridge, Sir James Hanway
Prescott, Sir Henry
Reynolds, Sir Barrington
Richards, Sir William
Rokeby, Lord
Rose, Sir Hugh Henry
Rowan, Sir William
Russell, Sir James
Scarlett, Hon. Sir James Yorke
Schoedde, Sir James H.
Scott, Sir Hopton S.
Scovell, Sir George
Seymour, Sir Geo. Francis
Seymour, Sir Michael
Sleigh, Sir James W.
Smith, Sir Charles Felix
Somerset, Sir Henry
Steel, Sir Scudamore Winde
Stewart, Sir Houston
Stopford, the Hon. Sir Montagu
Storks, Sir Henry Knight
Stovin, Sir Frederick
Strode, Sir Edward Chetham
Tucker, Sir Edward
Vivian, Sir Robert John H.
Watson, Sir James
West, Sir John
Wetherall, Sir George A.
Williams, Sir William Fenwick, Bart.
Willshire, Sir Thomas, Bart.
Wilson, Sir Archdale, Bart.
Woodford, Sir John G.
Wymer, Sir George Peter

CIVIL KNIGHTS COMMANDERS.

(K.C.B.)

Abercromby, Hon. Sir Ralph
Barkly, Sir Henry
Beaufort, Sir Francis
Bligh, Hon. Sir John Duncan
Bloomfield, Lord
Bonham, Sir Samuel George, Bart.
Brooke, Sir James
Cautley, Sir Proby Thomas
Clerk, Sir George Russell
Crampton, Sir John Fiennes
Cubbon, Sir Mark
Davis, Sir John Francis, Bart.
Denison, Sir William Thomas
Elliot, Sir Charles
FitzRoy, Sir Charles Augustus
Grey, Sir George
Hawes, Sir Benjamin
Higginson, James M.
Howden, Lord
Hudson, Sir James
Lefevre, Sir John George Shaw
Light, Sir Henry
Magenis, Sir Arthur Charles
M'Gregor, Sir Duncan
Mayne, Sir Richard
Melvill, Sir James Cosmo
Nicholls, Sir George
Ouseley, Sir William Gore
Pakenham, Right Hon. Sir Richard
Phipps, Sir Charles Beaumont
Rawlinson, Sir Henry C.
Redington, Sir Thomas N.
Reid, Sir William
Routh, Sir Randolph J.
Shiel, Sir Justin
Stephen, Right Hon. Sir James
Trevelyan, Sir Charles Edward
Tulloch, Sir Alexander Murray
Wilson, Sir Belford Hinton
Wyse, Right Hon. Sir Thomas

HONORARY KNIGHTS COMMANDERS.

Bouat, General
Bouet-Willaumez, Rear-Admiral
Camou, General
Charner, Vice-Admiral
Dalesme, General
D'Autemarre, General
D'Allonville, General
D'Aurelles de Paladines, General
De Chabannes-Curton, Rear-Admiral
De la Gravière, Rear-Admiral
De Martimprey, General
Dulac, General
Durando, Lieut.-General
Herbillon, General
Hertsberg, Lieut.-Colonel Sir F. A. de
Heyden, Admiral Count de
Hugel, Lieut.-General Baron de
Levaillant, General
Lugeol, Rear-Admiral
Mellinet, General
Mensdorf, Count Alexander
Niel, General
Nugent, Field-Marshal Count
Odet Pellion, Rear-Admiral
Paté, General
Penaud, Rear-Admiral
Rigault de Genouilly, Rear-Admiral
Schriebershofer, Sir Maximilian
Thiry, General
Trotti, Lieut.-General
Walker, Sir Baldwin W., Bart.

THIRD CLASS.

MILITARY COMPANIONS.

(C.B.)

Abbott, Augustus
Abbott, Sir Frederick
A'Court-Repington, Charles Ashe
Adams, Frank
Adams, George
Adye, John Miller
Ainslie, William Bernard
Airey, James Talbot
Alexander, James
Alexander, Thomas
Alexander, George Gardiner
Anderson, Joseph
Anderson, William
Anderson, John Richard

APPENDIX.

Andrews, Augustus
Anstruther, Philip
Arbuthnot, Hon. Hugh
Armstrong, James Wells
Ashburnham, Hon. Thomas
Austin, Horatio T.
Backhouse, J. B.
Bainbrigge, Philip
Baker, Sir Henry
Balders, Charles Wm. Morley
Barker, George Robert
Baumgartner, Robert Julian
Baynes, Robert L.
Becher, Arthur Mitford
Beckwith, Charles
Bent, George
Belcher, Sir Edward
Bell, George
Bell, Thomas
Benson, Richard
Bethune, Charles R. D.
Biddulph, Edward
Birch, Richard James H.
Bisshopp, Cecil
Blair, Charles Devaynes
Blake, William W.
Blane, Robert
Blanshard, Thomas
Blundell, Frederick
Booth, William
Borlase, John
Borton, Arthur
Bowles, William
Bradford, John F.
Brandling, John James
Bray, Edward William
Brereton, William
Brock, Thomas Saumarez
Broke, Sir George Nathaniel, Bart.
Brooke, George
Brooke, Henry Vaughan
Brown, Gustavus
Browne, Fielding
Browne, Gore
Browne, Walter J.
Browne, James Frankfort M.
Brownrigg, John Studholme
Buckle, Henry Mason
Bunbury, Henry William
Bunbury, Thomas
Burghersh, Lord
Burlton, William
Burnett, William F.
Burton, Adolphus W. D.
Cadogan, Earl
Cadogan, Hon. George
Caffin, James Crawford
Caldwell, Henry
Cameron, Duncan Alexander
Cameron, George P.
Campbell, John
Campbell, Robert Parker

Campbell, Hugh Archibald Beauchamp
Campbell, George
Capon, David
Carmichael, Charles M.
Carnegie, Hon. Thomas Swynfen
Carnegy, Alexander
Carruthers, Richard
Carter, Thomas Wren
Cator, William
Chalmers, Sir William
Chamberlain, Neville Bowles
Chapman, Frederick Edward
Church, Sir Richard
Claremont, Edward Stopford
Clifford, Sir Augustus, Bart.
Clifford, William John C.
Cloete, Sir Abraham J.
Cochrane, Hon. Arthur A.
Codrington, Henry J.
Coke, John
Colborne, Hon. Francis
Cole, Arthur Lowry
Collier, Edward
Collinson, Richard
Colvin, John
Congreve, George
Conway, Thomas S.
Corbett, Stuart
Cotton, Henry
Couper, Sir George, Bart.
Craigie, P. Edmonstone
Cuninghame, Arthur A. T.
Cunliffe, Sir R. H. Bart.
Curtis, Sir Lucius, Bart.
Curtis, James G. W.
Curzon, Edward
Curzon, Hon. R. W. Penn
Custance, W. N.
Dacres, Sydney Colpoys
D'Aguilar, Charles Lawrence
Daly, Henry
Dalzell, Hon. Robert A. G.
Daubeney, H. C. Barnston
Daubeney, James
Deacon, Charles Clement
Deas, David
Delamaine, Charles A.
De la Motte, Peter
Despard, Henry
Dickson, Collingwood
Digby, George Stephen
Dixon, George
Doherty, Henry E.
Douglas, John
Douglas, John
Douglas, Robert
Douglas, Thomas Monteath
Drummond, Hon. James R.
Drake, W. Henry
Dumbreck, David
Dundas, W. Bolden
Dunmore, Thomas

Dupuis, John Edward
Dyneley, Thomas
Eckford, James
Eden, Charles
Eden, John
Edwardes, Herbert Benjamin
Edwards, Clement Alexander.
Ellice, Charles Henry
Ellicombe, Charles G.
Elliot, Richard Coffin
Elliot, Hon. C. G. J. B.
Elliot, Hon. George
Ellis, Samuel B.
English, Frederick
Evans, Thomas
Evelegh, Frederick Charles
Eyres, Harry
Fair, Alexander
Fanshawe, Arthur
Fanshawe, Edward
Farren, Richard T.
Ferryman, Augustus Halifax
Festing, Robert W. G.
Filder, William
Finch, Hon. John
Fisher, George
Fitzgerald, Charles
Fitzmayer, James William
Fleming, Edward
Foley, Hon. St. George
Forbes, John
Fordyce, Charles Francis
Franklyn, John Henry
Franklin, Charles T.
Freese, John Noble A.
Forrest, John
Forster, Henry
Franklin, Henry
Franks, Thomas Harte
Fraser, James
Fraser, Hugh
Frederick, Edward
French, James, M.D.
Fuller, Francis
Gairdner, William
Gaitskell, Frederick
Gambier, Gloucester
Geddes, William
George, Frederick Darley
Gibson, James Brown
Giffard, George
Glasse, F. H. H.
Godby, Christopher
Goldie, George L.
Goldsmith, George
Gordon, Hon. Alexander
Gordon, Charles
Gordon, John William
Gordon, Archibald
Gore, Hon. Charles
Gough, John B.
Gowan, George Edward

Graham, Charles
Graham, Fortescue
Grant, Sir James Robert
Grant, John Thornton
Grant, James Hope
Grant, Charles
Grattan, John
Greathed, Edward Harris
Green, Edward
Greenwood, William
Greville, Henry Francis
Griffith, Henry Darby
Gunning, John
Halkett, Hugh
Halkett-Craigie, John
Hall, Henry
Hall, William H.
Hall, William King
Haly, William O'Grady
Hamilton, Walter
Hamilton, Charles
Hamilton, Sir Charles J. John, Bart.
Hamilton, F. William
Harding, George J.
Harding, Francis Pym
Hardinge, Hon. Arthur Edward
Harrington, Earl of
Harrison, John B.
Harvey, Sir Robert J.
Hastings, Hon. G. Fowler
Hawkins, Francis Spencer
Hawkins, John P.
Hay, George James
Hay, Lord John
Heath, Leopold George
Henderson, Robert
Herbert, Charles
Herbert, Charles
Herbert, Robert
Herbert, Hon. Percy Egerton
Hervey, Andrew
Hewlett, Richard Strode
Heyland, Arthur Thomas
Hicks, George
Hill, Sir Robert C.
Hillyar, Henry Scank
Hodge, Edward Cooper
Hoggan, John
Holditch, Edward Alan
Honner, Robert W.
Hope, James
Hopkins, William Friend
Hopkinson, Sir Charles
Horn, Frederick
Horsford, Alfred Hastings
Hoste, Dixon Edward
Huish, George
Hume, Henry
Hunt, John P.
Hurdle, Thomas
Huthwaite, Edward
Hutt, George

Ingall, William Lenox
Irving, Alexander
Jackson, John
Jacob, John
Jeffries, Edmund Richard
Jenyns, Soame G.
Jessop, John
Johnstone, John Douglas
Jones, John
Jones, William
Jones, Lewis Tobias
Kellett, Henry
Kemball, Arnold Burrowes
Kenah, Thomas
Kennedy, Alexander, K.C.
Kennedy, James
Kennedy, James S.
Kennedy, John Jas.
Kennedy, John Clark
Key, Astley Cooper
King, George St. Vincent
Kingscote, Robert Nigel F.
Kuper, Augustus Leopold
Kynaston, Augustus Frederick
Lake, Noel Thomas
Lake, Henry Atwell
Lane, Charles Richard William
Lane, John Theophilus
Latour, Peter A.
Lawrence, Arthur J.
Leeke, Sir Henry John
Leslie, John Thomas
Le Geyt, George
Lewis, Griffith G.
Liddell, Sir John, M.D.
Lightfoot, Thomas
Lillie, Sir John Scott
Lindsay, Alexander
Linton, William
Lloyd, George W. Aylmer
Lloyd, John
Lluellyn, Richard
Lockwood, George Henry
Lockyer, Henry
Longfield, John
Loring, William
Lovell, John William
Low, John
Luard, J. Kynaston
Lugard, Edward
Lumsden, Thomas
Lushington, Franklyn
Lygon, Hon. E. P.
Lynche, Henry Blosse
Lysons, Daniel
Macbeath, George
M'Cleverty, James J.
Macdonald, Hon. James
Macdonald, Robert
Macdonell, Alexander
Macdonell, George
Macdowell, George James Mowatt

Mackinnon, George H.
M'Murdo, William S.
Macpherson, Robert B.
MacPherson, Philip
Maitland, Sir Thomas
Malcolm, George Alexander
Mansell, John
Maude, George Ashley
Maude, Frederick Francis
Mauleverer, James Thomas
Maxwell, George Vaughan
Maxwell, Alexander
McGregor, George Hall
McMahon, Thomas Westropp
Mends, William Robert
Michell, Frederic Thomas
Michell, John
Michel, John
Miller, Fiennes S.
Money, Archibald
Money, Rowland
Montgomery, A. Barry
Montgomerie, Patrick
Moore, Henry
Moore, John
Moore, R. Cornwallis
Moorsom, William
Morgan, John
Morris, Charles Henry
Morris, William
Morris, Edmund
Morshead, William H. A.
Mouat, James
Mundy, George V.
Munro, William
Murray, Hon. Henry
Napier, Thomas E.
Napier, G, Thomas C.
Nash, Joseph
Nias, Joseph
Norcott, William L. R.
O'Connor, Luke Smyth
Osborn, Sherard
Ouvry, Henry Aime
Owen, Henry C.
Pack-Reynell, Arthur
Paget, Lord George, A. F.
Paget, Lord Clarence
Pakenham, Hon. William Lygon
Parke, Thomas A.
Parkinson, Edward
Parlby, Brook
Parsons, James
Pattle, William
Paty, George William
Paulet, Lord George
Paulet, Lord William
Paulet, Lord Frederick
Payner, David William
Pears, Thomas Townshend
Pelham, Hon. Frederick Thomas
Pellew, Hon. Sir Fleetwood B.

Penny, Nicholas
Perceval, John M.
Poole, John
Powell, Richard Ashmore
Powell, Thomas Sidney
Power, William G.
Pratt, Thomas S.
Proctor, Henry A.
Purton, John
Rae, William, M.D.
Rainey, Henry
Ramsay, William
Ramsay, George
Reed, Thomas
Reginolds, Thomas Scott
Reid, Charles
Reid, Francis A.
Reilly, William Edmund Moyse
Rennie, James
Renny, Charles, M.D.
Reynardson, Edward Birch
Richards, Peter
Richardson, Sir John, M.D.
Richmond, Archibald F.
Ridley, C. William
Roberts, Abraham
Roberts, Henry T.
Rogers, Henry Downing
Rooke, Sir Henry Willoughby
Rowan, Henry
Russell, Lord Edward
Ryves, George F.
Salter, Henry F.
Sanders, Robert
Saxe-Weimar, Prince Edward of
Scott, James
Scott, John
Scott, Francis
Seaton, Thomas
Seymour, George Henry
Seymour, Francis
Sewell, William Henry
Shadwell, Charles Frederick Alex.
Sharpe, Alexander R.
Showers, St. George D.
Shirley, Horatio
Simmons, John L. Arabin
Simmons, Joseph
Simpson, William Henry
Smelt, William
Smith, Henry
Smith, James Webber
Smith, Robert
Smith, Richard Baird
Smith, John William Sidney
Smyth, Henry
Smyth, John Rowland
Somerset, Poulet H. G.
Somerset, Edward Arthur
Sotheby, Frederick Samuel
Sparks, James Pattoun
Spence, James

Spencer, Hon. Augustus Almeric
Spencer, Earl
Spratt, Thomas Abel B.
Stack, Maurice
Stanton, Edward
Staveley, Charles William Dunbar
Steel, James
Steele, Thomas Montagu
Stephenson, John Lionel
Stepney, Arthur St. George H.
Sterling, Anthony C.
Steuart, Charles
Stevens, Stephen James
Stewart, James Pattison
Stisted, Henry W.
Story, Philip Francis
Strange, Henry Francis
Straton, Robert J.
Street, John Alfred
Stuart, James
Stuart, John Ramsay
Sullivan, Bartholomew James
Sullivan, William
Sutherland, William
Symonds, Thomas M. C.
Tait, Thomas Forsyth
Talbot, Earl
Tarleton, John Walter
Tapp, Thomas
Taylor, Joshua N.
Taylor, John Robert
Taylor, Henry G. A.
Taylor, Richard Chambre Hayes
Thackeray, Frederick R.
Thomas, Henry
Thompson, John Armstrong
Thompson, William J.
Thomson, George
Timbrell, Thomas
Tombs, Henry
Troubridge, Sir Thomas St. Vincent H. C. Bart.
Trevelyan, Henry W.
Tritton, Edmund
Trollope, Charles
Tucker, Auchmuty
Tucker, Henry T.
Tulloch, Alexander
Tulloch, John
Turner, George
Turner, John
Turner, William West
Tweeddale, Marquess of
Tytler, James Macleod Bannatyne Fraser
Upton, Hon. George F.
Van Cortlandt, Henry Charles
Vansittart, Nicholas
Van Straubenzee, Charles T.
Vernon, H. C. E.
Waddington, Charles
Waddy, Richard
Wade, Hamlet Coote

APPENDIX.

Wade, Sir Claude M.
Waldegrave, Earl of
Walker, Edward W. F.
Ward, John R.
Warde, Col. Edward Charles
Warden, Frederick
Warre, Henry J.
Warren, Charles
Warren, William
Waters, Edmund Frederick
Watson, Rundle B.
Watts, George Edward
Welchman, John
Wellesley, George G.
Wemyss, Thomas J.
Wemyss, John Morris
West, Lord
Wetherall, E. Robert
Whinyates, Edward Charles
White, Henry D.
White, Michael
Whittingham, Ferdinand
Wilbraham, Richard
Wilcox, James
Wilkins, George
Wilkinson, Christopher Dixon
Wilkinson, Arthur P. S.
Williams, Thomas
Willoughby, Michael F.
Wilmot, Arthur P. E.
Wilson, George Davis
Wilson, Sir John Morillyon
Wilton, John Lucas
Windham, Charles Ash
Wodehouse, Edwin
Wood, David
Wood, Henry John
Wood, John Stewart
Wood, Robert Blucher
Wood, William
Woodburn, Alexander
Woodgate, William
Wright, Thomas
Wylde, William
Wyllie, William
Wynyard, Edward
Wynyard, Robert Henry
Yarborough, Charles Cook
Yelverton, Hastings Reginald
Yorke, John
Young, Charles Wallace
Young, William Laurieston M.

CIVIL COMPANIONS.

(C.B.)

Baldwin, Robert
Balfour, George
Bromley, Richard Madox
Browne, George
Brownrigg, Henry John
Buchanan, Andrew
Campbell, Thomas Edmund
Chadwick, Edwin
Churchill, Henry Adrian
Clarke, Sir Robert B.
Cole, Henry
Colebrooke, Sir Wm. M. G.
Crofton, Walter F.
Dawson, Robert Kearsley
De Rottenburg, George
Donnelly, William
Draper, William Henry
Fitzgerald, Charles
Gordon, Henry William
Hastings, Sir Thomas
Hay, John H. Drummond
Hodges, George L.
Horsford, Sir Robert Marsh
Jebb, Joshua
Macarthur, Edward
Maclean, John
MacDonnell, Sir Richard G.
Maxwell, John Hall
Milne, Alexander
Murray, Henry Charles A.
Northcote, Sir Stafford Henry, Bart.
Oliphant, Sir Anthony
Otway, Loftus Charles
Playfair, Dr. Lyon
Robe, Frederick Holt
Robinson, Sir John Beverley, Bart.
Romaine, William Govett
Rowe, Sir Joshua
Sandwith, Humphry
Scarlett, Hon. P. Campbell
Scotland, George
Smith, Peter
Strzelecki, Paul E.
Stewart, Alexander
Young, Sir Henry E. F.

HONORARY COMPANIONS.

Abahamson, Major
Anne-Duportal, Captain
Auger, Colonel
Augot, Military Intendant
Avinoff, Captain
Ballard, Lieut.-Colonel John Archibald
Barrel, Lieut.-Colonel
Baumbach, Major
Bazaine, General
Bertrand, Lieut.-Colonel
Beuret, General
Beuret, General
Bisson, General
Blanchard, General
Blanchot, Intendant General
Bodenhausen, Baron de
Bogdanowitch, Captain
Bondurand, Military Intendant
Borel de Bretizel, General
Bouet, Captain
Bourbaki, General
Brosin, Major-General
Cassaignolles, General
Chevillotte, Chef de Bataillon
Cler, General
Coffinières, General
Collineau, Colonel
Comignan, Colonel
Couston, General
Craquembourgh, Count de
Crespin, Colonel
Danner, Colonel
Dautin, Colonel
Darrican, Bon., Captain
De Bentzmann, Chef d'Escadron
De Berckheim, Chef d'Escadron
De Bertier, Colonel
De Beville, General
De Champéron, General
De Castagny, Colonel
De Cissey, General
De Cornély, Lieut.-Colonel
De Dompierre d'Hornoy, Captain
De Failly, General
De Ferrabouc, Colonel
De Forton, General
De la Bretonnier, Captain
De la Tour and Taxis, Prince
De la Martinière, Colonel
De la Motterouge, General
De la Rovere, Lieut.-Col.
De Lorencez, General
De Monet, Gen. Comte
De Puibusque, Colonel
De Rochebouet, Colonel
Desaint, Chef d'Escadron of Etat Major
De Saisset, Captain
De Sorbiers, Colonel
De Tournemine, General
De Vernon, Colonel
De Waubert de Genlis, Lieut.-Col.
Decaen, Colonel
Desusleau de Malroy, Lieut.-Col.
Dieu, Colonel
Di Negro, Captain Marquess
Douay, Colonel
Dufour de Montlouis, Captain
Duhesme, Colonel
Dupouy, Captain
Duprat de Larroquette, General
Dupré, Captain
Epautchoff, Captain Jean
Epautchoff, Captain Nicholas
Espinasse, General
Faucheux, General
Feray, General
Forgeot, Colonel
Frossard, General
Gagneur, Lieut.-Colonel
Garnault, Captain
Ginoux de la Couche, Captain
Govone, Major
Gorkum, Colonel Van
Goze, Colonel
Huchet de Centré, Captain
Hugon, Rear-Admiral
Jannin, General
Jarras, Colonel
Jourjon, Colonel
Krouschtoff, Captain
Lescure, Captain
Larrien, Captain
Le François, Colonel
Lefebvre, General
Lefevre, Colonel Auguste Henri
Lafont Villiers, General
Lallemand, Chef d'Escadron of Etat Major
Larchey, General
Laterrade, Colonel
Lebœuf, General
Lebzeltern, Colonel Wilhelm de
Lion, Colonel
Lugeol, Captain
Manèque, General
Maussion de Caudé, Captain
Méquèt, Captain
Montaudon, Colonel
Montenard, General
Morice, Captain N.
Niol, General
Ohier, Captain

Paris de la Bollardiere, Intendant-General
Paris, Captain
Pelissier, Lieutenant-Colonel
Pettite, Colonel Count
Penhoat, Captain
Picard, Colonel
Polhès de Bonnet Maurelhan, Colonel
Pothuau, Captain
Raoult, Lieut.-Colonel
Rebecque, Baron de
Reille, Lieut.-Colonel
Renson, Lieut.-Colonel
Ressayre, Colonel
Reybaud, Lieut.-Colonel
Robert, Captain J. B.
Rose, Colonel
Saurin, Colonel
Scrive, Principal Physician
Slade, Captain Adolphus, R.N.
Soleille, General
Sytin, Captain
Teesdale, Lieut.-Colonel Christopher Charles
Touchard, Captain
Trochu, General
Turpin, Captain
Uhrich, General
Vergé, General
Vinoy, General
Walsin Esterhary, General
Warnier de Wailly, Captain
Wimpffen, General

OFFICERS OF THE ORDER.

Dean of the Order—Richard Chevenix Trench, B.D., Dean of Westminster.
Genealogist and Blanc Coursier Herald—Walter Aston Blount, Esq.
Bath King-of-Arms—Algernon Greville, Esq.
Registrar and Secretary—Rear-Admiral Sir Michael Seymour, K.C.B.
Gentleman Usher of the Scarlet Rod, and Brunswick Herald—Albert William Woods, Esq.
Messenger—William Law, Esq.

THE VICTORIA CROSS.

ROYAL NAVY (INCLUDING THE NAVAL BRIGADE EMPLOYED ON SHORE) AND ROYAL MARINES.

Buckley, Cecil William
Burgoyne, Hugh Talbot
Roberts, John
Cooper, Henry
Trewavas, Joseph
Kellaway, Joseph
Day, George Fiott
Commerell, John Edmund
Rickard, William

NAVAL BRIGADE.

Peel, William, K.C.B.
Daniels, Edward St. John
Hewett, William Nathan Wright
Sullivan, John
Shepherd, John
Reeves, Thomas
Raby, Henry James

BALTIC.

Ingouville, George
Bythesea, John
Johnstone, William
Lucas, Charles D.

ROYAL MARINES.

Dowell, George Dare
Prettyjohn, John
Wilkinson, Thomas

ARMY.

Grieve, John
Parkes, Samuel
Dunn, Alexander Robert
Berryman, John
Andrew, Henry
Dixon, Matthew Charles
Arthur, Thomas
Graham, Gerald
Lennox, D.
Ross, John
Lendrim, William J.
Perie, John
Russell, Sir Charles, Bart.
Palmer, Anthony
Ablett, Alfred
Goodlake, Gerald Littlehales
Stanlock, William
Strong, George
Lindsay, Robert James
M'Kechnie
Reynolds, William
Prosser, Joseph
Maude, Frederick Francis
Connors, John
Hughes, Mathew
Norman, William
Moynihan, Andrew
Smith, Philip
Lyons, John
Bell, Edward W. D.
O'Connor, Luke
Shields, Robert
Coffey, William
Sims, John J.
Rowlands, Hugh
Madden Ambrose
M'Wheeney, William
M'Dermond, John
Walters, George
Owens, James

Beach, Thomas
Elton, Frederick C.
McCorrie, C.
Hamilton, T. De Courcy
Byrne, John
Park, John
Wright, Alex.
Alexander, John
Lumley, Charles Henry
Coleman, John
Clifford, Hon. Henry H.
Cuninghame, William James
Bourchier, Claude Thomas
Wheatley, F.
Knox, John
McGregor, R.
Humpston, Robert

Bradshaw, Joseph
Percy, Hon. Henry Hugh Manvers
Hope, William
Hale, Thomas Egerton
Conolly, John Augustus
Teesdale, Christopher Charles, C.B.
Malone, Joseph
Jones, Henry Mitchell
Esmonde, Thomas
Farrell, John
Symons, George
Craig, James
Sylvester, William Henry Thomas
Crowe, Joseph P. H.
Havelock, Sir Henry Marshman, Bart.
Hancock, Thomas
Purcell, John

REGULATIONS RESPECTING FOREIGN ORDERS.

1. No subject of Her Majesty shall accept a Foreign Order from the Sovereign of any foreign country, or wear the insignia thereof, without having previously obtained Her Majesty's permission to that effect, signified by a Warrant under Her Royal Sign Manual.

2. Such permission shall not be granted to any subject of Her Majesty, unless the Foreign Order shall have been conferred in consequence of active and distinguished service before the enemy, either at sea or in the field; or unless he shall have been actually and entirely employed, beyond Her Majesty's dominions, in the service of the Foreign Sovereign by whom the Order is conferred.

3. The intention of a Foreign Sovereign to confer upon a British Subject the Insignia of an Order, must be notified to Her Majesty's Principal Secretary of State for Foreign Affairs, either through the British Minister accredited at the Court of such Foreign Sovereign, or through His Minister accredited at the Court of Her Majesty.

4. If the service for which it is proposed to confer the Order has been performed during War, the Notification required by the preceding Clause must be made not later than two years after the exchange of the Ratifications of a Treaty of Peace.

If the service has been performed in time of Peace, the Notification must be made within two years after the date of such service.

5. After such Notification shall have been received, Her Majesty's Principal Secretary of State for Foreign Affairs shall, if the case comes within the conditions prescribed by the present Regulations, and arises from naval or military Services before the Enemy, refer it to Her Majesty's Principal Secretary of State for the War Department, previously to taking Her Majesty's pleasure thereupon, in order to ascertain whether there be any objection to Her Majesty's permission being granted.

A similar reference shall also be made to the Commander-in-Chief, if the application relates to an Officer in the Army, or to the Lords of the Admiralty, if it relates to an Officer in the Navy.

6. When Her Majesty's Principal Secretary of State for Foreign Affairs shall have taken the Queen's pleasure on such application, and shall have obtained Her Majesty's permission for the person in whose favour it has been made to accept the Foreign Order, and wear the Insignia thereof, he shall signify the same to Her Majesty's Principal Secretary of State for the Home Department, in order that he may cause the Warrant required by Clause 1 to be prepared for the Royal Sign Manual.

When such Warrant shall have been signed by the Queen, a Notification thereof shall be inserted in the Gazette, stating the service for which the Foreign Order has been conferred.

7. The Warrant signifying Her Majesty's permission, may, at the request and at the expense of the person who has obtained it, be registered in the College of Arms.

8. Every such Warrant as aforesaid shall contain a Clause providing that Her

Majesty's licence and permission does not authorize the assumption of any style, appellation, rank, precedence, or privilege appertaining to a Knight Bachelor of Her Majesty's Realms.

9. When a British Subject has received the Royal permission to accept a Foreign Order, he will at any future time be allowed to accept the Decoration of a higher Class of the same Order, to which he may have become eligible by increase of rank in the Foreign Service, or in the Service of his own country; or any other distinctive mark of honour strictly consequent upon the acceptance of the original Order, and common to every person upon whom such Order is conferred.

10. The preceding Clause shall not be taken to apply to Decorations of the Guelphic Order which were bestowed on British Subjects by Her Majesty's predecessors, King George IV. and King William IV., on whose heads the Crowns of Great Britain and of Hanover were united.

Decorations so bestowed cannot properly be considered as rewards granted by a Foreign Sovereign for services rendered according to the purport of Clause 2 of these Regulations. They must be rather considered as personal favours bestowed on British Subjects by British Sovereigns, and as having no reference to services rendered to the Foreign Crown of Hanover.

REGULATIONS RESPECTING FOREIGN MEDALS.

1. Applications for permission to accept and wear Medals which, not being the decoration of any Foreign Order, are conferred by a Foreign Sovereign on British subjects in the Army or in the Navy, for military or for naval services, should be addressed, as the case may be, to the Commander-in-Chief, the Master-General of the Ordnance, or the Lords of the Admiralty, who, if they see fit, may submit the same to Her Majesty's Principal Secretary of State for Foreign Affairs, for Her Majesty's sanction; upon obtaining which, they may grant such permission without any other formality.

2. Permission to wear a Foreign Medal cannot be granted to a British subject, unless such Medal is bestowed for military or naval services performed by the command or with the sanction of Her Majesty. But no permission is necessary for accepting a Foreign Medal, if such Medal is not to be worn.

(Signed)   CLARENDON.

Foreign Office, May 10, 1855.

THE LEGION OF HONOUR.

THE ARMY.

GRAND CROSSES.

Simpson, General Sir James | Brown, General Sir George

GRAND OFFICERS.

Burgoyne, Lieutenant-General Sir John Fox, Bart.
Evans, Lieutenant-General Sir De Lacy

Pennefather, Lieutenant-General Sir J. Lysaght
England, Major-General Sir Richard

APPENDIX.

COMMANDERS.

Lucan, Lord
Bentinck, Sir Henry J. William
Barnard, Henry William
Rokeby, Lord
Codrington, Sir William John
Scarlett, Hon. Sir James Yorke
Eyre, Sir William
Rose, Sir Hugh Henry
Buller, Sir George
Dacres, Sir Richard J.
Windham, Charles Ash
Dupuis, J. Edward

Terryman, A. Halifax
Campbell, R. Parker
Hay, A. S. Leith
Sibthorp, R. F. Waldo
Elrington F. Robert
Newdigate, Edward
Barker, G. Robert
Biddulph, M. A. Shrapnel
Devine, John
Lloyd, E. Thomas
Ewart, C. Brisbane

OFFICERS.

Steele, Thomas Montagu
Pakenham Hon. William L.
Hall, Dr. J.
Macmurdo, W. M. Scott
Paulet, Lord F.
Gordon, A.
Cunynghame, A. Augustus Thurloe
Herbert, P. E.
Wilbraham, R.
Brownrigg, S.
Sterling, Anthony
Paget, Lord G. A. Frederick
Shewell, F. G.
Ridley, C. W.
Upton, Hon. G. F.
Walker, E. W. F.
Paulet, Lord William
Straubenzee, C. T. Van
Horn, Frederic
Sackville, Charles Richard
West, Lord
Lyons, Daniel
Adams, Frank
Mauleverer, James Thomas
Cameron, Duncan Alexander

Spencer, Hon. A. Almeric
Garrett, Robert
Farren, R. Thomas
Warren, Charles
Trollope, Charles
Shirley, Horatio
Lawrence, A. Johnstone
Seymour, Francis
Fitzmayer, James William
St. George, John
Warde, Edwarde Charles
Wood, David Edward
Adye, John Miller
Gordon, Alexander
Chapman, Frederick Edward
Hamilton, F. William
Grant, J. Thornton
Smyth, Henry
Dickson, Collingwood
Hodge, E. Cooper
Haly, W. O'Grady
Sparks, James P.
Lockyer, Henry Frederick
Norcott, W. S. Ramsay
Lake, N. Thomas

KNIGHTS.

Saxe-Weimar, Prince Edward of
Maitland, C. L. Brownlow
Colville, Hon. William
Harding, Francis Pym
Shadwell, Lawrence
Hume, Gustavus
Mackenzie, Kenneth Douglas
Hallewell, E. Gilling

Wetherall, Edward Robert
Colborne, Hon. Francis
Airey, James Talbot
Mayow, George W.
Hardinge, Hon. Arthur E.
Thackwell, J. E.
Smith, Hugh
Sullivan, William

APPENDIX.

Blane, Robert
Wood, John Stewart
Dickson, Collingwood
Thompson, George Latham
Woodford, Charles John
Morris, William
Willis, Harry Smith
Vacker, F. Smith
Bellairs, William
Glyn, Julius Richard
Earle, A. Maxwell
Armstrong, James Wells
Maxwell, George Vaughan
Ellison, C. George
Daniell, C. F. Torrens
Barnston, Robert
Gordon, Archibald
Mouatt, James
Matthew, T. Patrick
Eliot, Richard Coffin
Alexander, Thomas
Brady, Thomas Clarke
Ligertwood, Thomas
Sylvester, Henry Thomas
Fair, George
O'Callaghan, Charles
Drake, William Henry
Smith, John William
Turner, Philip
Carpenter, F. Stanley
Darling, M. William
Osborne, Kean
Conolly, James
Elliot, James Hardy
MacCreagh, Michael
Percy, William
Herbert, Henry
Babbington, Charles
Elmsall, W. De Cardonnel
Keyle, William
Clarke, George Calvert
Rant, William
Low, Alexander
Gillam, David
Shute, Charles Cameron
Jeffreys, Richard
De Salis, Rodolph
Gray, William
Guttridge, George
Bambrick, John Thomas
Tremayne, Arthur
Johnson, T. G. John
Gordon, Sir William, Bart.
Brown, John
Hamilton, F. William
Percy, Hon. Hugh Manvers
Higginson, G. W. Alexander
Russell, Sir Charles
Balgownie, Viscount
Dawkins, W. Gregory
Strong, Clement W.
Armytage, Henry

Goodlake, G. Littlehales
Tower, Harvy
Stephenson, F. C. Arthur
Jocelyn, Hon. John Strange
Gipps, Reginald
Baring, Francis
Lindsay, R. James
Wells, Frederick
Todd, J. A. Ruddell
Brown, J. Martin
Hurt, Charles
Gillies, William
M'Kenna, Theobald
Crisell, Henry
Maude, F. Francis
Lewes, John
Roe, G. Noble
Williams, Thomas
Robertson, Patrick
Paton, James
Watt, Thomas
Turney, W. West
Pack, A. John
Hibbert, H. John
Appleyard, Ernest
Jones, H. Mitchell
Walker, G. Henry
Bell, Joseph
Raines, James
Brown, Henry Ralph
Scott, H. Bassett
Ryder, William
Cook, William
King, George
Tyler, G. Henry
Dwyer, John
Macdonald, John
Travers, J. Oates
Thompson, W. Dalrymple
Plant, John
Armstrong, A. W. S. Freeman
Hayman, M. Jones
Grant, John
Dowbiggin, Montagu Hamilton
Massey, W. G. Dunham
Rooke, J. L. Richard
Warden, Robert
Bright, R. Onesephorus
Chippindale, Edward
Lyons, John
Evelegh, E. F. Charles
Butler, C. R.
Rule, Arthur
Brown, Joseph
Kileen, Roger
Carlton, William Henry
Image, John George
Templeman, Arthur
Line, James
Banbury, H. William
Herbert, A. James
Bell, E. W. Deddington

APPENDIX.

Drewe, F. Edward
Stait, William
Shiels, Robert
Butler, P. Archer
Aplin, J. G. Rogers
Roberts, William
Orlebar, O. R. Hamond
Smith, Charles
Atcherley, F. Topping
Green, C. Mingaye
Gubbins, Stamer
Nagle, Richard
M'Cormick, John
Spence, Frederick
Eagar, Robert John
Mundy, G. Valentine
Collings, John Elias
Donovan, Edward Westby
Quayle, J. E. Taubman
Pretyman, William
MacCay, William
Goodenough, A. Cyril
Simpson, John
Guilt, John
Mortimer, John
Smith, W. Sidney
Dickins, C. A. Scrace
Ellis, W. Kidston
Jeeves, William Younge
Scott, John
Munro, William
Leckie, William
Carr, R. Edward
Jobberns, Joseph
Skipwith, George
Goodwyn, J. Edmund
Rowlands, Hugh
Graham, Lumley
Allan, William
O'Neil, James
Stockey, Peter
M'Leod, J. Chetham
Drysdale, John
M'Kinnon, W. Alexander
Wood, William
Christie, Charles
M'Mahon, William
Robinson, John
Preston, Richard
Gibbons, John
Thimbleby, Robert
Maxwell, Alexander
Dallas, George
Bond, William
Simpson, William
Lowndes, J. Henry
Villiers, James
Villiers, C. Courtney
Stevenson, C. Aldersey
Wilson, John
West, Frederick
Kelly, Thomas

Grant, J. Thornton
King, J. Hynde
Dewar, J. William
Adams, Cadwallader
Armstrong, T. P. St. George
Butler, James
Waddy, Richard
Wilton, John Lucas
Frampton, H. J.
Lock, A. C. Knox
Macpherson, Angus
Daubeney, H. C. Barnston
Hume, Robert
Elton, Frederick Cockayne
Hume, J. Richard
Barnston, William
Doyle, Joseph
Anderson, Richard
Butler, Henry
Forsyth, G. John
Cumming, George
Griffith, William
Burgess, Joseph
Daubeney, James
Gooch, Charles
Hunter, E. Henry
Newman, Joseph
Harris, Thomas
Elliot, H. Christopher
Smyth, Henry
Hamilton, Thomas de Courcy
Tucker, A. Harvey
Stadden, Henry
Fletcher
Ogden, John
Ready, Charles
Hope, William
Parke, William
Thellusson, Dalton
Rickman, William
Carden, Robert H.
Chawner, E. Henry
Borritt, Henry
Coonin, Thomas
M'Call, William
Hodgson, W. Chanval
Campbell, Henry Wotton
Young, James
Davie, William
Maxwell, E. Herbert
Stevens, Nathaniel
Browne, George Richard
Beresford, G. Robert
Goggins, Thomas
Grennan, Joseph
Aylmer, F. Charles
Boyle, W.
Cuppage, J. Macdonald
Fisher, John
Grove, Robert
Smith, Thomas
Wolsely, G. Joseph

Smaller, Joseph
Ewart, J. Alexander
Crowe, Robert
Cornwall, George
Knox, Alexander
Hume, Henry
Sargent, John Neptune
Massey, Hon. E. C. Henry
Carmichael, G. Lynedoch
Sexton, John
Abbott, Timothy
Ingram, Thomas
Legh, E. Cornwall
Lumley, C. Henry
Lawless, Peter
Stone, Peter John
Somerset, E. Arthur
Clifford, Hon. Henry
Brett, John
Murphy, Timothy
Wheatley, Francis
Macdonell, Alexander
Fyers, W. Augustus
Blackett, E. William
Knox, J. Simpson
Andrews, John
Bourchier, Claud Thomas
Wodehouse, Edwin
Dixon, W. M. Hall
Strange, H. Francis
Hamley, E. Bruce
Field, G. Thomas
Baddeley, J. F. Lodington
Boothby, J George
Singleton, John
Carthew, E. John
Hope, J. Edward
Bolton, William John
Owen, C. Henry
Broughton, S. Delves
Branding, J. James
Turner, John
Moubray, Edward
Reilly, W. E. Moyses
Lukin, W. W. Augustus
Miller, Frederick
Grant, W. J. Esten
Dickson, Philip
Mackenzie, Roderick
Campbell, Hugh A. Beauchamp
Richards, W. Powell
Spurway, John
Simpson, W. H. Randolph
King, A. Henry
Lyons, Joseph
Longley, R. Cytherus
Alderson, H. James
Keene, J. E. Ruck
Arbuthnot, Henry
Maxwell, Stuart
Ridout, Arthur
Conolly, H. Hamilton

Price, J. Andrew
Brown, J. Henry
Strangways, W. A. Fox
Markham, Edwin
Torriano, Charles Edward
Stirling, William
Vaughan, E. Courtenay
Tillard, H. Percy
Broughton, L. Delves
Walter de Winton, Francis
Hickes, H. J. F. Ellis
Harris, Noel Hamly
Hall, W. James
Elton, F. Coulthurst
Fasson, S. Hunter
Ward, W. Pearson
Park, Thomas
Taylor, A. Henry
Stockley, J. Surtees
Young, William
Lilley, J. Isaac
Hant, Arthur
Norton, William
Mervin, George
Mitchell, Joseph
Mitchell, Thomas
Devine, John
Kerr, George
Bruce, Robert
Hargreaves, John
Stevenson, John
Wheatley, Hugh
Todd, William
Hendry, William
Burke, Robert
Gibbs, John
MacVeight, John
Bent, George
Bourchier, Eustace Fane
Stanton, Edward
Browne, J. F. Manners
Montagu, Horace William
De Vere, Francis Horatio
Fisher, A. A'Court
Graham, Gerald
Cowell, J Clayton
Donelly, J. F. Dykes
Elphinstone, H. Crauford
Neville, Glastonbury
Anderson, W. Christian
Martin, C. Nassau
Drake, J. M. Cutliffe
Gordon, C. George
Landry, John
Macdonald, Henry
Stanton, Joseph
Jarvis, George
Leitch, Peter
Cole, Samuel
Paul, John
Collins, Joseph
Burghersh, Lord

APPENDIX.

Fielding, Hon. Percy
Bingham, Lord
Campbell, Hon. H. W.
Neville, Edward
Torrens, H. D'Oley
Whitmore, E. A.
Curzon, Hon. Leicester
Calthorpe, Hon. S. J. Gough
Clifton, T. H.
Gubbins, James
Carcur de Morel, Charles
Anderson, Arthur
Brush, J. Ramsay
Wyatt, John
Bostock, J. Ashton
Valpy de Lisle, R. F.
Lockwood, A. P.
Longmore, Thomas
Mackinnon, D. R.
Barlow, D. G.
Muir, G. M.
Fraser, John
St. Croix Crosse, J. B.
Gloag, J. G.
Wardlaw, R.
Sulivan, G. A. F.
Brown, G. J.
White, G. D.
Douglas, John
Evans, W. E.
Cooke, E. A.
Tipping, A.
Cameron, W. Gordon
Halkett, J.
Baring, C.
Shuckburgh, G. T. F.
Bell, George
Plunkett, Hon. C. D.

Huey, R. W.
Hunt, Joseph
Troubridge, Sir T. St. Vincent Hope Cochrane, Bart.
Borton, Arthur
Elmhurst, C.
Barlow, Maurice
M'Pherson, Philip
Gordon, William
Clement, A. Edwards
M'Gee, Edward
Massey, G. W. H.
Stevens, George
Crofton, Hugh Dennis
Campbell, Joseph
Bayly, Paget
Staunton, George
Foseland, George
Kelley, R. Denis
Finley, R. Newport
Rollo, Hon. Robert
Sayer, Frederick
Browne, Andrew
Campbell, C. Frederick
Hunter, F. Frederick
Riky, Benjamin
Lamb, G. Henry
Regan, Thomas
Werge, H. Reynolds
Margesson, W. George
Inglis, William
Ingall, Lennox W.
Carter, W. Frederick
M'Gowan, John
Blount, Herbert
Straton, Robert Jocelyn
Dixon, George

THE NAVY.

GRAND CROSSES.

Dundas, Vice-Admiral Sir James Whitley Deans.
Lyons, Rear-Admiral, Lord.

GRAND OFFICERS.

Stewart, Rear-Admiral Sir Houston
Stopford, Rear-Admiral the Hon. Sir Montague

Lushington, Rear-Admiral Sir Stephen
Keppel, Capt. the Hon. Henry

OFFICERS.

Lushington, Sir Stephen
Michell, T. Frederick
Graham, Charles
Carter, Thomas Wren
Keppel, Henry
Jones, Lewis Tobias
Peel, Sir William, K.C.B.
Moorsom, William
Mends, William Robert
Spratt, Thomas Abel B.

Osborne, Sherard
Hurdle, Thomas
Holloway, Thomas
Greville, H. Francis
Paulet, Lord George
Russell, Lord Edward
Dacres, Sidney Colpoys
King, G. St. Vincent
Drummond, Hon. James Robert
Deas, David

KNIGHTS.

Tatham, Edward
Ewart, C. J. Frederick
Cumberland, Octavius
Bowyear, George Le Geyt
Wiles, G. Gommanney
Bickford, J. Grant
Gordon, W. E. Alphonse
Derriman, S. H.
Porteus, F. Pender
Dench, C. Thomas
Anesley, C. Murray
Joliffe, W. Kynaston
Ross, J. Francis
Comber, H. Wandesford
Pym, W. Henry
Fairholme, Charles
Thompson, S. W. Heniker
Hudson, J. Samuel
Evered, J. G. C.
Paul, Henry
Bower, G. H. K.
Forbes, C. R. Pecco
Bullock, T. Thelwall
Sanctuary, W. Melancthon
Hunter, J. Edward
Hayward, C. Augustus
Carmichael, James
Mason, R. Denton
Reynolds, Vernon Eliakim
Irwin, Ahmutz
Thorne, Edward
Hamilton, William
Hewbz, Matthew
Cooper, Henry
Hayman, William
Rowe, George
Major, William
Barry, David
Henderson, Edward
Hewett, Henry
Roberts, H. Bradley
Joliffe, Charles
Festing, Francis Worgan
Pitman, William
Brookes, J. Rowland
Frere, J. J. B. Edward
Burnett, W. Farquharson
Heath, L. George
Hillyar, H. Schenk
Randolph, G. Granville
Hay, Lord John
Kynaston, A. Frederic
Powell, R. Ashmore
Borlase, John
Lambert, Rowley
Kennedy, J. James
Coles, C. Phipps
Rogers, Henry Downing
Dowell, W. Montague
Commerill, J. Edmund

Rolland, W. Rae
Lloyd, Henry
Bowden, William
Luce, J. Proctor
Jones, W. Gore
Armytage, William
M'Killop, H. Frederick
M'Kenzie, J. F. C.
Horton, William
Crang, J. Hay
Bull, James
Pritchard, Samuel
Whyte, J. William
Oldfield, R. Bryce
Urmston, W. Brabazon
Raby, H. James
Cavo, J. Halliday
Marryat, J. Henry
Day, G. Fiott
Campion, Hubert
Buckley, C. William
Gough, F. William
Byng, J. Clark
Grylls, C. Gerveys
Hardinge, Edward
Burgoyne, H. T.
Mitchell, Alfred
Noddal, C. T. Augustus
Mainprise, W. Thomas
Roberts, R. Wilson
Williams, George
Potter, Thomas
Arguimbeau, Narcissus
Ball, E. Codrington
Brooker, E. Wolfe
Llewellyn, F. R. Glyndsor
Parker, W. Henessey
Campbell, C. Andrew
Palmer, C. Frederic
Dalyell, O. W.
Hewett, W. N. Wright
Maitland, H. L. R. Lennox
Selby, W. D. D.
Kennedy, Andrew James
Parsons, George
Leet, H. Knox
Creagh, J. Brazier
Barnett, J. Barber
Pearson, T. Livingston
Lillingston, N. D. Foveran
Cooper, J. R. Dene
Armstrong, R. Ramsay
Hallowes, F. W.
Sinclair, G. C.
Wood, H. E.
Daniel, E. St. John
Simpson, D. James
Cleeve, Frederick
Rees, John
Walsh, James

Smart, W. E. Richard
Jenkins, James
Baker, Thomas
Murdoch, George
Langley, J. Henry
Rumble, W.
Harger, Frank
Beal, John
Muir, G. W.
Roberts, John
Hayles, John
Verey, Richard
Dunlop, G. Greenirk
Rowe, Richard
Spilsbury, Robert
Kellaway, Joseph
Shepherd, John
Rickards, W.
Cleverly, John
Taylor, John
Sullivan, John
Willis, C.
Allen, W.

Hanlon, Peter
Milestone, George
Trewavas, Joseph
Alexander, G. Gardiner
Hopkins, W. F.
March, W. H.
Digby, G. S.
Blyth, David
Brydges, George
Pym, F. George
Steele, A. Charles
Douglas, A. Alexander
Jull, H. John
Horner, Charles
Yule, George
Richards, Edwin
Jordan, John
Chappel, W.
Wilkinson, Thomas
Bull, John
Kerr, Thomas
Bunten, John
Osborn, John

THE FRENCH MILITARY WAR MEDAL.

Teevan, Rourke
Bond, Seth
Harrison, Thomas
Teehan, Cornelius
Kempton, W.
Scott, W.
Smeaton, Robert
Wood, Henry
Botfield, Robert
Gibson, George
Burrows, W. J.
Iles, Frederick
Douglas, John
Hewitt, W.
Cannell, James
M'Ardle, John
Hay, John
Perkins, Richard
Davis, George
Powell, John
Fitzsimons, C.
Adams, John
Ackland, John
Hamilton, James
Milligan, Joseph
Bower, John
O'Donohue, Michael
Malowney, M.
Fairfax, John
Magee, James
Hagan, John
Henderson, Charles

Jenkins, David
M'Garrity, James
Conway, Patrick
Bines, George
M'Grath, James
Flockhart, Walter
Browne, James
Sutherland, Angus
Norton, John
M'Claren, John
Vance, John
Knight, Patrick
Fenton, Matthew
Smith, Job
Buchanan, Joseph
Boggie, James
Smith, Joseph
M'Pherson, John
Bacchus, Henry
Woodbridge, Richard
Knight, Kester
Ross, John
Hanson, Robert
Conning, Walter
Perie, John
Sargeant, Charles
Archer, Isaac
Elger, Thomas
Hale, Aaron
King, James
Myers, William
Williams, William

APPENDIX.

Carter, Sheppard
Burnett, John
Reed, W.
Walden, George
Winter, John
Tutt, Charles
M'Gregor, W.
Badenoch, James
Lennox, James
Manson, David
Judd, John
Coulter, Joseph
Drummond, John
Sparks, W.
Moran, Daniel
Horsfall, John
Colver, James
Campbell, Andrew
Stewart, A. J.
Sullivan, W. J.
Hunter, Stephen
Mulvany, James
Pulfer, Charles
Lock, Frederick
O'Grady, W.
Fleming, Alexander
Marshall, Robert
Clarkson, John
Fitzgerald, John
Murray, Teddy
Murphy, James
Bell, Joseph
Watts, John
Laws, John
Poulton, Thomas
Hanlon, Patrick
Marshall, W.
Edwards, Michael
Godwin, James
Corry, Valentine
Tallman, Edward
Coopen, Thomas
Cooper, Thomas
Macdonald, John
Harrison, Robert
Caby, Thomas
Canty, Patrick
Dunne, Edward
Harvey, John
O'Donnell, Neil
Cox, John
Gleeson, John
Langton, Edward
Britts, John W.
Murphy, W.
Murphy, Thomas
Smith, W.
Strick, Henry.
Higgins, Hugh B.
Duffy, James
Moss, Joseph
Boxall, George

Brown, John
Brown, Joseph
Kirkham, George
Hennessy, W.
Gray, Henry
Higdon, John
Sim, James
Driscoll, Timothy
Kelly, Patrick
M'Phely, Michael
Russell, John
Crowley, Peter
Handley, W.
Collins, James
Hodden, Charles
Andrews, Robert
Boyse, James
Brown, John
Coviton, Charles
Cook, W.
Dunnery, George
Carson, James
Connell, Michael
Dunn, W.
Blake, John
Tobin, John
Richardson, John
Curran, Owen
M'Donough, Thomas
Byrne, Michael
Nicoll, W.
Quigley, C.
Smith, John
Foley, James
Stapleton, Richard
Ruth, James
Ryan, Lucky
Barwell, W.
Whelan, Patrick
Bacon, James
Crotty, Francis
Douglass, W.
Crane, W.
Menaing, W.
Quirk, W.
Haydon, John
Carney, W.
Loft, Thomas
Coffer, W.
Gill, W.
M'Fadden, Patrick
Walsh, John
Longheed, Robert
Brennan, Thomas
Clarke, Andrew
Murphy, Michael
Newhall, Benjamin
Davies, W.
Kelly, James
Garvey, Patrick
Kennelly, John
M'Quade, Thomas

Nelson, Charles
Rogerson, Martin
Ridley, Thomas
Strathearn, W.
M'Nair, Robert
M'Kenzie, Donald
Bennett, W.
Carmichael, Neil
Reddin, Denis
Brown, Thomas
Canty, Denis
Drenon, John
Edlow, James
Burnside, John
M'Carthy, Thomas
Harbour, Stephen
Blagdon, George
Watt, William
Hunt, James
Condon, Jeremiah
M'Donald, George
O'Loghlin, Connor
Gill
Bowler, W.
Flanagan, Daniel
Dillon, John
Dinneen, John
Francis, S.
Kelly, T.
Downey, J.
Vayng, G.
M'Coy, John
Pendridge, A.
Owens, Peter
Rooney, Michael
Thompson, John
M'Kenna, Robert
Foley, Robert
Ward, Lawrence
Hannan, Michael
Brennan, John
Cooney, W.
Turner, W.
Newcombe, Richard W.
Hendrick, Henry
Spencer, W.
M'Lachlan, W.
Wilson, Joseph
Toohey, James
M'Gill, Thomas
Wright, Alexander
Charleston, Murdock
Wilson, W.
M'Guire, W.
Quinlan, John
Spence, James
Goodbrand, A.
Campbell, C.
Bruce, Robert
Davie, W.
Wilkie, James
Conyngham, Stephen

Kelley, Hubert
Canty, Maurice
Ryan, Michael
M'Namara, Bernard
Handley, Thomas
Spellacy, Henry
Grant, John
Tremwith, John
Kinneally, Patrick
Lenaghan, Derby
Heffernan, W.
Campion, W.
Whelan, Jeremiah
Johnstone, Thomas
Dibbs, W.
Whittaker, Joseph
Lord, John
Hogan, Lewis
M'Cardle, John
Coughlan, John
Andrews, J. F.
Connell, Thomas
Kinnarney, W.
Murray, John
Gibbons, John
Delany, Peter
Finns, Patrick
Sims, James
Ferris, Wm.
Watson, Thomas
Ross, Charles
Duncan, Archibald
Alison, Thomas
Harper, John
M'Neish, Samuel
Sanderson, Charles
Alexander, John
Flaxman, Edward
Lawless, John
Bayley, Thomas
Goldsmith, John
Knox, Alexander
Crabtree, Archibald
M'Kenzie, William
Leslie, John
M'Kay, Peter
Forbes, John
Davidson, James
Cody, James
Dooley, Patrick
Linn, James
Webb, Samuel
English, James
Gallagher, Peter
Jacques, John
Donnellan, Patrick
Curran, Andrew
Jackson, Henry
Cotterill, John
M'Milty, Patrick
Newman, W.
Hicks, John

APPENDIX.

M'Mahon, Bernard
King, John
M'Cann, Patrick
Bailey, Henry
Davis, Thomas
Green, John
Waller, John
Fisher, Daniel
Harrywood, James
Burge, Thomas
Bradshaw, Joseph
Feough, Charles
M'Cormick, Michael
Joice, William
Cooke, Richard
Hogan, Patrick
Russell, J.
Griffith, S.
Stewart, W.
Lyons, W.
Edwards, T.
Norris, John
Bailey, Matthew
Savage, John
Greene, John
Tisley, George
Wilson, Andrew
Kelly, J. W.
Andrews, John
Guthrie, Thomas
M'Gregor, George
Wakefield, T. J.
Morton, Andrew
Monkes, Thomas
Pickworth, John
Macauley, Charles
Donaghue, James
Martin, John
Finch, W.
Cannings, J. W.
Earson, John
Johnson, Thomas G.
Davis, Richard
Dearlove, George
Fenton, John
Wooden, Charles
Shearingham, John
Nunnerly, James
Watson, Charles
Heves, W.
Brown, W.
Connors, John
Eagan, John
Hall, John
Walsh, John
Ripton, George
Firmin, Ezekiel
M'Mahon, D.
Farrell, Christopher
Redmond, John
Smith, Philip
Davis, John

Hogan, Richard
Lawless, Thomas
Vaughan, Benjamin
Boyle, Michael
Garrett, James
Lind, Lawrence
Pegram, George
Ryan, Michael
Reilly, W.
Brophy, Michael
M'Kee, James
Carney, Thomas
M'Carthy, John
Finnigan, Thomas
Hughes, Robert
Ward, James
Morris, W.
Ahern, W.
M'Gowan, John
Sullivan, Daniel
Hughes, James
Don, W.
Martin, Roger
Rattray, Alexander
Drake, Joseph
Davidson, M.
Borthwick, James
Polkinghorn, Humphrey
Smith, G. L.
Powley, Robert
Nurton, W.
Vile, Frederick
Bott, John
Attrill, George
Sharp, George
Clarke, Henry
Newth, James
Fitzpatrick, John
Bacon, W.
White, W.
Rielly, Andrew
Monagan, Michael
Stokes, Frederick
Brown, Thomas
Collins, Charles
Byrne, John
Rolins, George
Evans, Samuel
Callaghan, Patrick
Lowe, John
Ellis, Richard
Marshman, Edward
O'Neill, James
Parkinson, William
Gerraghty, Thomas
Hill, Jonathan
Tulley, Patrick
M'Allister, Hastings
M'Donald, Thomas
Spelman, John
Reid, Philip
M'Guire, Patrick

Smith, W.
Brophy, Clement
Moore, W.
Blackmore, James
Omealy, Thomas
Madden, Ambrose
Smith, John
Fox, George
Cromtie, Andrew
Donelan, James
Murray, Robert
Brommell, W.
Gooding, Leonard
Court, Robert
M'Dermond, John
Barnes, Charles
Reilly, W.
Hope, Peter
Dunn, James
Butler, James
Jones, John
Anderson, Thomas
Warren, James
M'Sharry, John
Brophy, John
Roberts, Arthur
Mitchell, Joseph
Donohue
Cousins, John
Laughlan, James
Gunn, Wm.

Sloan, James
Myers, John
Grannon, Richard
M'Keen, Henry
Hill, Henry
Whelan, Michael
Kiddie, James
Cobb, James
Ormond, Nathan
Harris, W.
Wedgworth, Francis
Fitzgerald, W.
Cornelius, R.
Eagle, W.
Munro, C. F.
Benn, Mark
Dencer, Charles
Walsh, Thomas
Trotter, John
Betts, Thomas
Margee, Thomas
Bower, J.
O'Brien, E.
Davis, Hugh
Ewing, Samuel
Hovendon, W.
Reynolds, T.
Ramsey, W.
M'Kown, J,
M'Murphy, John
Lendrim, W. James

THE SARDINIAN WAR MEDAL.

Brown, Sir George
England, Sir Richard
Bentinck, Sir H. J. W.
Rokeby, Lord
Scarlett, Sir J. Y.
Jones, Sir H. D.
Eyre, Sir W.
Dupuis, J. E.
Mayow, Wynell
Hope, Hon. Adrian
Curzon, Hon. L.
Mackenzie, K. D.
Smith, Hugh
Thackwell, J. Edwin
Ross, R. L.
Shadwell, Lawrence
Hamley, E. B.
Cathcart, Hon. A. M.
Kirkland, J. A. V.
Wing, V.
Fellowes, Edward
Hackett, John
Wortley, A. H. P. S.

Elliot, Hon. Gilbert
Faussett, W.
Snodgrass, A. C.
Colville, Hon. W. J.
Garrett, Algernon R.
Thesiger, F. A.
Pitcairn, Andrew
Luard, Richard G. A.
Pearson, Richard L. O.
Hammersley, Frederick
St. Clair, Charles W.
Ponsonby, Arthur E. V.
Jervoise, G. Clarke
Keith, Hon. C. J.
Swire, Roger
Mansfield, C. E.
Ellison, R. G.
Earle, W.
Day, H. Hooper
Stopford, G. Montague
Forrest, W. C.
Forster, F. R.
Evans, J.

M'Mahon, T. W.
Cattell, W.
Gamble, J.
Yorke, John
Campbell, George
Hill, John
Griffith, H. D.
Buchanan, George
Wilson, J.
Paget, Lord G. A. F.
Lowe, A.
Portal, R.
Waterson, W.
Hunt, E. D.
Hardy, J.
De Salis, R.
Tomkinson, C.
Wilson, W.
Parlby, W.
Yates, John
Davies, Robert
Oakes, T. G. A.
Smith, Percy Shawe
Gardiner, W.
Lawrenson, J.
Duncan, J.
Ranson, A.
Ridley, C. W.
Hay, Lord A.
Sturt, C. Napier
Verschoyle, H. W.
Hamilton, R. W.
Minor, R.
Sharpe, T.
Strong, C. W.
Fitzroy, Lord A. C. Lennox
Crawley, P. S.
Dunlop, Sir J. Bart.
Conolly, J. A.
Haynes, G.
File, F.
Walker, E. W. F.
Coke, Hon. W. C. W.
Frazer, Hon. A. E.
Blane, S. J.
Scott, J.
M'Blain, John
Stewart, J.
Montgomery, A. B.
Plunkett, Hon. C. D.
Rudd, W. F. J.
Cooksworthy, W. S.
Hope, F. H.
Henshall, R.
M'Dowell, W.
Urquhart, F. H.
Gillum, W. J.
Woodhouse, G.
Van Straubenzee, C. T.
Ambrose, G. J.
Fahey, J.
Hort, J. J.

Hamilton, F. F.
Sykes, A. J.
Howley, J.
M'Ardell, J.
Scannells, T.
Shipley, R. Y.
Heyland, J. R.
Hibbert, H. R.
Hope, W.
Barrack, W.
M'Guire, J.
Lister, Frederick D.
Nugent, W.
Donohue, P.
Barlow, Maurice
Alexander, Sir J. E.
Maycock, J. G.
Hopkins, W.
M'Kinstrey, A.
Gibson, H.
Kennedy, J. C.
Call, H. F. S.
Baker, T. D.
Weir, J.
Warden, R.
Uniacke, H. T.
Warburton, G. A.
Thompson, T.
Sherlock, J.
Halloran, J.
Horn, F.
Radcliffe, W. B.
Parkinson, C. E.
Vaughan, H. B.
Whybrow, J.
Rowe, P.
Sackville, C. R.
West, Lord
Boldero, G. N.
King, H.
Stephens, R.
Fowler, W.
Lysons, D.
Drewe, F. E.
Millett, S. C.
O'Connor, L.
Luby, E.
Symonds, T.
Adams, F.
Baumgartner, R. J.
Hallewell, E. G.
Maunsell, T.
Messiter, S. L. A. M.
Bell, T. L.
M'Loughlin, J.
Gleeson, W.
Mauleverer, J. T.
Pakenham, T. H.
Dillon, R.
Sanders, G. H.
Shaw, T.
Andrews, J.

APPENDIX.

Staunton, G.
Mundy, G. V. E.
Collings, J. E.
Wallis, A. B.
De Montmorency, R. H.
Clark, T.
Leary, P.
Bond, J.
Simpson, J.
Jordan, J.
Boyce, A. W.
Peel, F.
Pratt, J.
Coughlan, D.
Sparks, J. P.
Loftus, W. J.
Gaynor, C. W. S.
Ewen, A. J. A.
M'Guire, P.
Reynolds, T.
Hudson, T. W.
Bennett, T. W.
M'Cluskey, J.
Pratt, R.
Skipwith, G.
Bush, Stratton H.
Peddie, G.
Crawford, W.
Collins, P.
Cameron, D. A.
Cameron, A.
Montgomery, H.
Halkett, Sir P. A. Bart.
Dalgleish, D.
M'Millan, E.
Spencer, Hon. A. A.
Staveley, C. W. D.
M'Mahon, W.
Fletcher, W.
Baillie, R.
Wood, W. A.
Doole, W.
Woodgate, W.
Garrett, Sir. R.
Campbell, C. F.
Dunscombe, N.
Knapp, G. H.
Cullen, P.
Flinn, P.
Farren, R. T.
Villiers, J.
Lowndes, J. H.
Ward, Hon. B. M.
Buchanan, H. J.
Grant, W.
M'Mahon, E.
Cairnes, W. H.
Gatlin, R.
Brant, J. T.
King, J. H.
Chatfield, G. K.
Young, W.

Davis, J.
Holden, R.
Gibbons, J.
Waddy, R.
Wilton, J. L.
Weare, H. E.
Hibbert, E. G.
Clarke, M. De S. M'K. G. A.
Lamb, J.
Leary. A.
Reghan, T.
Warren, C.
Cure, A. C.
Johnson, W. B.
Scott, J.
Meara, J.
O'Donnell, J.
Street, J. A.
Forsyth, G. J.
Slade, A. F. A.
Norton, M.
Healy, J.
Trollope, C.
Ingall, W.
Cooch, C.
Wilkieson, G. H.
Warren, J.
Farrell, J.
Dalzell, Hon. R. A. G.
Fairtlough, E.
Paterson, T.
Ceaton, P.
Smyth, H.
Macbeath, G.
Grace, S.
Saunderson, F. De Luttrell
Burrows, S.
Magner, J.
Hackett, F. J.
Wemyss, J. O.
Gourley, H.
Cathcart, J.
Willis, G. H. S.
Willington, R. B.
Burton, R. G.
Humphrey, A.
Bushell, R.
Brown, G.
Douglas, J.
Taylor, R. H.
Clephane, R. D.
Stevenson, H. H.
Jameson, R.
Anderson, J.
Campbell, W.
Shirley, H.
Maxwell, G. V.
Brown, E. J. V.
Maynard, E. G.
Gore, T.
Riley, Edward
Priestly, G.

APPENDIX.

Sullivan, J.
Durwoode, W.
Egerton, C. R.
Hawley, R. B.
Skynner, L.
Scott, P.
Smith, Thomas
Perrin, J.
Wade, Herne J.
Kirkland, A.
Smith, W.
Ainslie, W. Bernard
Ewart, J. A.
Dalzell, J.
Cooper, R. A.
Allan, C.
Robertson, J.
Reyland, A. T.
Raines, J. A. R.
Macdonald, A. J. J.
Boothby, B.
Anney, F.
Keenan, J.
Burton, F.
Ware, G. H. H.
Browne, C. H.
Kemmy, M.
Moore, W.
Norcott, W. S. R.
Horsford, A. H.
Macdonnell, A.
Woodford, C. J.
Russell, Lord A. G.
Stuart, Hon. J.
Saunders, G. R.
Hudling, J.
Farrant, J.
Fremantle, Fitzroy W.
Moore, J.
Cherry, J.
Tarvish, E.
Ward, F, B.
Fortescue, J. W.
Morris, C. H.
Gordon, S. Enderby
Gage, Hon. E. T.
Henry, C. S.
Thomas, H. J.
Rippon, P. G.
Tupper, G. Le Marchant
Ingilby, C. H.
Yates, H. P.

Pennyquick, J. F.
Hawkins, A. C.
Shaw, G.
Moubray, E.
Barry, W. W.
Michell, J. E.
Sinclair, G. Henry
Penn, L. W.
Taddy, E.
L'Estrange, P. W.
Champion, R. H.
Andrews, W. G.
Le Mesurier, W. G.
Humfrey, B. G.
Campbell, Sir J. W. Bart.
Ward, E. J.
Anley, F. A.
Browne, C. O.
Mauley, H. B.
Roberts, C. F.
Perry, W.
Bowen, E.
Troop, A.
Beardsley, J.
Hamilton, J.
Hamilton, J.
Dowling, D.
Symons, G.
Hunter, M.
Ewing, S.
Cambridge, D.
Ramsay, W.
Collier, H.
O'Brien, E.
M'Garry, J.
Arthur, T.
Death, J.
Barrett, J.
Gordon, J. W.
Chapman, F. E.
Stanton, E.
Browne, J. F. M.
Montagu, H. W.
Hassard, F. C.
Ewart
De Vere, F. H.
Lennox, W. O.
Leahy, A.
Pratt, F. E.
Baker, W.
M'Caughey, A.
Tumble, W.

ORDER OF THE MEDJIDIE.

OFFICERS OF THE BRITISH ARMY.

FIRST CLASS.

Campbell, Sir Colin
Codrington, Sir William J.
Lucan, Earl of

SECOND CLASS.

Bentinck, Sir Henry J. W.
Pennefather, Sir John L.
Cardigan, Earl of
Jones, Sir Harry D.
Airey, Sir Richard

Scarlett, Hon. Sir James Yorke
Buller, Sir George
Eyre, Sir William
Dacres, Sir Richard J.
Windham, Charles Ash

THIRD CLASS.

Rokeby, Lord Henry
Rose, Sir Hugh Henry
Dupuis, John Edward
Hodge, Edward Cooper
Paget, Lord George Augustus Frederick
Ridley, Charles William
Hamilton, Frederick W.
Cadogan, Hon. George
Gordon, Hon. Alexander
Upton, Hon. George F.
Paulet, Lord Frederick
Steele, Thomas Montagu
Walker, Edward W. F.
Straubenzee, Charles Thomas Van
Borton, Arthur
Barlow, Maurice
Edwards, Clement
Horn, Frederick
West, Lord Charles Richard
Lysons, Daniel

Adams, Frank
Cameron, Duncan Alexander
Spencer, Hon. Augustus A.
Garrett, Sir Robert
Haly, William O'Grady
Warren, Charles
Trollope, Charles
Shirley, Horatio
Lockyer, Henry F.
Lawrence, Arthur J.
Norcott, William S. R.
Paulet, Lord William
Herbert, Hon. Percy E.
Wilbraham, Richard
Pakenham, Hon. W. L.
Dickson, Collingwood
Gordon, John William
Chapman, Frederick E.
Hall, Sir John
Filder, William

FOURTH CLASS.

Yorke, John
Griffith, Henry Darby
Parlby, William
Lawrenson, John
Percy, Hon. Henry H. M.
Brownrigg, John Studholme
Saxe Weimar, His Serene Highness Prince William Augustus Edward of
Seymour, Francis

Berkeley, Charles A. F.
Wetherall, Edward R.
Somerset, Poulett G. H.
Bell, George
Huey, Richard William
Troubridge, Sir Thomas St. Vincent Hope Cochrane, Bart.
McPherson, Philip
Staunton, George

Smyth, Henry
Ferryman, Augustus H.
Sullivan, William
Cunynghame, Arthur A. T.
McMurdo, William M. S.
Lake, Noel Thomas
St. George, John
Warde, Edward Charles
Wood, David Edward
Fitzmayer, James William
Barker, George Robert
Low, Alexander
White, Henry Dalrymple
Douglas, John
Airey, James Talbot
Stephenson, Frederick C. A.
Montgomery, Alexander B.
Williams, Thomas
Wood, John Stewart
Evelegh, Frederick Charles
Baumgartner, Robert J.
Mauleverer, James T.
Sparks, James Pattoun
Smith, John William S.
Munro, William
Farren, Richard Thomas
Grant, John Thornton

Armstrong, James Wells
Waddy, Richard
Wilton, John Lucas
Daubeney, Henry C. B.
Street, John Alfred
Straton, Robert Jocelyn
Dixon, George
Douglas, John
Maxwell, George Vaughan
Ainslie, William Bernard
Hume, Henry
Heyland, Alfred Thomas
Sterling, Anthony Coningham
Mayow, George Wynell
Morris, William
Adye, John Miller
Stopford, George Montague
Linton, William
Cumming, Alexander
Dumbreck, David
Forrest, John
Lawson, Robert
Macdonnel, Alexander S.
Maclean, Sir George
Adams, George
Drake, William Henry
Carpenter, Frederick S.

OFFICERS ON THE STAFF OF THE OTTOMAN ARMY.

Cadell, Robert
Morgan, George Augustus
O'Reilly, Eugene

Green, William H. R.
Farquhar, Alexander

OFFICERS OF THE BRITISH ARMY—Continued.

FIFTH CLASS.

Spottiswoode, Andrew
Jones, Henry Richmond
Pole, Edward
Doherty, Charles Edmund
Lewis, Charles Algernon
Newton, William Samuel
Ridley, William John
Tyrwhitt, Charles
Murray, Lord James Charles Plantagenet
Haines, Frederick Paul
Riky, Benjamin
Denny, William
Smith, James Webber
McMahon, Thomas Westropp
Wardlaw, Robert
De Salis, Rodolph
Wilkie, John
Benson, Henry Roxby
Bradford, Ralph

Maitland, Charles L. Brownlow
Hay, Lord Arthur
Montresor, Henry Edward
Ponsonby, Henry Frederick
Ellison, Cuthbert George
Wood, William Mark
Cocks, Charles Lygon
Halkett, James
Carleton, Dudley Wilmot
Fitzroy, Lord Augustus Charles Lennox
Stepney, Arthur St. George Herbert
Burdett, Charles Sedley
Canning Ulick, Lord Dunkellin
Dawkins, William Gregory
Strong, Clement William
Burghersh, Lord Francis W. H.
Hardinge, Hon. Arthur E.
Fielding, Hon. Percy R. B.
Baring, Charles

APPENDIX.

Le Couteur, John Halkett
Dalrymple, John Hamilton E.
De Bathe, Henry Percival
Buchan, George W. F.
Moorsom, Robert
Hepburn, Henry Poole
Haygarth, Francis
Jocelyn, Hon. John Strange
Vane-Tempest, Lord Ad. F. C. W.
Scarlett, Hon. William F.
Meyrick, Augustus W. H.
Holder, Charles
Neville, Edward
Haythorn, Edmund
Going, Richard
Paterson, James
Hort, John Josiah
Reynell-Pack, Arthur J.
Shipley, Reginald Y.
Elmhirst, Charles
Lister, Frederick D.
Kerr, Lord Mark
Holcombe, Alexander E. F.
Cole, Arthur Lowry
Bourke, Oliver Paget
Kennedy, John Clark
Sanders, Robert
McGee, Henry E.
Crofton, Hugh D.
Stuart, John R.
Browne, Hon. James L,
Bunbury Henry William
Herbert, Arthur James
Whitmore, Edmund A.
Kelly, Thomas C.
Johnstone, John D.
Mundy, George V. E.
Erskine, George
Kelly, Richard D.
Goodenough, Arthur C.
Tinley, Robert N.
Goodwyn, Julius E.
Pratt, Robert
Tulloch, Thomas
Rollo, Hon. Robert
Cameron, Alexander
Staveley, Charles W. D.
Fielden, Robert
Maxwell, Alexander
Fordyce, Charles F.
Lys, George M.
Whimper, Frederick A.
Cure, Alfred C.
Warre, Henry J.
Ingall, William L.
Dalzell, Hon. Robert A. G.
Fairtlough, Charles E.
Macbeath, George
Ready, Charles
Sharp, Richard P.
Parke, William
Taylor, Richard C. H.

Jeffreys, Edmund R.
Brown, Edward J. V.
Egerton, Caledon R.
Aylmer, Frederick C.
Purnell, William P.
Hay, Alexander S. L.
Hope, Hon. Adrian
Ingram, Thomas O. W.
Bradford, Wilmot H.
Horsford, Alfred H.
Somerset, Edward A.
Foley, Hon. St. George G.
Claremont, Edward S.
Walker, Charles P. B.
Nedham, William R.
Morris, Henry J.
Taylor, Arthur J.
Maclean, George
Francklyn, John H.
Gambier, Gloucester
Irving, Alexander
Rowan, Henry S.
Freese, John N. A.
Paynter, David W
Phillpotts, Arthur T.
Wodehouse, Edwin
Maude, George A.
Thomas, Henry J.
Forrest, William C.
Custance, William N.
Sulivan, George A. F.
Clarke, George C.
Shute, Charles C.
Peel, Edmund
Fyler, Lawrence
Higginson, George W. A.
Daveney, Burton
Plunkett, Hon. Charles D.
Urquhart, Francis G.
Hawkins, Thomas S.
Byrne, Tyrrell M.
Maude, Frederick F.
Smith, Hugh
Thomson, George L.
Turner, William W.
Heyland, John R.
Alexander, Sir James E.
Gordon, William
Call, George Frederick S.
Warden, Robert
Bright, Robert O.
Kirkland, John A. V.
Harding, Francis Pym
Bell, Edward W. D.
Hallewell, Edmund G.
Lindsell, Robert H.
Butler, Percy A.
Pakenham, Thomas H.
Spence, Frederick
Collings, John E.
Donovan, Edward W.
Simpson, John

Gwilt, John
Loftus, William J.
Strachan, Henry A.
Graham, Lumley
MacMahon, William
Browne, Andrew
Campbell, Colin F.
Villiers, James
Lowry, Robert W.
Hamilton, Henry M.
Lowndes, John H.
Sankey, William
King, John H.
Adams, Cadwallader
Weare, Henry E.
Maxwell, Hon. James P.
Inglis, William
Lea, Frederick P.
Daubeney, James
Harries, Thomas
Blount, Herbert
Patton, Walter D. P.
Willis, George H. S.
Carden, Henry R.
McCall, William
Clephane, Robert D.
Maxwell, Edward H.
Grove, Robert
Smith, Thomas
Mackenzie, Kenneth D.
Gordon, Charles H.
Ewart, John A.
Legh, Edmund C.
Macdonnell, Alexander
Elrington, Frederick R.
Russell, Lord Alexander G.
Glyn, Julius R.
Fyers, William A.
Curzon, Hon. Leicester
Macdonald, Hon. James W. B.
Blane, Robert
Colborne, Hon. Francis
Thackwell, Joseph E.
Conolly James
Clifton, Thomas H.
Napier, William C. E.
Broughton, Spencer D.
Campbell, Hugh A. B.
Dixon, Matthew C.
Turner, John
Strange, Henry F.
Fortescue, John C. W.
Morris, Charles H.
Henry, Charles S.
Hamley, Edward B.
Biddulph, Michael A. S.
Gordon, Samuel Enderby
Gage, Hon. Edward T.
Owen, Henry C. C.
Bourchier, Eustace F.
Browne, James F. M.
Stanton, Edward

Briggs, George
Thompson, Richard
Harrison, Broadley
Greville, Arthur C.
Hood, Charles
Lewis, John
Bartley, John C.
Rutherford Archibald
Dowbiggin, Montagu H.
Watson, Charles E.
Fitzgerald, William H. D.
Bethune, Duncan M.
Leslie, Charles H.
Browne, Henry Ralph
King, George
Cox, John W.
Budd, Ralph
Ruttledge, Thomas O.
Armstrong, William A.
Lawrie, John
Shadwell, Lawrence
Radcliffe, William P.
Butler, Charles R.
Hobbs, Thomas F.
Dalyell, John T.
Rose, James
Dickson, Graham Le Fevre
Bayley, Paget
Pocock, George F. C.
Eagar, Robert J.
Ellis, Henry Disney
Pretyman, William
Peel, John
Farrer, James S. H.
Hackett, Samuel
Wolfe, William Clarges
Hudson, Thomas W.
Meredith, Henry Warter
Skipwith, George
Steward, Richard O. F.
Murray, Charles
Wilkinson, Frederick Green
Pitcairn, Andrew
Vesey, Arthur G.
Hardy, William
West, Frederick
Nason, John
Hibbert, Edward G.
Brown, Thomas S.
Rynd, M'Kay
Carter, William F.
Somerville, Thomas H.
Campbell, R. D.
Hope, William
Mackenzie, James
Thellusson, A. D.
Hackett, John
Rickman, William
Hunt, Andrew
O'Brien, Bartholomew
Burke, John Hardman
Bourke, Hon. J. J.

Skynner, Leslie
Hawley, Robert B.
White, Hans R.
Ross, Robert L.
Cathcart, Hon. A. M.
Dennis, John F. T.
Sargent, John N.
Burton, Fowler
Woods, Henry George
Hardinge, Henry
Erroll, William H. Earl of
Clifford, Hon. H. H.
Evans, William E.
Morel, Charles C. de
Gubbins, James
McDonald, A. McIan
Kane, F. A. C.
Wortley, A. H. P. S.
Forster, Francis R.
Burton, A. W. D.
Inglis, William
Elliot, A. J. H.
Elmsall, William de Cardonelly
Brown, George J.
Hutton, Thomas
Portal, Robert
Manley, Robert G.
Tomkinson, Edward
Chetwode, George
Calthorpe, Hon. S. J. G.
Thompson, John W.
Cook, Edwin A.
Fellowes, Edward
Jenyns, Soame G.
Tremayne, Arthur
White, Robert
Tipping, Alfred
Horsey, William H. B. de
Fox, Augustus H. L.
Thesiger, Frederick A.
Burnaby, Edward S.
Cameron, William G.
Russell, Sir Charles, Bart.
Pearson, Richard Lyons Otway
Armytage, Henry
Thellusson, Arthur J. B.
Crawley, Philip Sambrook
Goodlake, Gerald L.
Bingham, Lord George
Boyle, Hon. W. G.
Conolly, John Augustus
Maxse, Henry F. B.
Shuckburgh, George T. F.
Astley, John Dugdale
Coke, Hon. Wenman C. W.
Fraser, Hon. Alexander E.
Gipps, Reginald
Baring, Francis
Lindsay, Robert James
Stewart, William Little
Neville, Henry Draper
Mein, Frederick R.

Whitmore, Francis Locker
Wells, Frederick
Ambrose, George James
Walker, Mark
Robertson, Patrick
Hibbert, Robert Hugh
Appleyard, Frederick E.
Baynes, Robert Stuart
Hawes, George Harrington
Dwyer, John
Douglas, William
Hammersley, Frederick
McKinstry, Alexander
O'Connor, Richard John Ross
Brice, George Tito
Cormick, John
Armstrong, Anthony W. S. F.
Hayman, Jones Matthew
Chippindall, Edward
Hay, James George
Boldero, George Neeld
Torrens, Henry D'Oyley
Aplin, John Guise Rogers
Maunsell, Thomas
Roberts, William
Godley, Henry Robert Crewe
Campbell, Archibald
Atcherley, Francis Topping
Green, Charles Mingaye
Fitzgerald, Henry Charles
Vacher, Frederic Smith
Quayle, John Edward T.
Maxwell, James
Warry, William
Jordan, Joseph
Brown-Westhead, George Edward
Harman, George Byng
Hume, Gustavus
Daniell, Charles Frederick T.
Daniel, Ludford Harvey
Snodgrass, Archibald Campbell
Currie, Robert Hamilton
Rowlands, Hugh
Graham, Charles Campbell
Faussett, William
Robinson, John
Preston, Richard
Fletcher, William
Wombwell, Arthur
Garrett, Algernon Robert
Shervington, Charles Robert
Dallas, George Frederick
Villiers, Charles Courteney
Elgee, Charles
Hunter, Fitzwilliam Frederick
Sykes, Cam
Deshon, Frederick G. T.
Bellairs, William
Dewar, James William
Lock, Andrew Campbell Knox
Tupper, Daniel William
Werge, Henry Reynolds

APPENDIX.

Hume, Robert
Elton, Frederick Cockayne
Hassard, Jason
Earle, Arthur Maxwell
Cooch, Charles
Lewis, John Edward
Finch, Hon. Daniel Greville
Savage, Frederick Stukely
Luard, Richard George A.
Hodgson, William Chauval
Maynard, Edmund Gilling
Steevens, Nathaniel
Boyle, William
Cuppage, John Macdonald
Crealock, Henry Hope
Raines, Julius Augustus Robert
Massey, Hon. Eyre Challoner H.
Sibthorp, Richard Francis W.
Lumley, Charles Henry
Walker, Hercules
Newdigate, Edward
Elliot, Hon. Gilbert
Colville, Hon. William James
Churchill, Charles Henry S.
Stuart, Hon. James
Warren, Arthur Frederick
Bourchier, Claude Thomas
D'Aguilar, Charles Lawrence
Ward, Francis Beckford
Brandling, John James
Rogers, Henry
Anderson, John Richard
Clifford, Miller
Adye, Mortimer
Franklin, Charles Trigance
Hawkins, Alexander Cæsar
Grant, William James Esten
Shaw, George
Lennox, Augustus Frederick F.
Pipon, Philip Gosset
Shakespear, John Davenport
Field, George Thomas
Fraser, Hon. David M'Dowell
Strange, Charles John
Newton, Horace Parker
Yelverton, Hon. William C.
Milman, Gustavus Hamilton L.
Baddeley, John Fraser Lodington
Arbuthnot, Charles George
Hastings, Francis William
Moubray, Edward
Chermside, Henry Lowther
Boothby, John George
Barstow, George
Craufurd, Robert Emilius F.
Tupper, Gaspard Le Marchant
Hoste, Dixon Edward
Singleton, John
Reilly, William Edmund Moyses
Fitz-Hugh, Henry Terrick
Soady, France James
Barry, William Wigram

Carthew, Edmund John
Michell, John Edward
Henry, George Cecil
Ingilby, Charles Henry
Yates, Henry Peel
Williams, William John
Pennycuick, James Farrell
Oldershaw, Charles Edward
Turner, Nathaniel Octavius S.
Dickson, Philip
Hope, John Edward
Brendon, Algernon
Lukin, William Windham A.
Walcott, Charles Edmund
Bredin, Edward Grantham
Bolton, William John
Sinclair, James
Penn, Lewis William
Taddy, Edward
Miller, Frederick
Owen, Charles Henry
Milman, George Alderson
L'Estrange, Paget Walter
Burt, Charles Edward
Irvine, Hazlitt
Champion, Reginald Henry
Andrews, William Gilly
Mackenzie, Roderick
Le Mesurier, William George
Keane, Hon. Hussey Fane
Gibb, Charles John
Hassard, Fairfax Charles
Lovell, John Williamson
Montagu, Horace William
Cooke, Anthony Charles
Armit, Louis John Amédée
Ewart, Charles Brisbane
Porter, Whitworth
Ravenhill, Philip
Nicholson, Lothian
Sedley, Charles Herbert
Vere, Francis Horatio de
Fisher, Arthur A'Court
Elphinstone, Howard Craufurd
M'Creagh, Michael
Halford, Charles Augustus D.
Stocks, Michael
Hunter, Robert Scott
Keith, Hon. Charles James
Hunt, Edmund D'Arcy
Seagar, Edward
Fitclarence, Hon. Frederick C. G.
Rosser, Charles Potts
Trevelyan, Harrington Astley
Oakes, Thomas George Alexander
Smith, Percy Shawe
Gordon, Sir William, Bart.
Barnard, William Andrew M.
Alexander, Claud
Ponsonby, Arthur Edward V.
Sturt, Charles Napier
Verschoyle, Henry William

APPENDIX. 401

Bathurst, Frederick Thomas A. H.
Hamilton, Robert William
Tower, Harvey
Dangan, Viscount William Henry
Heneage, Michael Walker
Blackett, Christopher Edward
Jervoise, Henry Clarke
Campbell, Hon. Henry W.
Wigram Godfrey James
Rose, George Ernest
Blane, Seymour John
Gordon, George Grant
Farquharson, James Ross
Tottenham, Charles George
Sharp, John Edward
Chrystie, John Alexander
Rudd, William Frederick J.
Gregory, Thomas John
O'Connell, Morgan James
Burningham, Henry George C.
Hamilton, Francis Fisher
Sheppard, Thomas
Eccles, Cuthbert
Mure, Charles Reginald
Cooper, Joshua Harry
Browne, Lord Richard Howe
Jones, Lewis John Fillis
Wilkinson, Henry John
Daunt, William
Straubenzee, Frederick Van
Montgomery, Robert Blackall
Jones, Hugh Maurice
Newman, Charles Cecil
Maycock, John Gittens
Smyth, Ralph
Dyer, Swinnerton Halliday
Swire, Roger
Taylor, William O'Brien
Barrett, Richard Doyle
Clay, George
Uniacke, Henry Turner
Bayley, Edward Robert Warde
Parkinson, Charles Edward
Dickins, William Drummond S.
Warren, Augustus Riversdale
Dowglasse, George
Hawker, Samuel William Henry
Sheffield, John Charles
Sayer, Frederick
Duff, James
Vane, Frederick Fletcher
Millett, Sydney Crohan
Bigge, Thomas Scovell
Messiter, Sussex L. A. B.
Hackett, Simpson
Morgan, Hill Faulconer
O'Brien, John
Williamson, Augustus Henry
Macpherson, Lachlan
Swaffield, Charles James O.
Schreiber, Arthur John
Barrett, Charles Carter

Nugent, Walter George
Carr, John Ralph
Scott, Arthur
Addington, Hon. Charles J.
Brooksbank, Arthur
Quicke, Sidney Godolphin
Pocklington, Frederick
Milligan, Charles
Macdonald, Norman
Lowry, Armar Graham
Kingscote, Fitzhardinge
Fitzroy, Charles Vane
Montgomery, Henry
Ward, William Crofton
Grove, Joseph Charles Ross
Scott, Francis Cunningham
Gregory, Frederick William
Thoroton, Levett
Handcock, Hon. Henry
Piper, Robert William
Nicholas, Albert
McAlester, Charles Somerville
Forde, Thomas Douglas
Lowry, James Armar
Buchanan, Henry James
Lucas, Jasper
Ellison, Richard George
Lovett, John Richard
Knight, William Henry
Trent, Francis Constantine
Lamb, George Henry
Marchant, Edward Le
Hopkins, John
Earle, William
Fitzgerald, Charles
Antrobus, Edward Crawfurd
Thompson, John
England, Richard
Richards, William Hamilton
Morgan, George Anthony
Harkness, John Granville
Brown, William Edward
Venables, Cavendish
Ingham, Joshua Cunliffe
Wilkieson, George Hampden
Hay, Graham
Hunter, Edward Henry
Cubitt, Charles Campbell
Paterson, Falkland L. T.
Magnay, Christopher J.
Bowles, Vere H.
Wybergh, Archibald
Shuttleworth, Charles U.
Fitzroy, Cavendish C.
Vaughan, Herbert
Battiscombe, Henry L.
Loftus, Henry
Parker, Arthur C.
Stuart, Robert C. W.
Kirkwall, Viscount George W. H.
Rocke, Richard
Buchanan, Richard D.

APPENDIX.

Kent, Henry
Acton, William M. C.
Willington, Richard B.
Butts, Frederick J.
M'Barnet, Alexander C.
Cuming, Edward W.
Stevenson, Henry H.
Sheehy, William
Pearson, William C.
Heycock, Charles
Pery, William C. G.
Hall, Savage
Wade, James Herne
Magenis, Richard H.
Wolseley, Garnet J.
Burroughs, Frederick W.
Stewart, William G. D.
Macdonald, William D.
Probart, Francis G. C.
Carmichael, George L.
Brinkley, Matthew
Whitehead, Robert C.
Nixon, Arthur James
Pellew, Hon. Barrington R.
Bramston, Thomas H.
Legge, Hon. George B.
Thynne, William F.
Cuninghame, William J. M.
Anson, Hon. Augustus H. A.
Morgan, Frederick C.
Thompson, Arnold
Johnson, George V.
Pigou, Arthur Comyn
Anson, Archibald, E. H.
Wilson, Willoughby J.
Morris, William
Jones, Dashwood
Whinyate, Frederick T.
Heyman, Henry
Davis, Gronow
Wilkinson, Bathurst E.
Hampton, Thomas L.
Glyn, Richard George
Moodie, Daniel
Hunt, George W.
Weir, Archibald
Mussenden, William
Jameson, Robert O'Brien
Gardner, George
Hope, Frederick H.
Stuart, Edward A.
Manners, Richard A.
Willis, Sherlock V.
Freeborn, William
Cox, Talbot Ashley
Laurie, John W.
Maule, Henry B.
Grinlinton, John J.
Bennet, Adrian
McQueen, John
Cobham, George H.
Wilson, Charles M.

Gordon, Alexander
Coote, Charles J.
Kemp, William
Hotham Charles
Goren, Ames
Vaughan, Hector B.
Lee, Vaughan H.
Clair, Stanislas Graham Bower-St.
O'Connor, Luke
Waldy, Edward G.
Campbell, John P.
Austin, Alfred J.
Leeson, Ralph
Owens, John
Boyce, Abel W.
Wyse, John Francis
Cochrane, Rupert I.
Thackwell, William de Wilton R.
Smyth, James G.
Hill, Henry Seymour
Lowry, Edward L. B.
Wilson, John
Cobham, Alexander W.
Knapp, George H.
Townshend, Edward
Jones, Percy M.
Palmer, Thomas
Stokes, Henry B. G.
Horne, Edmund G.
Clarke, Montague de Salis McKenzie Gordon Augustus
Lee, Thomas Denote
Lamb, James
Burke, Henry
Williams, Francis
Slade, Alfred F. A.
Shute, Henry D. M.
Palmer, Herrick A.
Davenport, William B.
Bonham, Francis
Campbell, George
Stewart, John C.
Vesey, Charles C. W.
Currie, Francis G.
Leith, John M.
Budgen, Edward H.
Vernor, Robert
Perceval, Ernest
Robinson, Barnes S.
Cooper, Richard A.
McBean, William
Benison, Jonathan
Wield, Robert
Stockwell, John W. I.
Robertson, George
Aylmer, Fenton J.
Browne, Charles H.
Saunders, George Robert
Singer, James
Harward, George S.
Browne, John T. B.
Ogilvie, Alexander, W. A.

Taylor, Markham Le Fer
Pearse, Arthur T. G
Treadcroft, Charles L.
Doyne, Henry A.
Biddulph, Robert
Hill, Peter E.
Cuthbert, Edmund C
Lloyd, M. Ernest A.
Griffiths, Leonard
Briscoe, Henry W.
Ward, Edward J.
Southhouse, Charles E.
Geary, Henry Le Guay
King, Augustus H.
Neville, Glastonbury
Lennox, Wilbraham O.
Graham, Gerald
Philips, George
Martin, Charles N.
Pratt, Francis E.
Drake, John M. C.
James, Edward R.
Newsome, William
Leahy, Arthur
Cowell, John C.
Wilkin, Henry J.
Duncan, James
Phelps, John S.
Slack, James
Scott, William F.
Allen, George
McGill, William
Moore, Thomas
Hume, Thomas D.
Logan, Thomas G.
Williams, James E.
Jameson, Thomas R.
O'Flaherty, Richard J.
Tice, John Charles G.
Prendergast, Joseph S.
Hunter, Thomas
Anderson George
Moore, James G. P
Roberts, Frederic
Hadley, Henry
Paynter, Joshua
Wood, John G.
Home, William
Downes, Henry
Davies, John
Smith, Henry F.

Combe, Matthew
Hyde, George
Jephson, William H.
Baxter, Francis H.
Massy, Hampden H.
Blenkins, George E.
Hearn, Charles B.
Thornton, Robert
Howard, Edward
Mackinnon, David R.
Watt, William G.
Dowse, Richard R.
Scott, James E.
Furlong, John S.
O'Leary, T. Connor
Franklyn, E. James
Scot, T. Goldie
Munro, William
Elliot, R. Coffin
Burt, John
Perry, William
Walshe, H. Crawford
Fitzgerald, Thomas G.
Robinson, Frederick
Elkington, A. Guy
Greer, Arthur J.
Milroy, David
Lawlor, Digby W.
Hannan, James
Burton, R. Graves
Miller, Ormsby B.
Harris, William
Pollard, W. Henry
Porter, W. Henry
Longheed, Joseph F.
Fogo, A. Scott
Haughton, William
Chapple, Robert A.
Gloag, John W.
Morse, Henry B.
Routh, Leonce
M'Mahon, E. John
Darling, Montague W.
Osborn, Kean
Power, W. J. Tyrone
De Fonblanque, E. Barrington
Crookshank, A. Crowder
Rolleston, Philip
Romaine, W. Govett
Fitzgerald, David

OFFICERS ON THE BRITISH STAFF ATTACHED TO THE OTTOMAN ARMY.

Macintyre, J. M'Kenzie
Holmes, John W.
Le Mesurier, Frederick
Bird, S. Dougan

Buzzard, Thomas
Edwards, Charles F.
Turner, Charles

OFFICERS OF THE ROYAL NAVY.

FIRST CLASS.

Stewart, Vice-Admiral Sir Houston.

THIRD CLASS.

Slade, Adolphus   Borlase, John

OFFICERS OF THE LATE TURKISH CONTINGENT.

FIRST CLASS.

Vivian, Lieutenant-General Sir Robert John Hussey.

SECOND CLASS.

Michel, John
Cunynghame, A. A. Thurlow

Shirley, Arthur
Dickson, Collingwood

THIRD CLASS.

Stevens, S. James
Graham, J. John
Wetherall, E. Robert
Morris, William
Forbes, Francis

Holmes, John
Abbott, John R.
Crewe, Richard
Hall, George

FOURTH CLASS.

Grant, W. Colquhoun
Westmacott, R. Marsh
Carey, Robert
Carruthers, G. Travers Sayer
Coates, William
Boudier, Edward W.
Mayne, James E.
Stephen, J. Grant
Brett, R. Best
Wray, Edward
Plowden, E. W. Chricheley
Stokes, John
De Courcy, John
Richardson, Roland
Gordon, C. A. Boswell
Gore, Frederick W.
Elkington, J. H. Ford
Hartman, Gustavus A.
Miller, Frederick
Austen, Albert G.
Sutton, W. Griffin
Payn, William

Hill, James M.
Melville, G. J, Whyte
Goldsmid, F. John
Vaughan, J. Luther
Whitmore, G. Stoddart
Mercer, E. Smyth
Pasley, G. Malcolm
Greene, Dawson Cornelius
Plasket, Thomas H.
Pattinson, Richard
Gosling, William C. F.
Stack, Frederick R.
Warde, George
McDonald, William C. R.
Grant, Ewin
Swaby, George
Hughes, Robert J.
Robeson, George H.
Garstin, Marcus A.
Campbell, Archibald H.
Owen, Edward H. M.
Rishton, Alfred Louis

Cuming, William H.
Francis, Henry
McNeill, Donald
Smyth, Edmund
Broome, Arthur
Robison, Hugh G.
Walker, William
Lucas, Charles P.
Desborough, Charles
McDowell, James V. V.
Wyndham, Charles
Sullivan, George
Bogle, Andrew H.

Grierson, William M.
Heathorn, Thomas B.
Holder, Frederick
Thornton, Charles McLeod J.
Whitmore, Montagu S.
Hearn, Charles S.
Philips, Henry
Brown, David P.
M'Pherson, Duncan
Vaughan, James
Ainger, Major
Paton, Robert
Hynde, Lawrence

FIFTH CLASS.

Johnson, Charles H.
Keeling, James H.
M'Dowall, Alexander A.
M'Dowall, Cameron
Irvine, Alexander

Sutherland, George S.
Williamson, J.
Edwards, Ernest
Gunn, Francis L.
Coleman, William W.

OFFICERS OF THE LATE OSMANLI IRREGULAR CAVALRY AND HORSE ARTILLERY.

OSMANLI IRREGULAR CAVALRY.

SECOND CLASS.

Smith, Major-General Michael William.

THIRD CLASS.

Watt, Edward
Havelock, Charles F.
Brett, De Renzie J.

Crofton, Edward W.
Skene, James H.

FOURTH CLASS.

Ring, William F.
Green, Malcolm S.
Pittman, Richard
Sankey, Francis
Brenan, Edward FitzGerald
Heyman, Henry
Ling, John T.
Wemyss, Charles T.

Rumbold, Sir Carlo A. H., Bart.
Williams, James
Stuart, W. Edington
Villiers, William G. V.
Walmsley, Hugh M.
Jones, Humphrey S.
Cockburn, Archibald W.

OSMANLI HORSE ARTILLERY.

Mundy, R. Miller
Bent, Hugh
Plunkett, Hon. E. Sidney
Colclough, George

Bredin, E. Grantham
Murray, A. Henry
Carleton, George
Murray, Augustus

OFFICERS OF THE BRITISH ARMY.

THIRD CLASS.

Barnard, Major-General Sir Henry William.

FOURTH CLASS.

Campbell, Robert P.   Rooke, J. L. Richard

FIFTH CLASS.

Tottenham, W. H.
Powell, Thomas S.
Steevens, George
Woodford, Charles J.
Balgonie, Viscount
Dunlop, Sir J. Bart.
Barnston, Roger

Perrin, James
Dashwood, H. W. John
Day, Henry Hooper
Dalzell, James
Jeffcock, Charles E.
Grahame, Nicol
Anderson, W. Christian

OFFICERS OF THE LATE TURKISH CONTINGENT.

THIRD CLASS.

Neill, James George   Evans, Dacres Fitzherbert

FOURTH CLASS.

Young, James   Moore, John   Quin, Charles W.

INDEX.

A.

Agriculture, Medal of, 221, Prussia.
Albert the Bear, 1, Anhalt Koethen, Dessau and Bernberg, Plate 2, No. 2.
Albert, 270, Saxony, Plate 79, No. 10.
Alcantara, 306, Spain, Plate 87, Nos. 5, 6.
Alexander Newsky, 230, Russia, Plate 70, No. 8.
Annunciation, 250, Sardinia, Plate 76, Nos. 1, 2.
Apostolic Order of St. Stephen, 10, Hungary, Plate 4, Nos. 5, 6, 7, and Plate 5, No. 14.
Aviz, St. Benedict of, 187, Portugal, 61, Nos. 3, 4, 5.

B.

Bath, 104, England, Plate 30.
Bavarian Crown, 54, Bavaria, Plate 12, Nos. 12, 13, 14.
Belgian Lion, 145, Holland, Plate 46, Nos. 7, 8, 9.
Black Eagle, 198, Prussia, Plate 65, Nos. 1, 2, 3.

C.

Calatrava, 301, Spain, Plate 87, Nos. 3, 4.
Charles III, 310, Spain, Plate 88, Nos. 12, 13, and Plate 89, No. 19.
Charles XIII. 338, Sweden and Norway, Plate 93, Nos. 12, 13.
Charles Frederick, 42, Baden, Plate 9, Nos. 3, 4.
Christ, 172, Papal States, Plate 55, Nos. 4, 5, 6.
Christ, 189, Portugal, Plate 62, Nos. 8, 9, and Plate 63, No. 12.
Civil Cross of Merit, 40, Austria, Plate 8, Nos. 3, 4.
Civil Merit, Medal of, 55, Bavaria, Plate 15, No. 32.
Civil Cross of Honour, 35, Austria, Plate 7, Nos. 25, 29.
Civil Medal of Honour, 36, Austria, Plate 7, No. 31.
Constantine, 291, the Two Sicilies.
Crimean Campaign, 111, England, Plate 33.
Crescent, 344, Turkey, Plate 96, No. 3.
Cross of the Bohemian Nobility, 37, Austria.
Cross of Honour for the Campaigns of 1814 and 1815, 223, Principalities.
Cross of Honour, 120, Greece, Plate 34, Nos. 3, 4.
Cross of Honour for Military Chaplains, 36, Austria, Plate 7, No. 21.
Cross of Merit, 134, Hesse (Electorate), No. 9.
Cross of Merit, 76, Brunswick, No. 6.
Cross of Military Distinction for sub-officers and soldiers, 135, Hesse (Electorate), No. 11.
Cross of the South, 71, Belgium, Plate 17, Nos. 3, 4.
Crown of Wurtemberg, 356, Wurtemberg, Plate 98, No. 1, and Plate 99, No. 6.

D.

Danneborg, 83, Denmark, Plate 25, Nos. 4, 5, 6, 8, 9, 10.
Decoration for Civil and other Merits, 128, Hanover.
Decoration for Field Service, 45, Baden, Plate 10, Nos. 11, 12.
Decoration for Field Service, 139, Hesse (Grand-Duchy), No. 9.
Decoration for eight and sixteen years Loyal Service, 88, Denmark, Nos. 11, 12.
Decoration of Honour, 78, Brunswick, No. 9.
Decoration of Honour, 87, Denmark.
Decoration of Honour, 152, Lippe-Detinol (Principality), Plate 48, Nos. 1—4.

Decoration of Honour, 154, Lucca, Plate 49.
Decoration of Honour, 156, Luxembourg (Grand-Duchy), Plate 50, Nos. 1, 2.
Decoration of Honour, 175, Papal States, Plate 57.
Decoration of Honour, 140, Hohenzollern-Hechingen, and Hohenzollern-Sigmaringen, Plate 44.
Decoration of Honour, 148, Holland, Plate 47.
Decoration of Honour, 161, Modena.
Distinction and Badge of Confidence, 38, Austria, Plate 6, No. 18.
Distinction of Merit, 44, Baden, Plate 10, No. 10, and Plate 9, Nos. 5, 6, 7.
Ducal House of Peter Frederick Louis, 167, Oldenburg, Plate 54, Nos. 1—6.

E.

Elephant, 81, Denmark, Plate 24, Nos. 1, 2, 3.
Elizabeth, Theresa, 17, Austria, Plate 5, No. 15.
Ernest Augustus, 128, Hanover.

F.

Family Order of the Golden Lion, 132, Hesse (Electorate), Plate 40, Nos. 1—5.
Family Order of Loyalty, 41, Baden, Plate 9, Nos. 1, 2.
Female Order and Institution of St. Ann of Munich, 59, Bavaria, Plate 13, Nos. 18, 19.
Female Order of the St. Ann Institution at Warsburg, 61, Bavaria, No. 20.
Francis I, 294, the Two Sicilies, Plate 86, Nos. 11, 12, 13.
Francis Joseph, 38, Austria, Plate 8, Nos. 32, 33, and Plate 16, *A, B, C.*
Frederick, 358, Wurtemberg, Plate 98, No. 4.

G.

Garter, 97, England, Plate 28, Nos. 1—4.
General Decoration of Merit, 128, Hanover.
Golden Fleece, 6, Austria, Plate 4, Nos. 1—8.
Golden Fleece, 310, Spain, Plate 88, Nos. 9, 10.
Golden Spurs, 173, Papal States, Plate 57, No. 12.
Guelphic Order, 123, Hanover, Plate 36, Nos. 1, 2, 5.
Guelphic Medal, 125, Hanover, Plate 36, No. 6.

H.

Hamburg, Distinction of Military Service, 131, Hanse Towns.
Henry the Lion, 75, Brunswick, 22, Nos. 1—5.
Holy Sepulchre, 347, Turkey, Plate 96, Nos. 1, 2.
House of Hohenzollern, 208, Prussia, Plate 66, No. 9.

I.

India, Medal for distinguished service in, 112, England, Plate 33, Nos. 24, 25.
Initials in Diamonds, 128, Hanover.
Iron Crown, 18, Austria, Plate 5, Nos. 12, 13, and Plate 6, No. 16.
Iron Cross and Medal, 67, Belgium, Plate 18, Nos. 7, 8, 9.
Iron Cross, 204, Prussia, Plate 66, Nos. 10, 11.
Iron Cross of Honour, 130, Hanse Towns, Plate 94, No. 5.
Iron Helmet, 134, Hesse (Electorate), Nos. 7, 8.
Isabella the Catholic, 318, Spain, 90, Nos. 22, 23.

J.

July, the Cross of, 94, France, No. 7.
July, the Medal of, 95, France.

L.

Legion of Honour, 90, France, Plate 26, Nos. 1, 2, and Plate 27, Nos. 5, 6.
Leopold, 14, Austria, Plate 11, Nos. 10, 11, and Plate 5, No. 9.
Leopold, 66, Belgium, Plate 17, Nos. 1—5.
Lion and the Sun, 184, Persia, 60.
Lion of Zachringen, 43, Baden, Nos. 8, 9, 13.
Louis, 136, Hesse (Grand Duchy), Plate 42, Nos. 1, 2, 3.
Louisa, 210, Prussia, 67, No. 14.

M.

Madonna of Guadaloupe, Order of the, 160, Mexico, (Republic).
Malta, (St. John), 29, Austria, Plate 7, Nos. 23, 24.
Maria Theresa, 8, Austria, Plate 4, Nos. 2, 3, 4.
Maria Louisa, 314, Spain, Plate 89, No. 14.
Maria Isabella Louisa, 319, Spain, Plate 90, No. 24.

INDEX.

Maximilian Joseph, Military Order of, 52, Bavaria, Plate 12, Nos. 8, 9, 10.
Maximilian, Order of, for Art and Science, 65, Bavaria, Plate 16, No. 35.
Medal of Civil Service, 45, Baden.
Medal of Deeds of Self Devotion or Sacrifice, 67, Belgium, Plate 19, Nos. 11, 12, and Plate 20, Nos. 14, 15, 16.
Medal for Artizans, Mechanics, and the Working Classes, 69, Belgium, Plate 19, No. 13.
Medal for Vaccination, 68, Belgium, Plate 18, No. 10.
Medal of Honour for the Spanish-Portuguese Campaign, 78, Brunswick, Plate 23, No. 10.
Medal of Honour, 88, Denmark.
Medal for Saving from Drowning, 88, Denmark.
Medal for Noble Deeds, 88, Denmark.
Medal of Merit for Saving from Danger, 129, Hanover.
Medal of Remembrance and Honour, 135, Hesse (Electorate), No. 10.
Medals of Merit in Gold and in Silver, and general Decorations of Honour, 127, Hanover.
Medals and Decorations of Honour, 163, Nassau, (Duchy), Plate 52, Nos. 1, 5.
Medals and Decorations of Honour, 162, Montenegro (Principality).
Medals and Decorations of Honour, 157, Mecklenburg-Schwerin (Grand Duchy), Plate 51.
Medals and Decorations of Honour, 169, Oldenburg (Grand Duchy), Plate 54.
Medals and Decorations of Honour, 195, Portugal.
Medals and Decorations of Honour, 218, Prussia, Plate 68.
Medals and Decorations of Honour, 245, Russia, Plate 73, 74, 75.
Medals and Decorations of Honour, 262, Sardinia, Plate 77, Nos. 10, 11.
Medals and Decorations of Honour, 282, Saxe-Weimar.
Medals and Decorations of Honour, 275, Saxe (Grand Duchies), Plate 81.
Medals and Decorations of Honour, 286, Schwarzburg-Sonderhausen, Plate 83, Nos. 2, 3, 4.
Medals and Decorations of Honour, 319, Spain.
Medals and Badges of Honour, 339, Sweden and Norway.
Medal of the Tenth August, 342, Switzerland, Plate 94, No. 2.
Medal of 1815, 341, Switzerland, Plate 94, No. 1.
Medal, 347, Turkey.
Medals and Decorations of Honour, 354, Tuscany.
Medals and Decorations of Honour, 361, Wurtemburg.
Medjidie, 345, Turkey, Plate 96, No. 6.
Memento for the Bavarian Auxiliary Corps, 119, Greece, Plate 34, No. 6.
Memento for the Bavarian Volunteers, 119, Plate 34, No. 5.
Merciful Brethren of the Holy Ghost, 178, Papal States.
Merit, Order of, 268, Saxony, Plate 79, Nos. 6, 7, 8.
Merit, Medal of, of 1771, 88, Denmark.
Merit, and of the House of Philippe-le-Bon, Order of, 43, Plate 11, Nos. 7, 8.
Merit, Order of, 202, Prussia, Plate 66, No. 9.
Merit, Medal of, of 1793, 88, Denmark.
Merit, Military Order of, 359, Wurtemberg, Plate 98, Nos. 1, 2, and Plate 99, No. 7.
Merit of the Dockyards, Medal of, 87, Denmark, Plate 25, No. 7.
Military Decoration of 1814, 37, Austria, Plate 7, No. 30.
Military Merit, 353, Tuscany.
Military Medal, 95, France, Plate 27, Nos. 7, 8.
Military Service, 138, Hesse (Grand Duchy), Plate 43, No. 5.
Military Decoration of Honour, 285, Schwarzburg-Rudolstadt, Plate 83, No. 1.
Military Order of Merit, 133, Hesse (Electorate), No. 6.
Military Distinction and Decorations of Honour, 63, Bavaria, Plate 15, Nos. 31, 33, 34, and Plate 13, No. 21.
Military Merit, 244, Russia, Plate 73, Nos. 22, 23.
Military Medal, 151, Lippe-Schaumburg, (Principality), Plate 48, Nos. 5, 6.
Military Medal of Honour, 36, Austria, Nos. 27, 28.

N.

Naval Actions, Medals for, 110, England.
Nichani-Iftchar, 345, Turkey, Plate 96, Nos. 1, 2.
Nichan, the, 343, Tunis, Plate 95, No. 3.
National Guard, Decoration of Honour for the, 150, Holland, Plate 47, No. 7.

O.

Oaken Crown, 155, Luxembourg (Grand Duchy), Plate 50, Nos. 4, 5.
Our Lady of the Conception of Villa Vicosa, 193, Plate 64, Nos. 14, 15.
Our Lady of Montesa, 308, Spain, Plate 88, Nos. 7, 8.

P.

Pedro, 70, Brazil, Plate 20, Nos. 1, 2.
Peninsula, Medal for Actions in the, 110, England, Plate 32.
Pius, Order of, 175, Papal States, Plate 57, No. 18.
Polar Star, or "The Black Ribbon," 336, Sweden and Norway, Plate 92, Nos. 7, 8, 9.

R.

Redeemer, 118, Greece, Plate 34, Nos. 1, 2.
Red Eagle, 200, Prussia, Plate 65, Nos. 4, 5, 6, 7, 8.
Rose, 72, Brazil, Nos. 5, 6.
Royal Louis Order, 56, Bavaria, Plate 14, Nos. 27, 28; Plate 15, No. 30.
Rue Crown, Order of the, 264, Saxony, 78, Nos. 1, 2.

S.

Saving Medal, 80, Brunswick, Tab. II. No. 12.
Savoy, Royal Military Order of, 257, Sardinia, 77, Nos. 6, 7.
Savoy, Civil Order of, 259, Sardinia, 77, Nos. 8, 9.
Star Cross, 22, Austria, Plate 6, No. 22.
Saxe-Ernest, Family Order of, 272, Grand Duchies of the Saxe-Gotha Branch of the Ernestine Line, Plate 80.
Seraphine, or the "Blue Ribbon," 329, Sweden and Norway, 91, Nos. 1, 2, 3.
St. Ann, Order of, 231, Russia, Plate 70, Nos. 9, 10, 11.
St. Andrew, Order of, 226, Russia, Plate 69, Nos. 1, 2, 6.
St. Benedict of Aviz and St. Jacob of the Sword and the Order of Christ, 73, Brazil, Plate 21, No. 6, 7, 8.
St. Catherine. 228, Russia, Plate 69, Nos. 3, 4, 5.
St. Constantine, Order of, 179, Parma, (Grand Duchy), Plate 59.
St. Elizabeth, 58, Bavaria, Tab. IV. Nos. 25, 26.
St. Faustin and of the Legion of Honour, the Orders of, 121, Haiti, Plate 35, Nos. 1, 2.
St. Ferdinand and of Merit, 288, the Two Sicilies, Plate 84, Nos. 3, 4, Plate 85, No. 10, and Plate 86, No. 15.
St. Ferdinand, Military Order of, 316, Spain, Plate 89, Nos. 15, 16, 17, 18.
St. Gregory the Great, 171, Papal States, Plate 55, Nos. 1, 2, 3.
St. George, Military Order of, 153, Lucca, Plate 49, Nos. 1, 2.
St. George, 122, Hanover, Plate 37, No. 11, Plate 36, No. 10.
St. George of the Reunion, 293, the Two Sicilies, Plate 85, Nos. 6, 7, 8, 9, 14.
St. George, Military Order of, 234, Russia, Plate 71, Nos. 12, 13, 14.
St. Hubert, 47, Bavaria, Plate 11, Nos. 1, 2, 3.
St. Hermingilde, Military Order of, 315, Spain, 90, Nos. 20, 21.
St. Henry, Military Order of, 265, Saxony, Plate 78, Nos. 3, 4, 5.
St. James of Compostella, Military Order of, 297, Spain, Plate 87, Nos. 1, 2.
St. James, Order of, 188, Portugal, 62, Nos. 6, 7.
St. Januarius, 287, the Two Sicilies, 84, Nos. 1, 2.
St. Helena, Medal, 96, France, Plate 27, No. 9.
St. John of Jerusalem, 176, Papal States.
St. John, 238, Russia.
St. John, 205, Prussia, Plate 66, Nos. 12, 13.
St. John, 296, Spain, Plate 56, Nos. 7, 8, 9.
St. Joseph, 352, Tuscany, Plate 97, Nos. 3, 4.
St. Isabella, 194, Portugal, Plate 64, No. 16.
St. Louis, Order of, for Civil Merit, 154, Lucca, Plate 49, No. 3.
St. Louis, 182, Parma (Grand Duchy), 59.
St. Maurice and Lazarus, 253, Sardinia, Plate 76, Nos. 3, 4, 5.
St. Michael, Order of Merit, 56, Bavaria, Plate 13, Nos. 15, 16, 17, and Plate 14, No. 29.
St. Michael and St. George, 107, England, Plate 31.

St. Olaf, Order of, 165, Norway, Plate 53, Nos. 1, 2, 3.
St. Patrick, Order of, 102, England, Plate 29, Nos. 5, 9.
St. Patrick, 50, Bavaria, Plate 2, No. 5, 6, 7, Plate 3, No. 11.
St. Stanislaus, 242, Russia, Plate 72, Nos. 19, 20.
St. Stephen, 351, Tuscany, Plate 97, Nos. 1, 2.
St. Wladimir, 238, Russia, Plate 71, Nos. 15, 16.
Swan, Order of the, 211, Prussia, Plate 67, No. 16.
Sword, or of the "Yellow Ribbon," Order of the, 333, Sweden and Norway, Plate 91, Nos. 4, 5, 6.

T.

Teutonic Order, 24, Austria, Plate 6, Nos. 19, 20.
Teutonic Order, 146, Holland.
Theresa, Order of, 62, Bavaria, Plate 14, No. 23.
Thistle, 100, England, Plate 29, Nos. 6, 8.
Tower and Sword, 192, Portugal, Plate 63, Nos. 10, 11.

V.

Victoria Cross, 112, England, Plate 33, No. 28.

Vasa, 337, Sweden and Norway, Plate 92, No. 11, and Plate 93, No. 14.

W.

War Medal, 130, Hanse Towns, Plate 94, No. 3.
War Medal for the Volunteers in the British German Legion, until the conclusion of the Peace at Paris, Plate 36, No. 13.
War Medal for the Volunteers in the Hanoverian Army in the Year 1813. 126, Hanover, Plate 36, No. 12.
Waterloo Medal, 77, Brunswick, Plate 36, No. 11.
Waterloo Medal, 125, Hanover, Plate 23, No. 9.
Waterloo Medal, 111, England, Plate 32, No. 22.
White Cross, 353, Tuscany.
White Eagle, 239, Russia, Plate 72, Nos. 17, 18.
White Falcon, or, Vigilance, 279, Grand Duchy of Saxe-Weimar, Plate 82, Nos. 1—5.
William Cross and William Medal, 126, Plate 36, Nos. 8, 14.
William, Military Order of, 144, Holland, Plate 45, Nos. 1, 2, 3.

THE END.

LONDON:
Printed by A. Schulze, 13, Poland Street.

www.ingramcontent.com/pod-product-compliance
Lightning Source LLC
Chambersburg PA
CBHW060415300426
44111CB00018B/2859